SACRAMENTO PUBLIC LIBRARY
828 "I" Street
Sacramento, CA 95814
02/16

You may be reading the wrong way!

In keeping with the original Japanese comic format, this book reads from right to left, so action, sound effects and word balloons are reversed. This preserves the orientation of the original artwork. Check out the diagram below to get the order of things, and then turn to the other side of the book to get started!

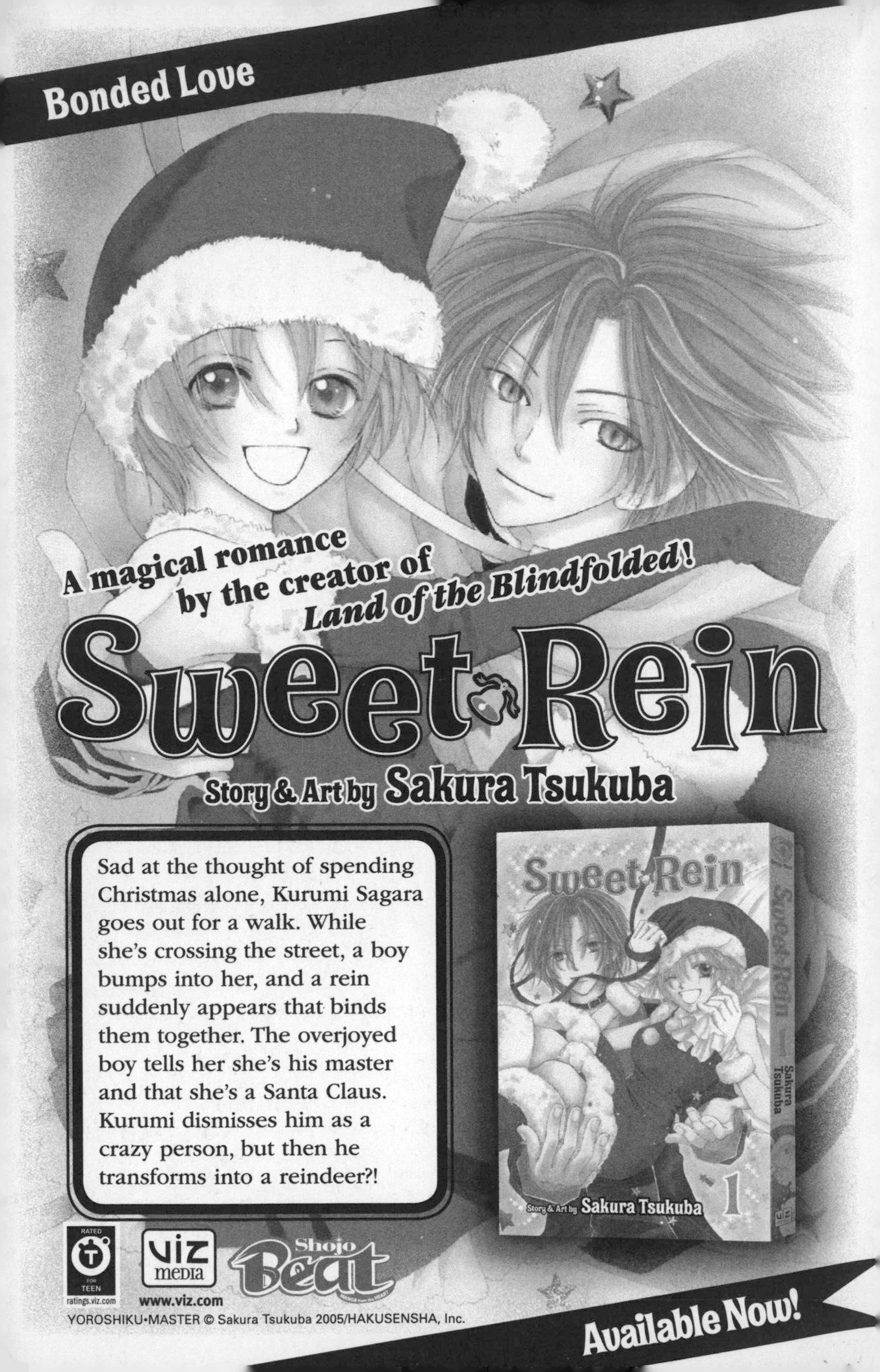
Bonded Love
A magical romance by the creator of *Land of the Blindfolded*!
Sweet Rein
Story & Art by Sakura Tsukuba
Sad at the thought of spending Christmas alone, Kurumi Sagara goes out for a walk. While she's crossing the street, a boy bumps into her, and a rein suddenly appears that binds them together. The overjoyed boy tells her she's his master and that she's a Santa Claus. Kurumi dismisses him as a crazy person, but then he transforms into a reindeer?!
Sweet Rein
Story & Art by Sakura Tsukuba
1
RATED T FOR TEEN
ratings.viz.com
VIZ media
www.viz.com
Shojo Beat
YOROSHIKU•MASTER © Sakura Tsukuba 2005/HAKUSENSHA, Inc.
Available Now!

Voice Over!
Seiyu Academy

Story and Art by
Maki Minami

She's ready to shine, and nothing is going to stand in her way!

A new series by the author of the best-selling S·A!

Hime Kino's dream is to one day do voice acting like her hero Sakura Aoyama from the Lovely ♥ Blazers anime, and getting accepted to the prestigious Holly Academy's voice actor department is the first step in the right direction! But Hime's gruff voice has earned her the scorn of teachers and students alike. Hime will not let that stand unchallenged. She'll show everyone that she is too a voice acting princess, whether they like it or not!!

VIZ MEDIA
www.viz.com

Shojo Beat

RATED TEEN
ratings.viz.com

Available now!

SEIYU KA! © Maki Minami 2009/HAKUSENSHA, Inc.

Ouran High School

Host Club BOX SET

Story and Art by
Bisco Hatori

Escape to the world of the young, rich and sexy

**All 18 volumes
in a collector's box
with an Ouran High
School stationery
notepad!**

In this screwball romantic
comedy, Haruhi, a poor girl at
a rich kids' school, is forced to
repay an $80,000 debt by working
for the school's swankiest, all-
male club—as a boy! There she
discovers just how wealthy the six
members are and how different
the rich are from everybody else...

VIZ MEDIA
www.viz.com

Shojo Beat

RATED **T** TEEN
ratings.viz.com

Ouran Koko Host Club © Bisco Hatori 2002/HAKUSENSHA, Inc.

Natsume's
BOOK of FRIENDS

STORY and ART by
Yuki Midorikawa

Make Some Unusual New Friends

The power to see hidden spirits has always felt like a curse to troubled high schooler Takashi Natsume. But he's about to discover he inherited a lot more than just the Sight from his mysterious grandmother!

Available at your local bookstore or comic store.

www.shojobeat.com

Natsume Yujincho © Yuki Midorikawa 2005/HAKUSENSHA, Inc.

RATED T FOR TEEN
ratings.viz.com

VIZ MEDIA

www.viz.com

Kamisama Kiss

Story and art by **Julietta Suzuki**

What's a newly fledged godling to do?

Now a hit anime series!

Nanami Momozono is alone and homeless after her dad skips town to evade his gambling debts and the debt collectors kick her out of her apartment. So when a man she's just saved from a dog offers her his home, she jumps at the opportunity. But it turns out that his place is a shrine, and Nanami has unwittingly taken over his job as a local deity!

Available now!

viz.com

Kamisama Hajimemashita © Julietta Suzuki 2008/HAKUSENSHA, Inc.

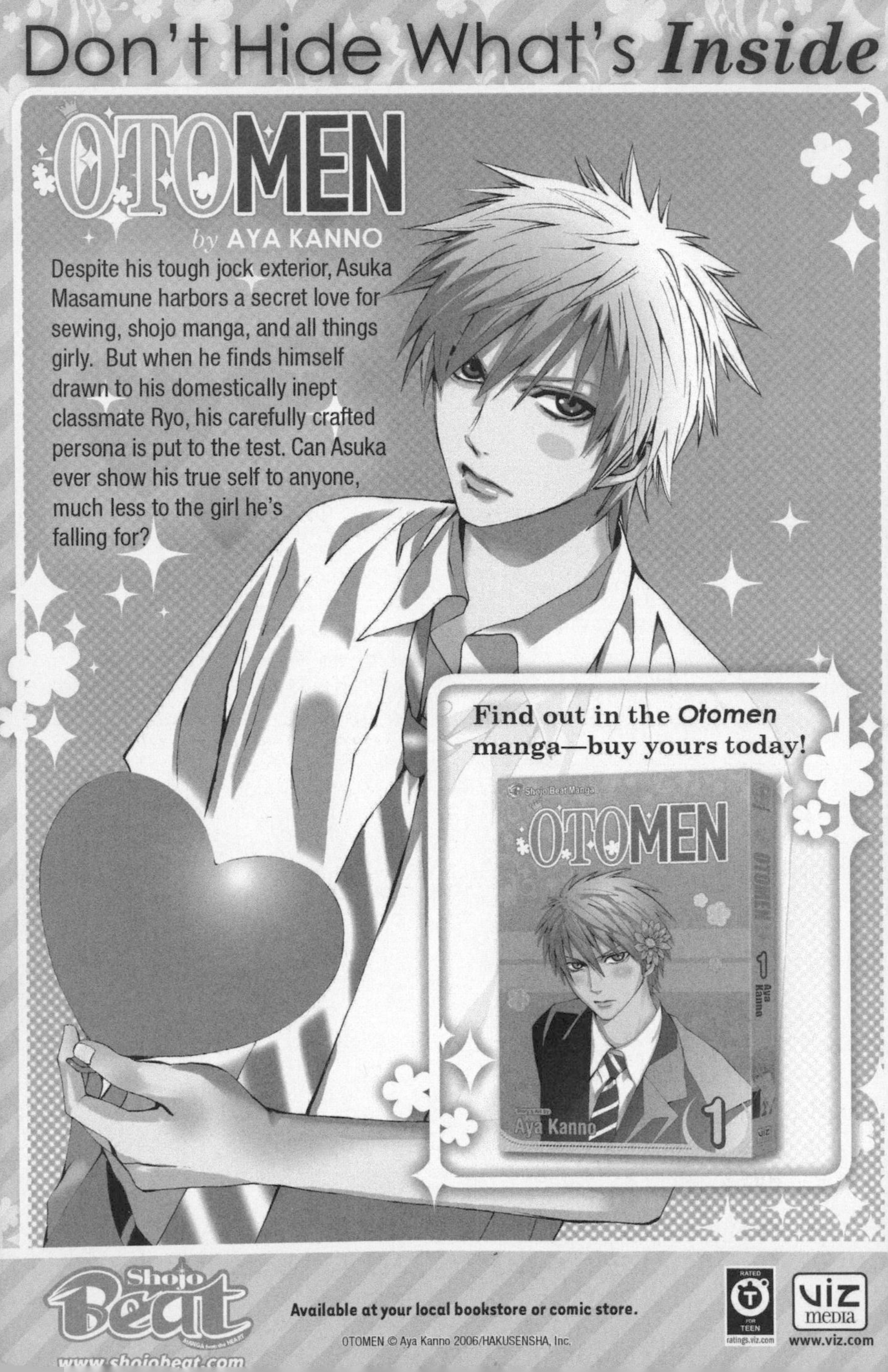

Don't Hide What's Inside
OTOMEN
by AYA KANNO
Despite his tough jock exterior, Asuka Masamune harbors a secret love for sewing, shojo manga, and all things girly. But when he finds himself drawn to his domestically inept classmate Ryo, his carefully crafted persona is put to the test. Can Asuka ever show his true self to anyone, much less to the girl he's falling for?
Find out in the Otomen manga—buy yours today!
Shojo Beat Manga
OTOMEN
Aya Kanno
1
Shojo Beat
Available at your local bookstore or comic store.
OTOMEN © Aya Kanno 2006/HAKUSENSHA, Inc.
RATED T FOR TEEN
ratings.viz.com
viz media
www.viz.com
www.shojobeat.com

Komomo Confiserie
Shojo Beat Edition
Volume 3

STORY AND ART BY
Maki Minami

Supervisor: Tsuji Shizuo Ryori Kyoiku Kenkyujo/Hiromi Kosaka
Special thanks to Tsujicho Group

Translation/Christine Dashiell
Touch-Up Art & Lettering/John Hunt
Design/Yukiko Whitley
Editor/Nancy Thistlethwaite

Komomo Confiserie by Maki Minami
© Maki Minami 2014
All rights reserved.
First published in Japan in 2014 by HAKUSENSHA, Inc., Tokyo.
English language translation rights arranged with HAKUSENSHA, Inc., Tokyo.

The stories, characters and incidents mentioned in this publication are entirely fictional.

No portion of this book may be reproduced or transmitted in any form or by any means without written permission from the copyright holders.

Printed in the U.S.A.

Published by VIZ Media, LLC
P.O. Box 77010
San Francisco, CA 94107

10 9 8 7 6 5 4 3 2 1
First printing, March 2016

www.viz.com   www.shojobeat.com

PARENTAL ADVISORY
KOMOMO CONFISERIE is rated
T for Teen and is recommended
for ages 13 and up.
ratings.viz.com

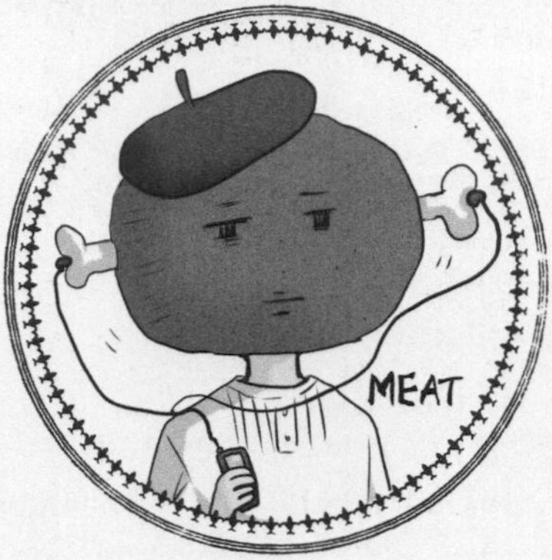
MEAT

Maki Minami is from Saitama Prefecture in Japan. She debuted in 2001 with *Kanata no Ao* (Faraway Blue). Her other works include *Kimi wa Girlfriend* (You're My Girlfriend), *Mainichi ga Takaramono* (Every Day Is a Treasure) and *Yuki Atataka* (Warm Winter). *S•A* and *Voice Over! Seiyu Academy* are published in English by VIZ Media.

Shojo Beat

Komomo Confiserie

Volume 3
Story & Art by Maki Minami

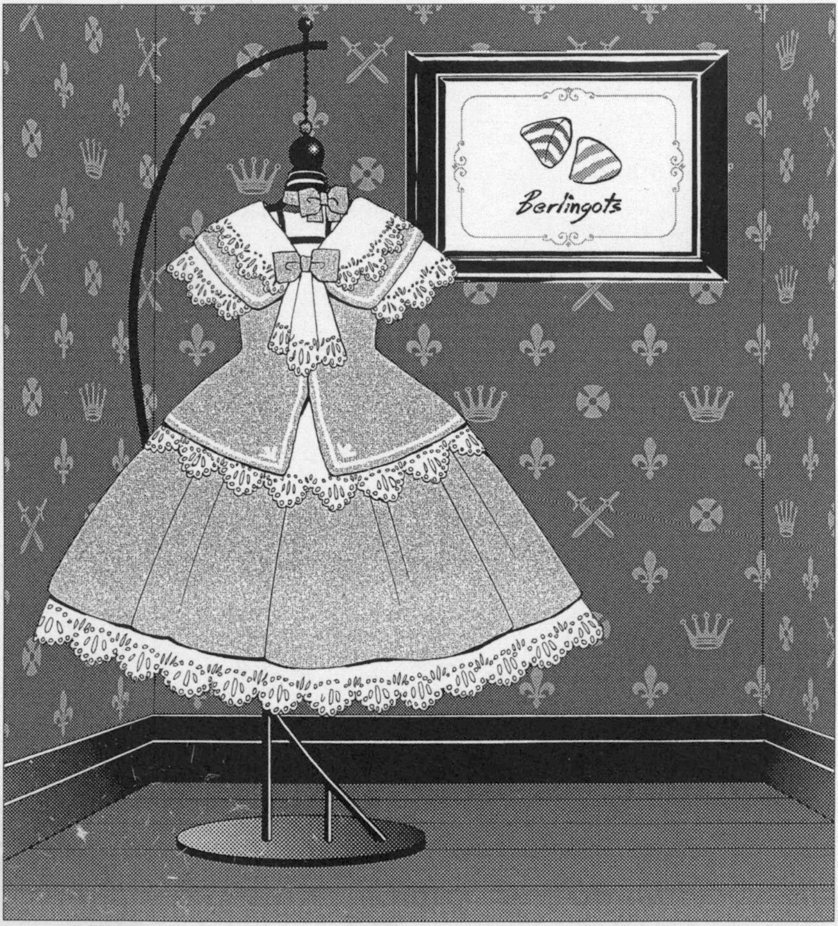
Berlingots

Komomo Confiserie

CONTENTS

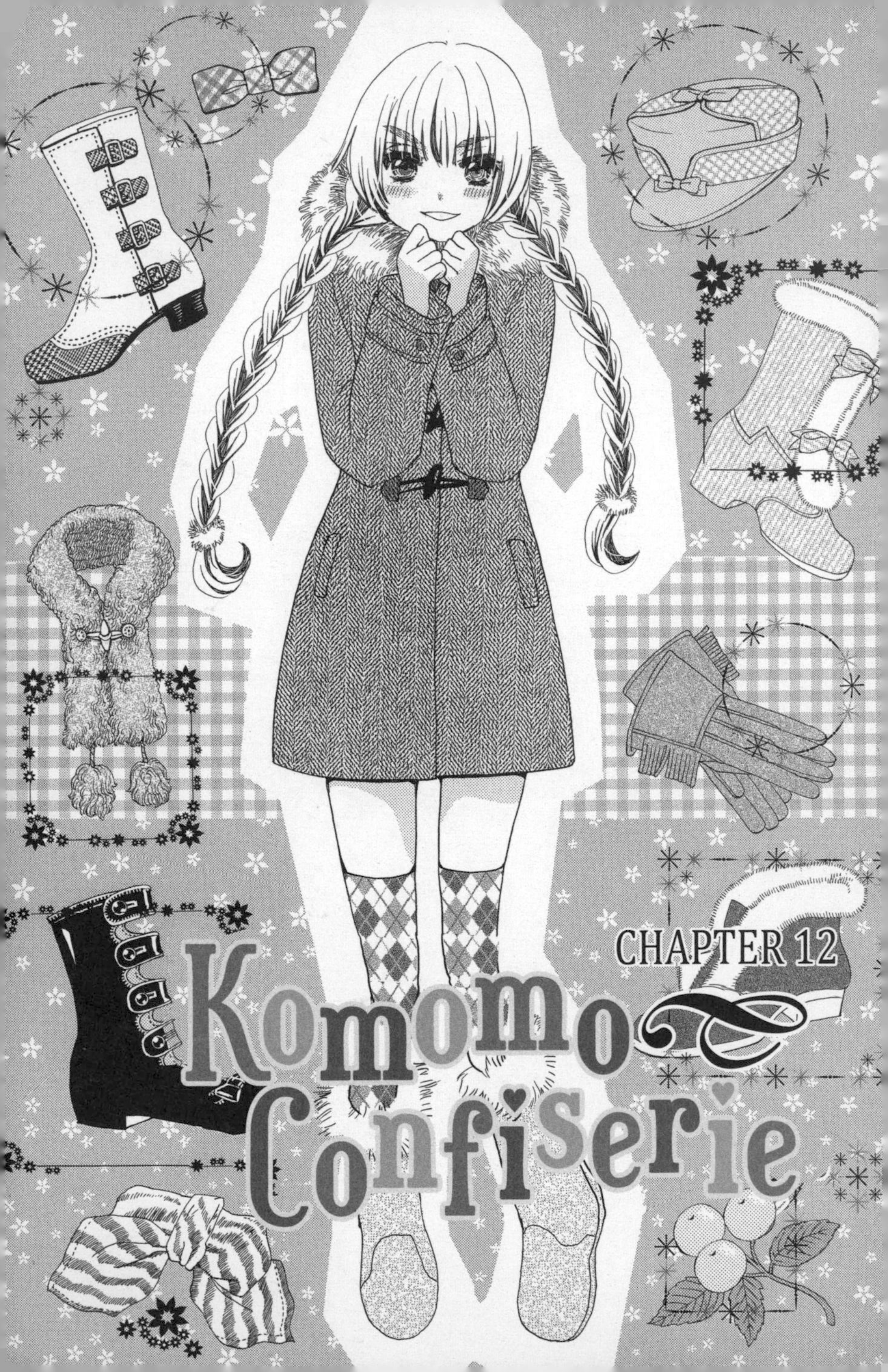
CHAPTER 12
Komomo Confiserie

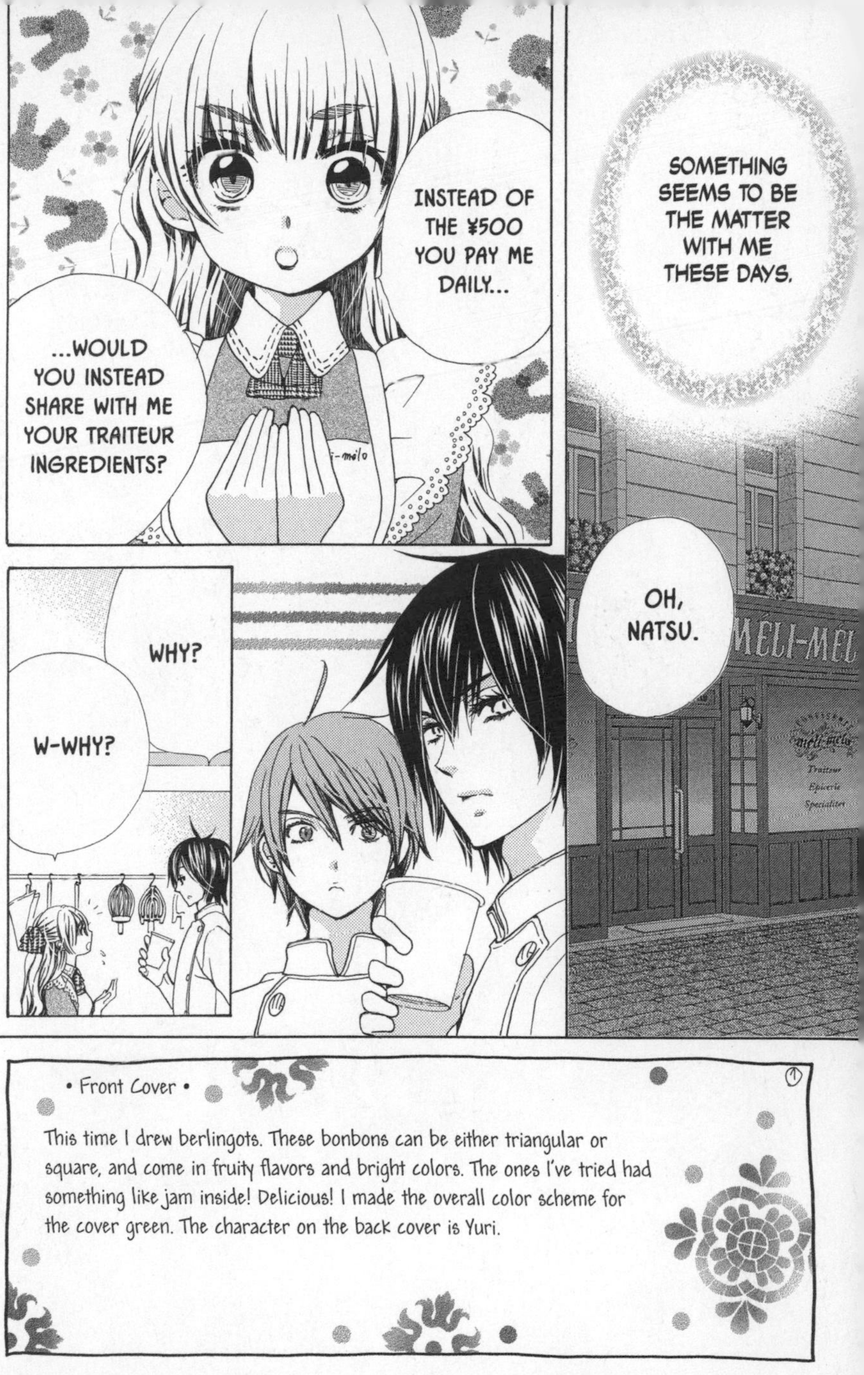
SOMETHING SEEMS TO BE THE MATTER WITH ME THESE DAYS.
OH, NATSU.
INSTEAD OF THE ¥500 YOU PAY ME DAILY...
...WOULD YOU INSTEAD SHARE WITH ME YOUR TRAITEUR INGREDIENTS?
WHY?
W-WHY?

• Front Cover • ①

This time I drew berlingots. These bonbons can be either triangular or square, and come in fruity flavors and bright colors. The ones I've tried had something like jam inside! Delicious! I made the overall color scheme for the cover green. The character on the back cover is Yuri.

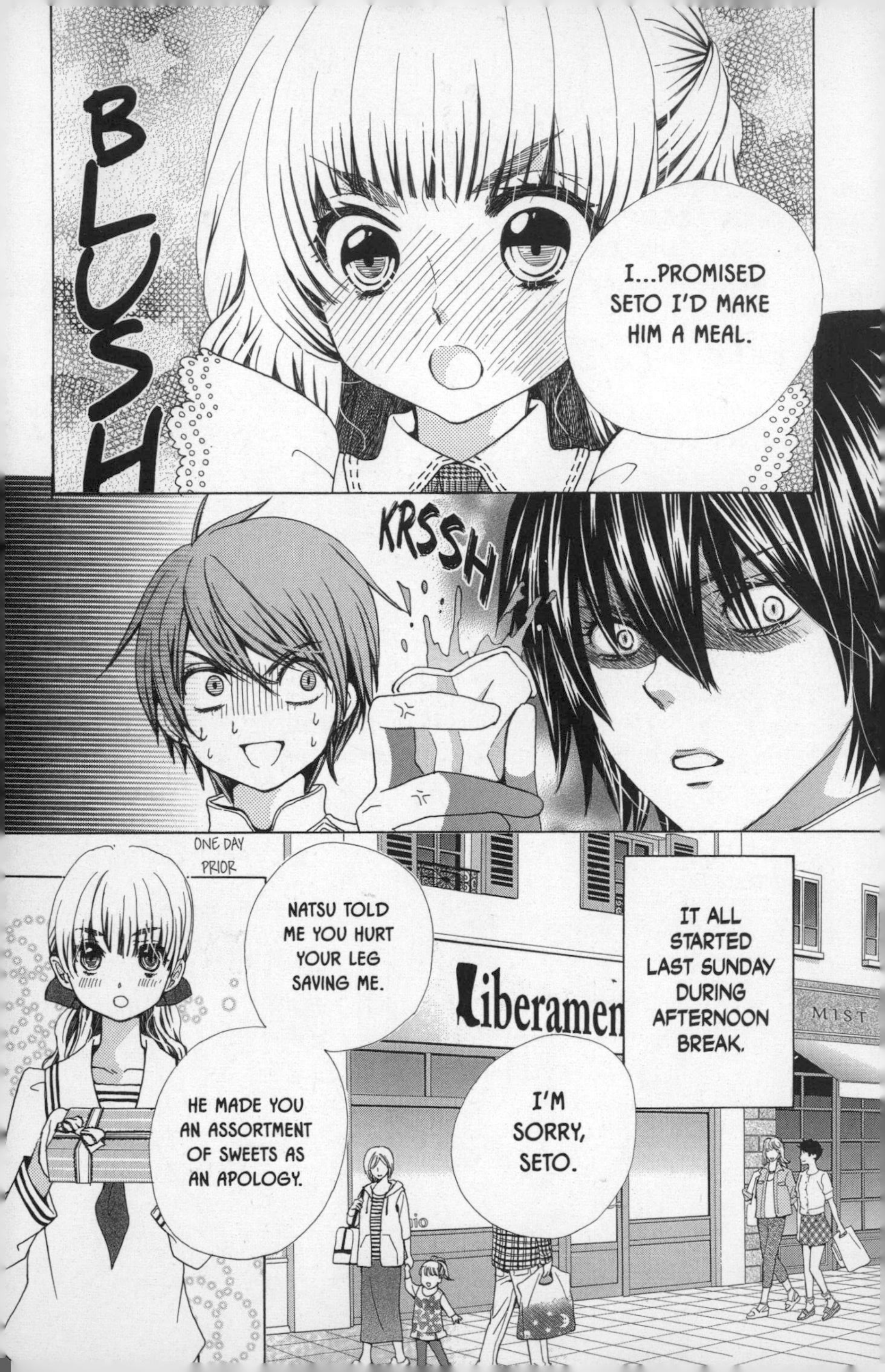
I...PROMISED SETO I'D MAKE HIM A MEAL.
BLUSH
KRSSH
IT ALL STARTED LAST SUNDAY DURING AFTERNOON BREAK.
MIST
Liberamen
NATSU TOLD ME YOU HURT YOUR LEG SAVING ME.
ONE DAY PRIOR
I'M SORRY, SETO.
HE MADE YOU AN ASSORTMENT OF SWEETS AS AN APOLOGY.

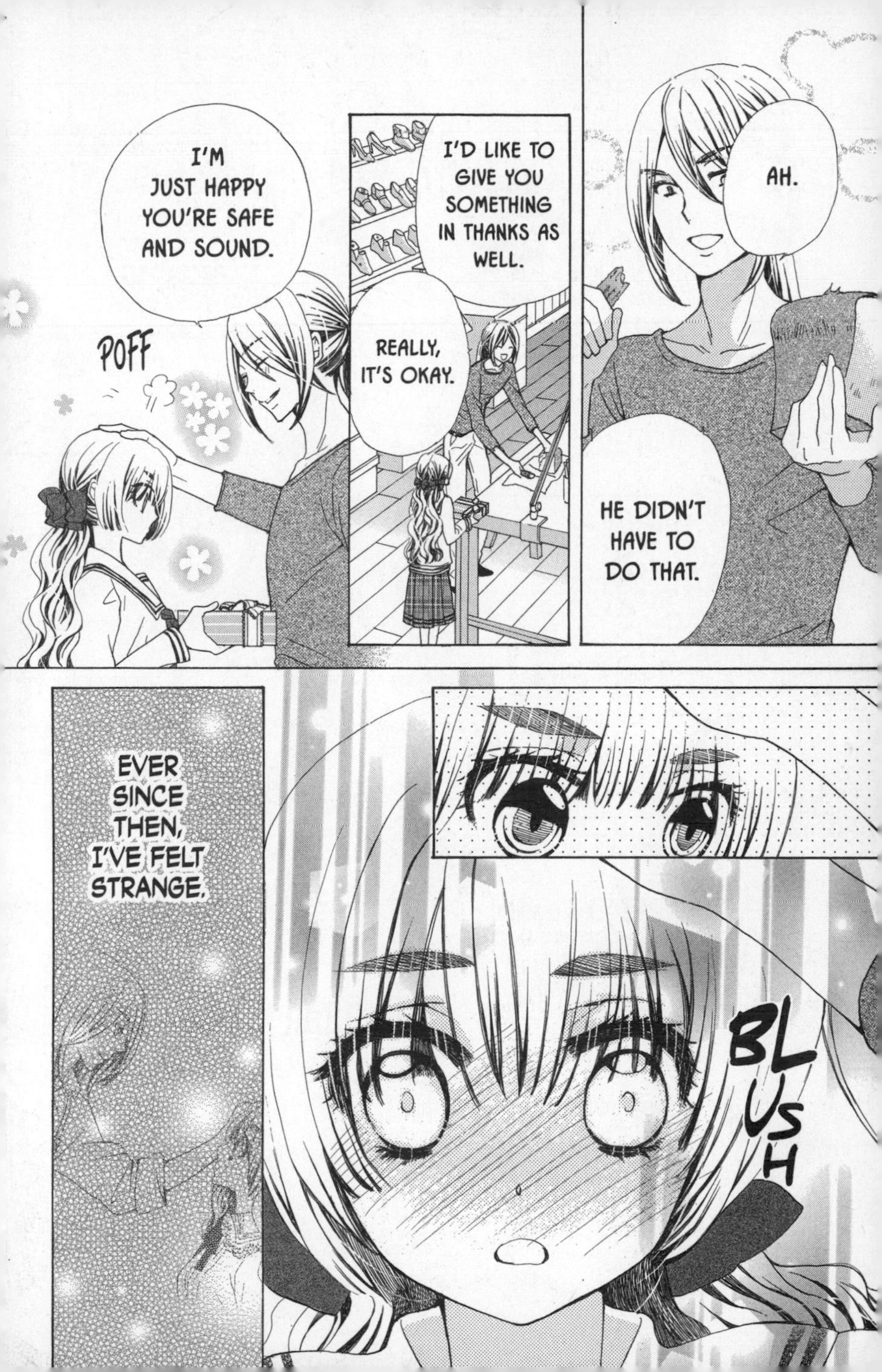
AH.
HE DIDN'T HAVE TO DO THAT.
I'D LIKE TO GIVE YOU SOMETHING IN THANKS AS WELL.
REALLY, IT'S OKAY.
I'M JUST HAPPY YOU'RE SAFE AND SOUND.
POFF
BLUSH
EVER SINCE THEN, I'VE FELT STRANGE.

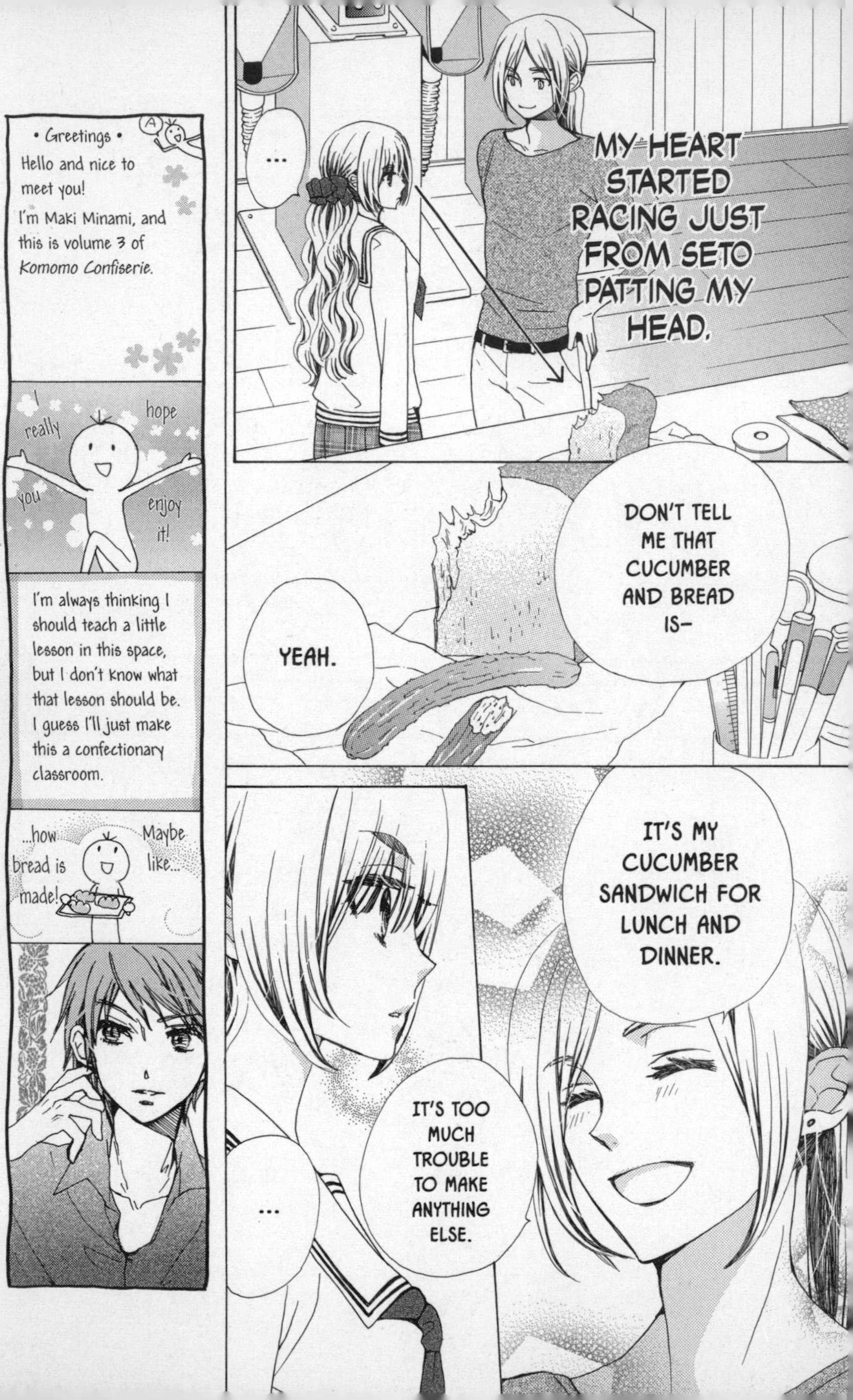
MY HEART STARTED RACING JUST FROM SETO PATTING MY HEAD.
...
DON'T TELL ME THAT CUCUMBER AND BREAD IS–
YEAH.
IT'S MY CUCUMBER SANDWICH FOR LUNCH AND DINNER.
IT'S TOO MUCH TROUBLE TO MAKE ANYTHING ELSE.
...
• Greetings •
Hello and nice to meet you!
I'm Maki Minami, and this is volume 3 of *Komomo Confiserie*.
I really hope you enjoy it!
I'm always thinking I should teach a little lesson in this space, but I don't know what that lesson should be. I guess I'll just make this a confectionary classroom.
Maybe like...
...how bread is made!

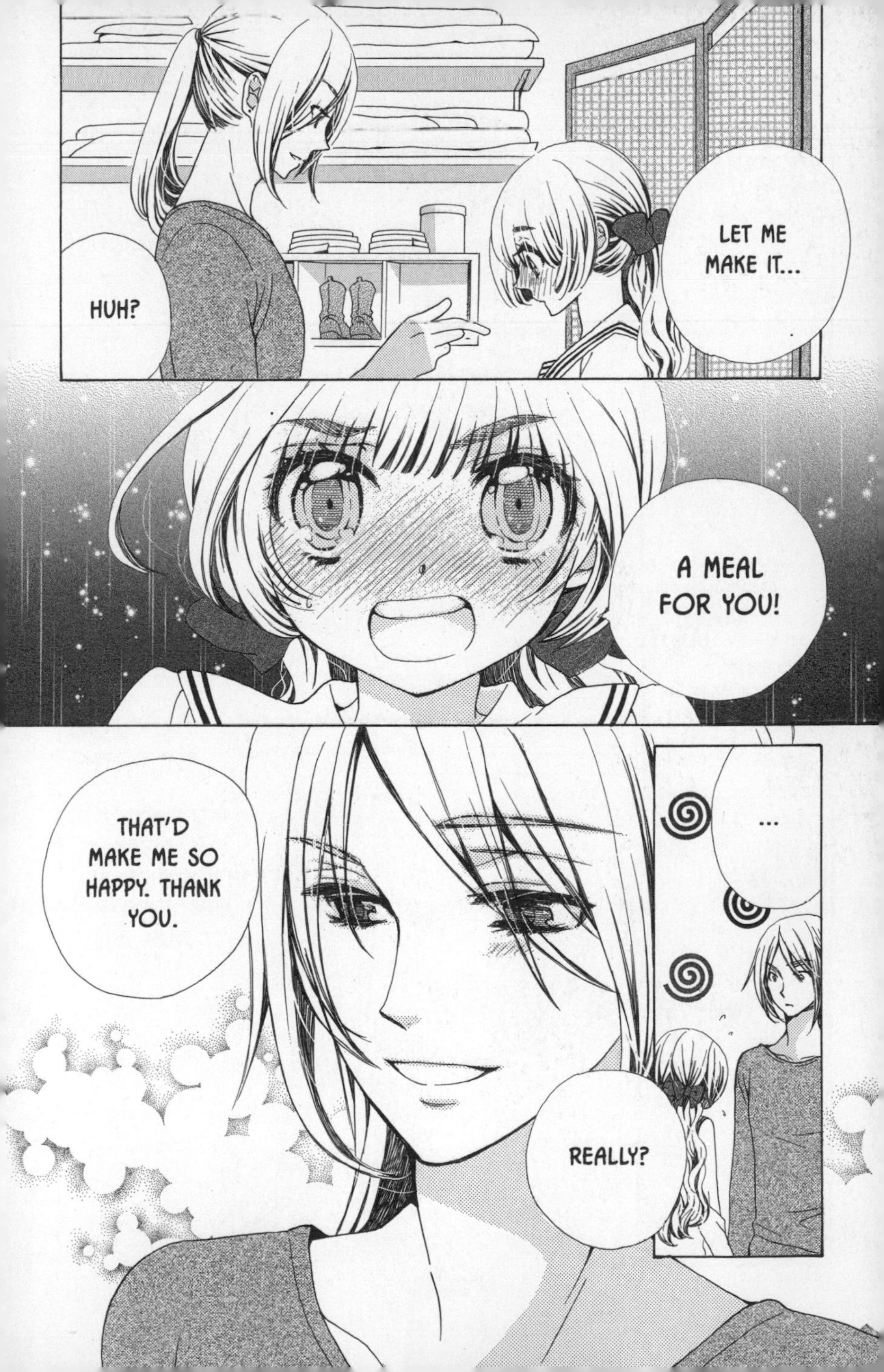
LET ME MAKE IT...
HUH?
A MEAL FOR YOU!
...
THAT'D MAKE ME SO HAPPY. THANK YOU.
REALLY?

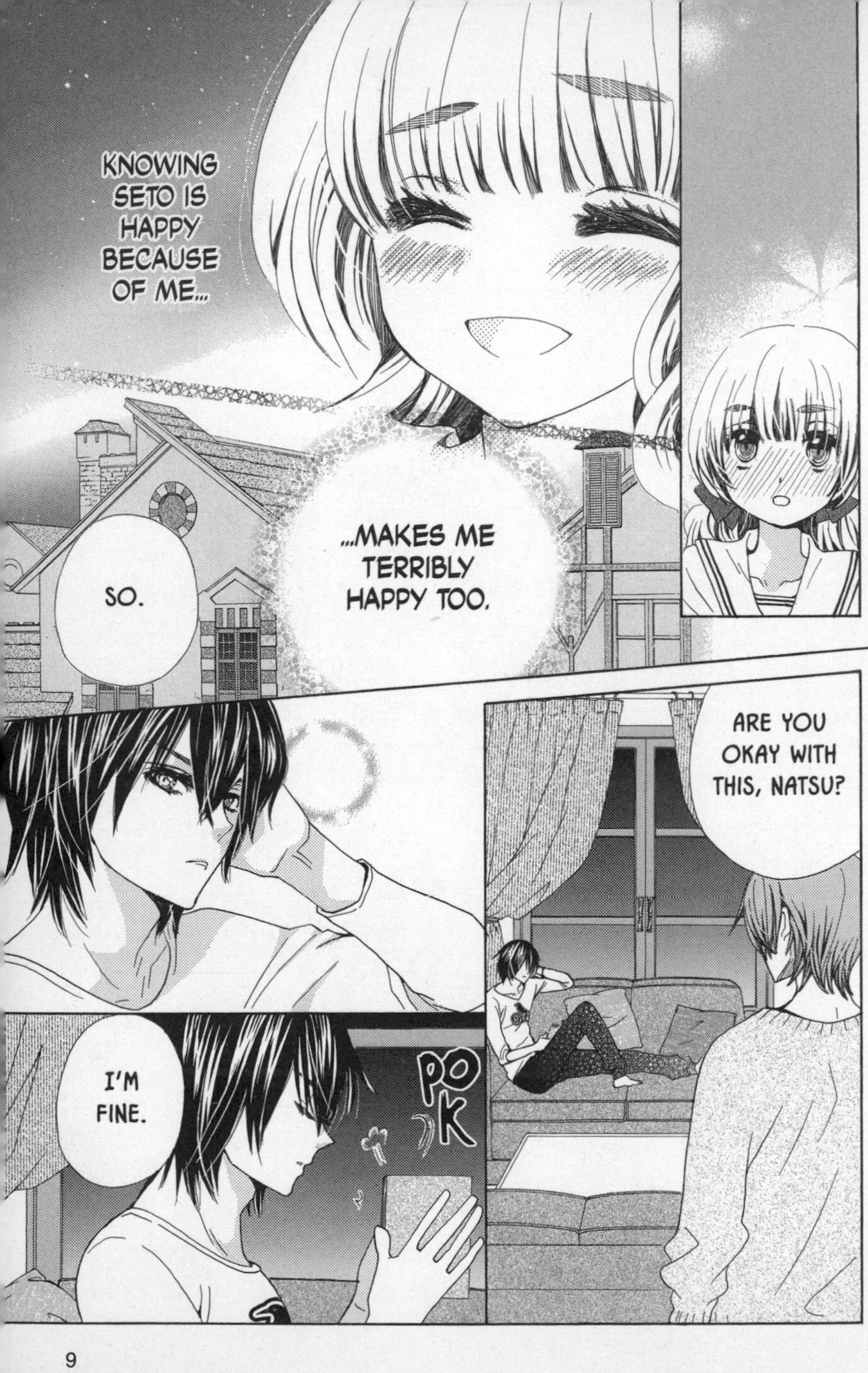
KNOWING SETO IS HAPPY BECAUSE OF ME...
...MAKES ME TERRIBLY HAPPY TOO.
SO.
ARE YOU OKAY WITH THIS, NATSU?
I'M FINE.
POK

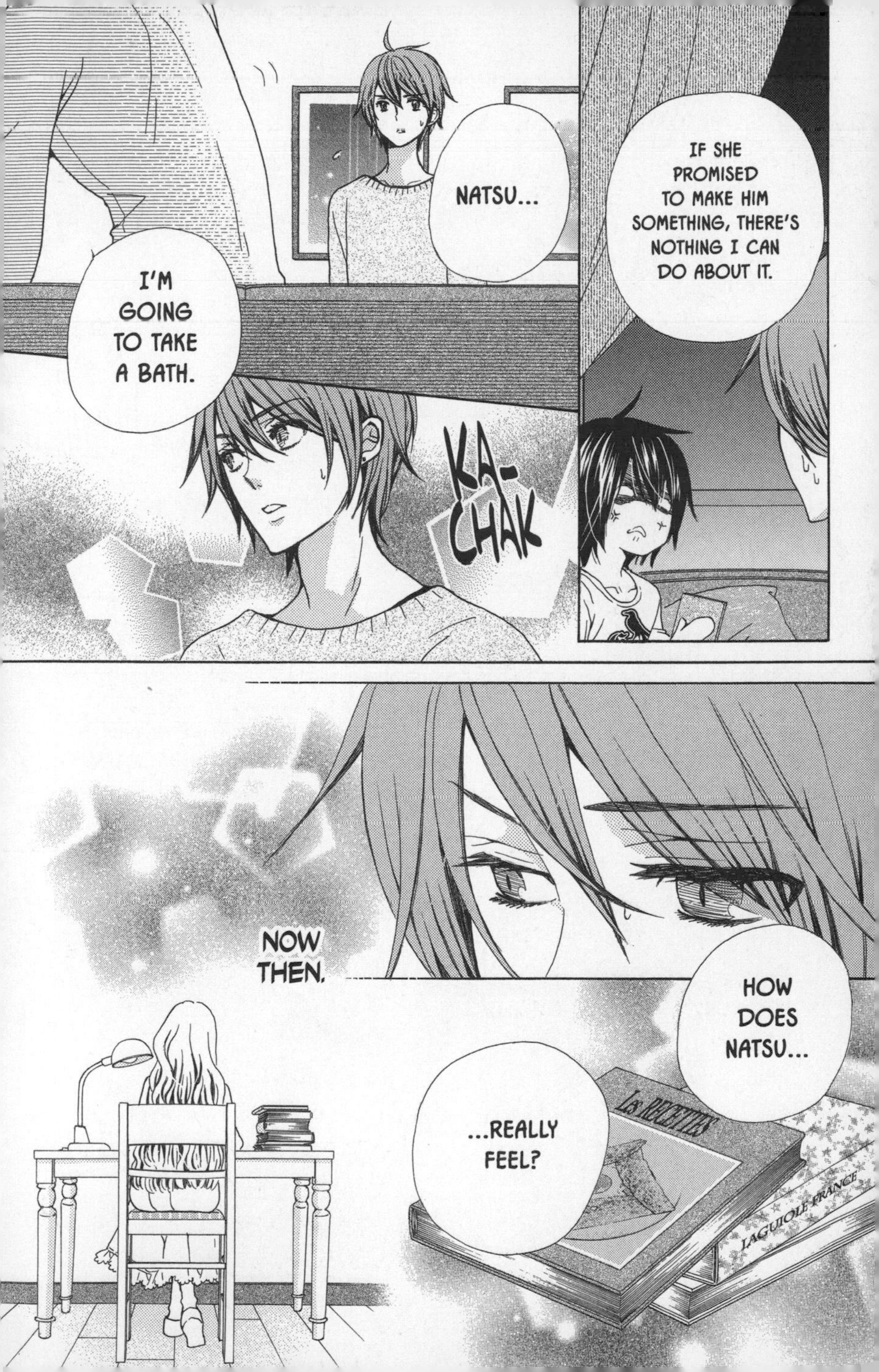
IF SHE PROMISED TO MAKE HIM SOMETHING, THERE'S NOTHING I CAN DO ABOUT IT.
NATSU...
I'M GOING TO TAKE A BATH.
KA-CHAK
NOW THEN.
HOW DOES NATSU...
...REALLY FEEL?
Les RECETTES
LAGUIOLE FRANCE

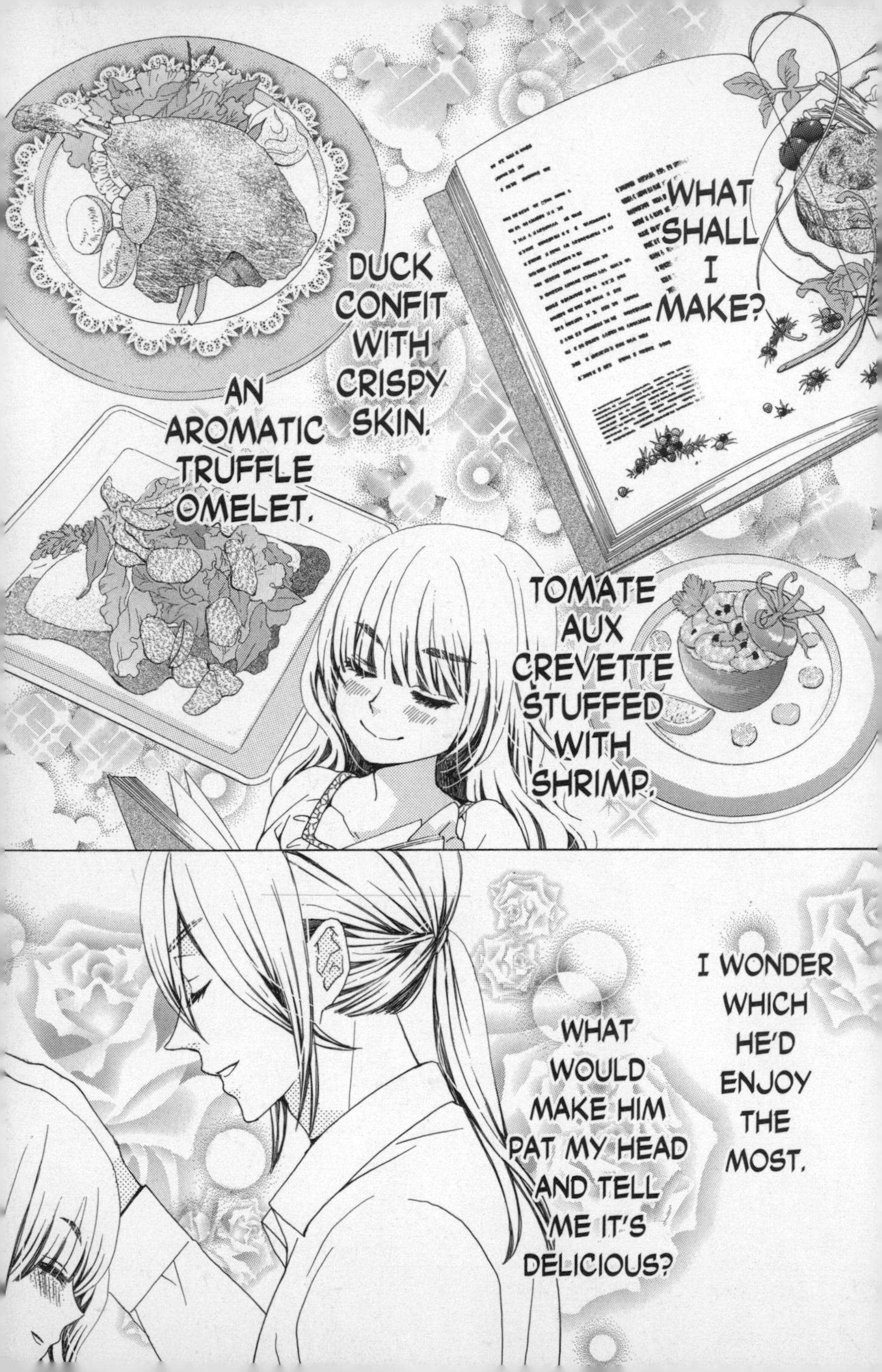
WHAT SHALL I MAKE?
DUCK CONFIT WITH CRISPY SKIN.
TOMATE AUX CREVETTE STUFFED WITH SHRIMP.
AN AROMATIC TRUFFLE OMELET.
I WONDER WHICH HE'D ENJOY THE MOST.
WHAT WOULD MAKE HIM PAT MY HEAD AND TELL ME IT'S DELICIOUS?

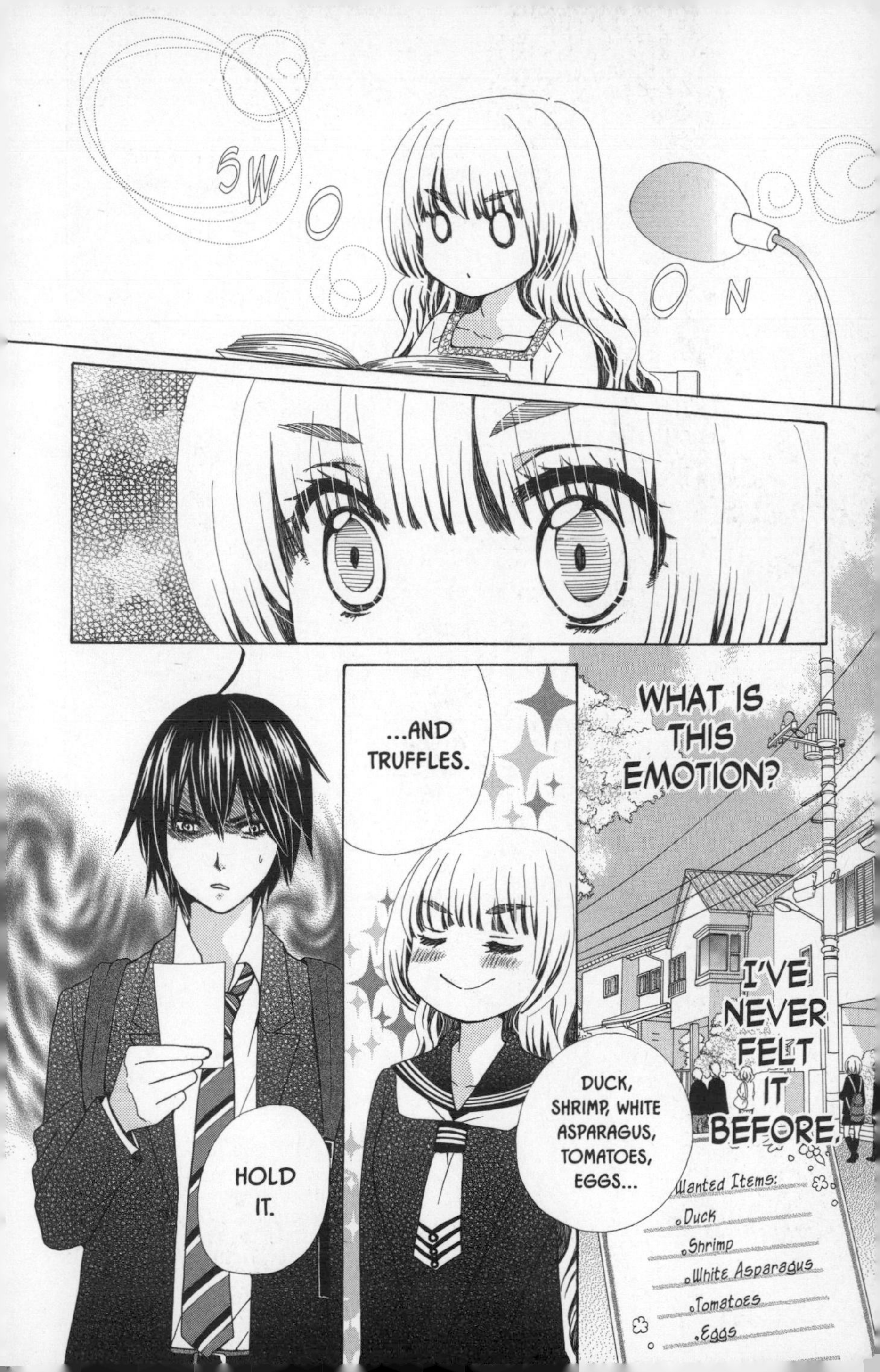
SWOOOON
WHAT IS THIS EMOTION?
I'VE NEVER FELT IT BEFORE.
Wanted Items:
Duck
Shrimp
White Asparagus
Tomatoes
Eggs
DUCK, SHRIMP, WHITE ASPARAGUS, TOMATOES, EGGS...
...AND TRUFFLES.
HOLD IT.

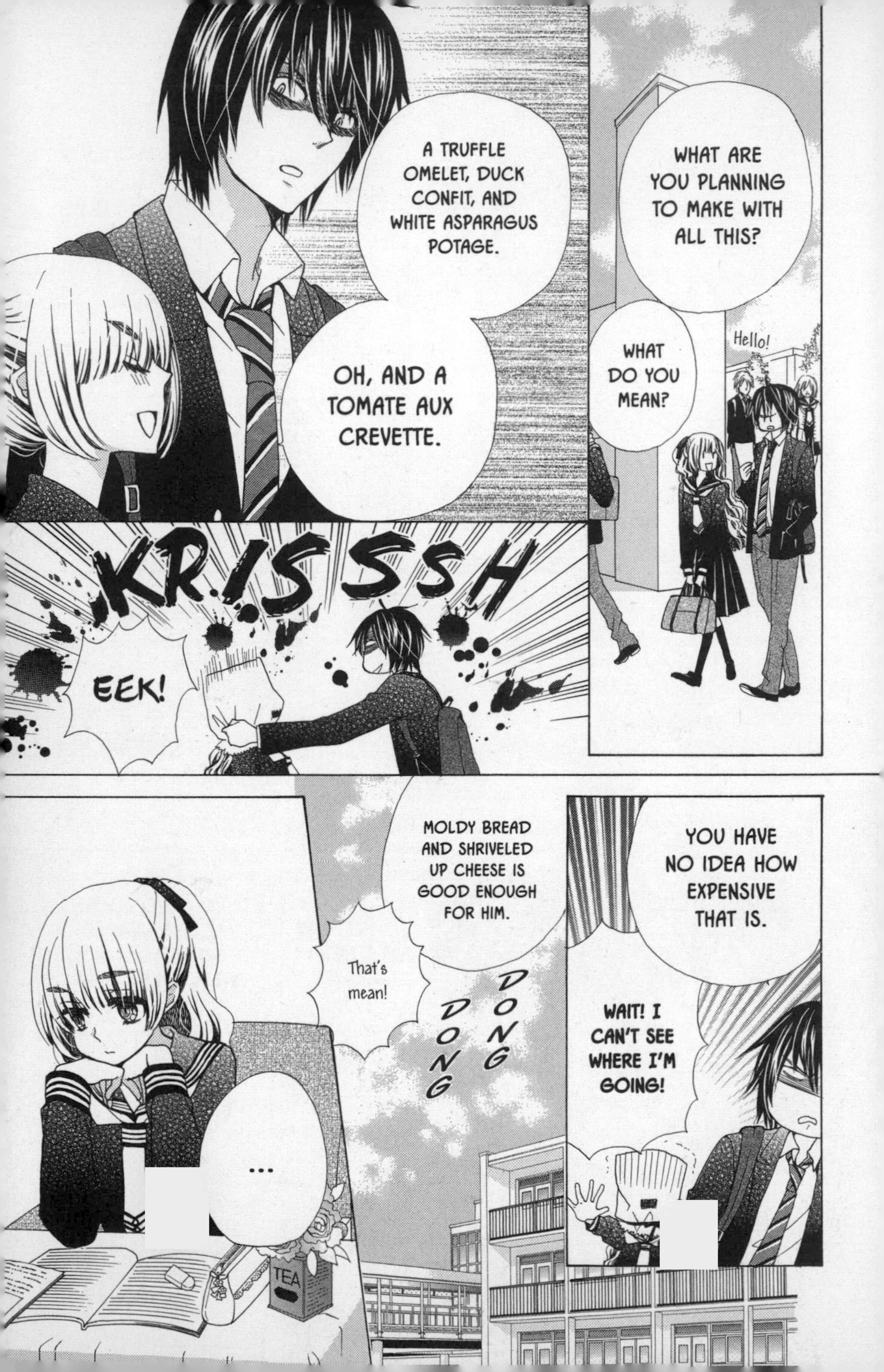
WHAT ARE YOU PLANNING TO MAKE WITH ALL THIS?
WHAT DO YOU MEAN?
Hello!
A TRUFFLE OMELET, DUCK CONFIT, AND WHITE ASPARAGUS POTAGE.
OH, AND A TOMATE AUX CREVETTE.
KRISSSH
EEK!
YOU HAVE NO IDEA HOW EXPENSIVE THAT IS.
WAIT! I CAN'T SEE WHERE I'M GOING!
MOLDY BREAD AND SHRIVELED UP CHEESE IS GOOD ENOUGH FOR HIM.
That's mean!
DONG
DONG
...

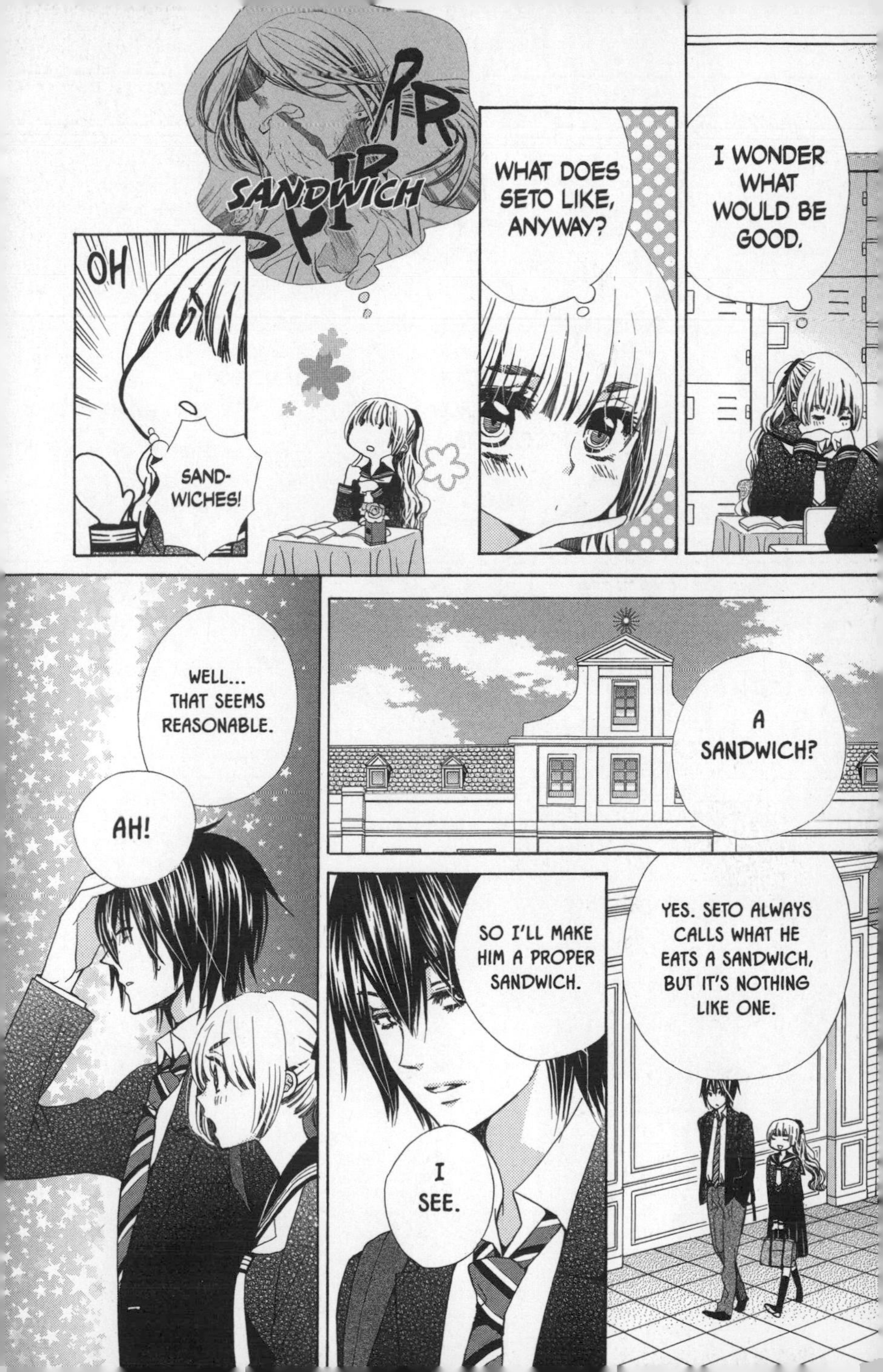
I WONDER WHAT WOULD BE GOOD.
WHAT DOES SETO LIKE, ANYWAY?
SANDWICH
OH
SAND-WICHES!
A SANDWICH?
YES. SETO ALWAYS CALLS WHAT HE EATS A SANDWICH, BUT IT'S NOTHING LIKE ONE.
SO I'LL MAKE HIM A PROPER SANDWICH.
I SEE.
WELL... THAT SEEMS REASONABLE.
AH!

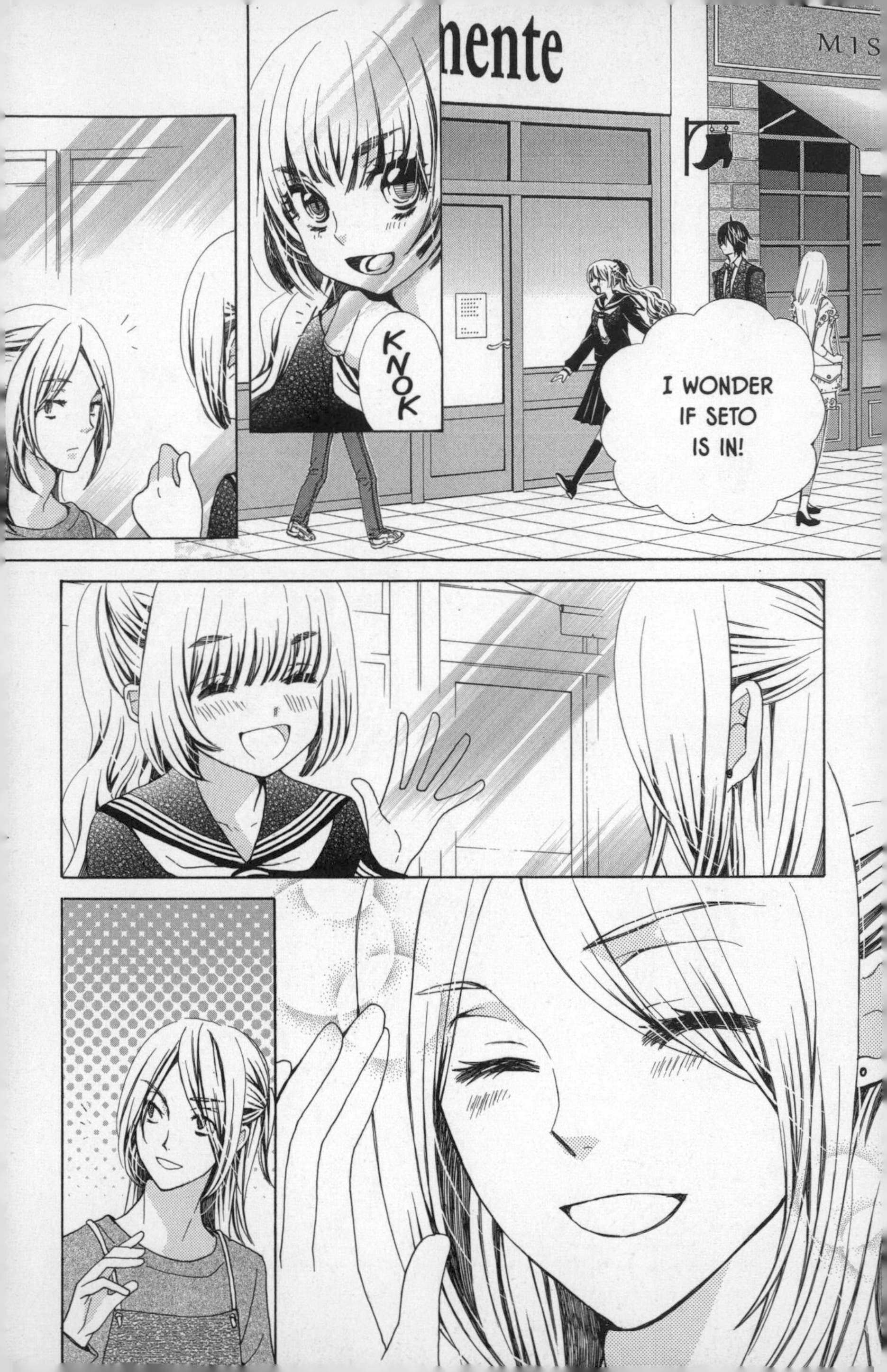
nente
MIS
I WONDER IF SETO IS IN!
KNOK

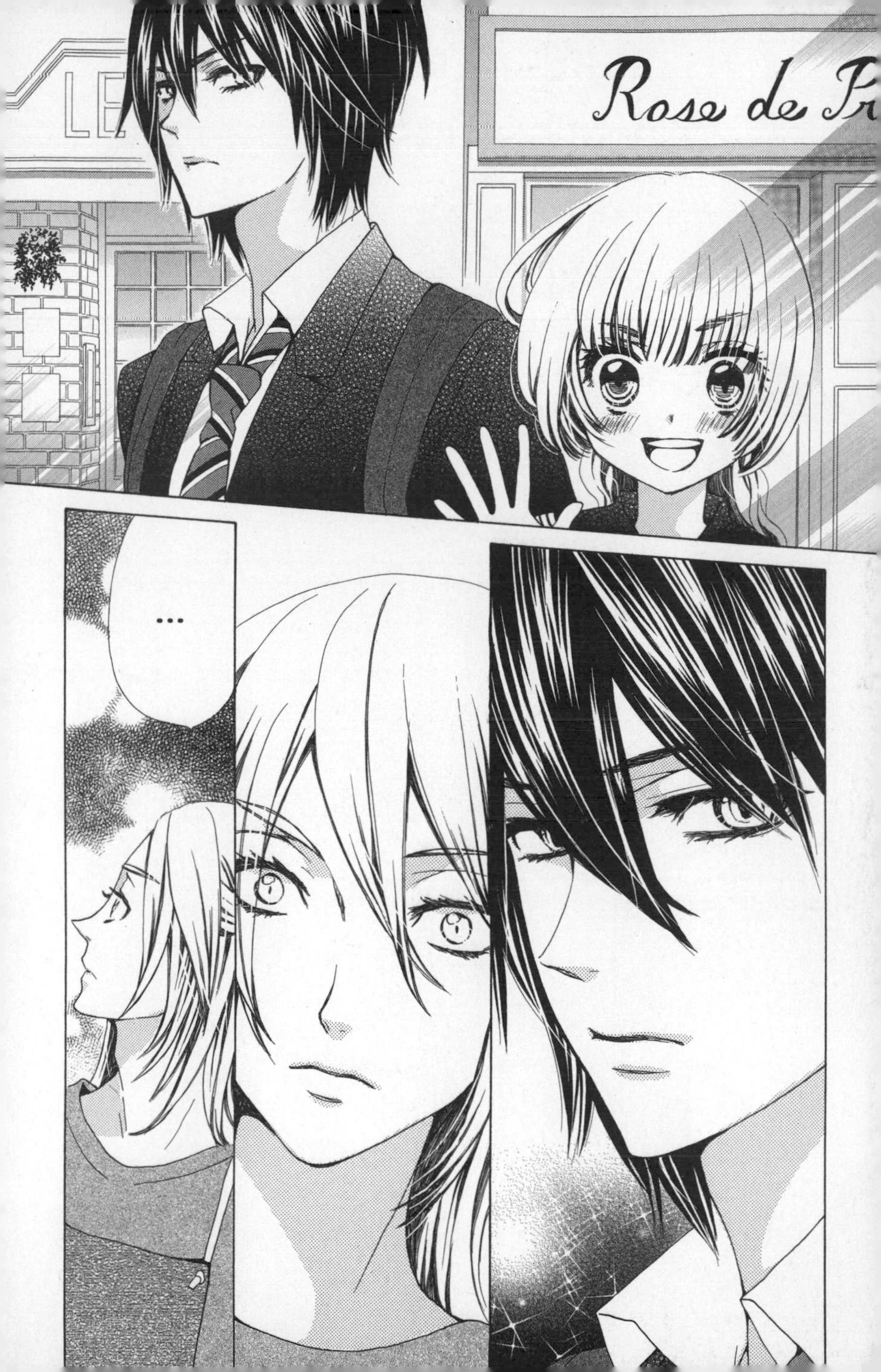

LE
Rose de Pr
...

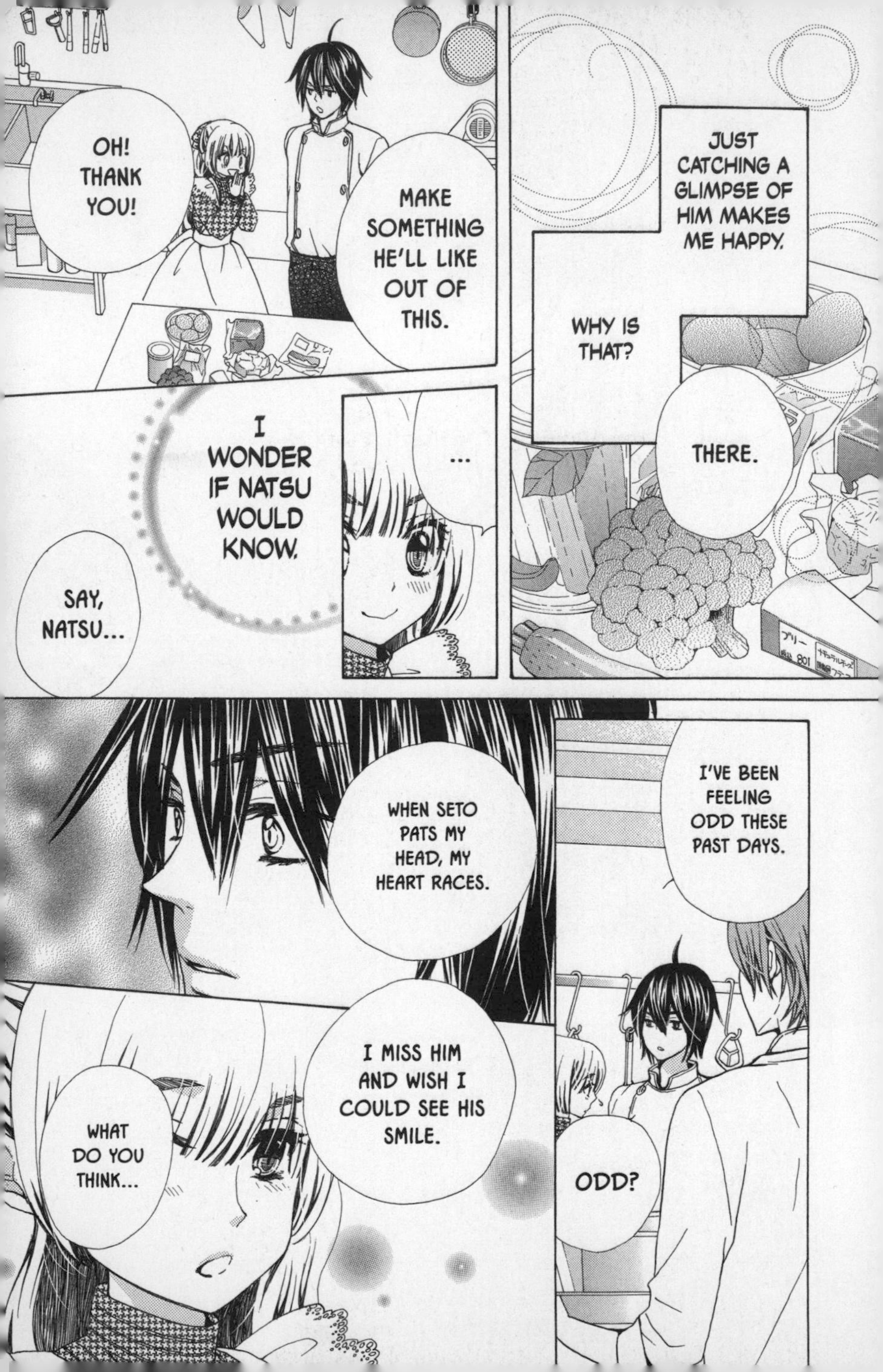
JUST CATCHING A GLIMPSE OF HIM MAKES ME HAPPY.
WHY IS THAT?
THERE.
MAKE SOMETHING HE'LL LIKE OUT OF THIS.
OH! THANK YOU!
...
I WONDER IF NATSU WOULD KNOW.
SAY, NATSU...
I'VE BEEN FEELING ODD THESE PAST DAYS.
ODD?
WHEN SETO PATS MY HEAD, MY HEART RACES.
I MISS HIM AND WISH I COULD SEE HIS SMILE.
WHAT DO YOU THINK...

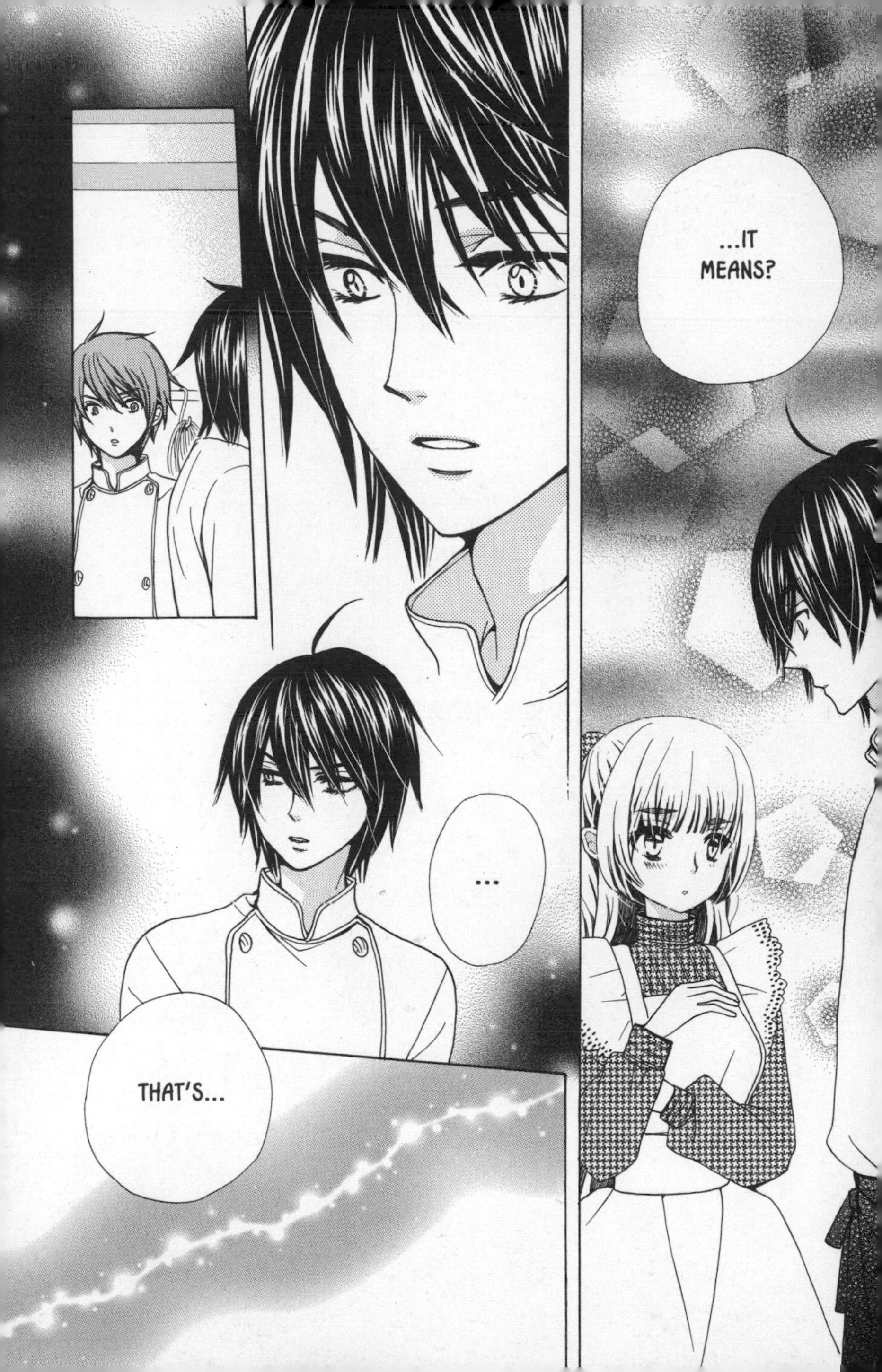
...IT MEANS?
...
THAT'S...

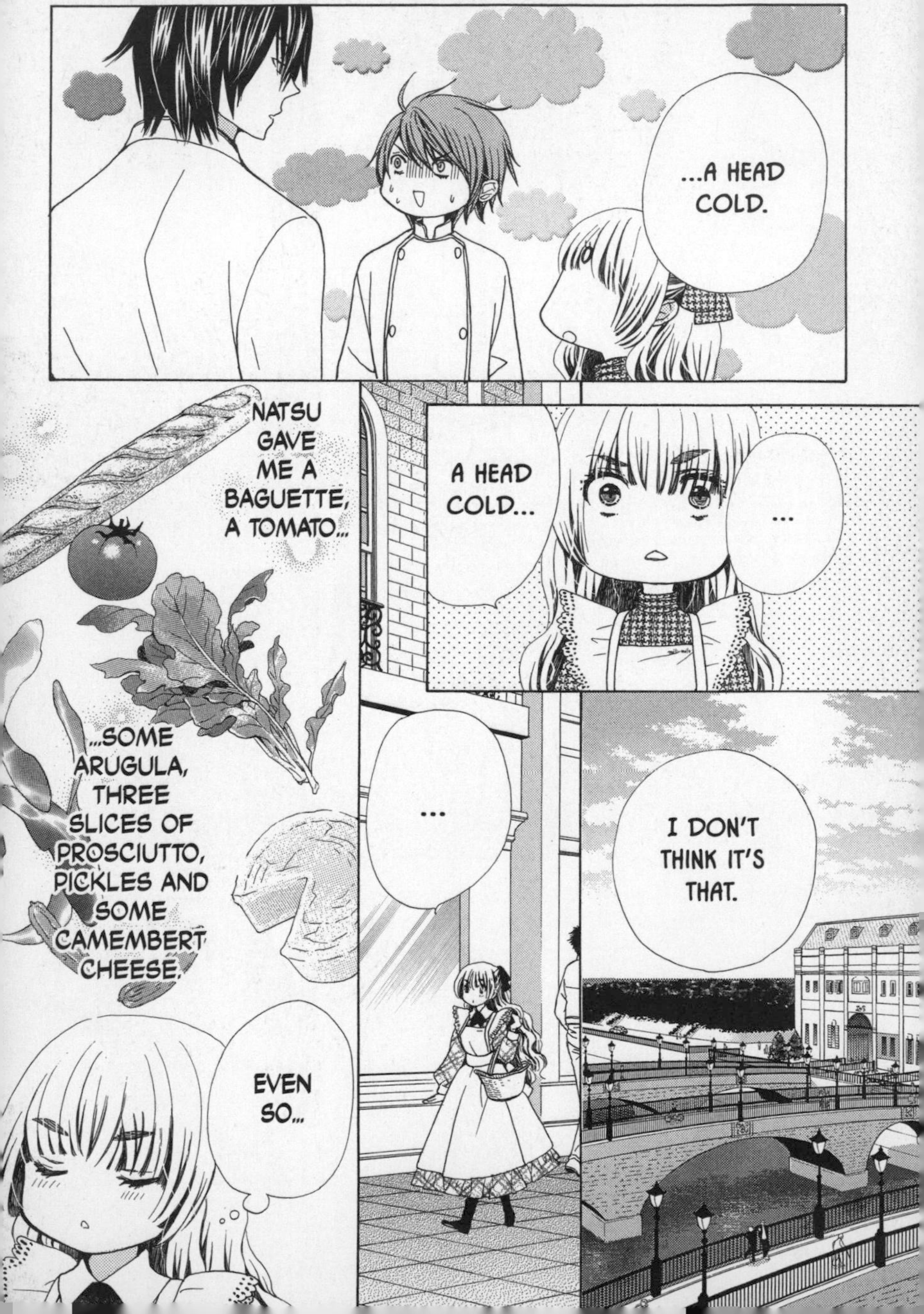
...A HEAD COLD.
A HEAD COLD...
...
I DON'T THINK IT'S THAT.
...
NATSU GAVE ME A BAGUETTE, A TOMATO...
...SOME ARUGULA, THREE SLICES OF PROSCIUTTO, PICKLES AND SOME CAMEMBERT CHEESE.
EVEN SO...

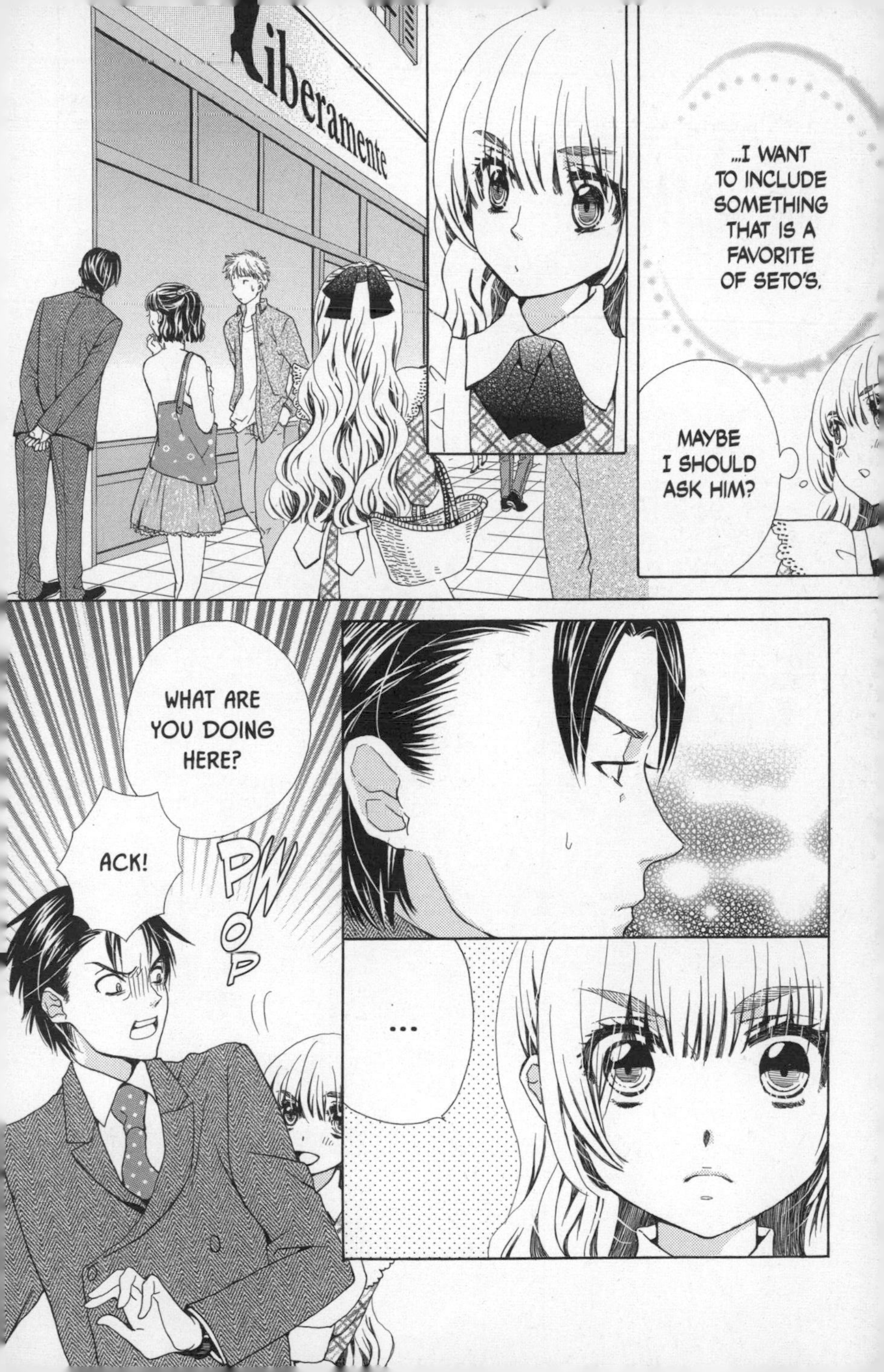
...I WANT TO INCLUDE SOMETHING THAT IS A FAVORITE OF SETO'S.
MAYBE I SHOULD ASK HIM?
iberamente
...
WHAT ARE YOU DOING HERE?
ACK!
PWOP

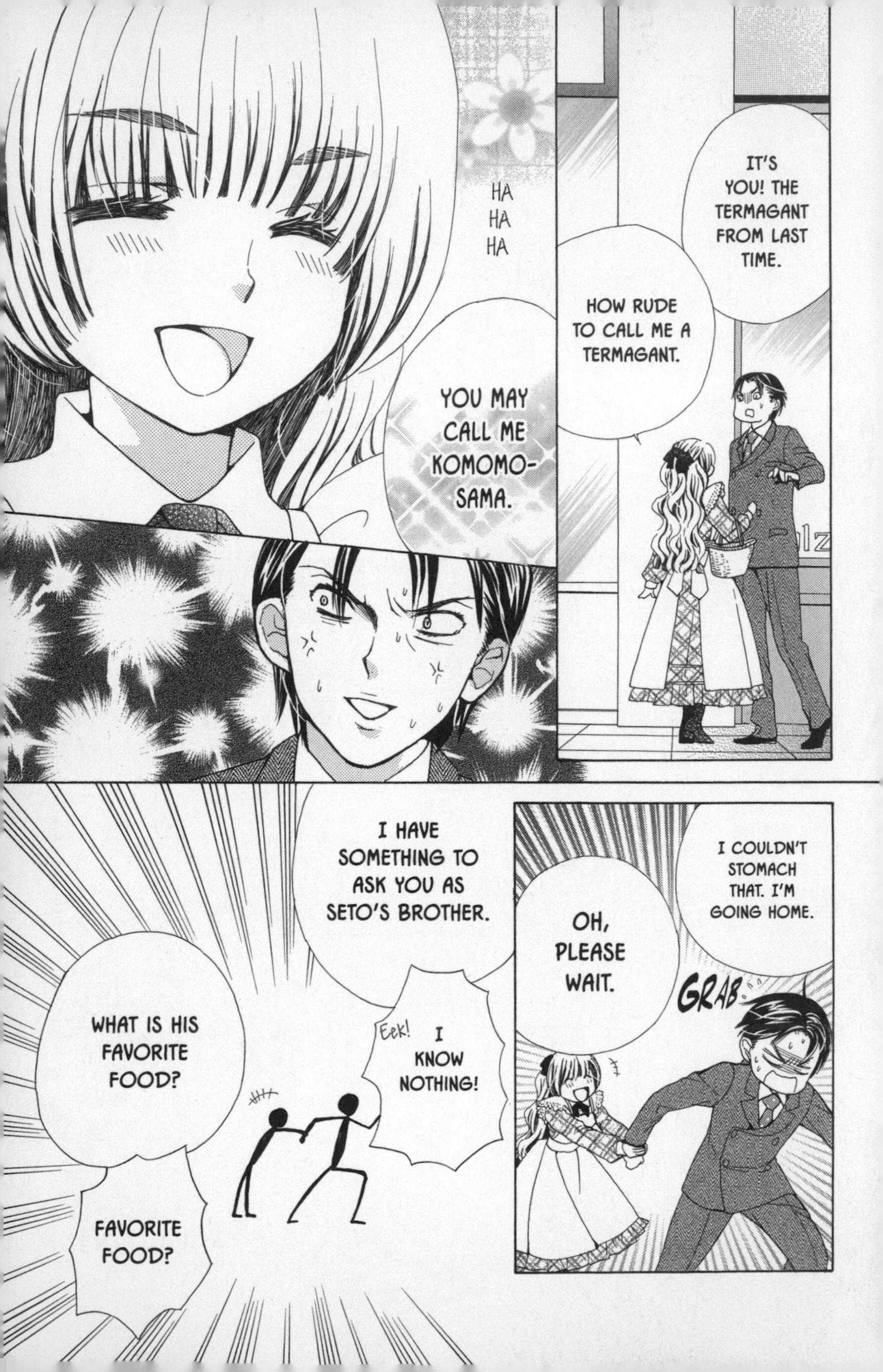
IT'S YOU! THE TERMAGANT FROM LAST TIME.
HOW RUDE TO CALL ME A TERMAGANT.
HA HA HA
YOU MAY CALL ME KOMOMO-SAMA.
I COULDN'T STOMACH THAT. I'M GOING HOME.
GRAB
OH, PLEASE WAIT.
I HAVE SOMETHING TO ASK YOU AS SETO'S BROTHER.
Eek!
I KNOW NOTHING!
WHAT IS HIS FAVORITE FOOD?
FAVORITE FOOD?

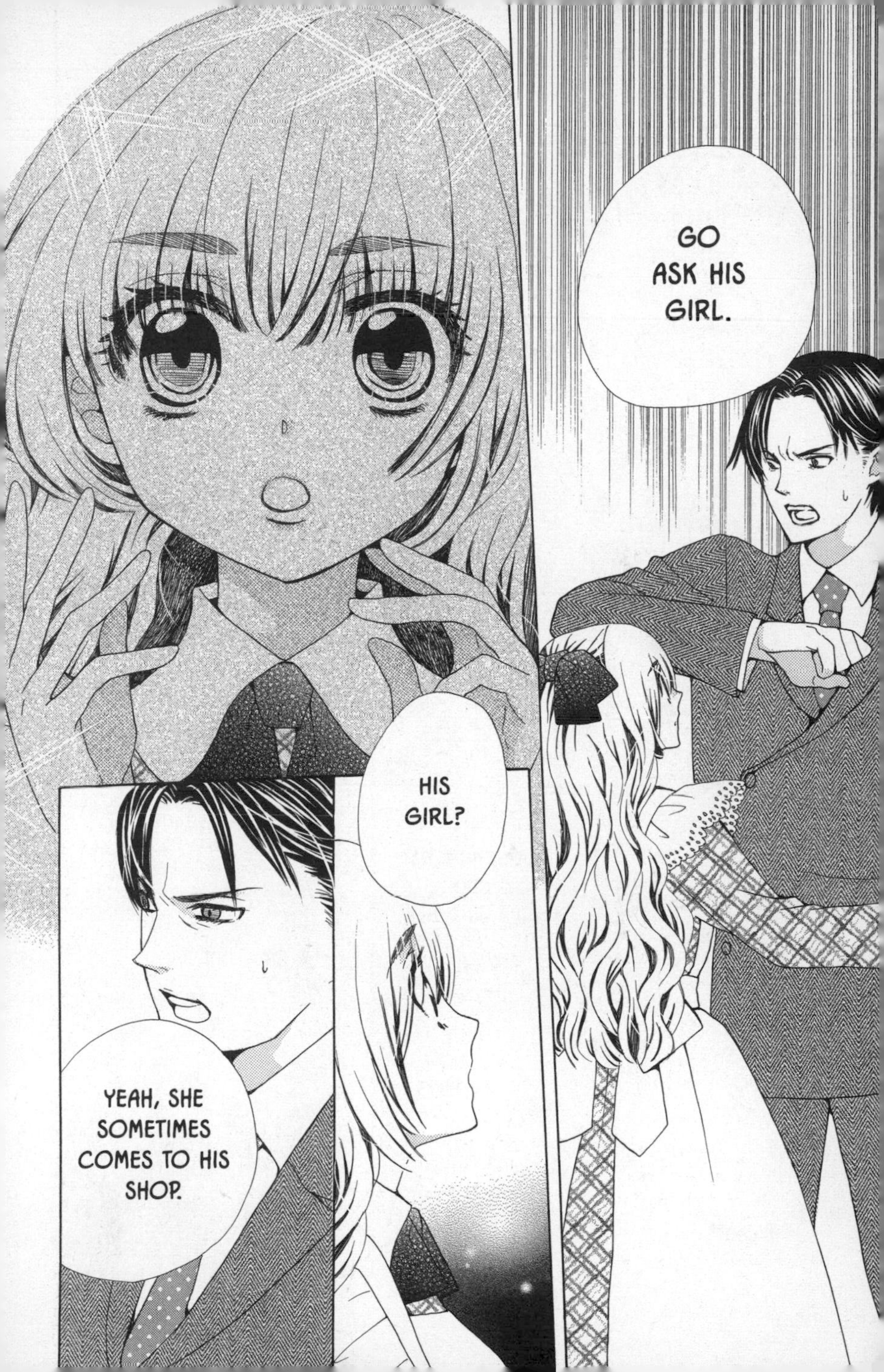
GO ASK HIS GIRL.
HIS GIRL?
YEAH, SHE SOMETIMES COMES TO HIS SHOP.

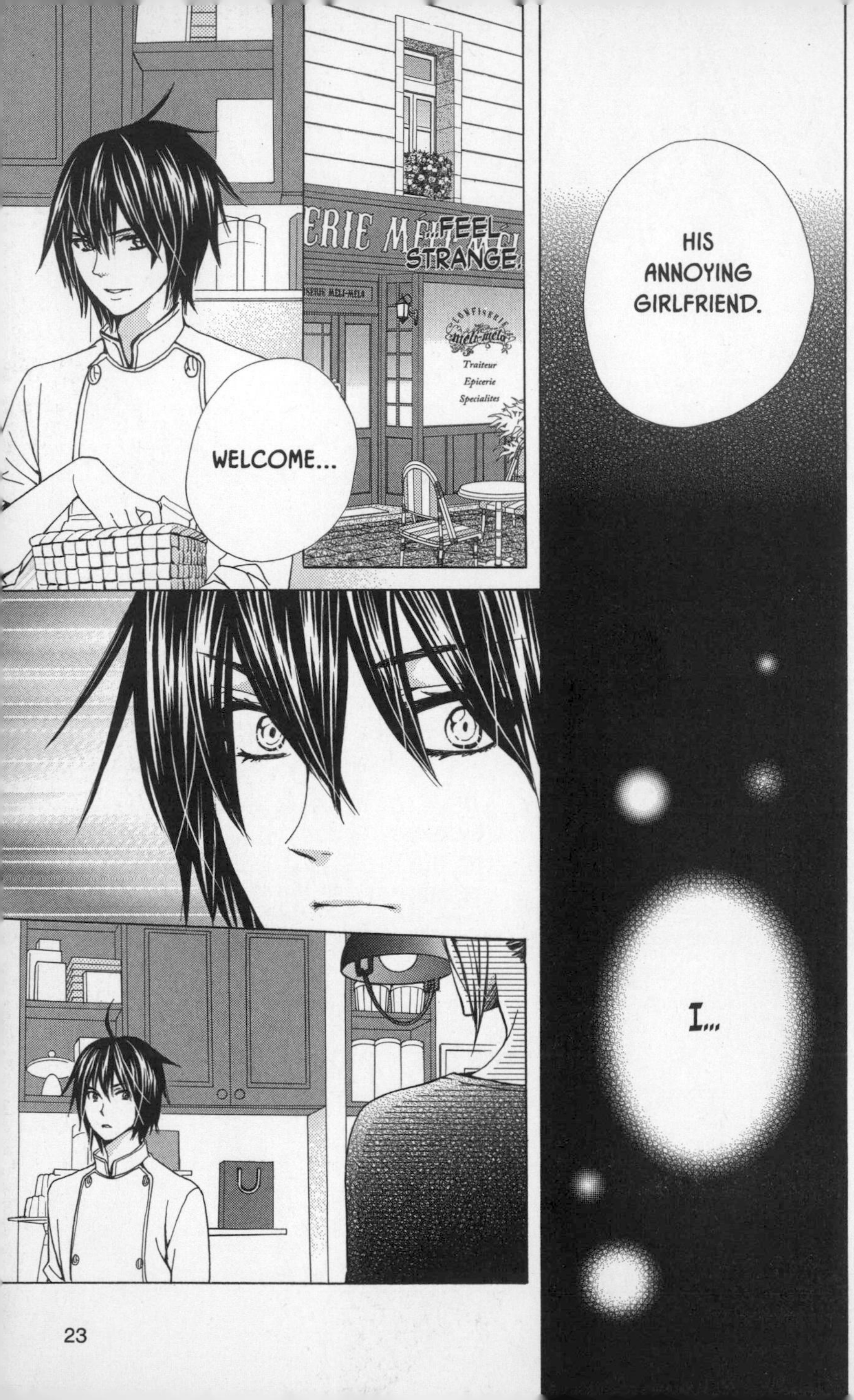
HIS ANNOYING GIRLFRIEND.
I...
...FEEL STRANGE.
Traiteur
Epicerie
Specialites
WELCOME...

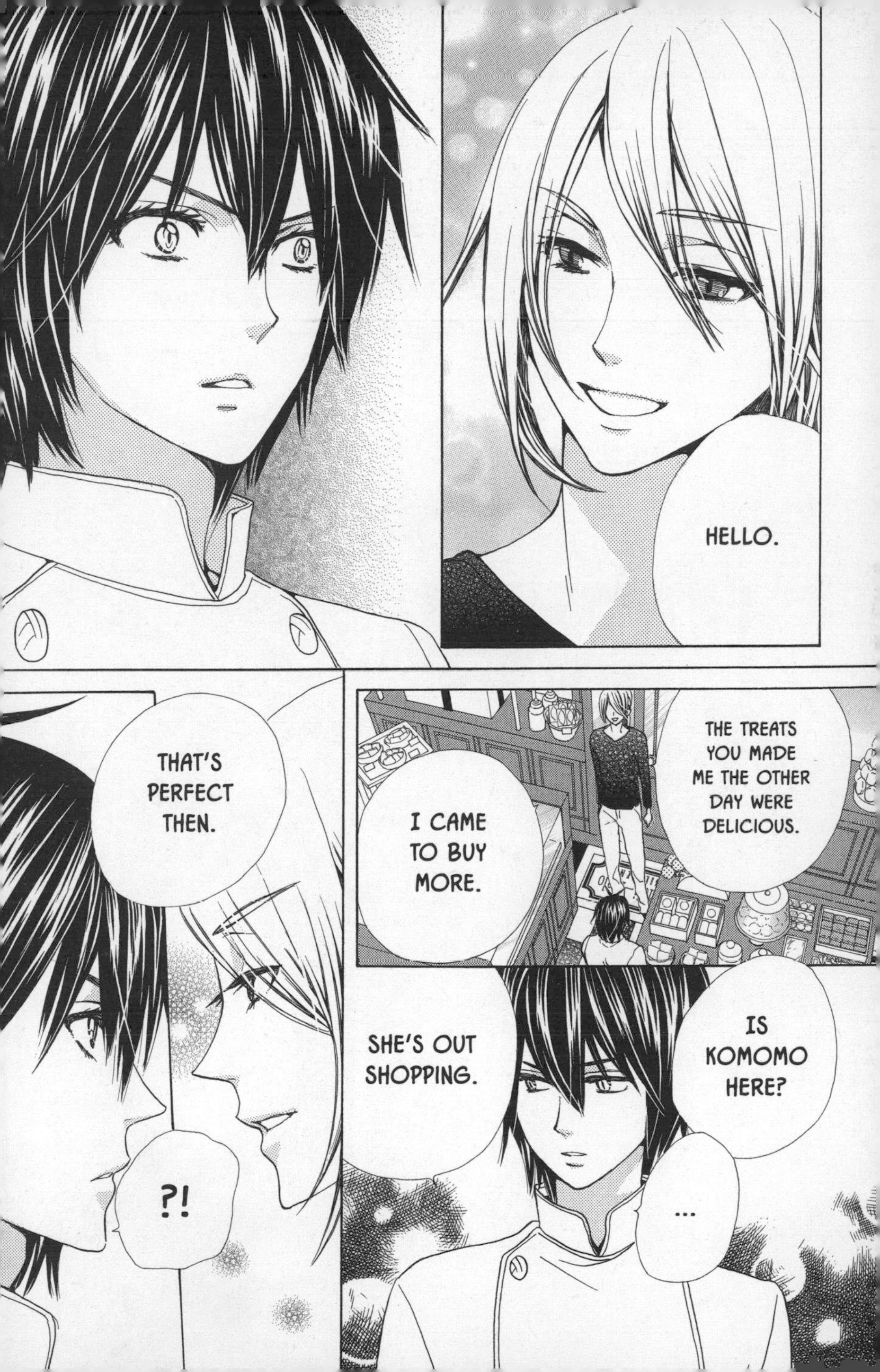
HELLO.
THE TREATS YOU MADE ME THE OTHER DAY WERE DELICIOUS.
I CAME TO BUY MORE.
IS KOMOMO HERE?
SHE'S OUT SHOPPING.
...
THAT'S PERFECT THEN.
?!

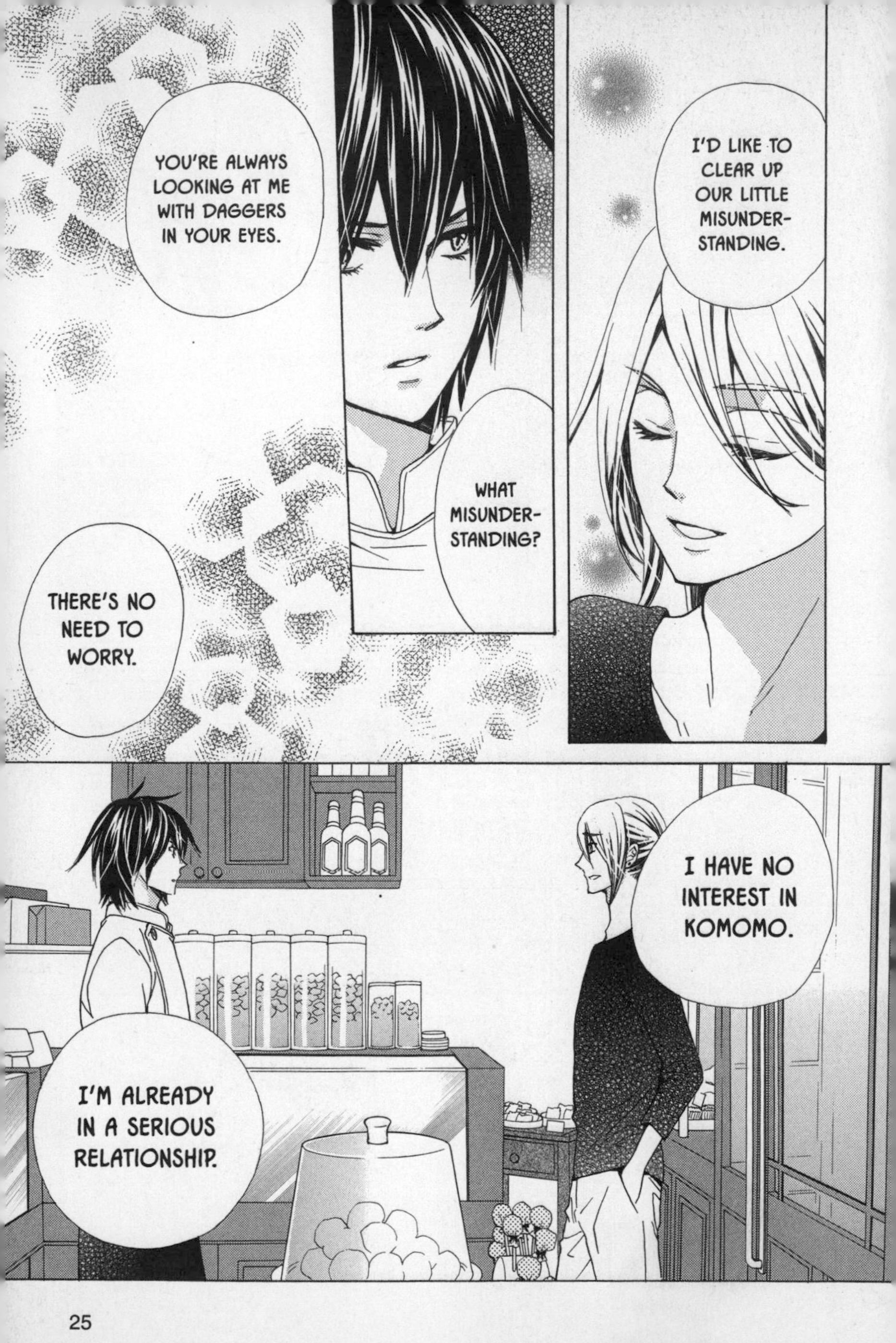
I'D LIKE TO CLEAR UP OUR LITTLE MISUNDERSTANDING.
WHAT MISUNDERSTANDING?
YOU'RE ALWAYS LOOKING AT ME WITH DAGGERS IN YOUR EYES.
THERE'S NO NEED TO WORRY.
I HAVE NO INTEREST IN KOMOMO.
I'M ALREADY IN A SERIOUS RELATIONSHIP.

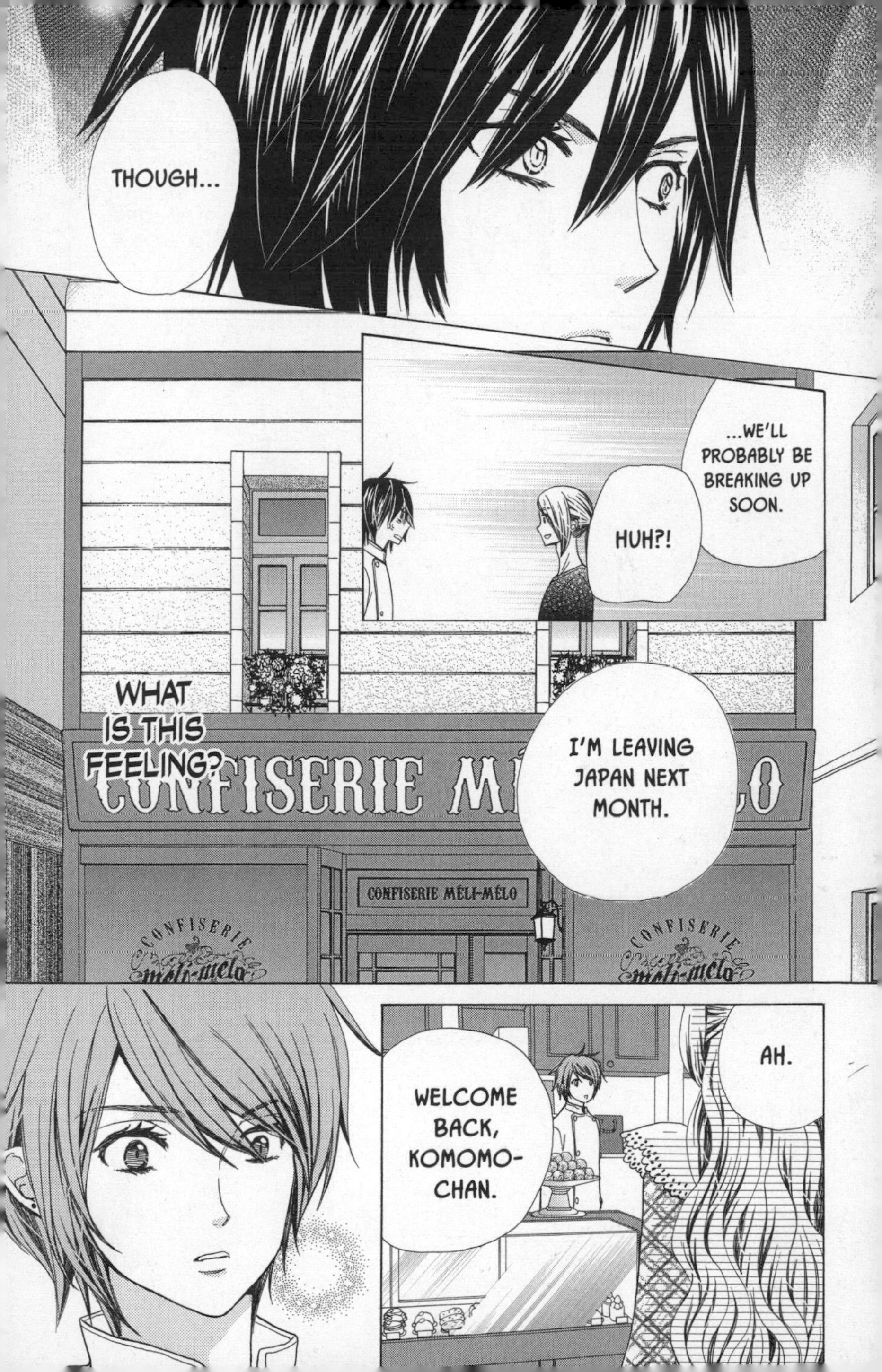
THOUGH...
...WE'LL PROBABLY BE BREAKING UP SOON.
HUH?!
I'M LEAVING JAPAN NEXT MONTH.
WHAT IS THIS FEELING?
CONFISERIE MÉLI-MÉLO
AH.
WELCOME BACK, KOMOMO-CHAN.

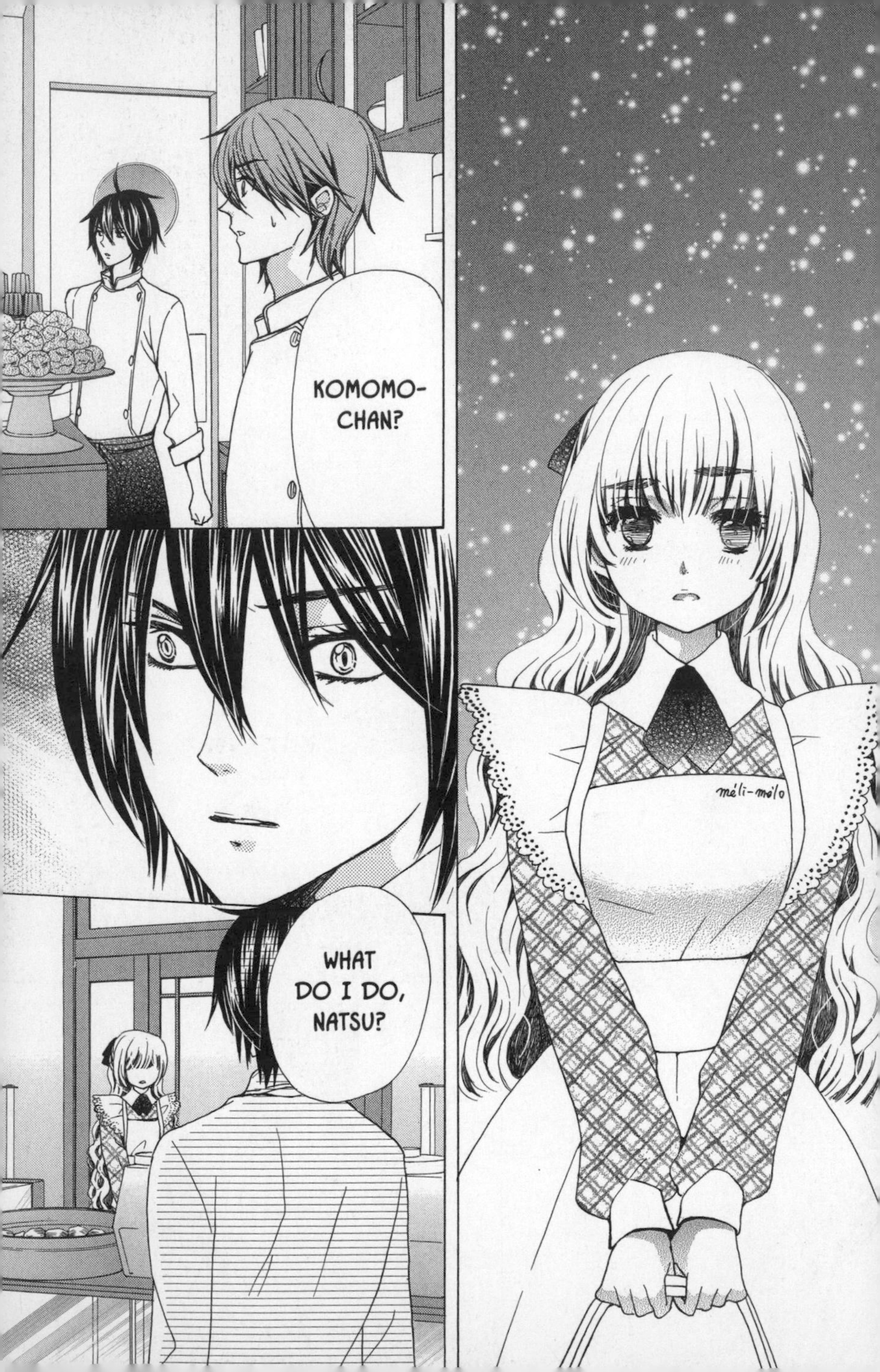
méli-mélo
KOMOMO-CHAN?
WHAT DO I DO, NATSU?

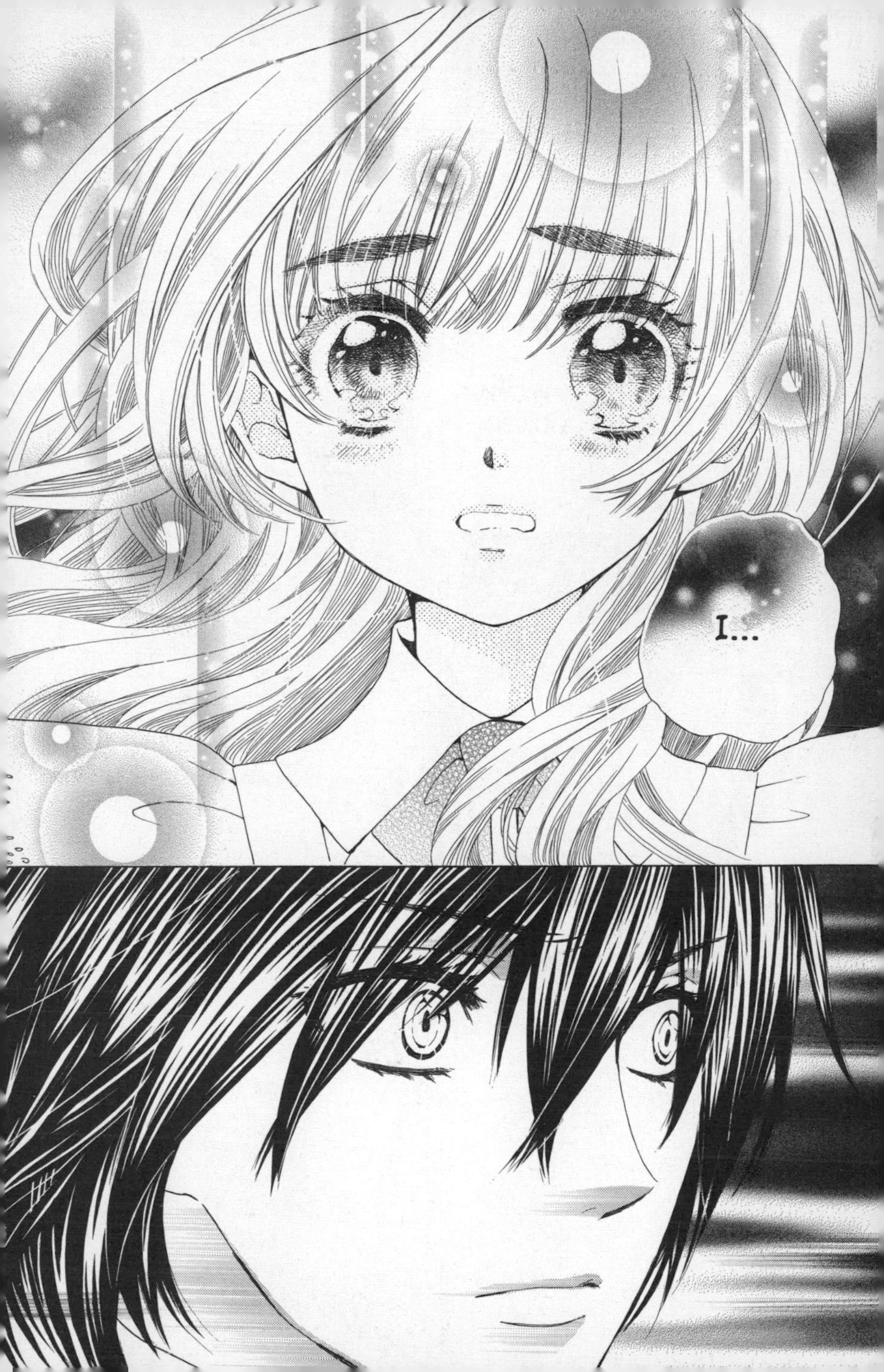
I...

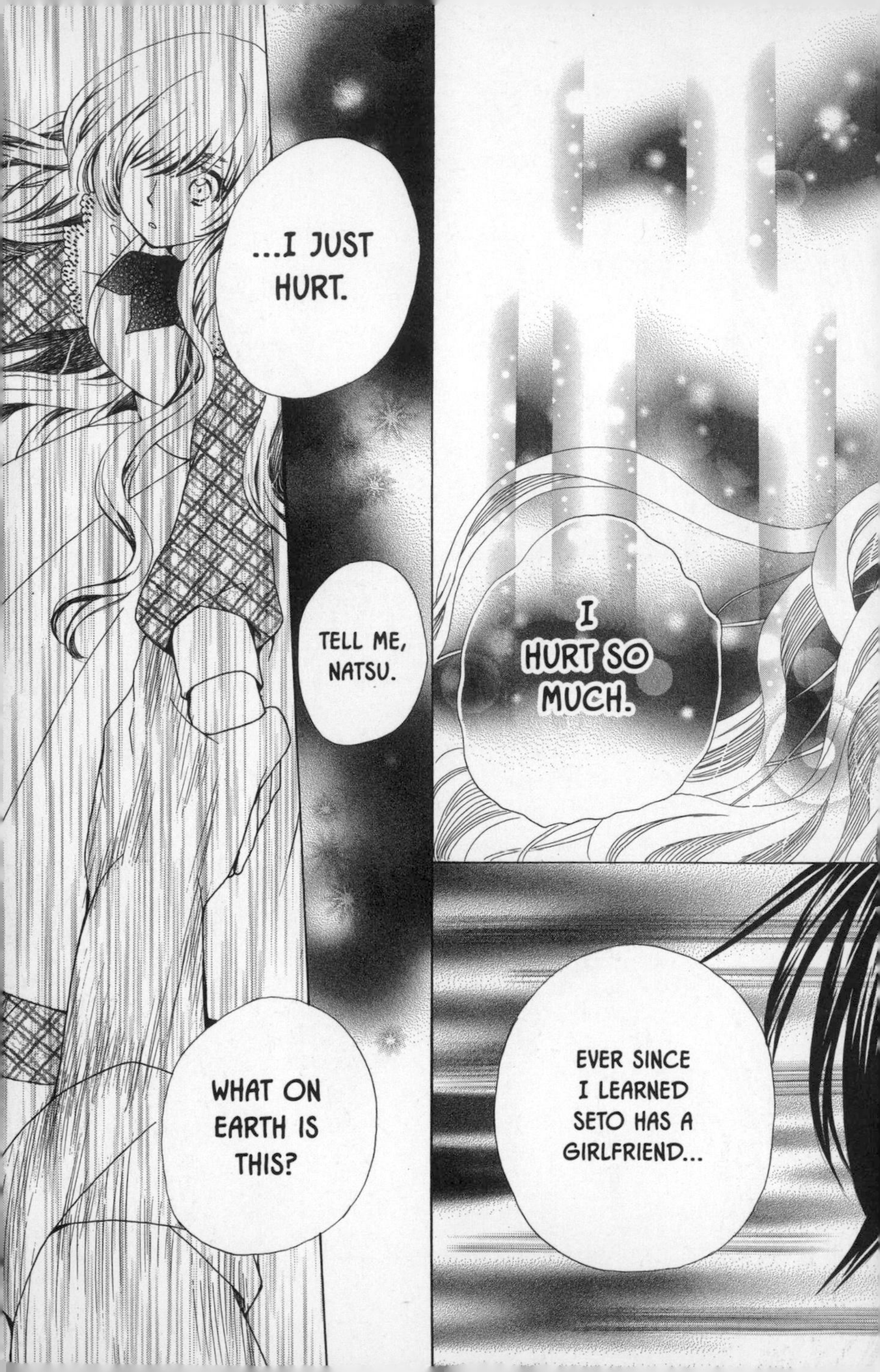
I HURT SO MUCH.
EVER SINCE I LEARNED SETO HAS A GIRLFRIEND...
...I JUST HURT.
TELL ME, NATSU.
WHAT ON EARTH IS THIS?

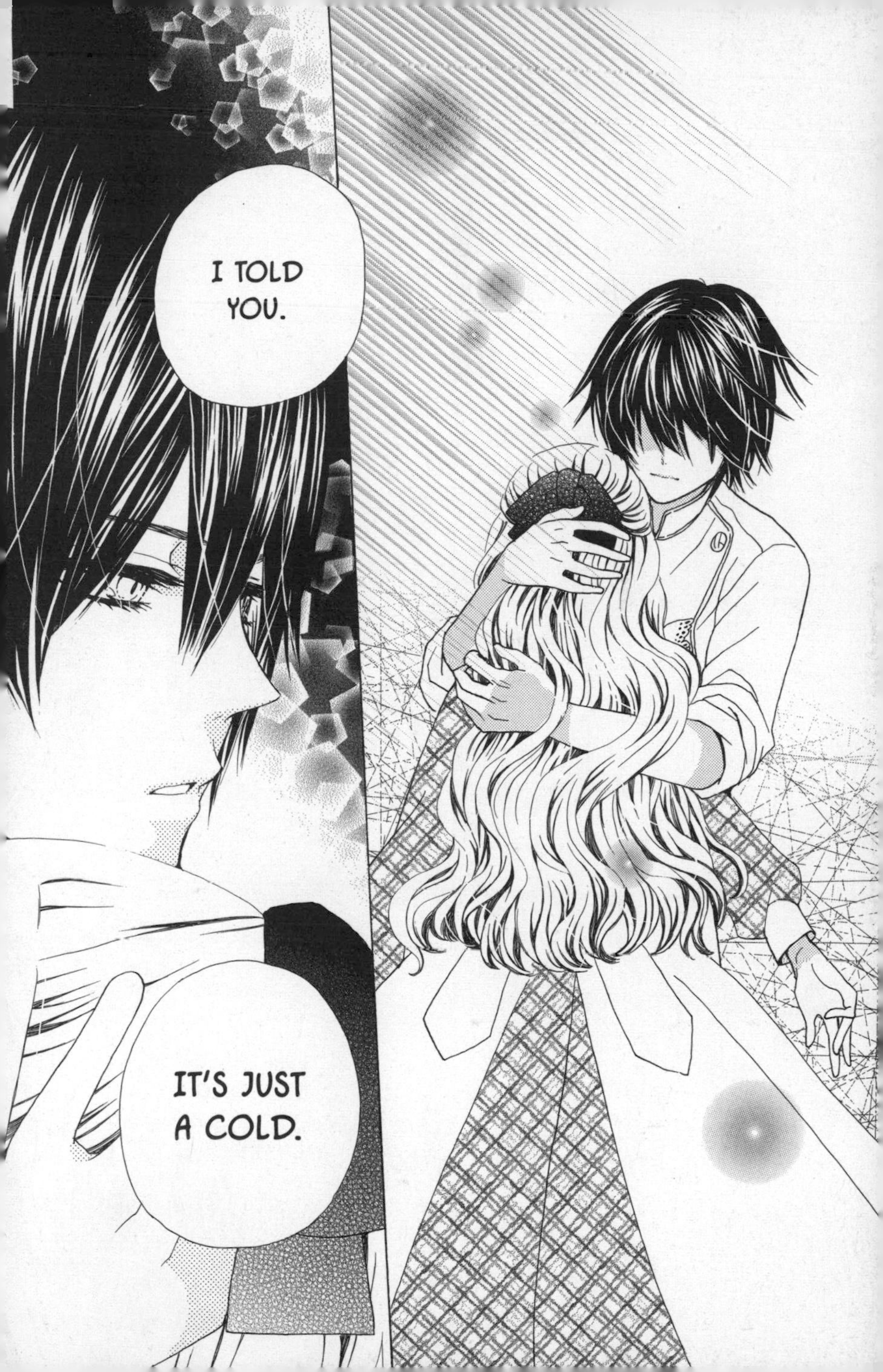
I TOLD YOU.
IT'S JUST A COLD.

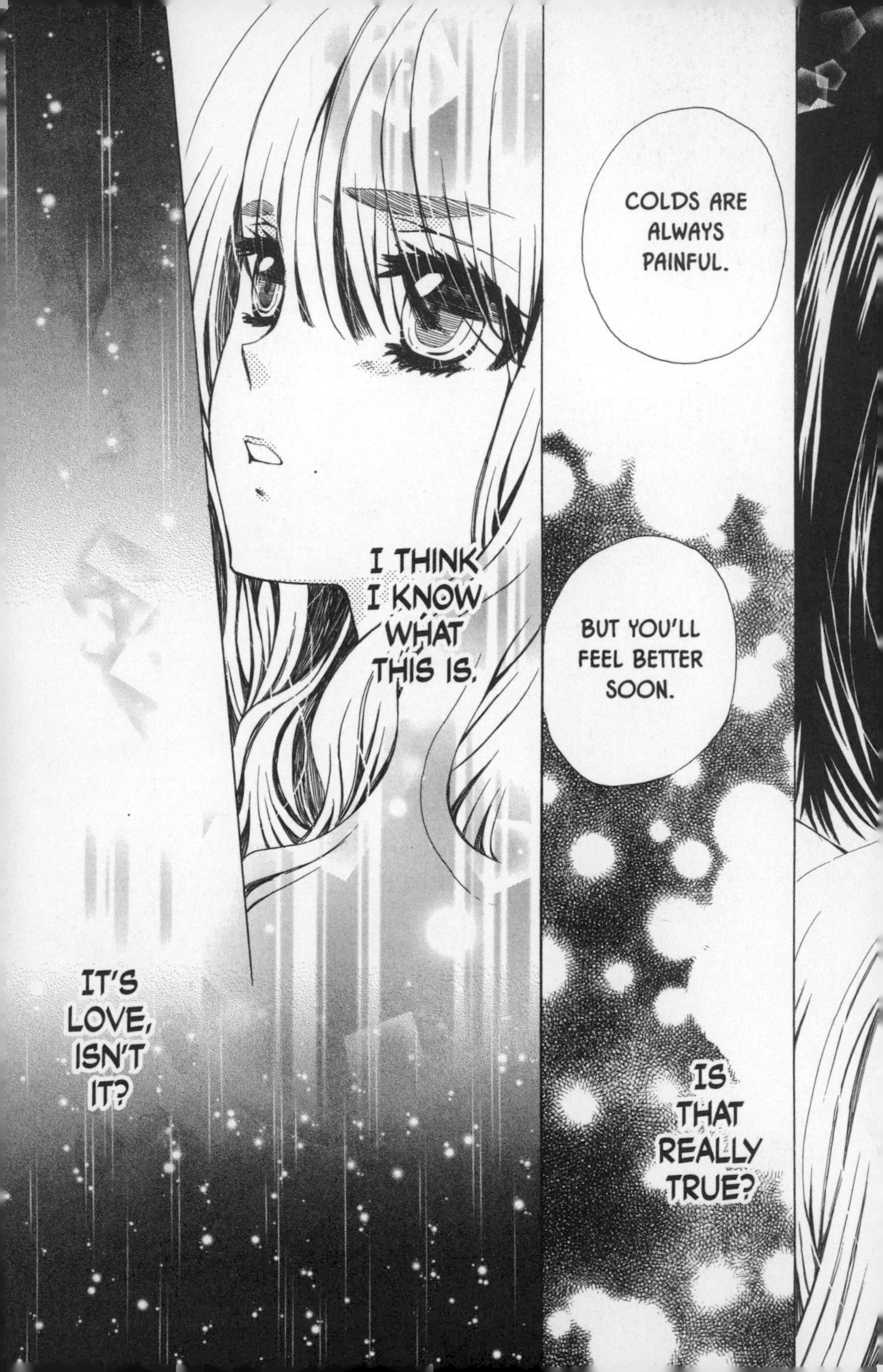
COLDS ARE ALWAYS PAINFUL.
BUT YOU'LL FEEL BETTER SOON.
IS THAT REALLY TRUE?
I THINK I KNOW WHAT THIS IS.
IT'S LOVE, ISN'T IT?

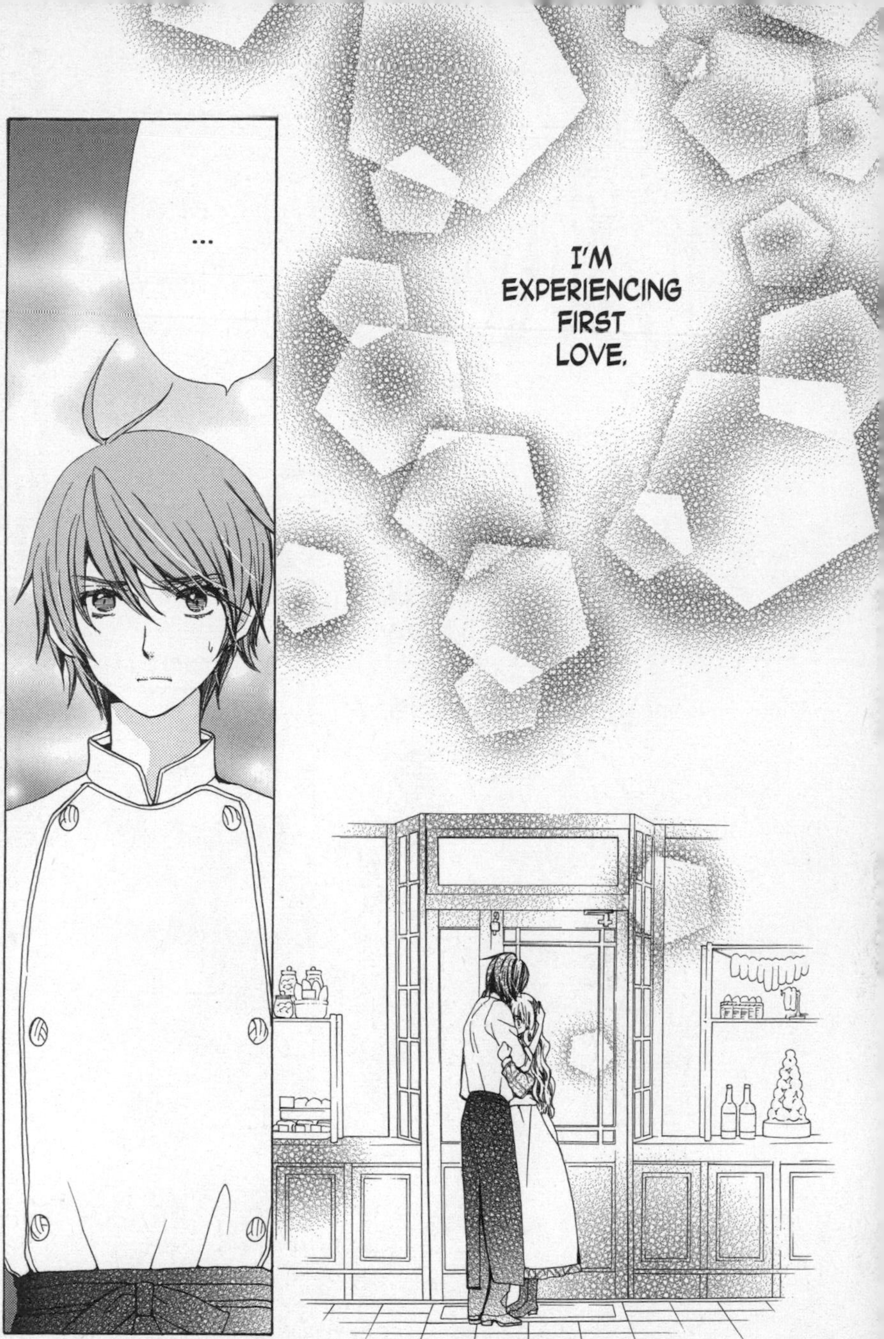
I'M EXPERIENCING FIRST LOVE.
...

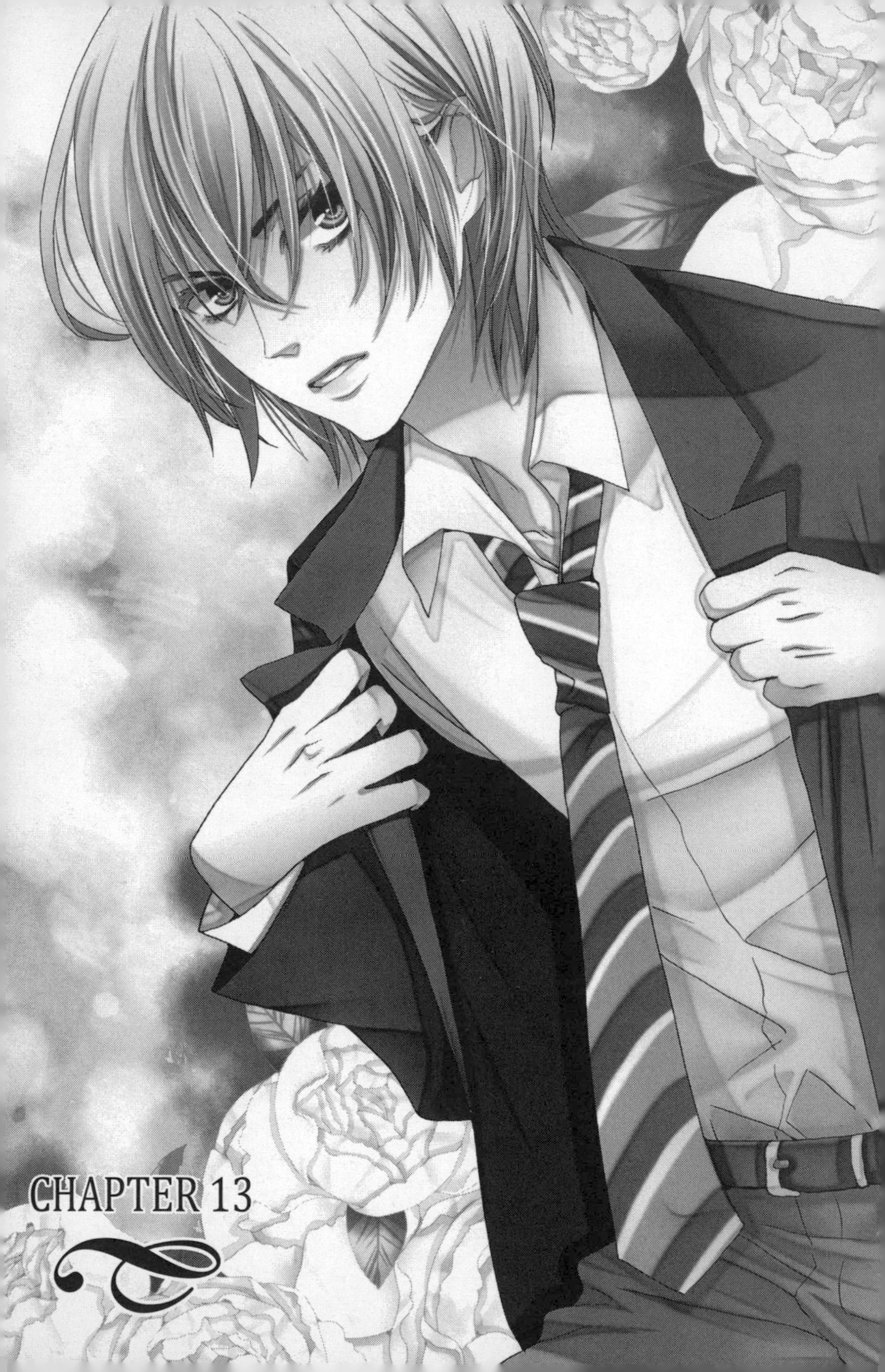
CHAPTER 13

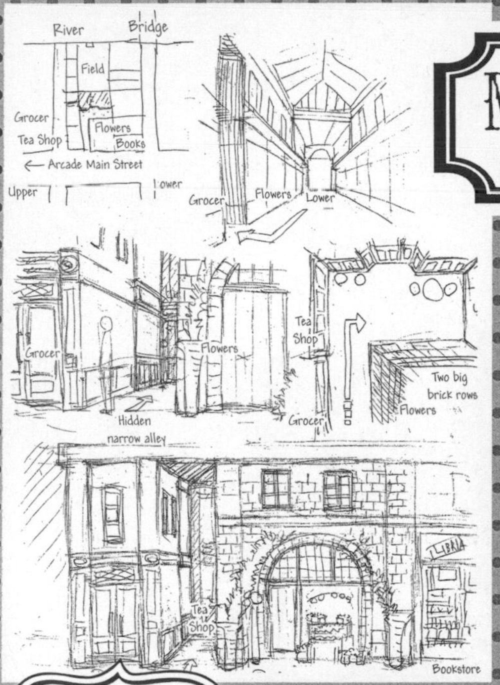
River
Bridge
Field
Grocer
Tea Shop
Flowers
Books
← Arcade Main Street
Upper
Lower
Grocer
Flowers
Lower
Grocer
Flowers
Hidden narrow alley
Tea Shop
Two big brick rows
Flowers
Grocer
LIBRIA
Tea Shop
Bookstore

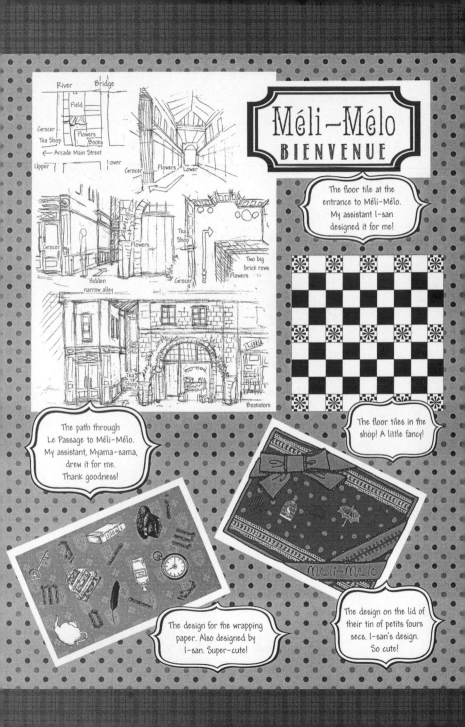

Méli-Mélo
BIENVENUE

The floor tile at the entrance to Méli-Mélo. My assistant I-san designed it for me!

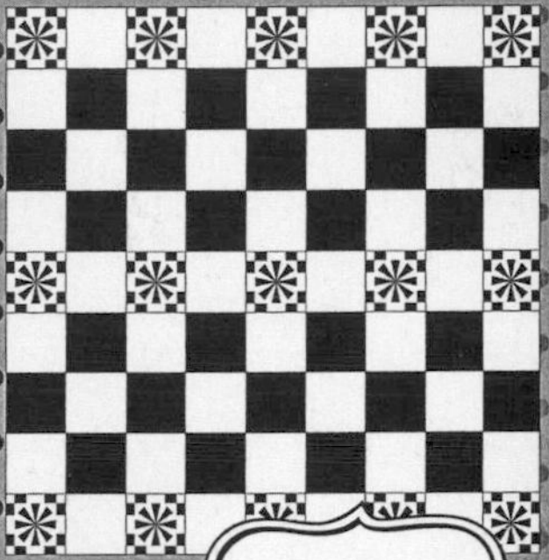

The path through Le Passage to Méli-Mélo. My assistant, Myama-sama, drew it for me. Thank goodness!

The floor tiles in the shop! A little fancy!

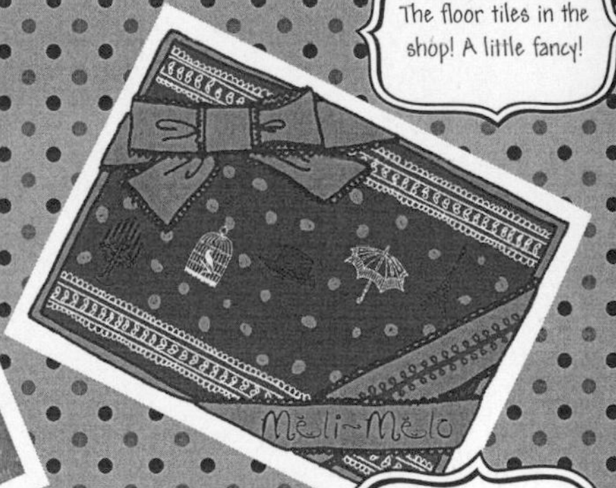
Méli~Mélo

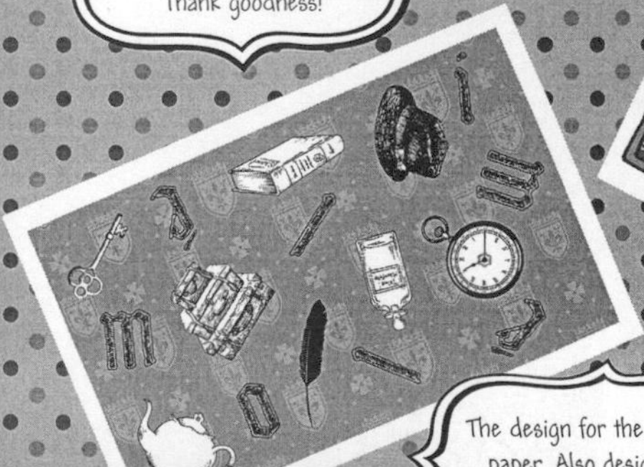

The design for the wrapping paper. Also designed by I-san. Super-cute!

The design on the lid of their tin of petits fours secs. I-san's design. So cute!

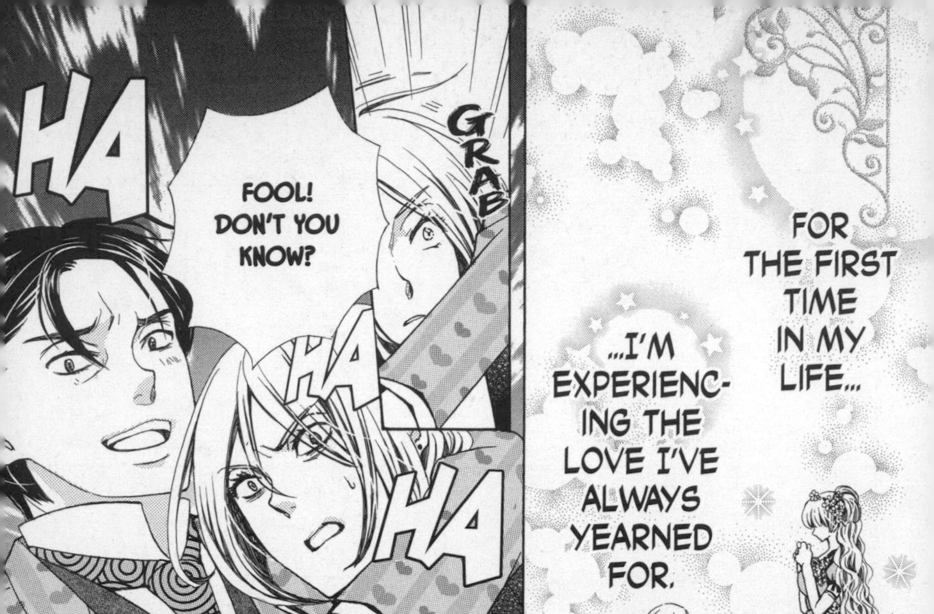
FOR THE FIRST TIME IN MY LIFE...
...I'M EXPERIENCING THE LOVE I'VE ALWAYS YEARNED FOR.
GRAB
HA
FOOL! DON'T YOU KNOW?
HA
HA
HA
HA
HA
HE'S ALREADY IN LOVE WITH SOMEONE ELSE!

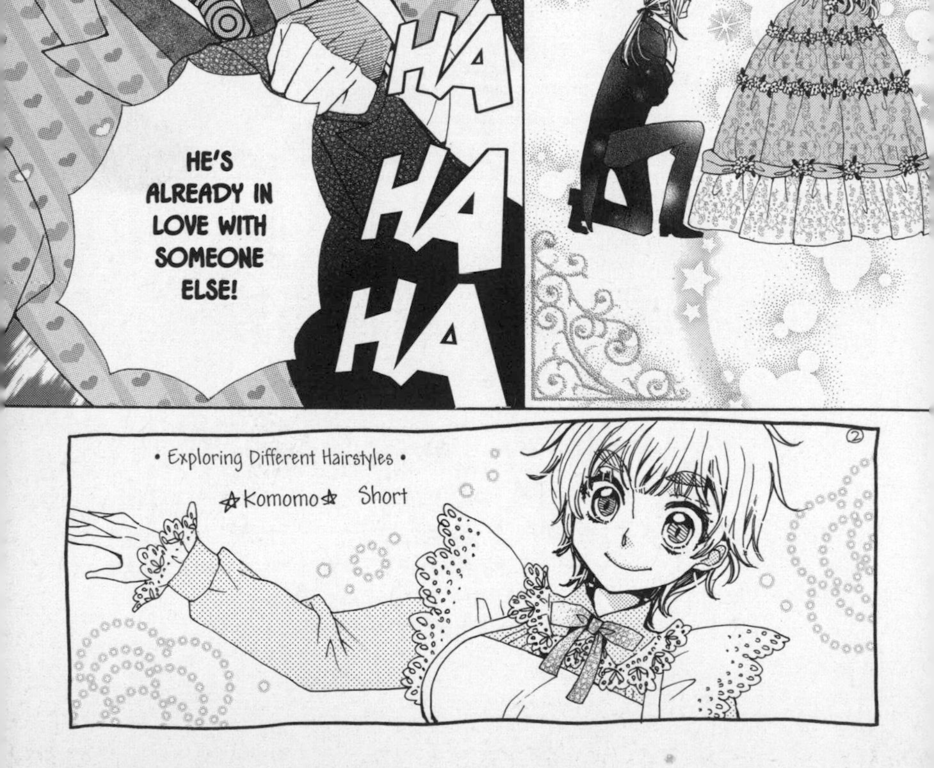
2
• Exploring Different Hairstyles •
☆Komomo☆ Short

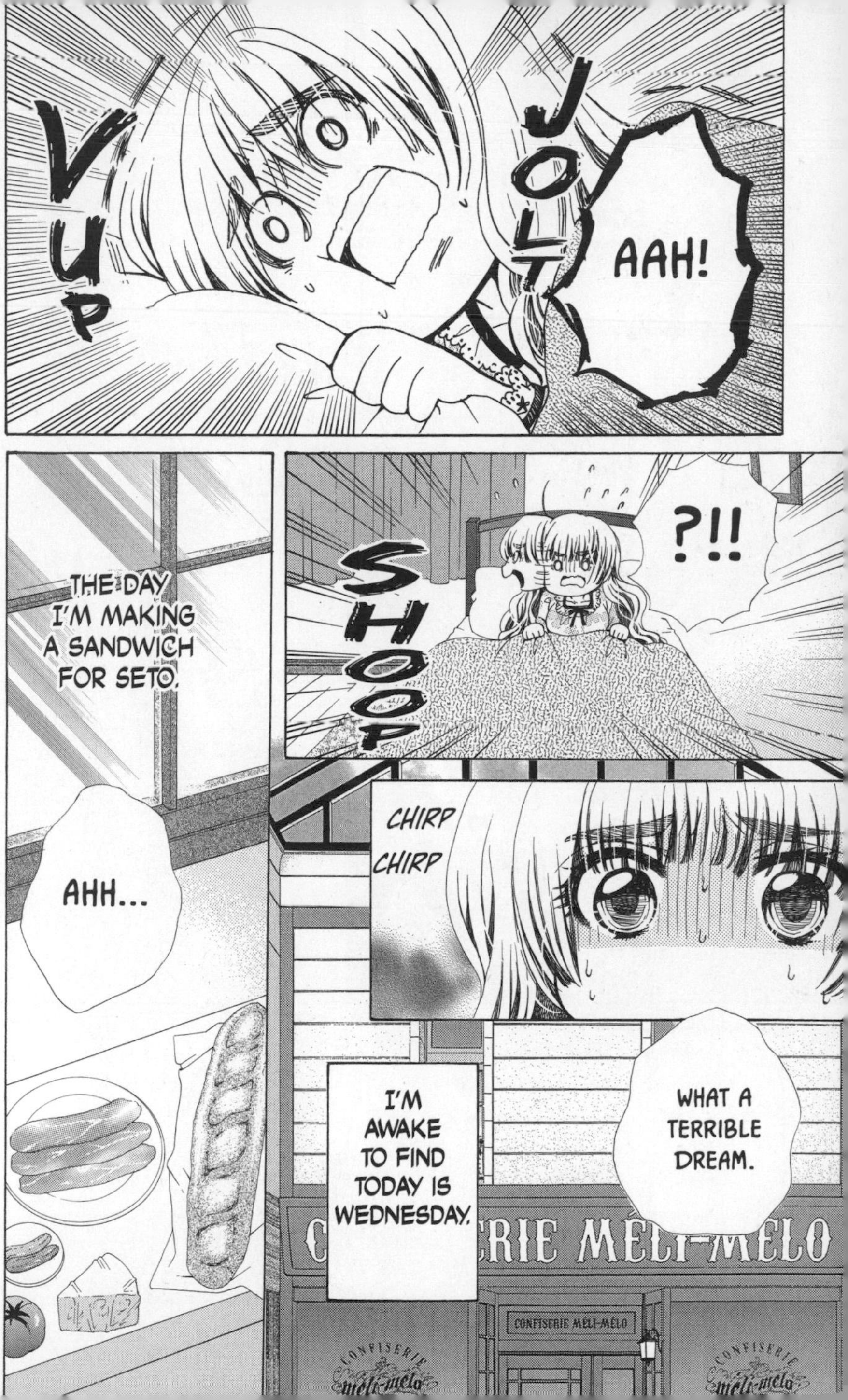
AAH!
JOLT
VUP
?!!
SHOOP
CHIRP
CHIRP
WHAT A TERRIBLE DREAM.
I'M AWAKE TO FIND TODAY IS WEDNESDAY.
ERIE MÉLI-MÉLO
CONFISERIE MÉLI-MÉLO
CONFISERIE méli-mélo
CONFISERIE méli-mélo
THE DAY I'M MAKING A SANDWICH FOR SETO.
AHH...

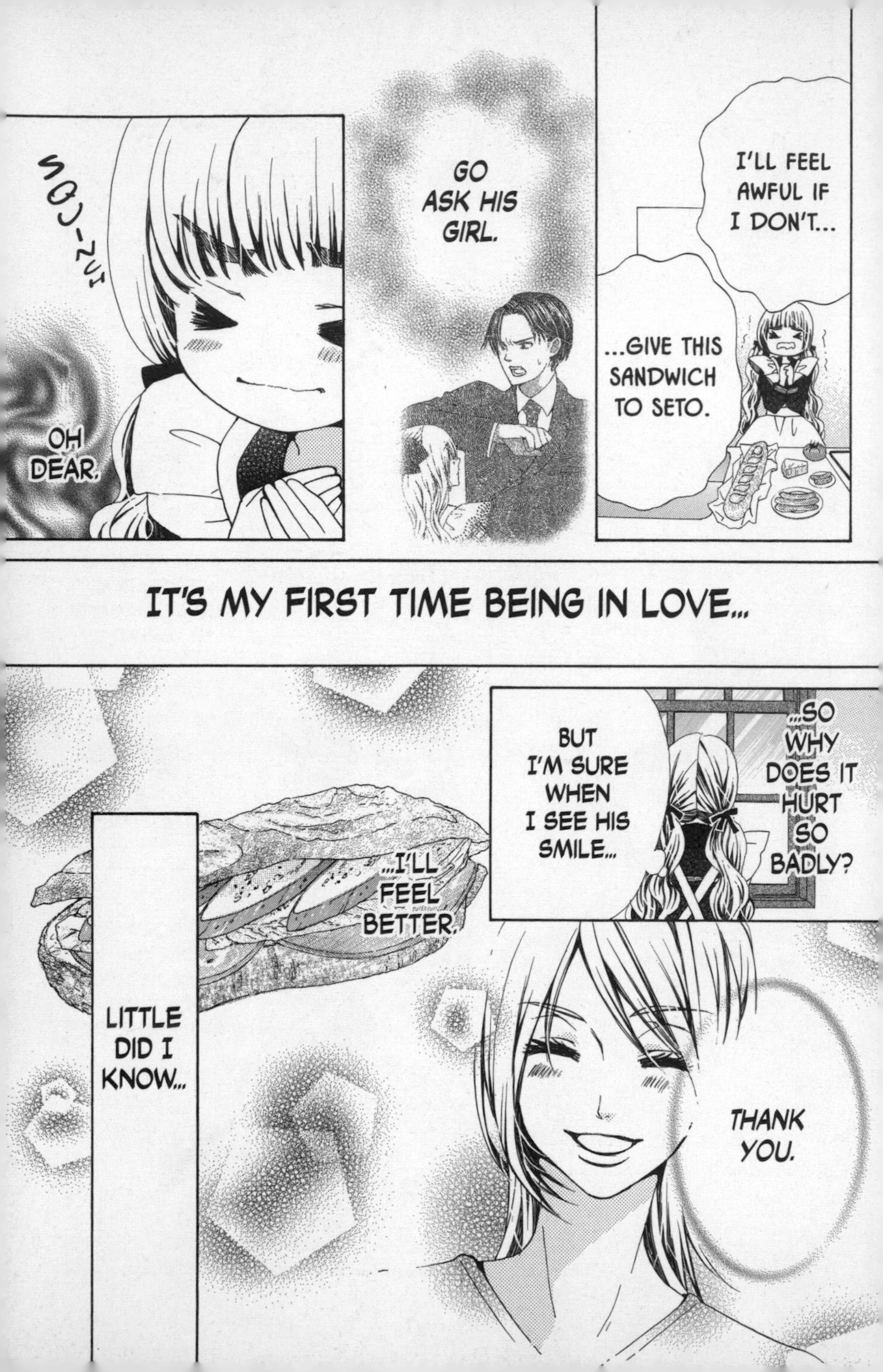
I'LL FEEL AWFUL IF I DON'T...
...GIVE THIS SANDWICH TO SETO.
GO ASK HIS GIRL.
OH DEAR.
IT'S MY FIRST TIME BEING IN LOVE...
...SO WHY DOES IT HURT SO BADLY?
BUT I'M SURE WHEN I SEE HIS SMILE...
...I'LL FEEL BETTER.
THANK YOU.
LITTLE DID I KNOW...

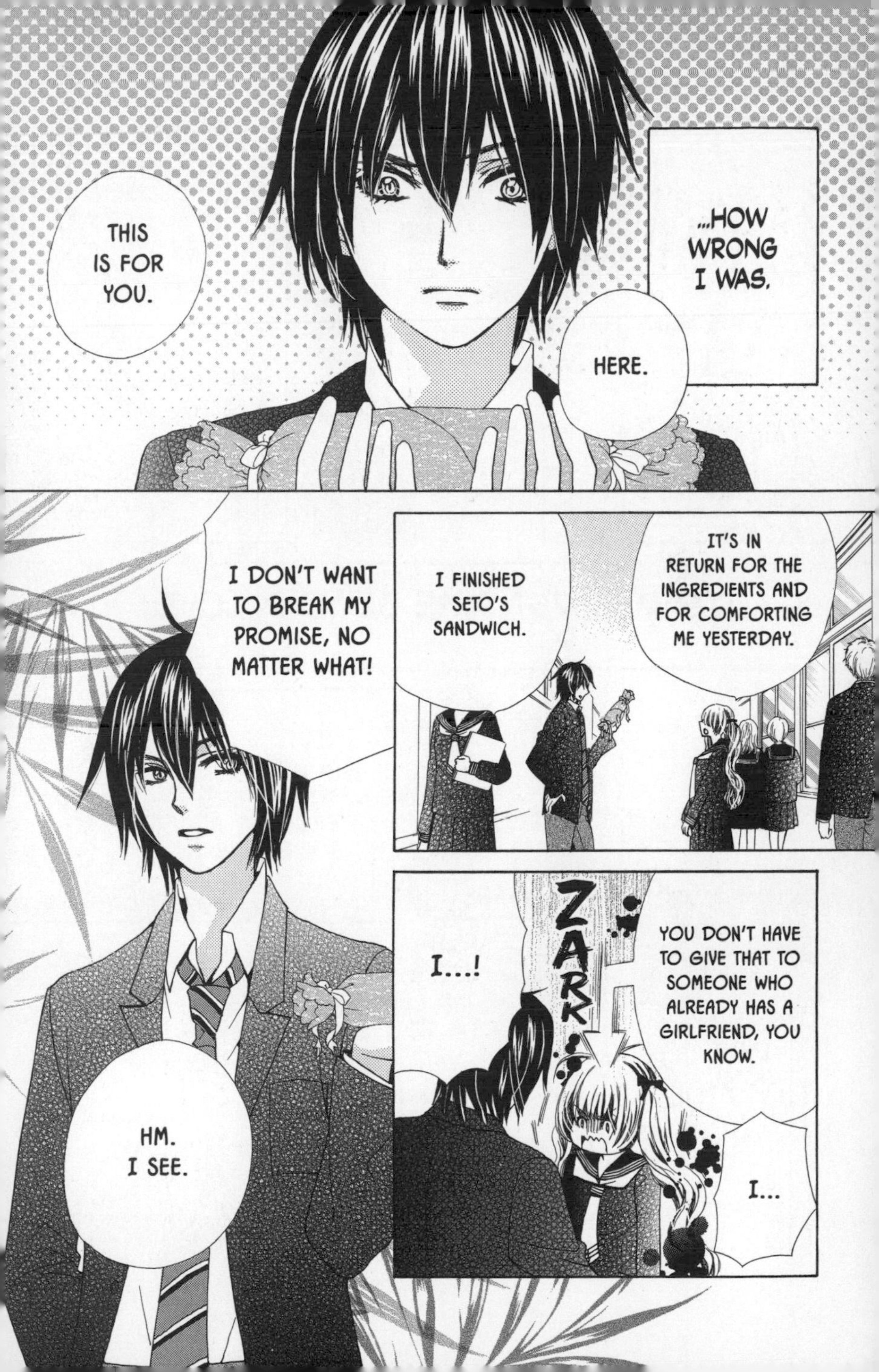
...HOW WRONG I WAS.
HERE.
THIS IS FOR YOU.
IT'S IN RETURN FOR THE INGREDIENTS AND FOR COMFORTING ME YESTERDAY.
I FINISHED SETO'S SANDWICH.
YOU DON'T HAVE TO GIVE THAT TO SOMEONE WHO ALREADY HAS A GIRLFRIEND, YOU KNOW.
ZARK
I...!
I...
I DON'T WANT TO BREAK MY PROMISE, NO MATTER WHAT!
HM. I SEE.

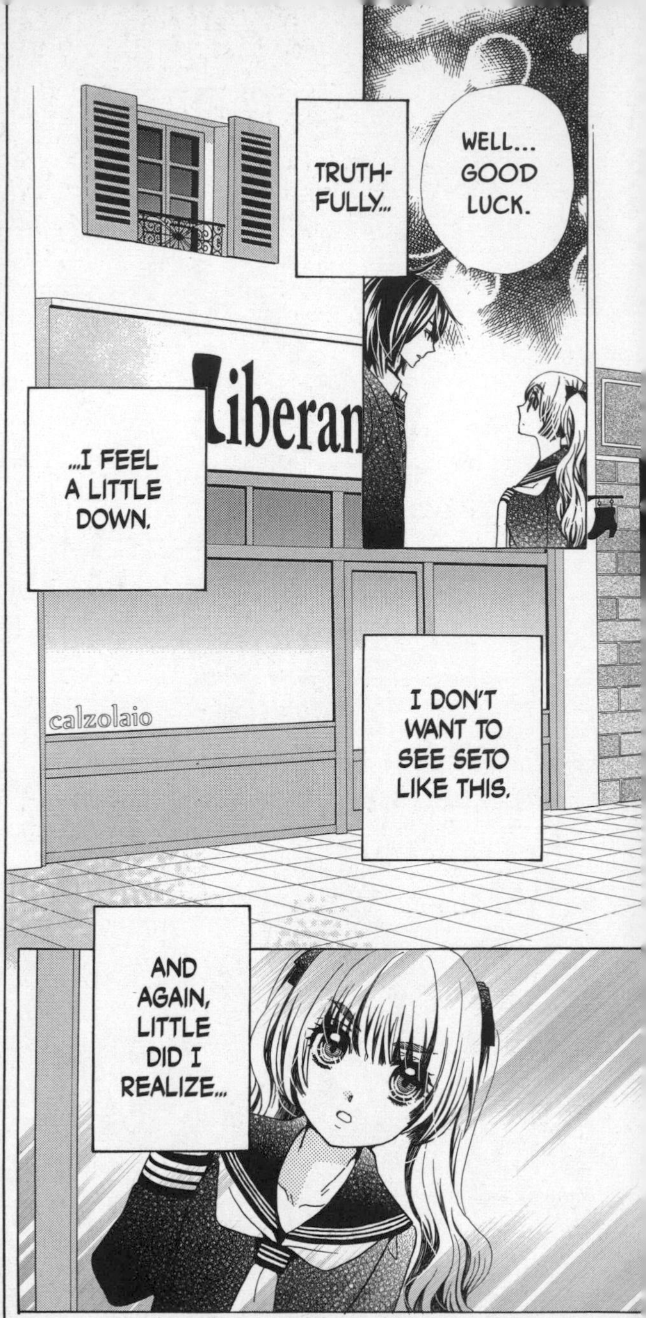
WELL... GOOD LUCK.
TRUTH-FULLY...
...I FEEL A LITTLE DOWN.
Liberan
calzolaio
I DON'T WANT TO SEE SETO LIKE THIS.
AND AGAIN, LITTLE DID I REALIZE...

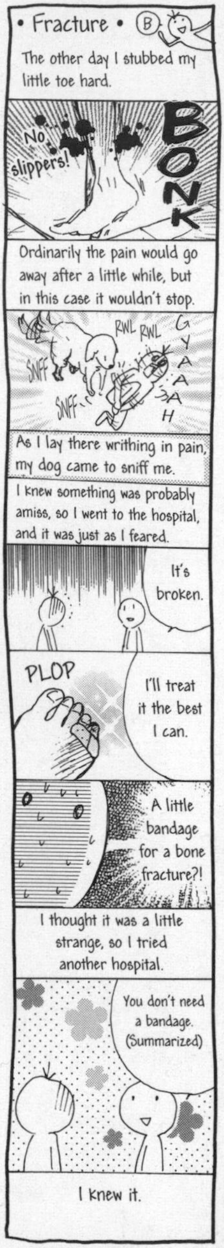
• Fracture • B
The other day I stubbed my little toe hard.
No slippers!
BONK
Ordinarily the pain would go away after a little while, but in this case it wouldn't stop.
RWL RWL
GYAAAAH
SNIFF
SNIFF
As I lay there writhing in pain, my dog came to sniff me.
I knew something was probably amiss, so I went to the hospital, and it was just as I feared.
It's broken.
PLOP
I'll treat it the best I can.
A little bandage for a bone fracture?!
I thought it was a little strange, so I tried another hospital.
You don't need a bandage. (Summarized)
I knew it.

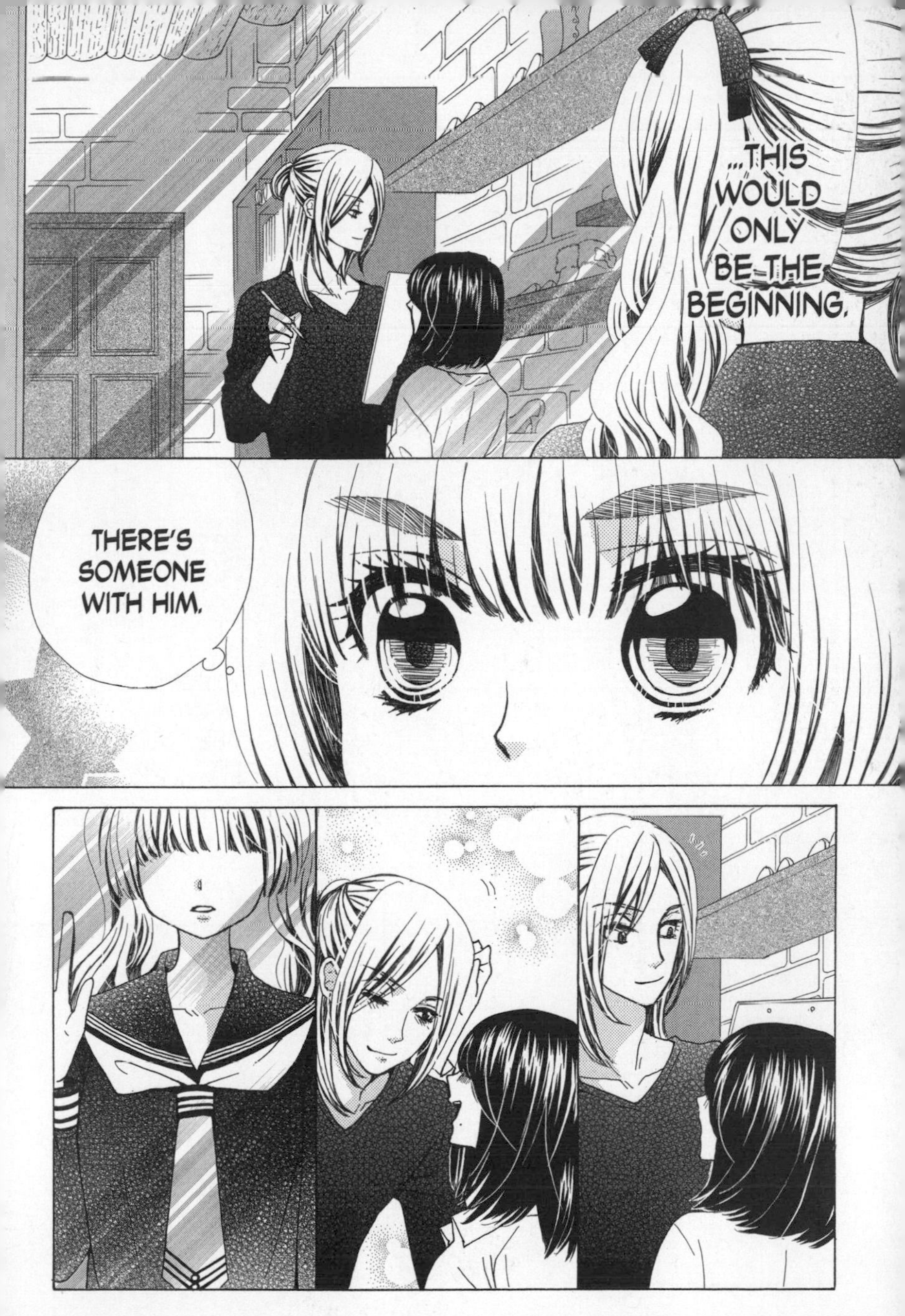
...THIS WOULD ONLY BE THE BEGINNING.
THERE'S SOMEONE WITH HIM.

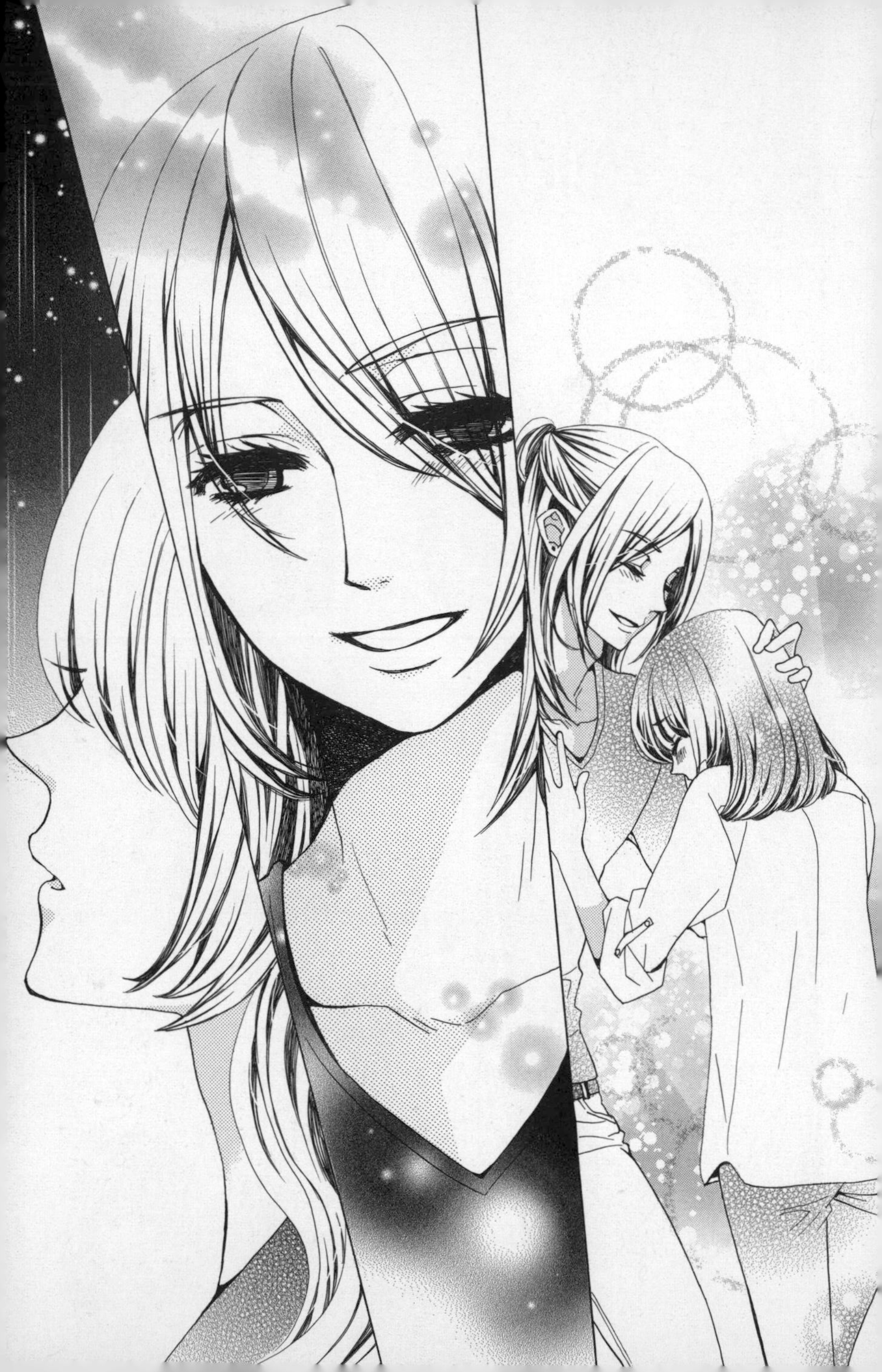

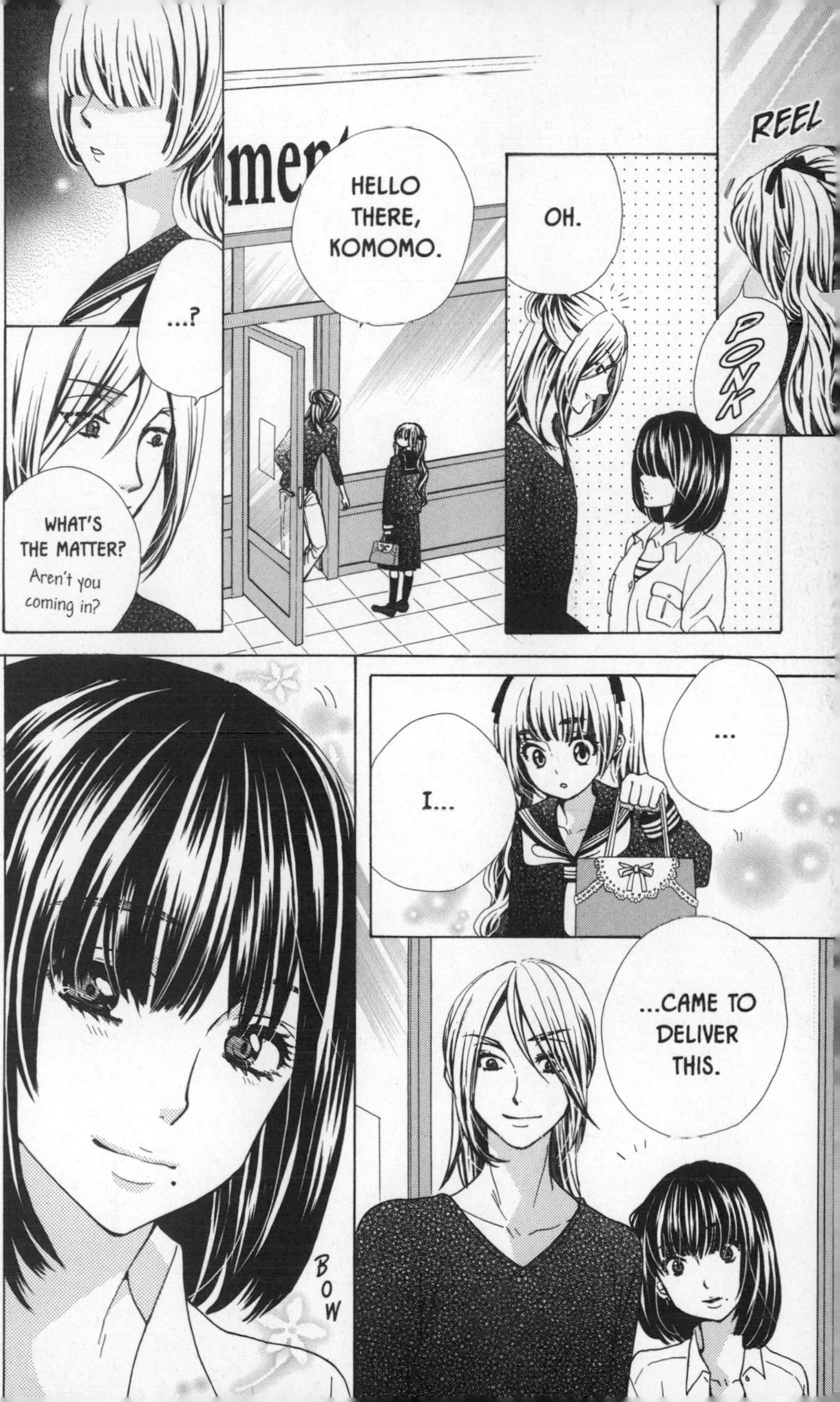
REEL
PONK
OH.
HELLO THERE, KOMOMO.
...?
WHAT'S THE MATTER?
Aren't you coming in?
...
I...
...CAME TO DELIVER THIS.
BOW

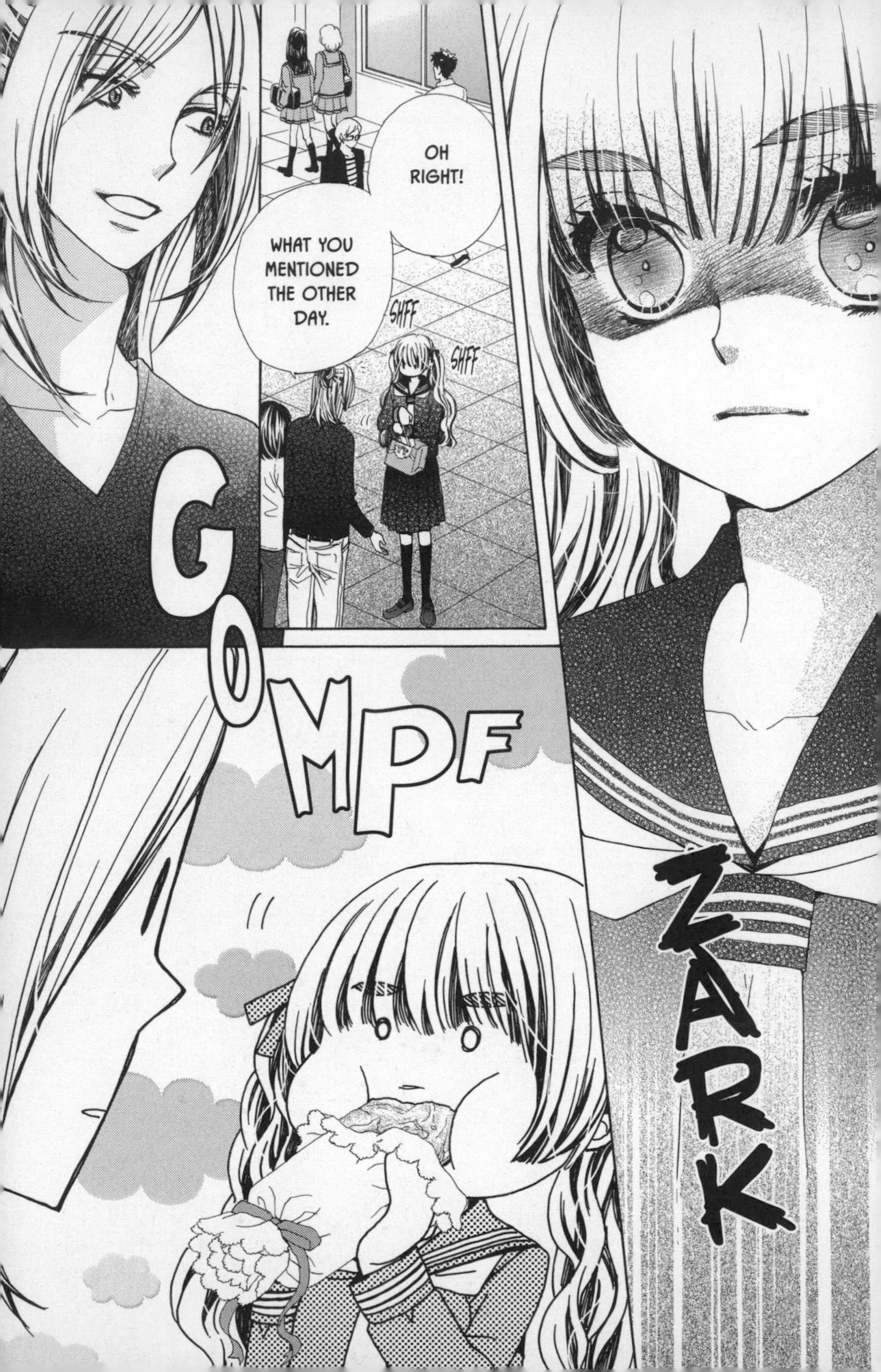
ZARK
OH RIGHT!
WHAT YOU MENTIONED THE OTHER DAY.
SHFF
SHFF
GOMPF

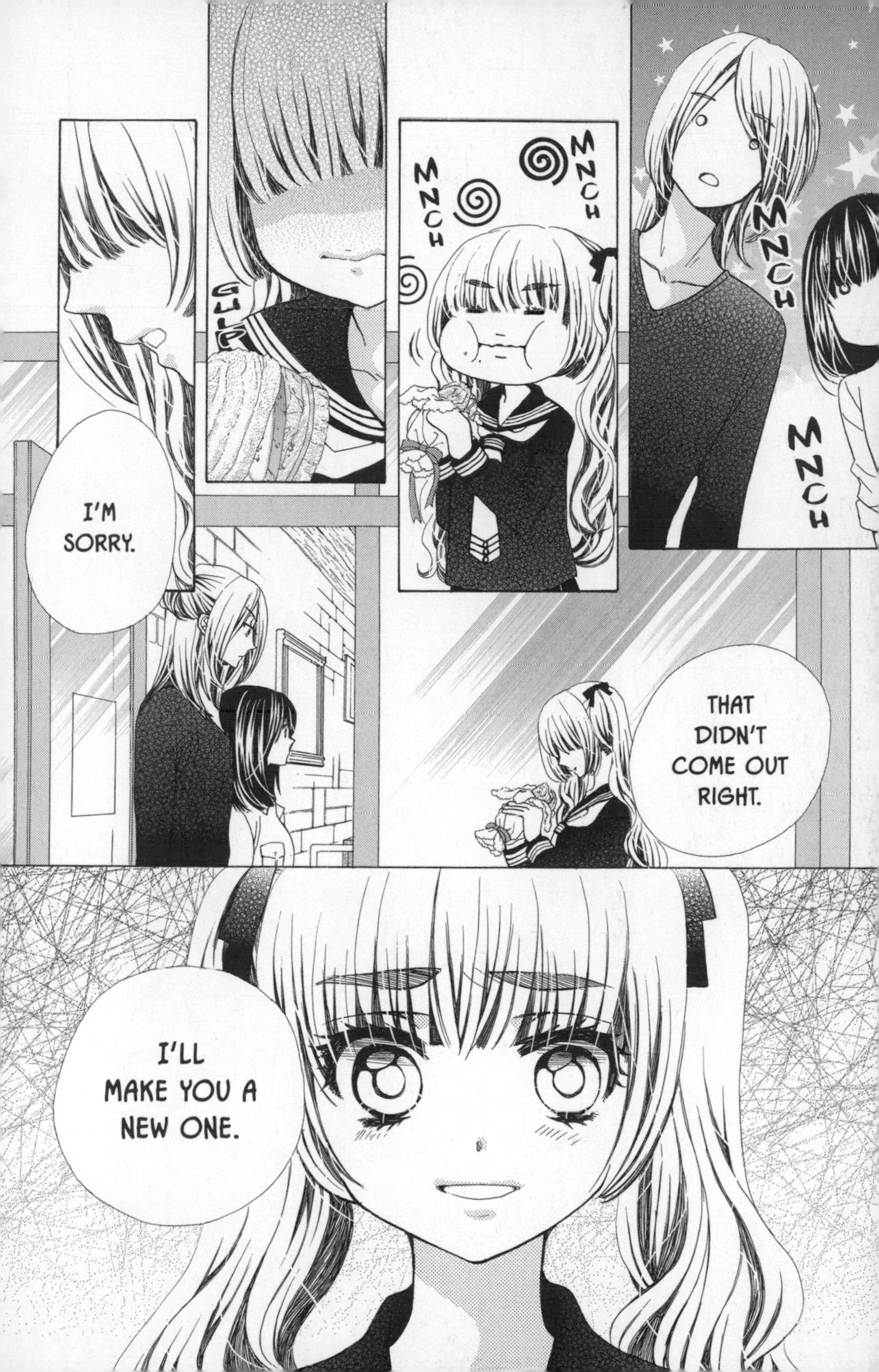
MNCH
MNCH
MNCH
MNCH
GULP
THAT DIDN'T COME OUT RIGHT.
I'M SORRY.
I'LL MAKE YOU A NEW ONE.

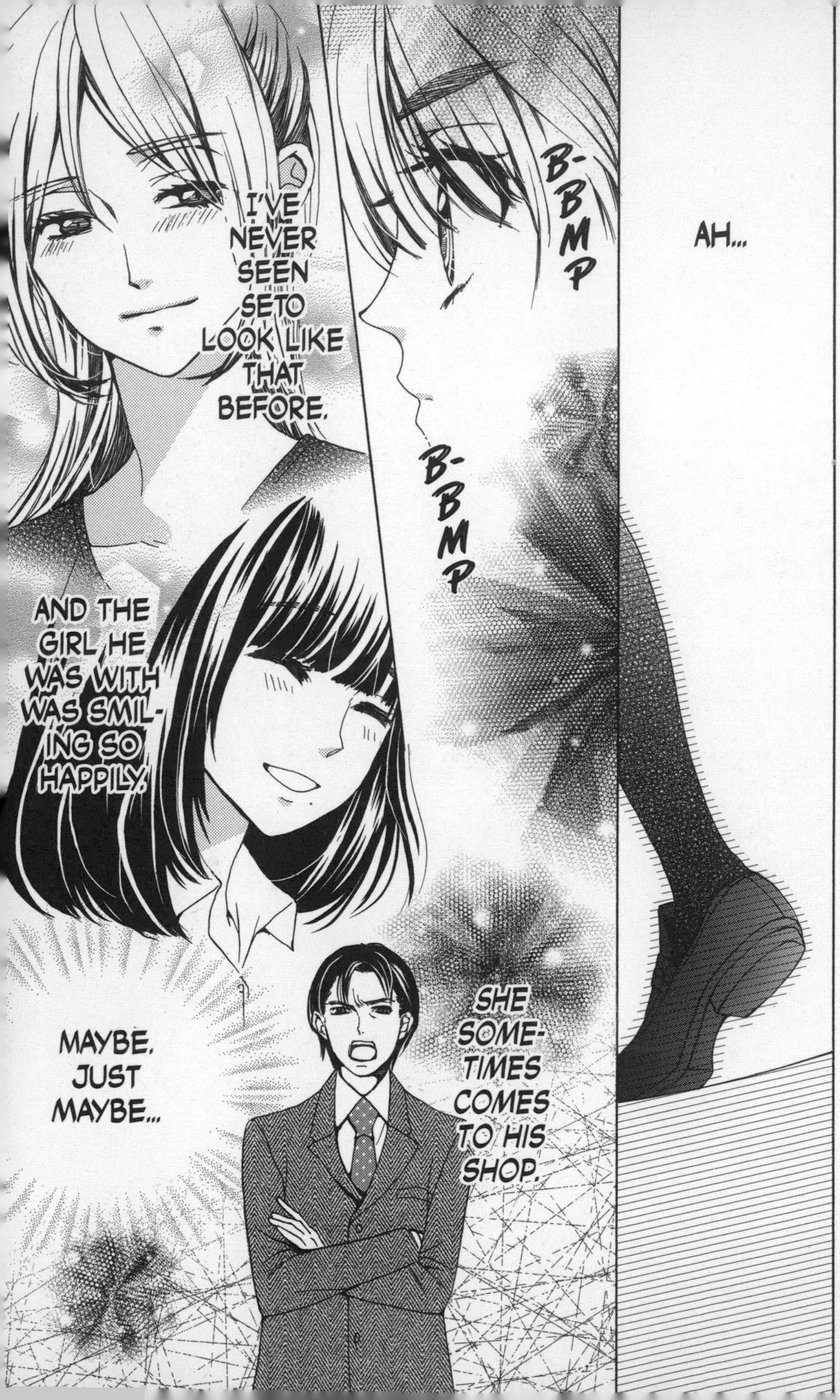
AH...
B-BBMP
B-BBMP
I'VE NEVER SEEN SETO LOOK LIKE THAT BEFORE.
AND THE GIRL HE WAS WITH WAS SMIL-ING SO HAPPILY.
SHE SOME-TIMES COMES TO HIS SHOP.
MAYBE. JUST MAYBE...

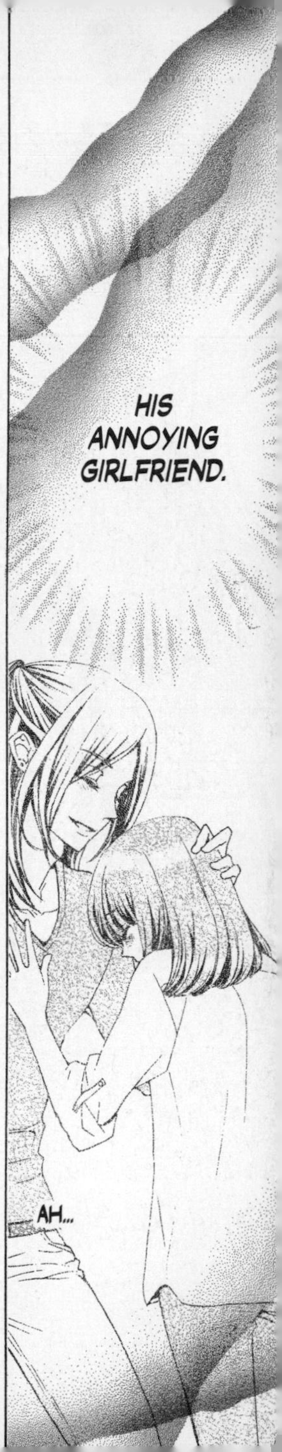
HIS ANNOYING GIRLFRIEND.
AH...
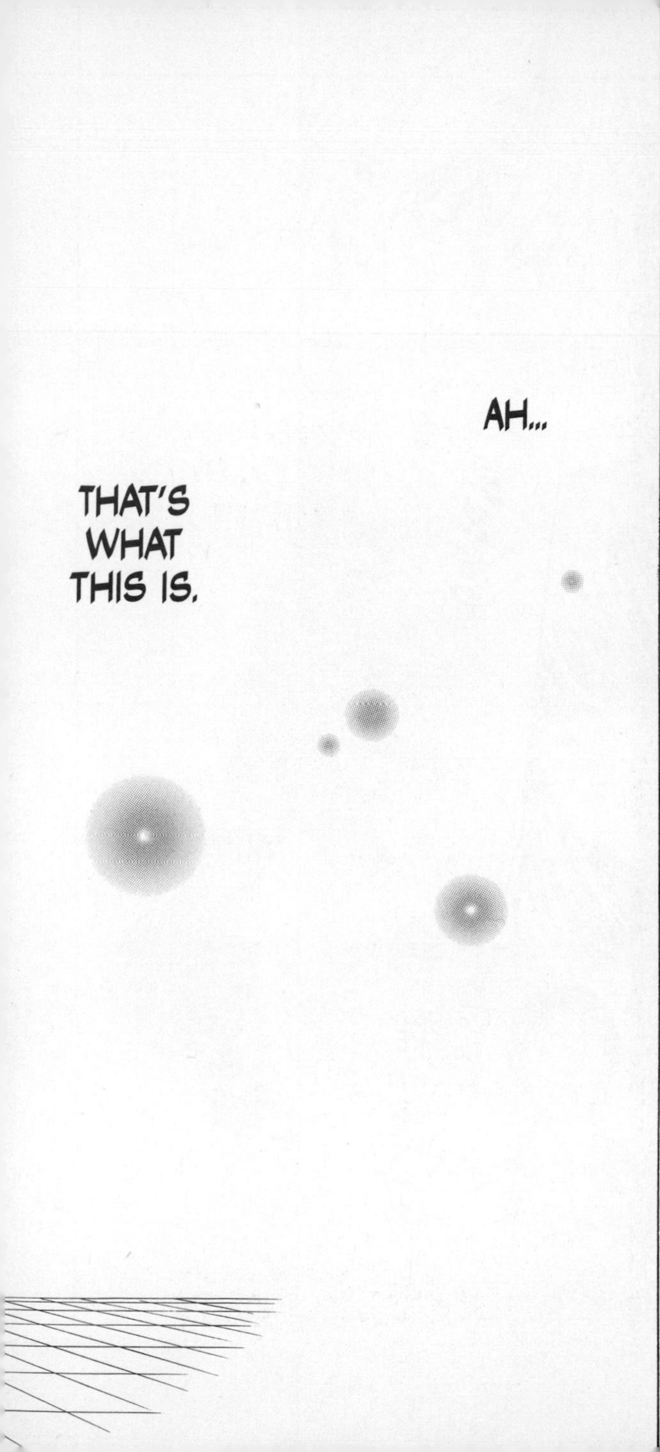
AH...
THAT'S WHAT THIS IS.

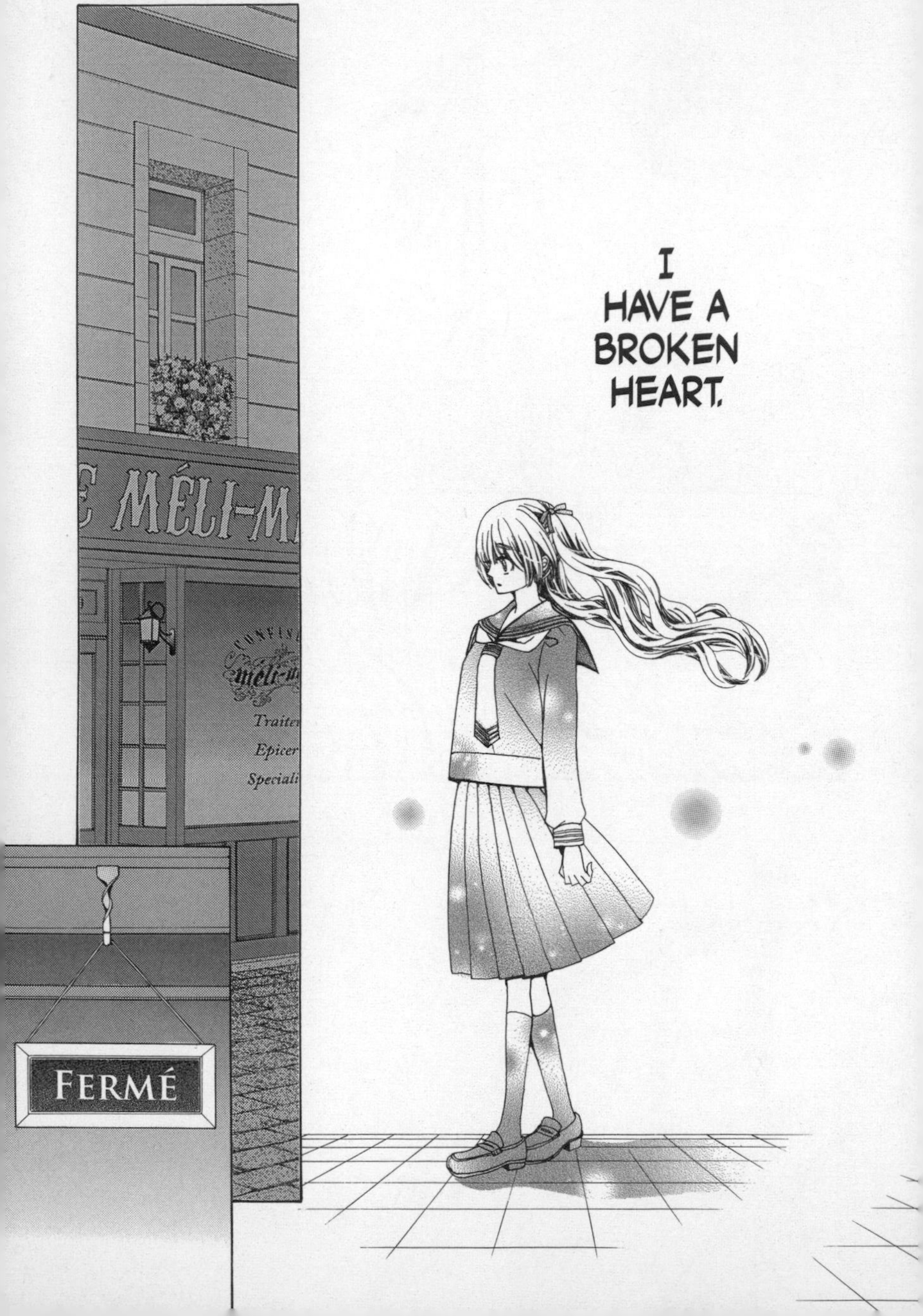
I HAVE A BROKEN HEART.
MÉLI-M
Traiter
Epicer
Speciali
FERMÉ

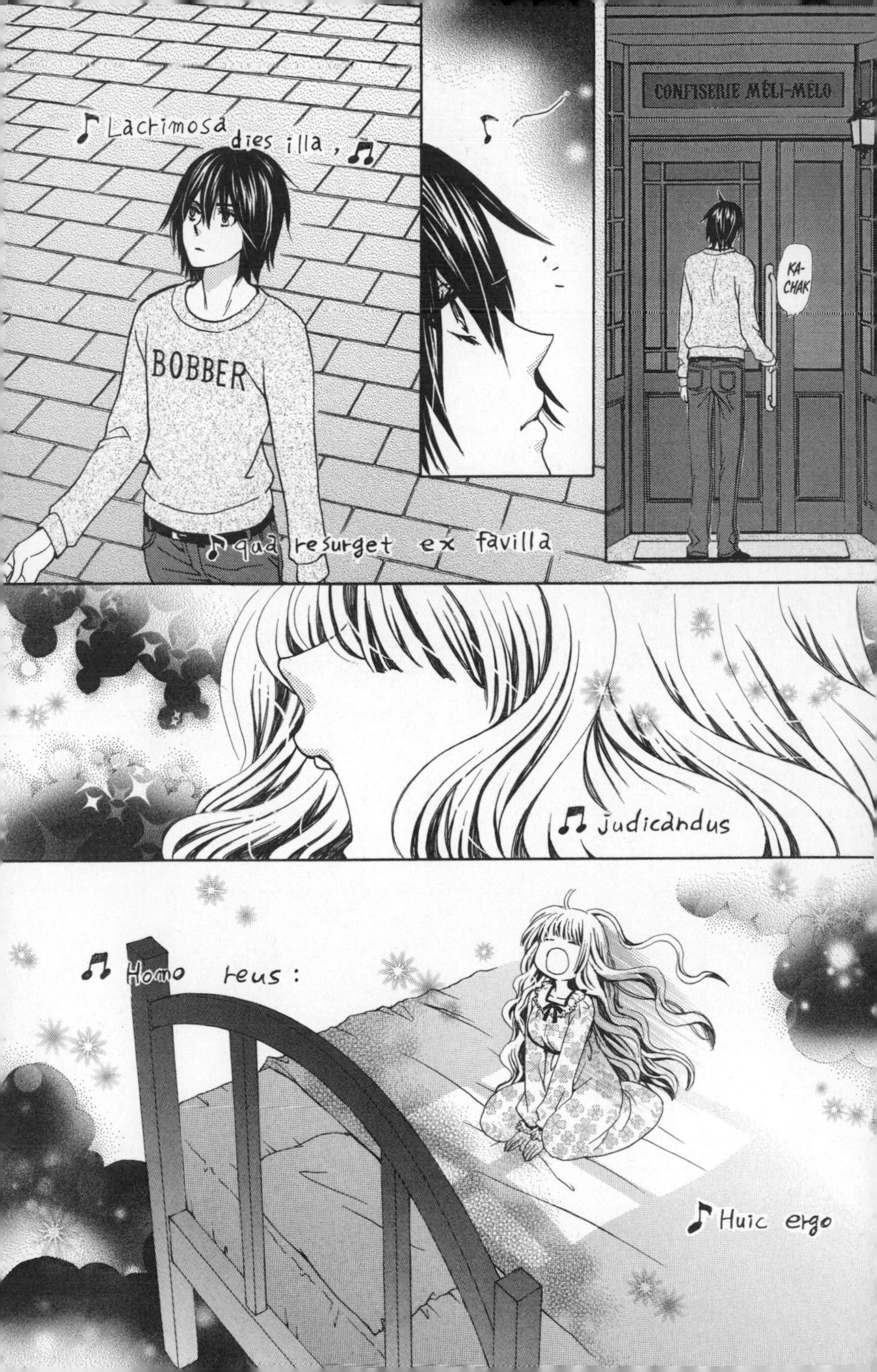

CONFISERIE MÉLI-MÉLO
KA-CHAK
Lacrimosa dies illa,
qua resurget ex favilla
judicandus
Huic ergo
Homo reus:

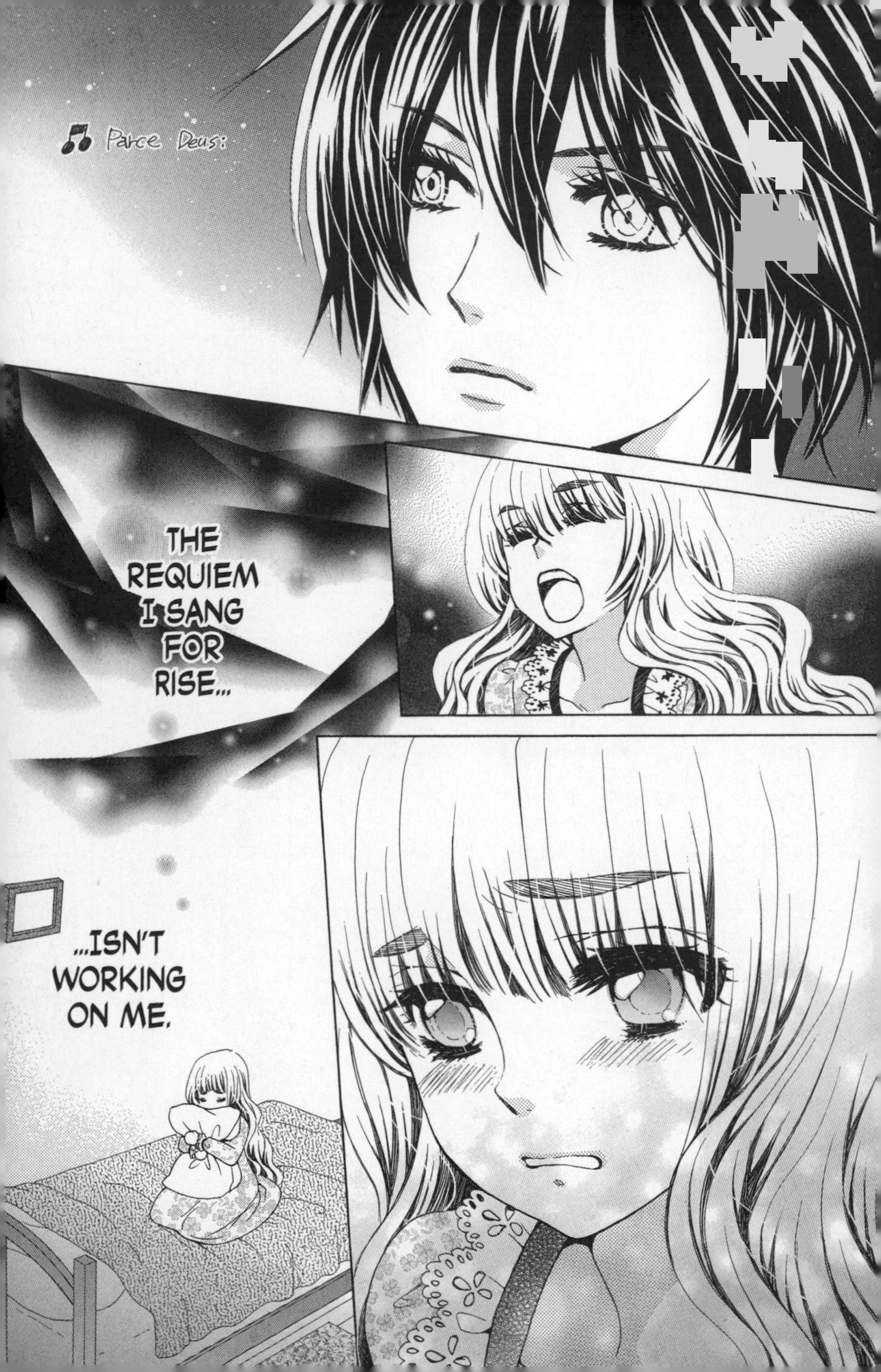
Parce Deus:
THE REQUIEM I SANG FOR RISE...
...ISN'T WORKING ON ME.

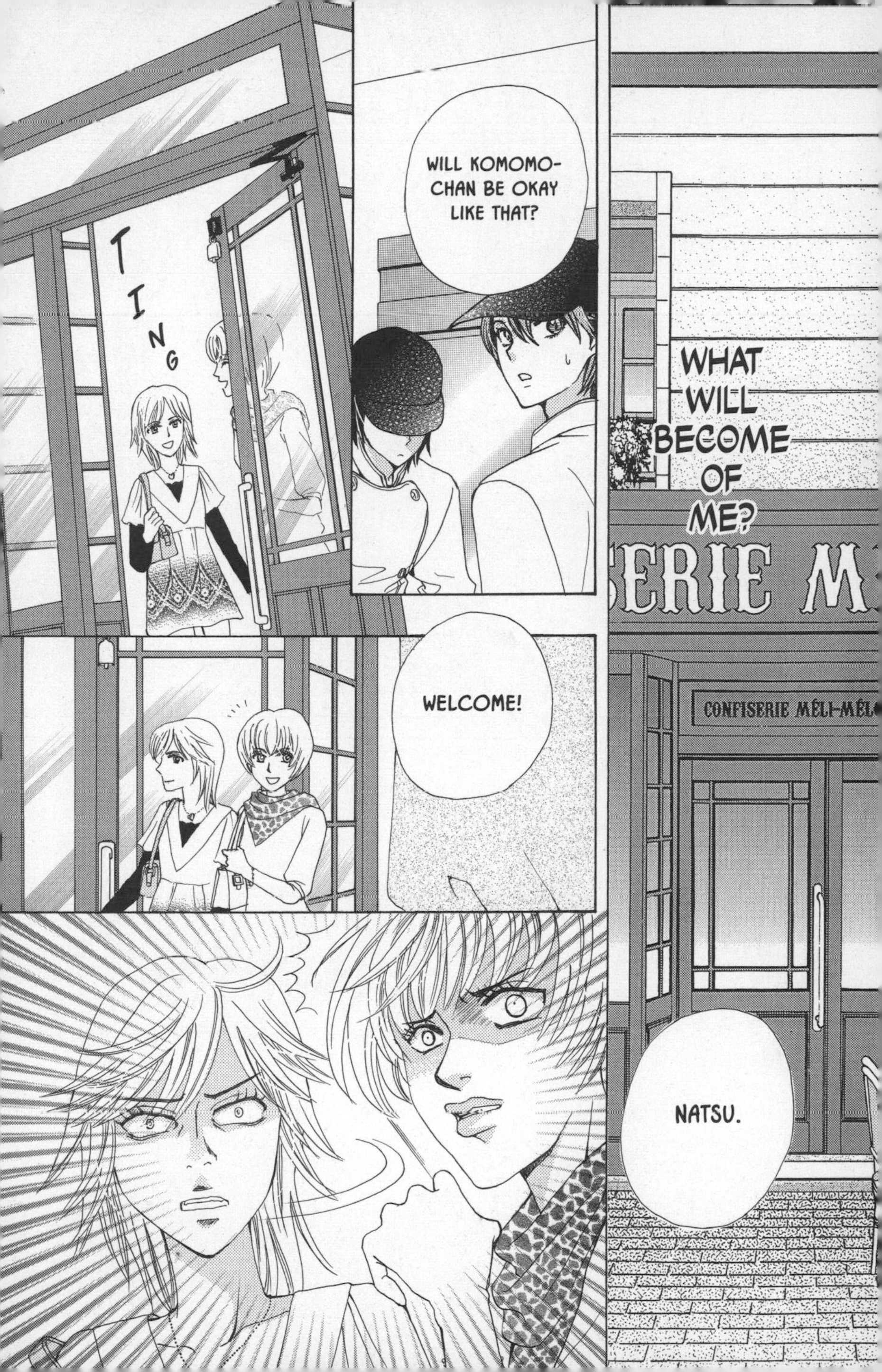
WHAT WILL BECOME OF ME?
SERIE M
CONFISERIE MÉLI-MÉLO
NATSU.
WILL KOMOMO-CHAN BE OKAY LIKE THAT?
TING
WELCOME!

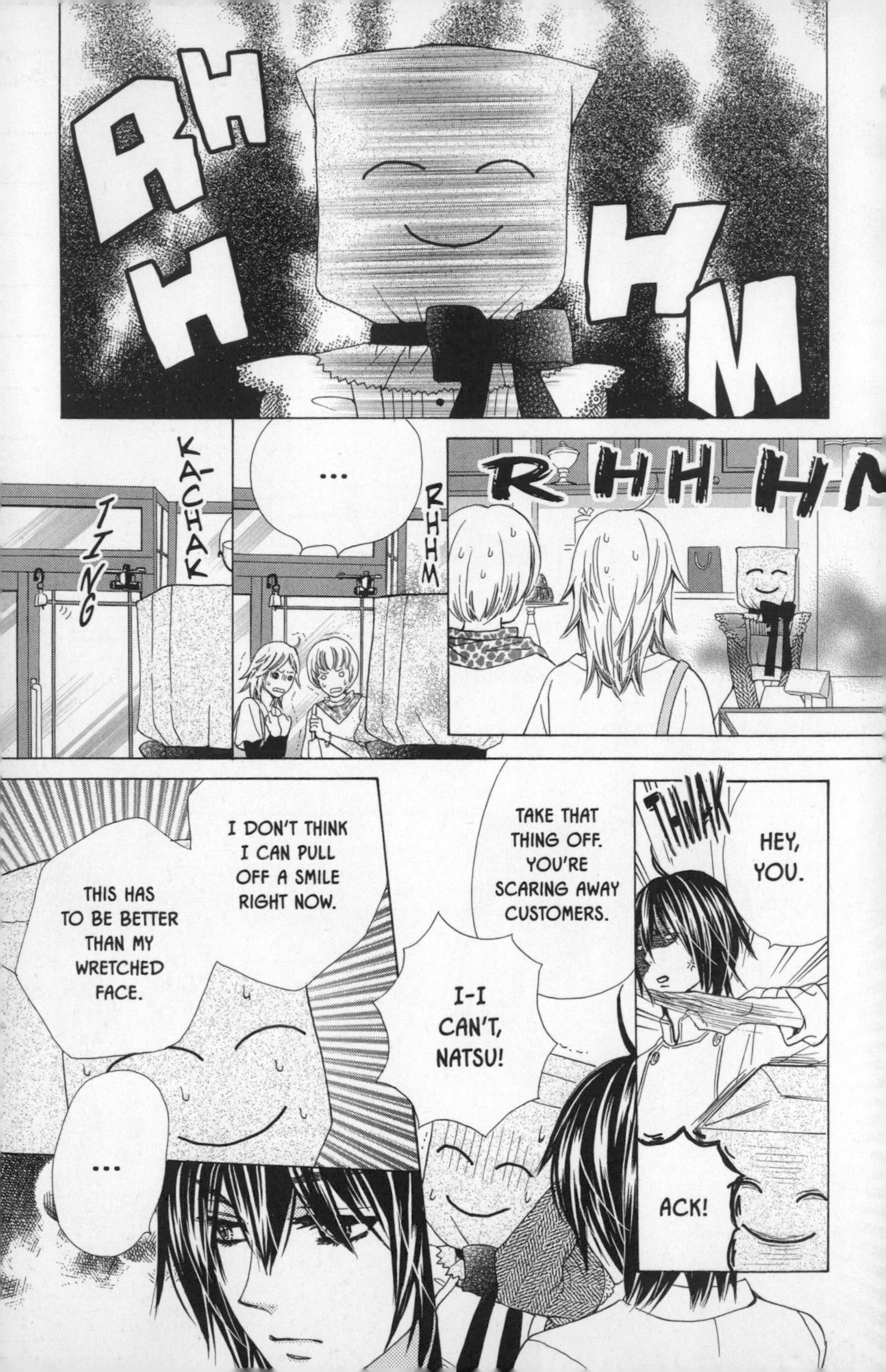
RHH
HHM
RHHHHM
...
RHHM
KA-CHAK
TIING
THWAK
HEY, YOU.
ACK!
TAKE THAT THING OFF. YOU'RE SCARING AWAY CUSTOMERS.
I-I CAN'T, NATSU!
I DON'T THINK I CAN PULL OFF A SMILE RIGHT NOW.
THIS HAS TO BE BETTER THAN MY WRETCHED FACE.
...

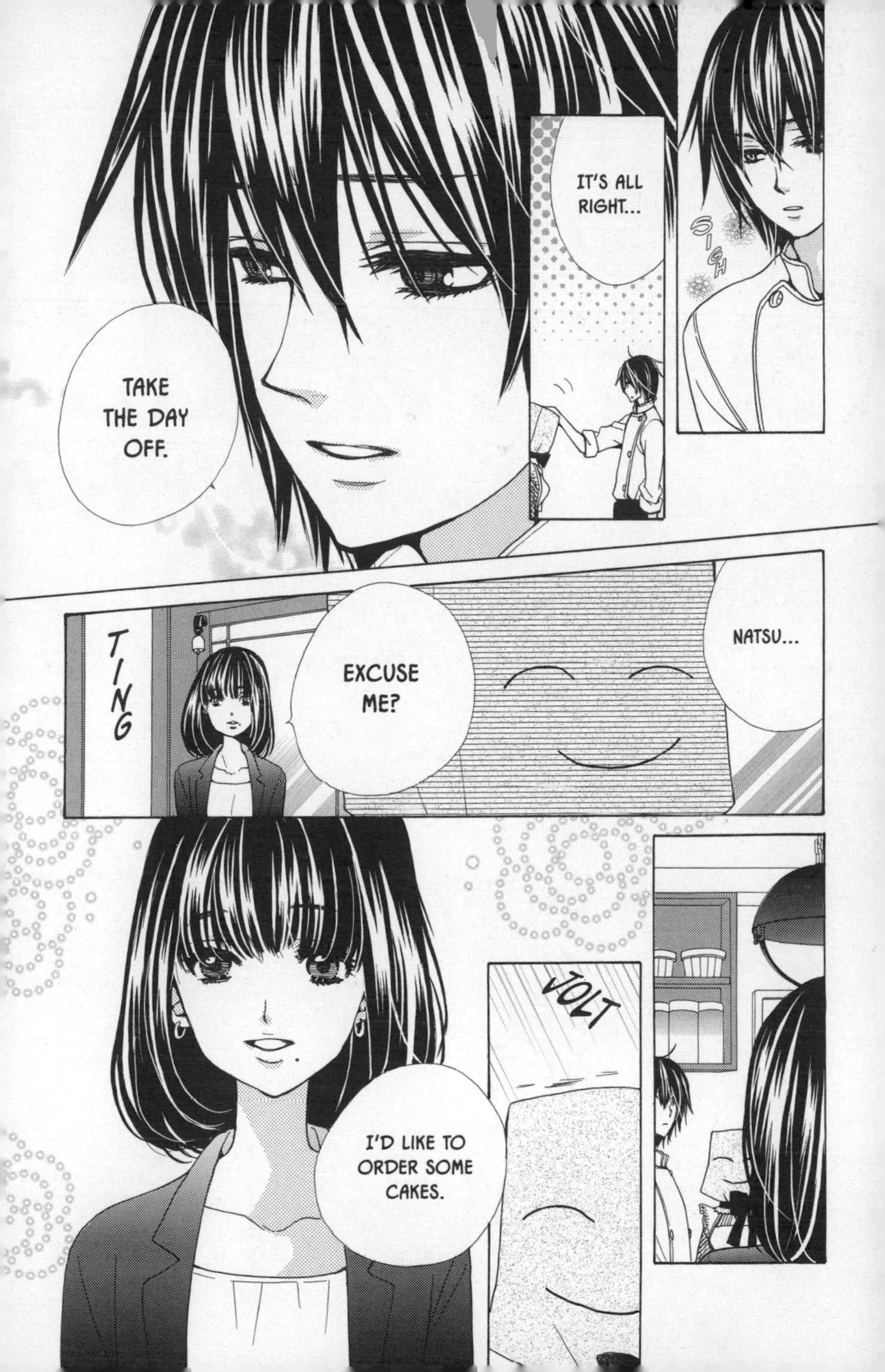
SIGH
IT'S ALL RIGHT...
TAKE THE DAY OFF.
NATSU...
EXCUSE ME?
TING
VOLT
I'D LIKE TO ORDER SOME CAKES.

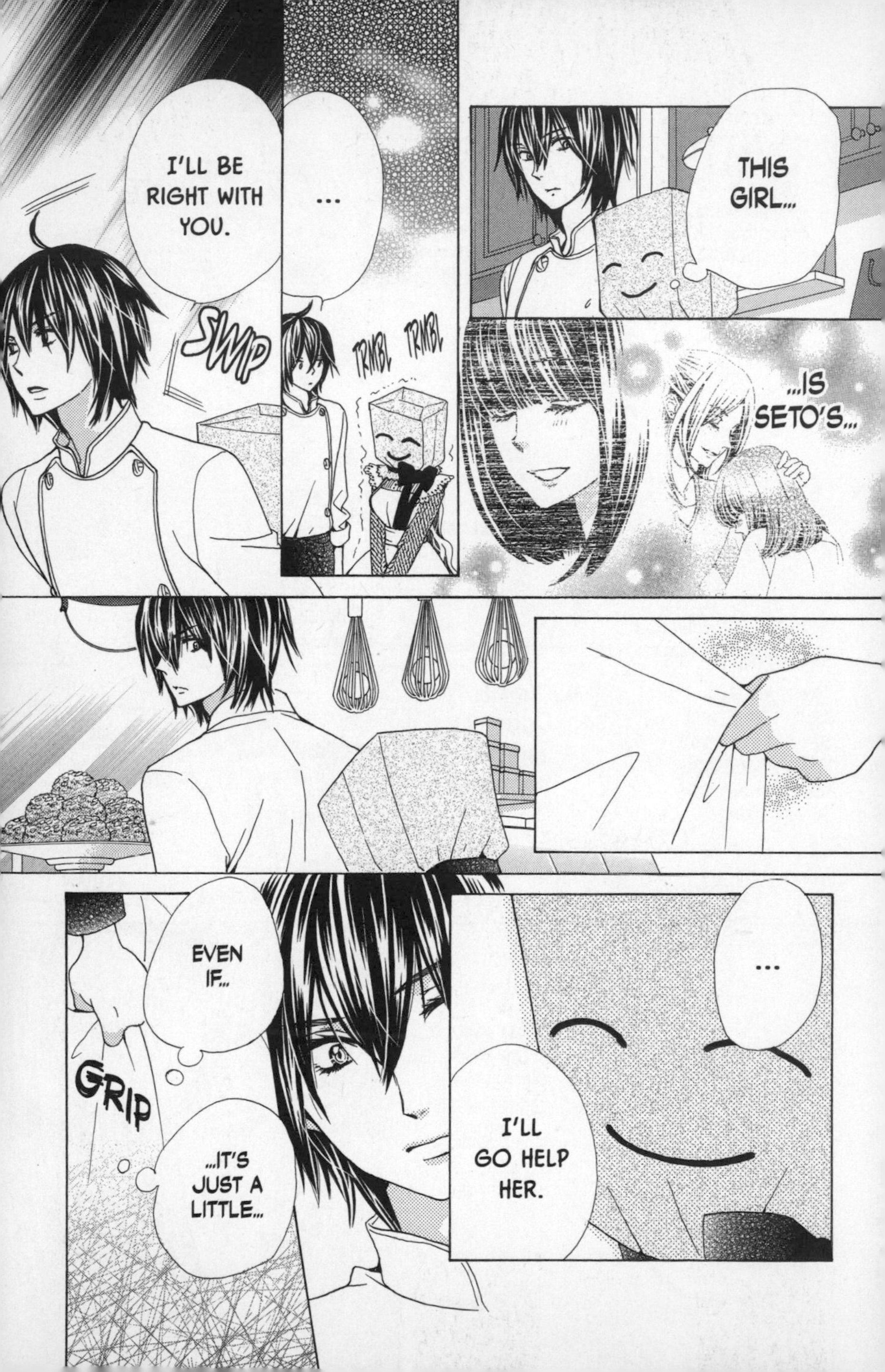
THIS GIRL...
...IS SETO'S...
...
TRMBL TRMBL
I'LL BE RIGHT WITH YOU.
SWIP
...
I'LL GO HELP HER.
EVEN IF...
...IT'S JUST A LITTLE...
GRIP

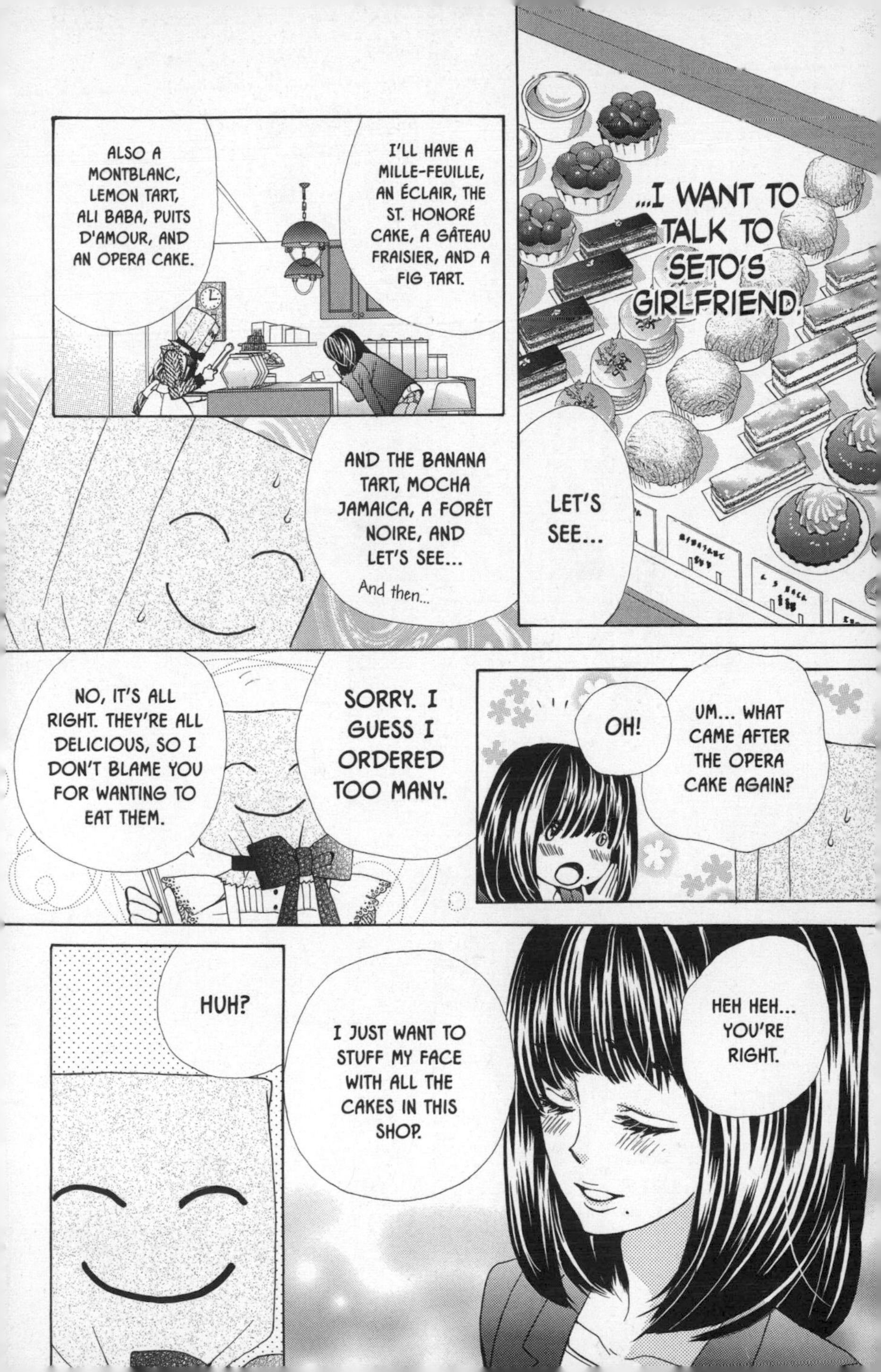
...I WANT TO TALK TO SETO'S GIRLFRIEND.
LET'S SEE...
I'LL HAVE A MILLE-FEUILLE, AN ÉCLAIR, THE ST. HONORÉ CAKE, A GÂTEAU FRAISIER, AND A FIG TART.
ALSO A MONTBLANC, LEMON TART, ALI BABA, PUITS D'AMOUR, AND AN OPERA CAKE.
AND THE BANANA TART, MOCHA JAMAICA, A FORÊT NOIRE, AND LET'S SEE...
And then...
UM... WHAT CAME AFTER THE OPERA CAKE AGAIN?
OH!
SORRY. I GUESS I ORDERED TOO MANY.
NO, IT'S ALL RIGHT. THEY'RE ALL DELICIOUS, SO I DON'T BLAME YOU FOR WANTING TO EAT THEM.
HEH HEH... YOU'RE RIGHT.
I JUST WANT TO STUFF MY FACE WITH ALL THE CAKES IN THIS SHOP.
HUH?

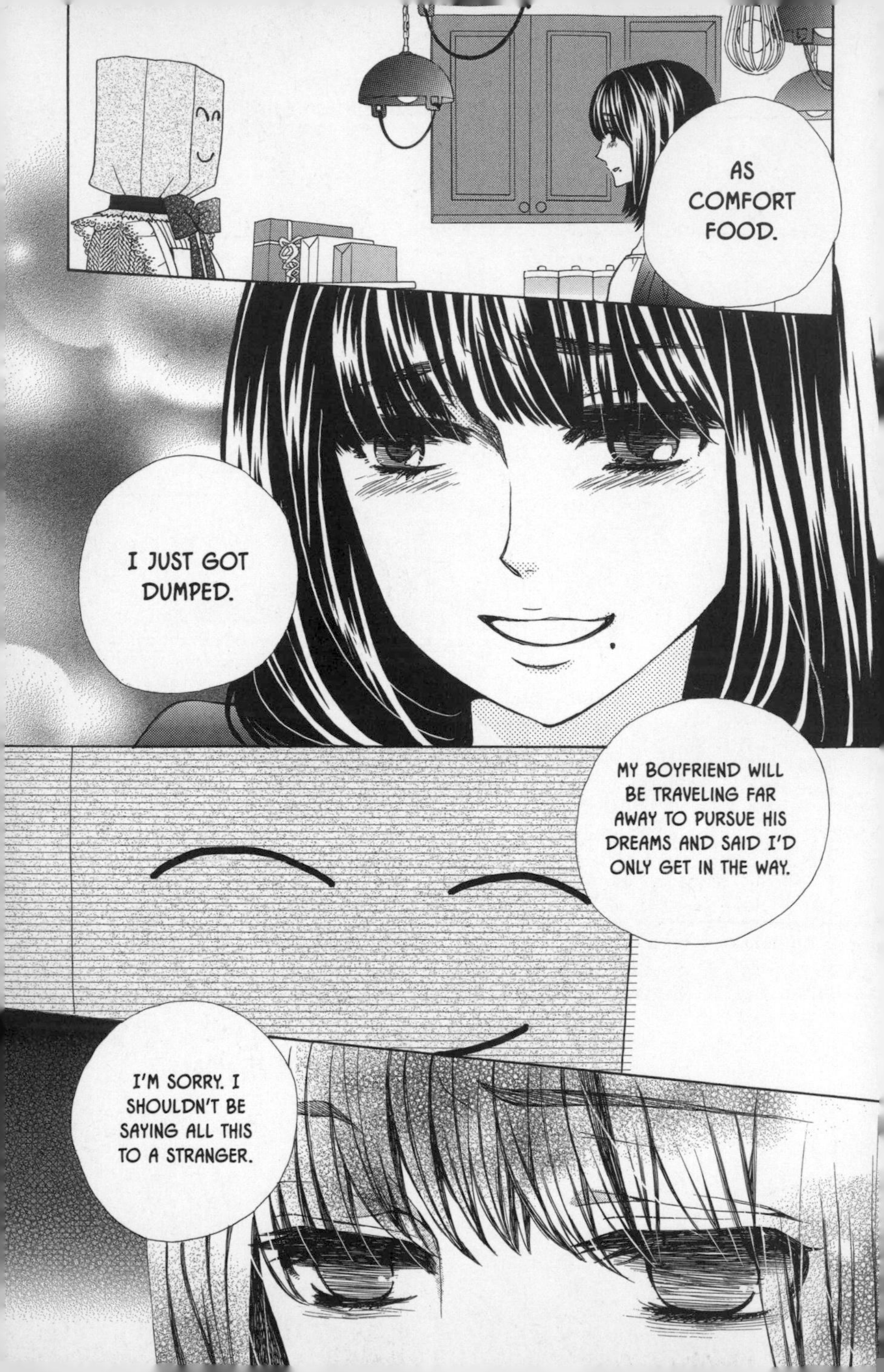
AS COMFORT FOOD.
I JUST GOT DUMPED.
MY BOYFRIEND WILL BE TRAVELING FAR AWAY TO PURSUE HIS DREAMS AND SAID I'D ONLY GET IN THE WAY.
I'M SORRY. I SHOULDN'T BE SAYING ALL THIS TO A STRANGER.

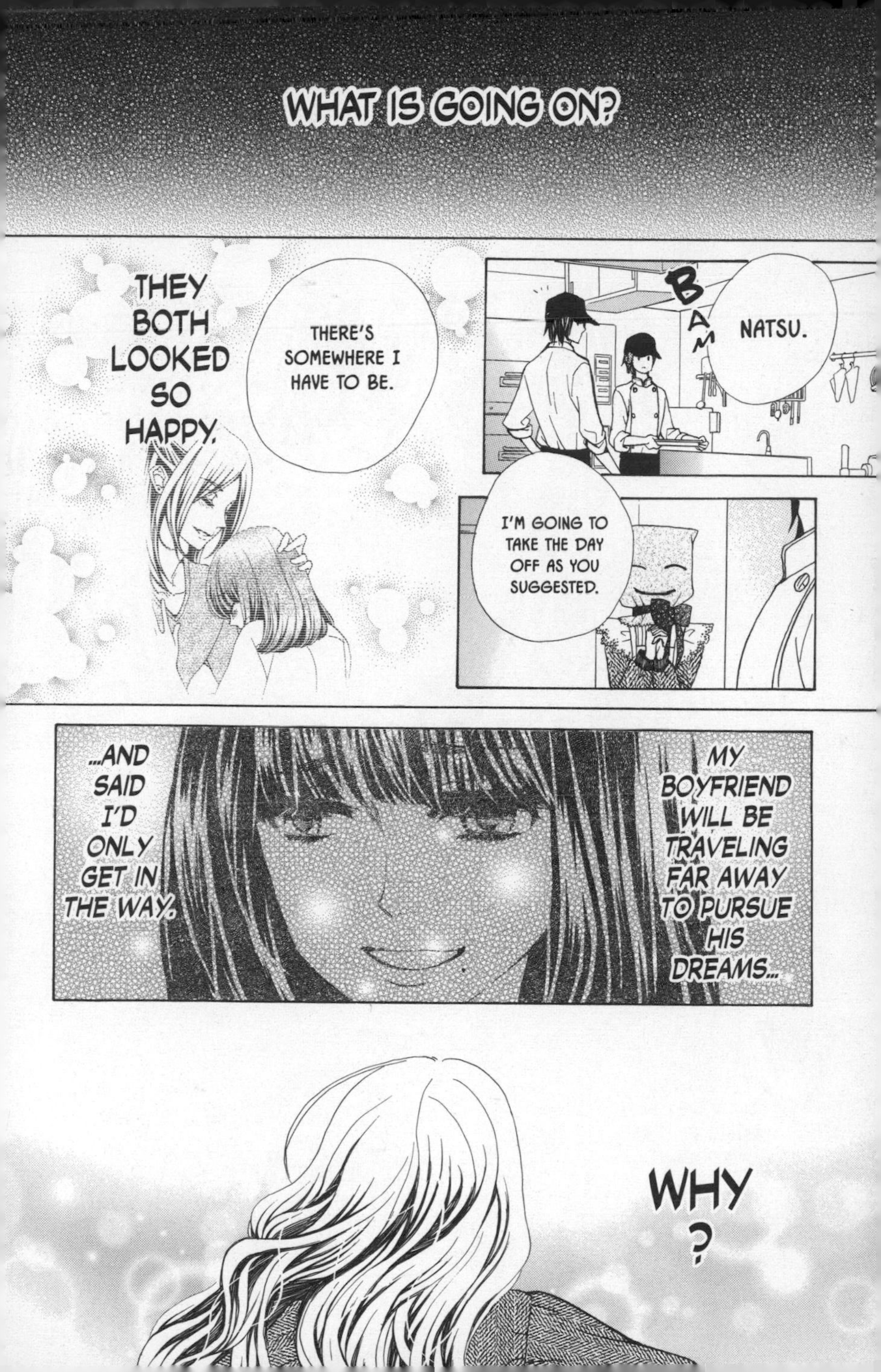
WHAT IS GOING ON?
BAM
NATSU.
I'M GOING TO TAKE THE DAY OFF AS YOU SUGGESTED.
THERE'S SOMEWHERE I HAVE TO BE.
THEY BOTH LOOKED SO HAPPY.
MY BOYFRIEND WILL BE TRAVELING FAR AWAY TO PURSUE HIS DREAMS...
...AND SAID I'D ONLY GET IN THE WAY.
WHY?

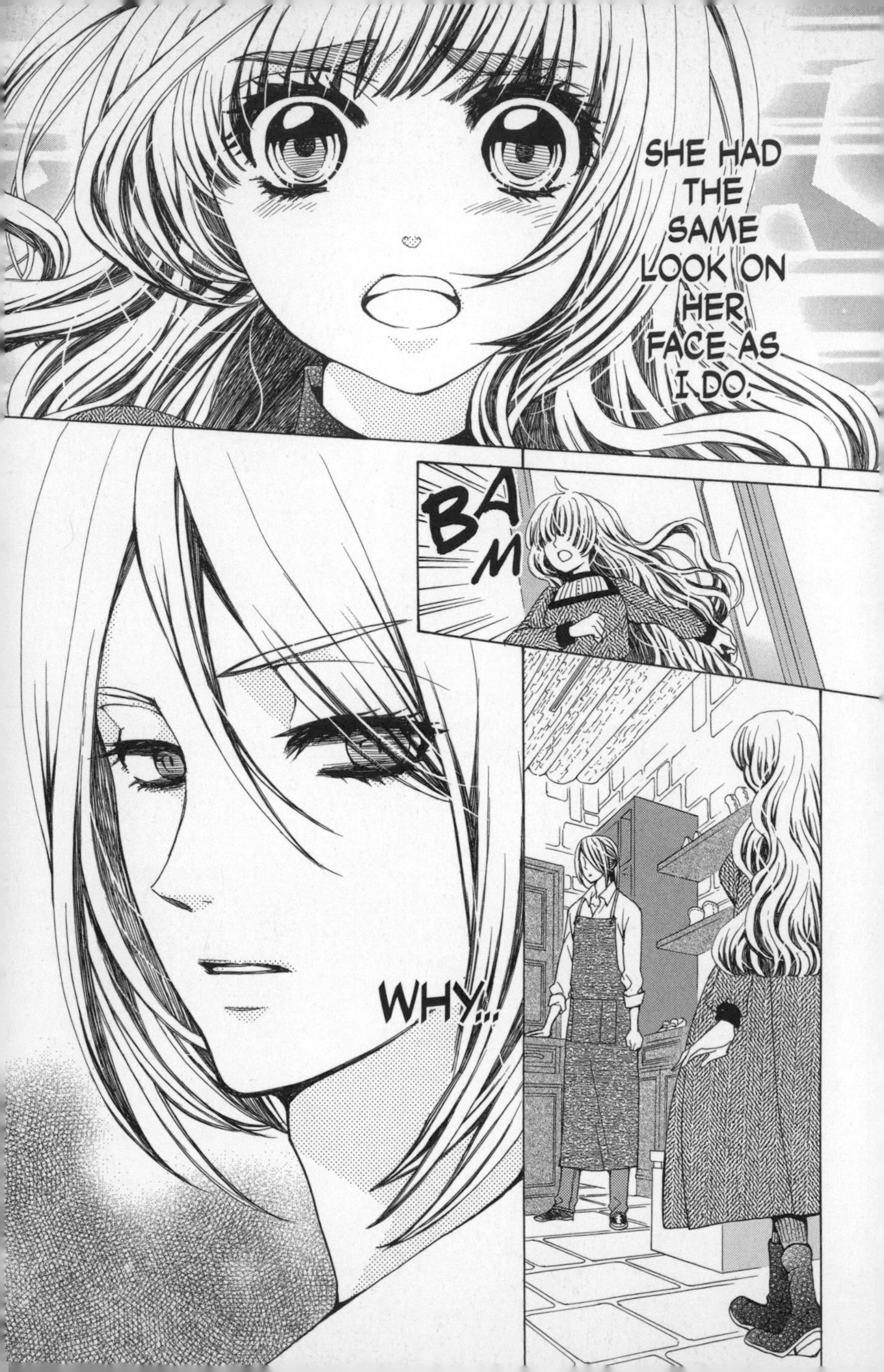
SHE HAD THE SAME LOOK ON HER FACE AS I DO.
BAM
WHY...

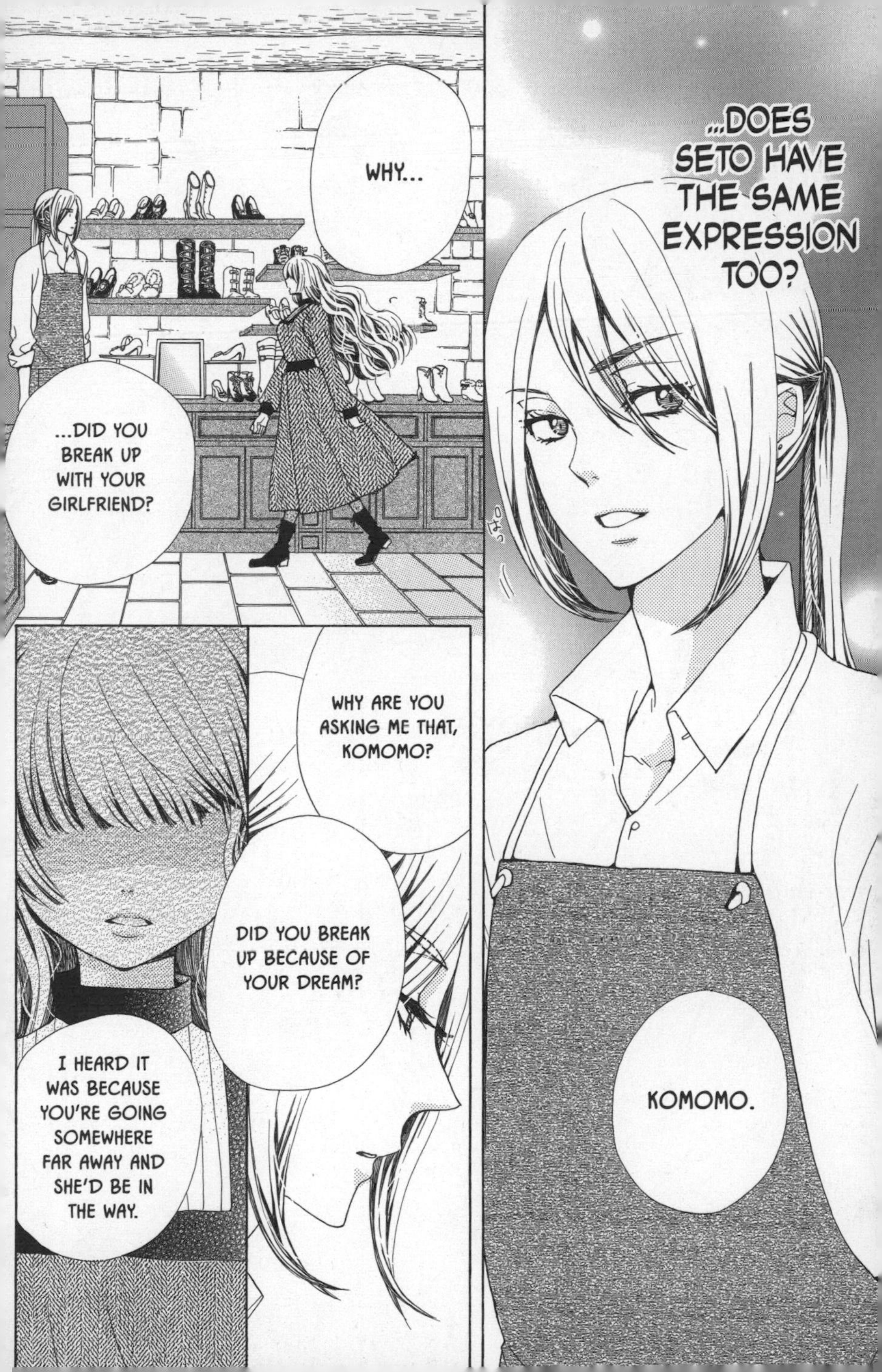
...DOES SETO HAVE THE SAME EXPRESSION TOO?
KOMOMO.
WHY...
...DID YOU BREAK UP WITH YOUR GIRLFRIEND?
WHY ARE YOU ASKING ME THAT, KOMOMO?
DID YOU BREAK UP BECAUSE OF YOUR DREAM?
I HEARD IT WAS BECAUSE YOU'RE GOING SOMEWHERE FAR AWAY AND SHE'D BE IN THE WAY.

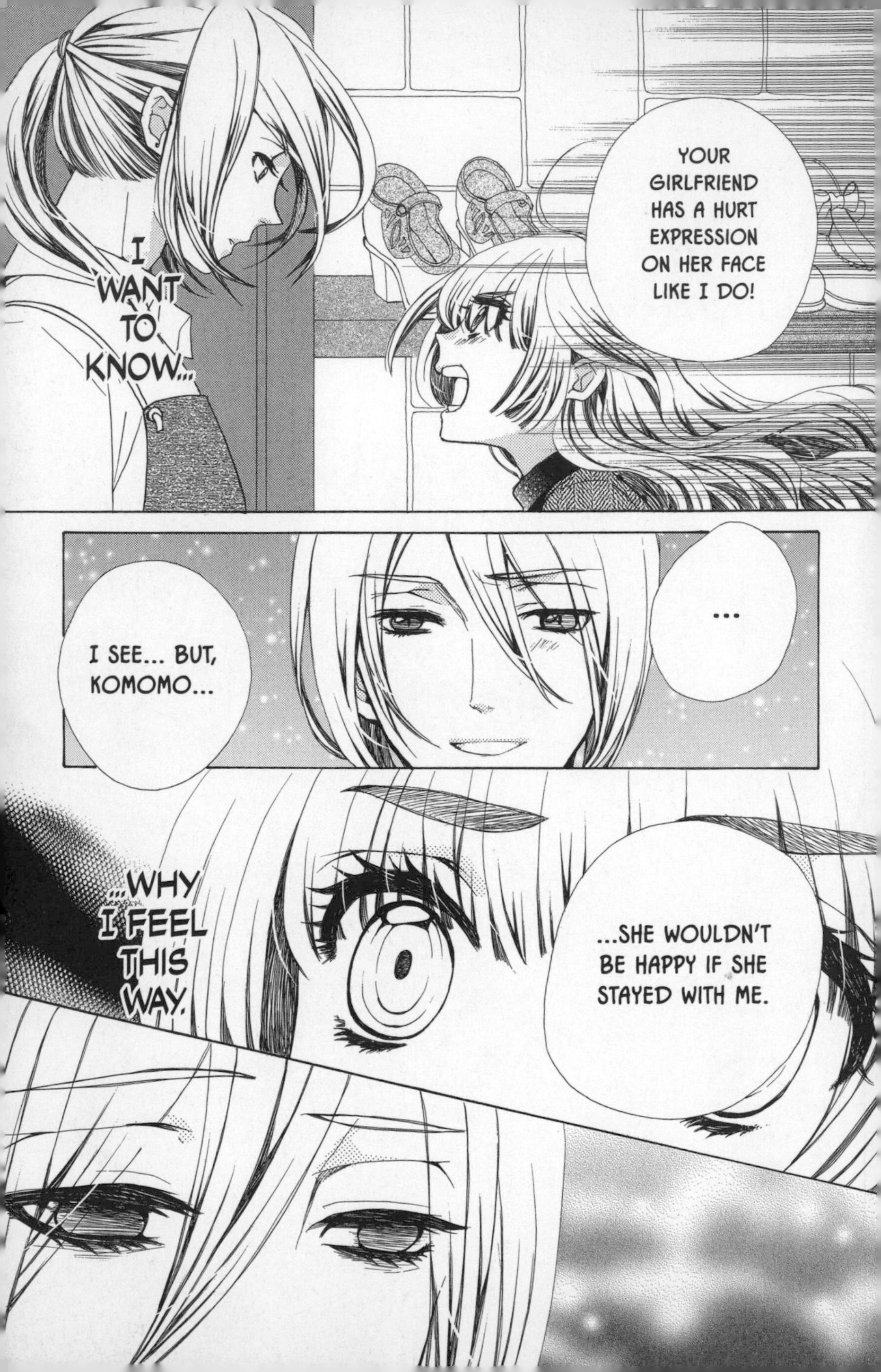
YOUR GIRLFRIEND HAS A HURT EXPRESSION ON HER FACE LIKE I DO!
I WANT TO KNOW...
...
I SEE... BUT, KOMOMO...
...SHE WOULDN'T BE HAPPY IF SHE STAYED WITH ME.
...WHY I FEEL THIS WAY.

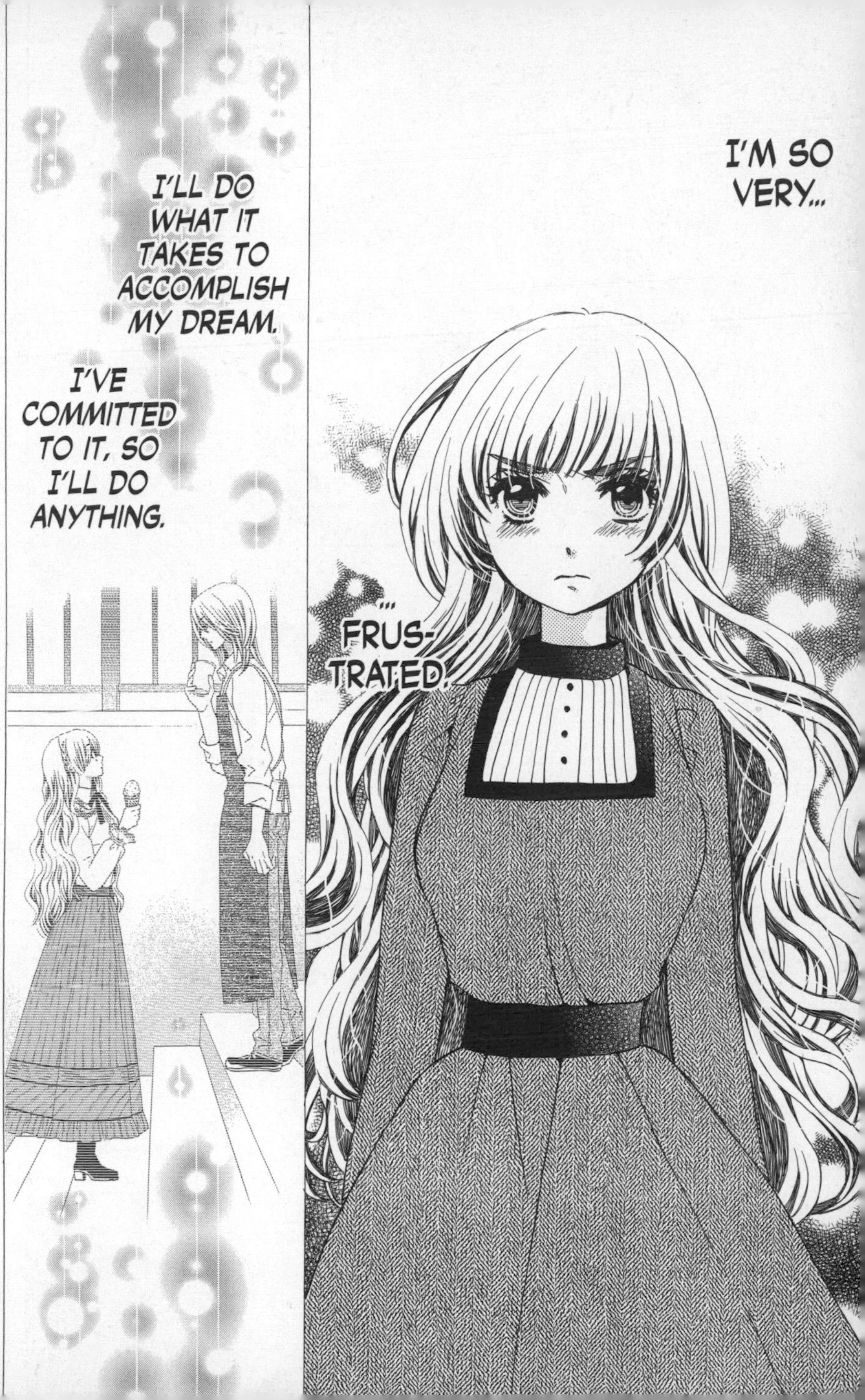
I'M SO VERY...
...FRUS-TRATED.
I'LL DO WHAT IT TAKES TO ACCOMPLISH MY DREAM.
I'VE COMMITTED TO IT, SO I'LL DO ANYTHING.

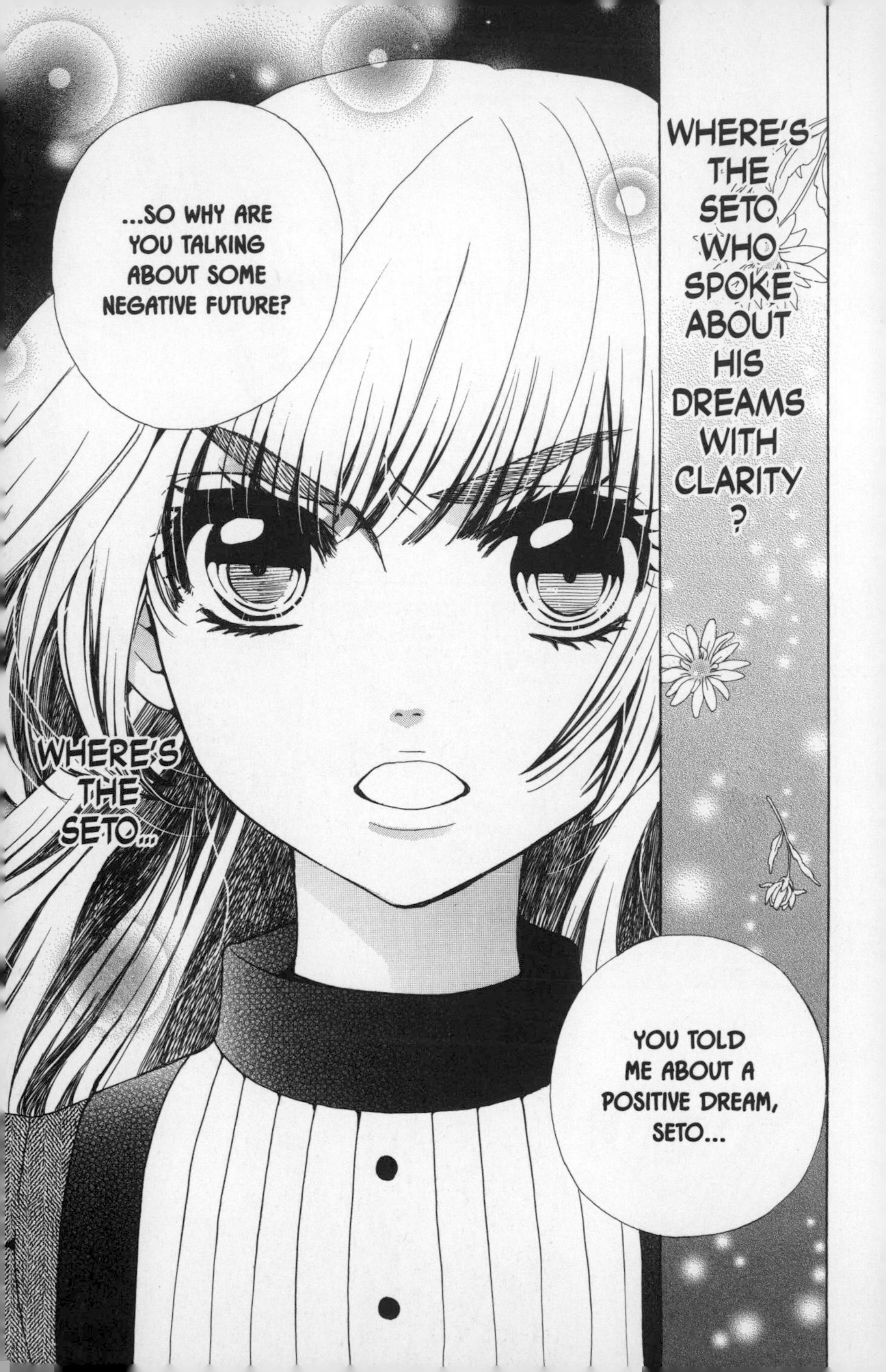
YOU TOLD ME ABOUT A POSITIVE DREAM, SETO...
...SO WHY ARE YOU TALKING ABOUT SOME NEGATIVE FUTURE?
WHERE'S THE SETO...
WHERE'S THE SETO WHO SPOKE ABOUT HIS DREAMS WITH CLARITY?

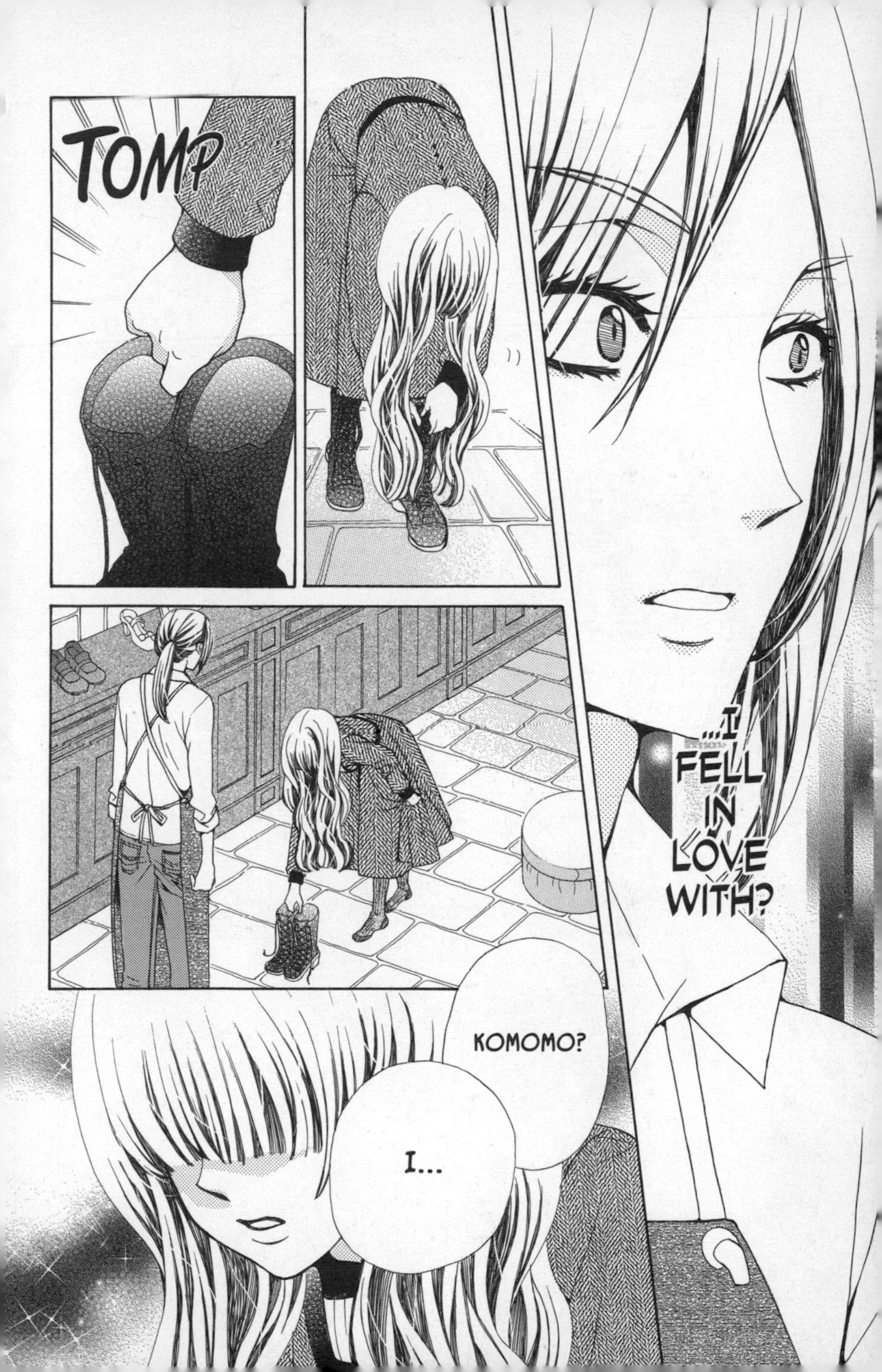
...I FELL IN LOVE WITH?
TOMP
KOMOMO?
I...

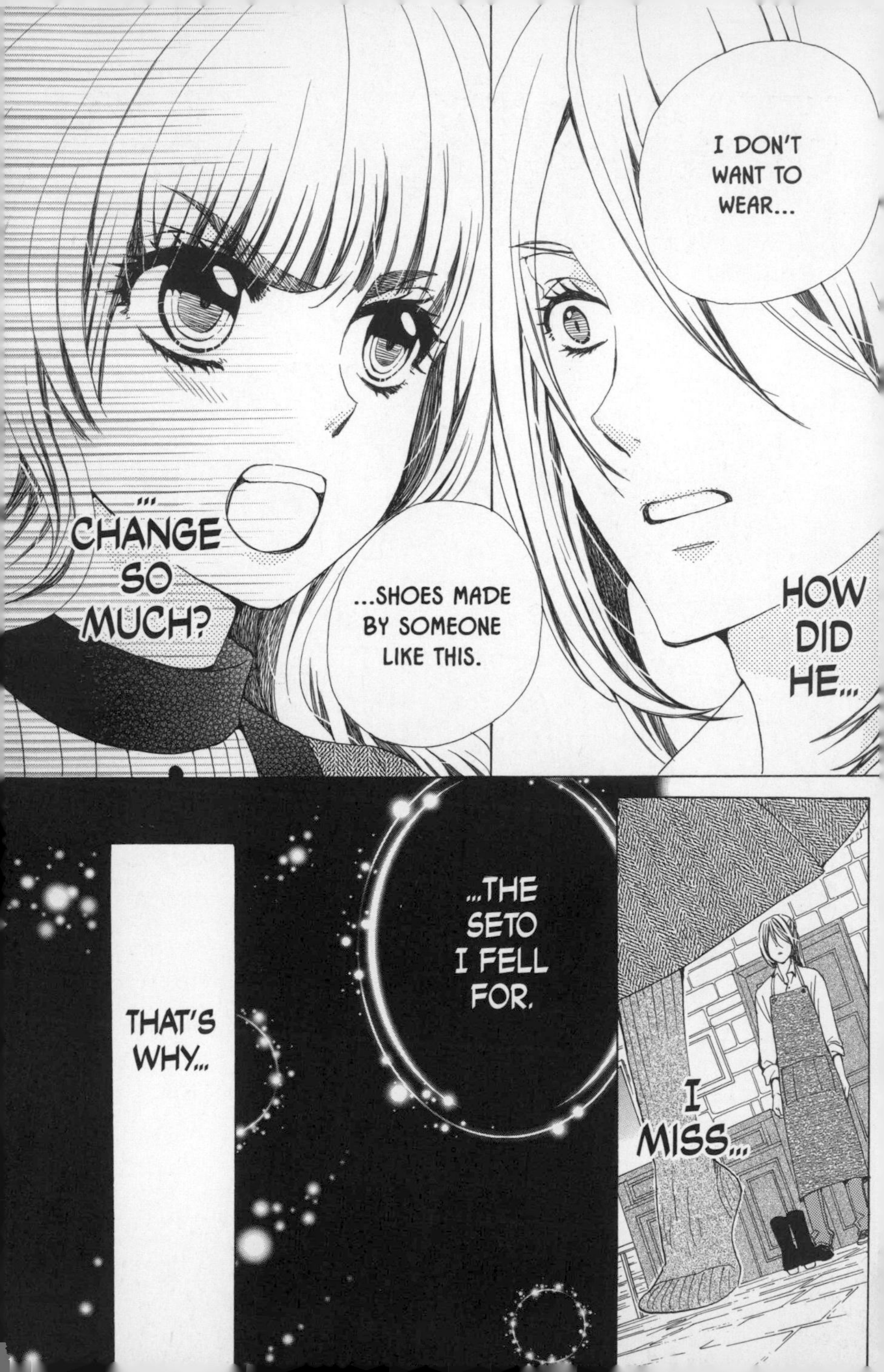
I DON'T WANT TO WEAR...
HOW DID HE...
...SHOES MADE BY SOMEONE LIKE THIS.
...CHANGE SO MUCH?
I MISS...
...THE SETO I FELL FOR.
THAT'S WHY...

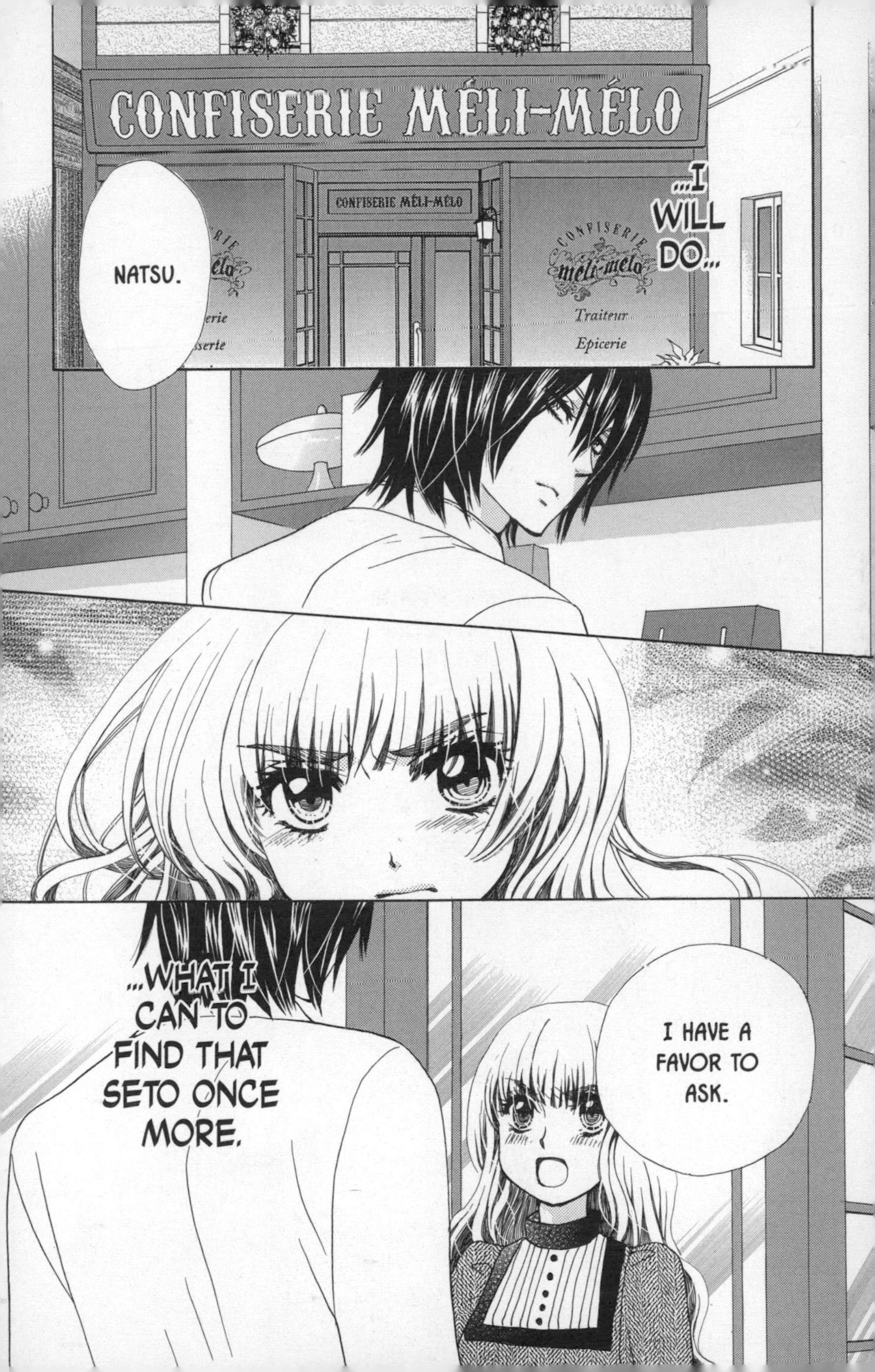
CONFISERIE MÉLI-MÉLO
CONFISERIE MÉLI-MÉLO
CONFISERIE méli-mélo
Traiteur
Epicerie
...I WILL DO...
NATSU.
I HAVE A FAVOR TO ASK.
...WHAT I CAN TO FIND THAT SETO ONCE MORE.

~ My Personal Takes on Different Pastries ~

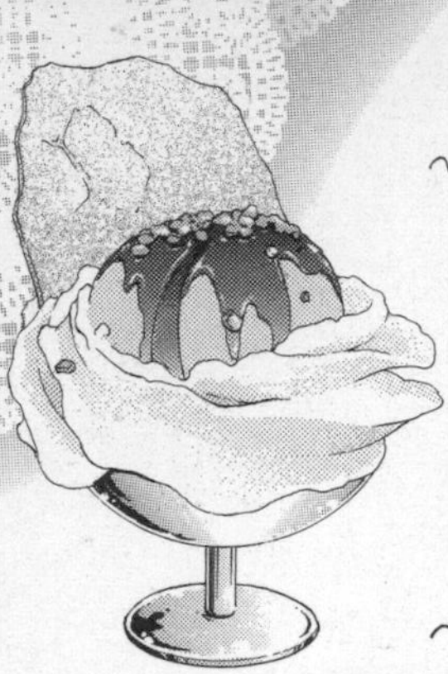

~Pêche Melba~

I first ate this as a child when my parents brought me to a cake shop called Lenôtre. It came in a bowl made of crispy cookies. It featured vanilla ice cream and peach compote topped with sliced almonds and thick whipped cream. Even as a child I was impressed by how tasty it was. But I did think to myself, "How is this any different than a parfait...? Ha ha!" But that's all I'll share of my young impressions.

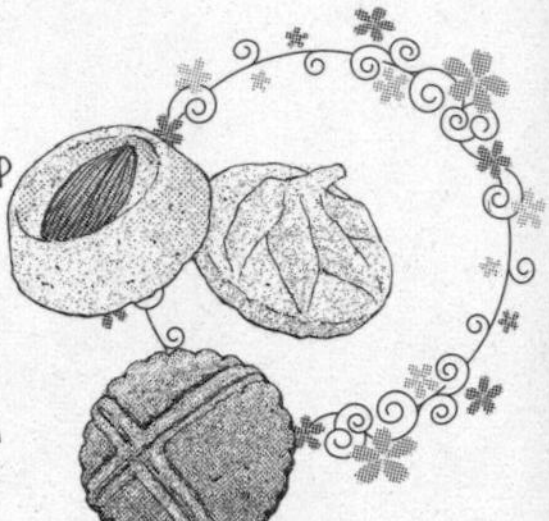

~ Sablé ~

This is the first recipe I learned from a confectionary shop that I used to frequent a few years ago. The difference between these and regular cookie-cutter cookies is that rather than kneading the dough together completely, you only do it until it has a "sand-like texture." Sablés really melt in your mouth, while typical cookies are tougher and have more of a crunch to them. I love both, of course. ♥

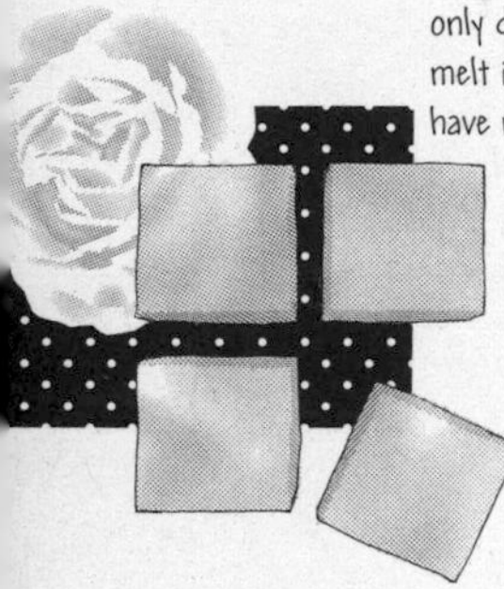

~ Rose Caramel ~

I've technically never had these before. I imagine they're very good when coated with white chocolate. Of course caramel and chocolate coating are both so delicious, it's sure to be a delectable! I think it's so romantic to use real roses in candy. Yes. Mm-hm.

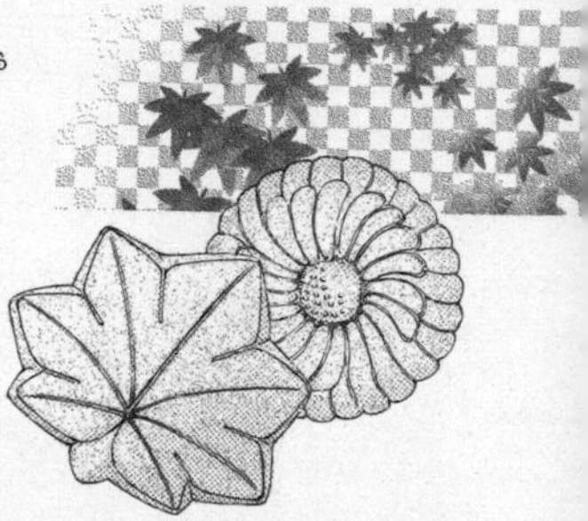

~Monaka~

This is a candy you want to pair with Japanese tea. The monaka they sell at sweets shops have the shells and bean filling separate so that when you eat it, you can put it together however you like. It's really good with whipped cream!

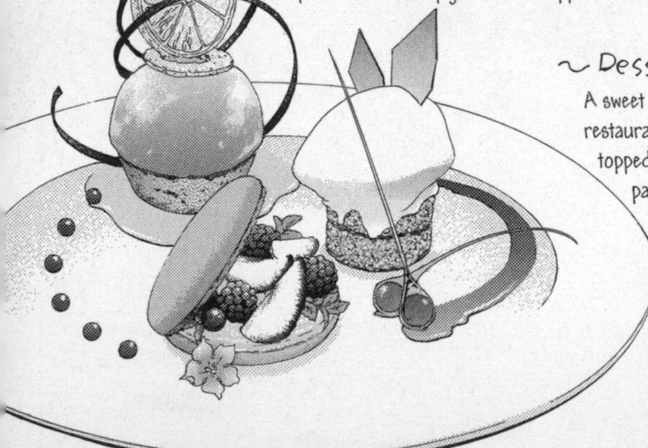

~Dessert~

A sweet you eat on a plate like they offer at restaurants. "Dessert" can be ice cream and topped with all sorts of sauces, or it can be a parfait. It's typically arranged in a way that's pleasing to the eye, and sometimes you may not even know what you are eating. All you know is that it's delicious and you can't wait to eat the next bite.

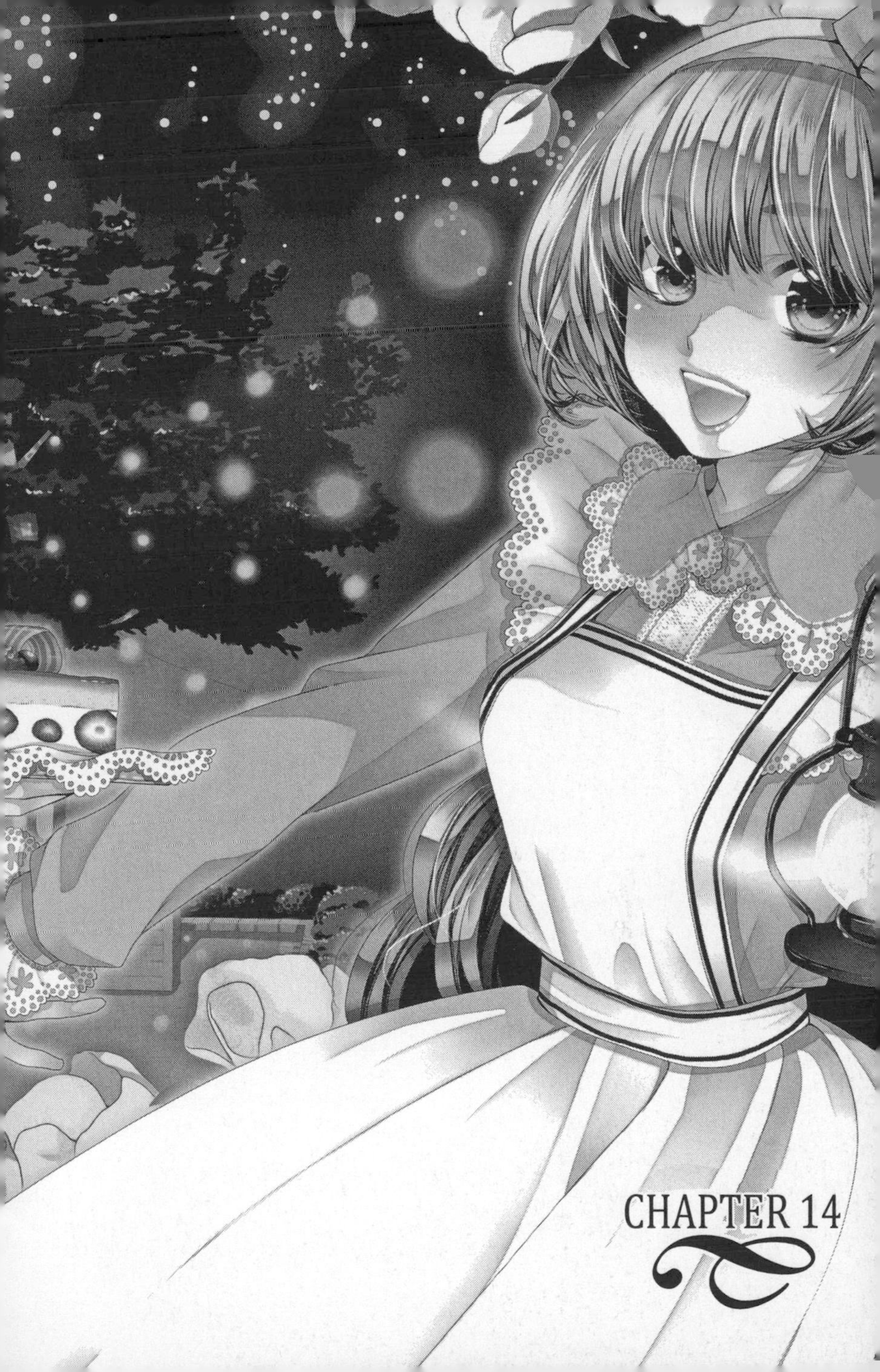
CHAPTER 14

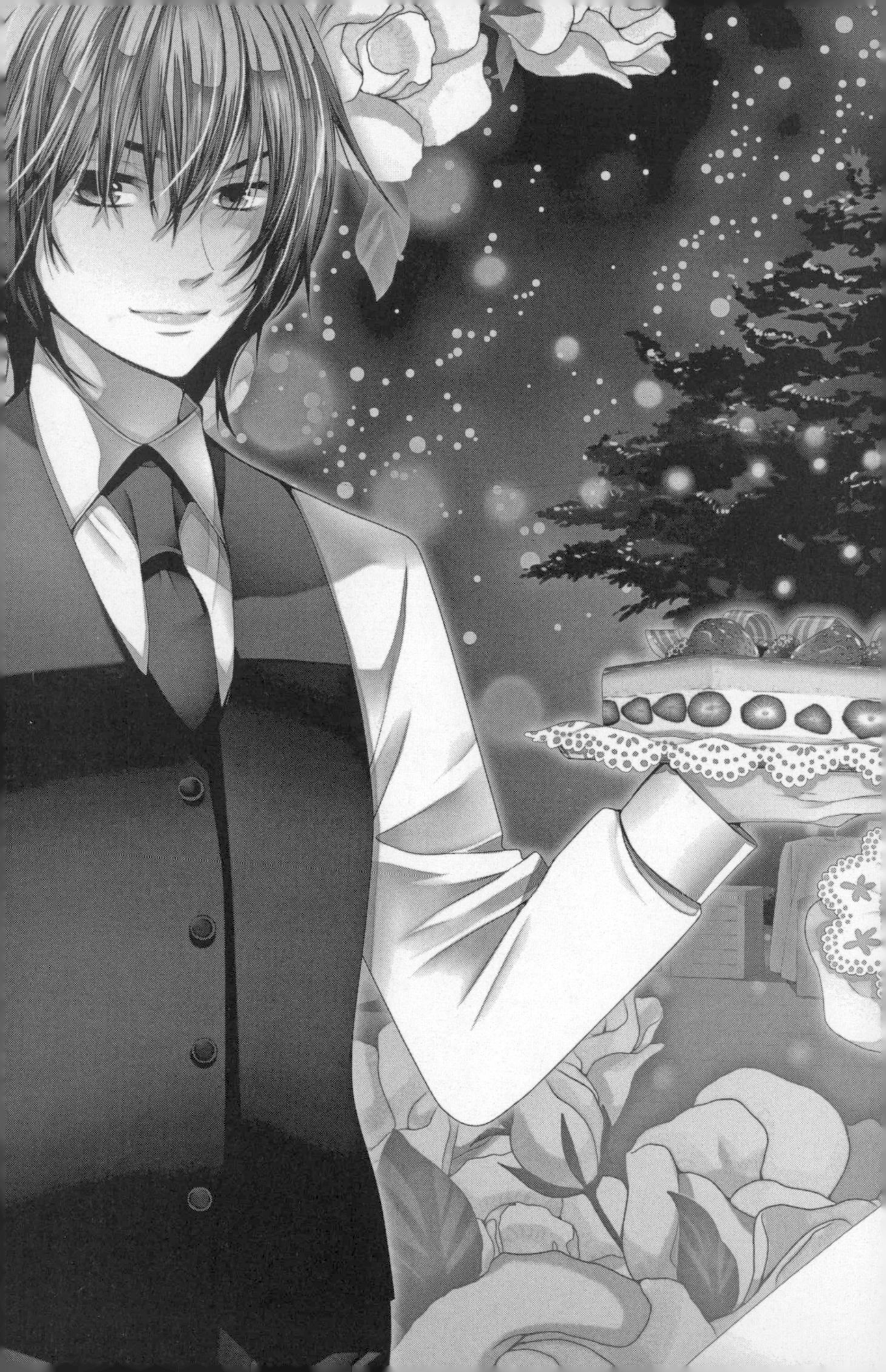

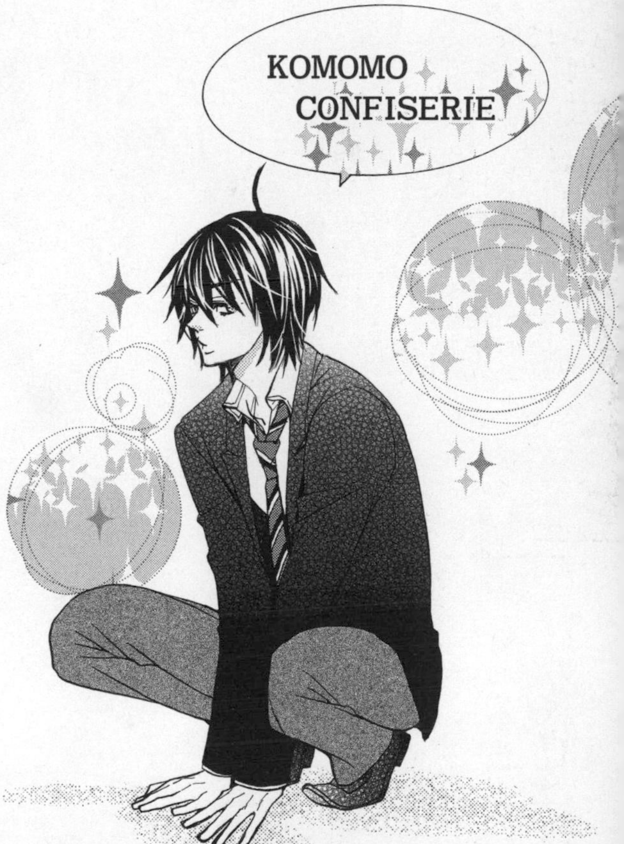
KOMOMO CONFISERIE

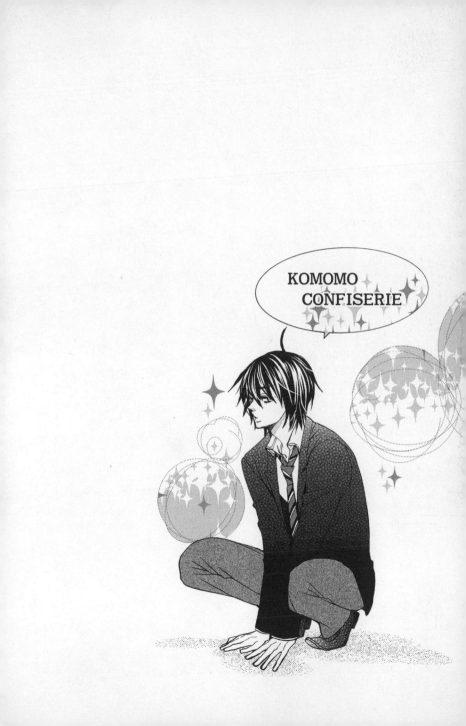

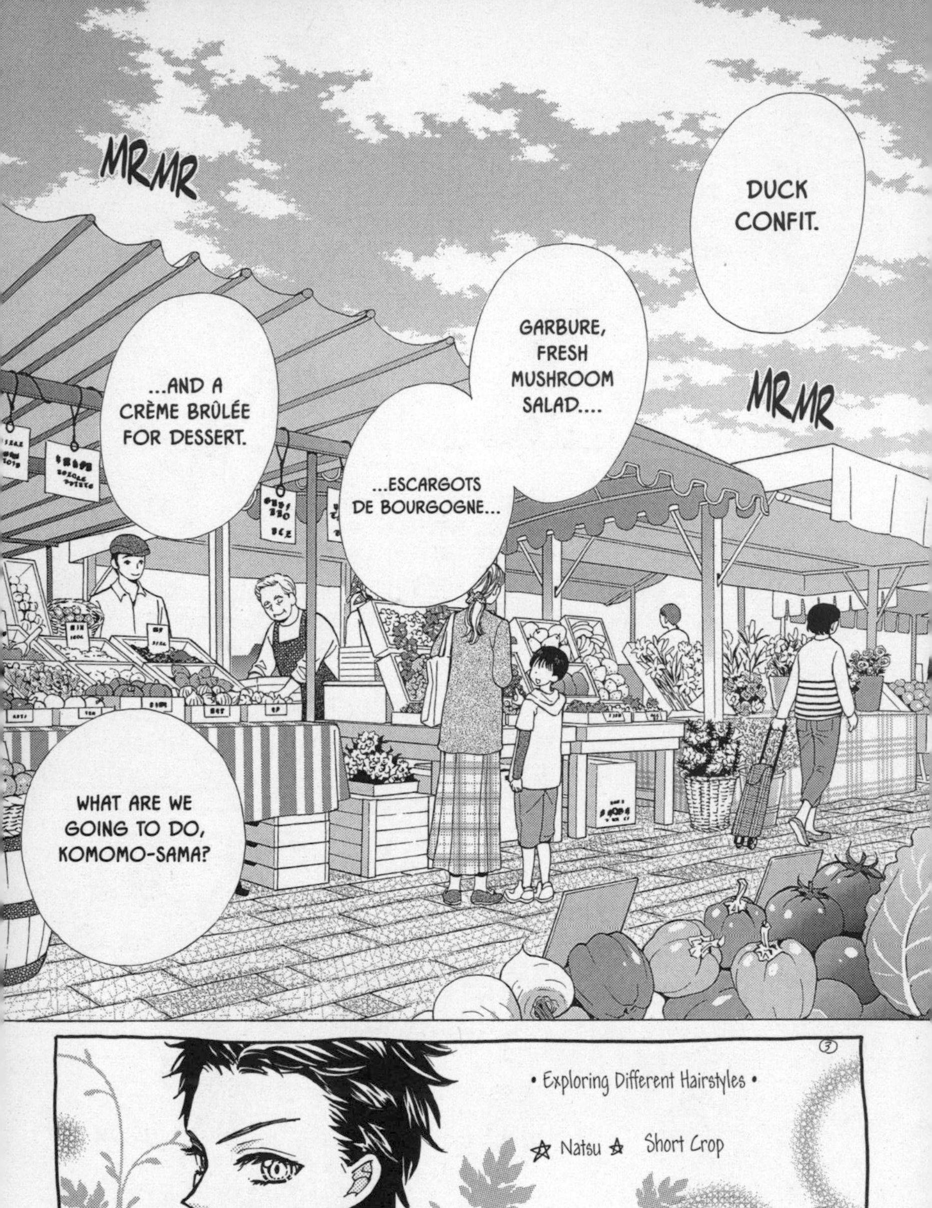
DUCK CONFIT.
MRMR
GARBURE, FRESH MUSHROOM SALAD....
...ESCARGOTS DE BOURGOGNE...
...AND A CRÈME BRÛLÉE FOR DESSERT.
MRMR
WHAT ARE WE GOING TO DO, KOMOMO-SAMA?

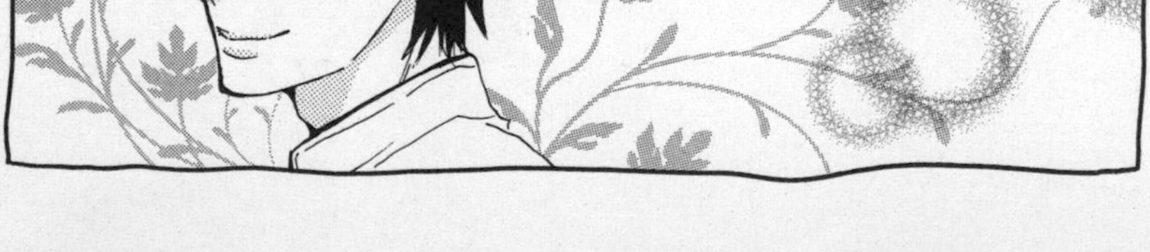
3
• Exploring Different Hairstyles •
☆ Natsu ☆ Short Crop

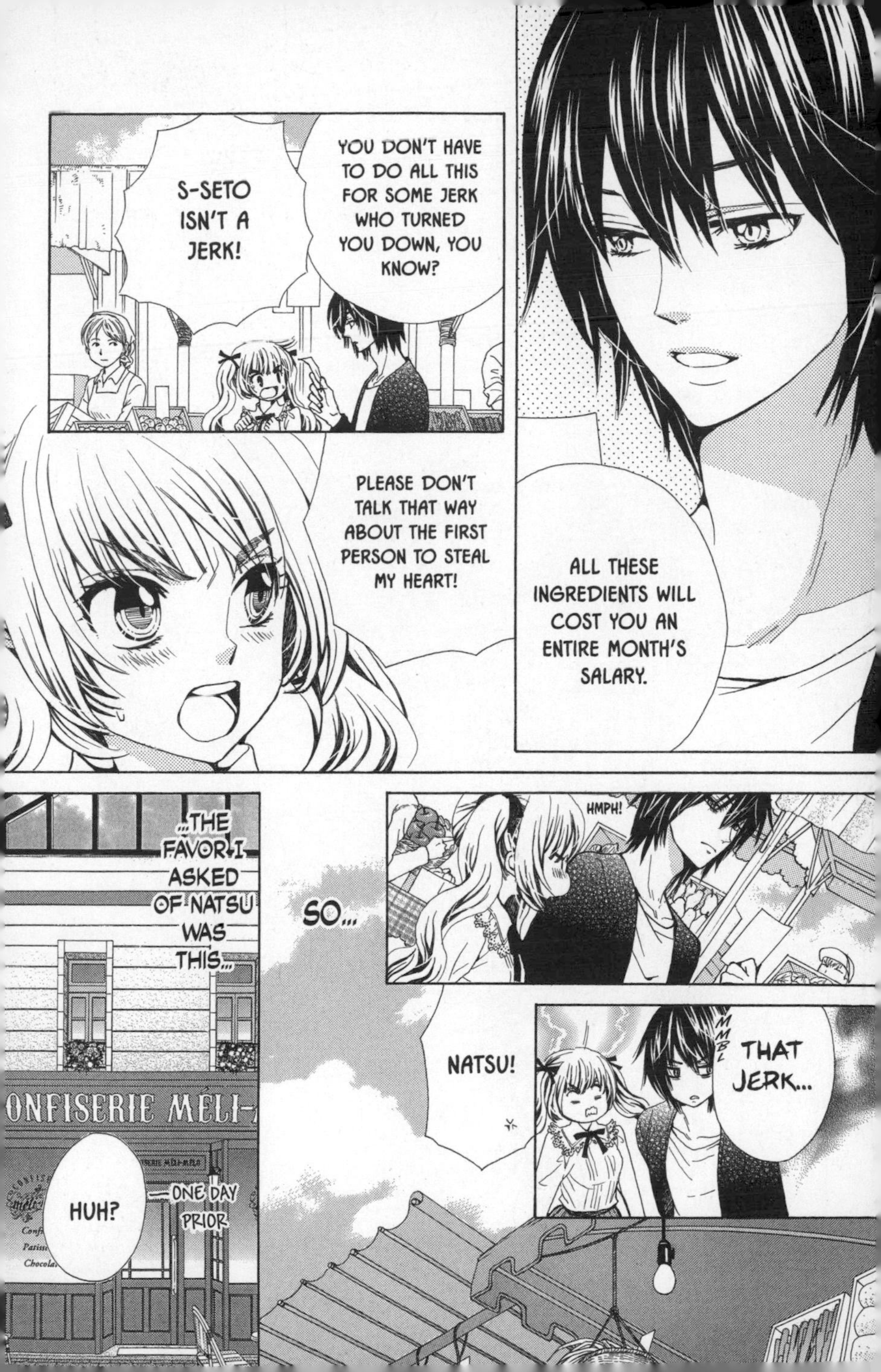
ALL THESE INGREDIENTS WILL COST YOU AN ENTIRE MONTH'S SALARY.
YOU DON'T HAVE TO DO ALL THIS FOR SOME JERK WHO TURNED YOU DOWN, YOU KNOW?
S-SETO ISN'T A JERK!
PLEASE DON'T TALK THAT WAY ABOUT THE FIRST PERSON TO STEAL MY HEART!
HMPH!
MMBL
THAT JERK...
NATSU!
SO...
...THE FAVOR I ASKED OF NATSU WAS THIS...
—ONE DAY PRIOR
HUH?

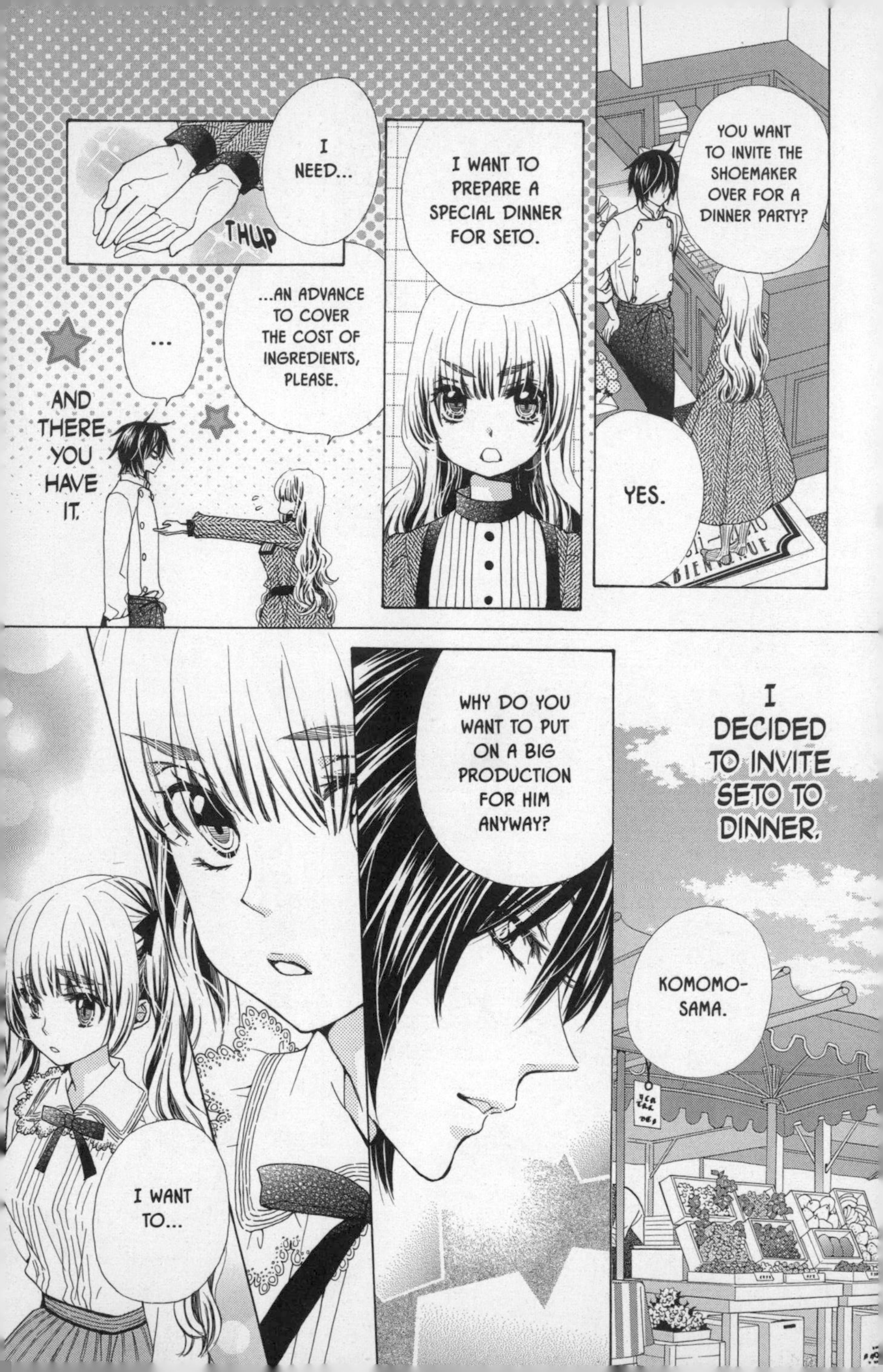
YOU WANT TO INVITE THE SHOEMAKER OVER FOR A DINNER PARTY?
YES.
I WANT TO PREPARE A SPECIAL DINNER FOR SETO.
I NEED...
THUP
...AN ADVANCE TO COVER THE COST OF INGREDIENTS, PLEASE.
...
AND THERE YOU HAVE IT.
I DECIDED TO INVITE SETO TO DINNER.
KOMOMO-SAMA.
WHY DO YOU WANT TO PUT ON A BIG PRODUCTION FOR HIM ANYWAY?
I WANT TO...

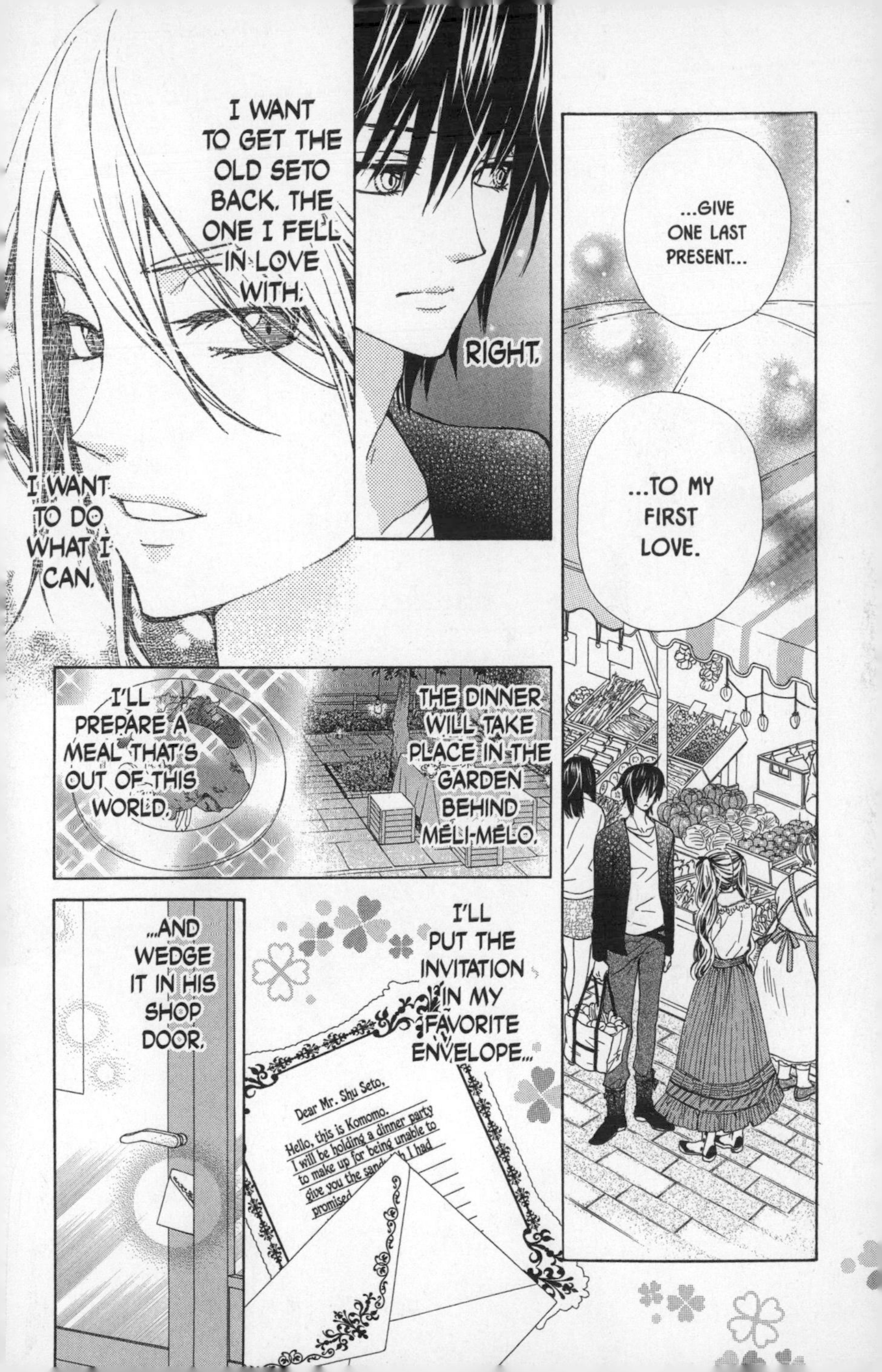
I WANT TO GET THE OLD SETO BACK. THE ONE I FELL IN LOVE WITH.
RIGHT.
I WANT TO DO WHAT I CAN.
THE DINNER WILL TAKE PLACE IN THE GARDEN BEHIND MELI-MELO.
I'LL PREPARE A MEAL THAT'S OUT OF THIS WORLD.
I'LL PUT THE INVITATION IN MY FAVORITE ENVELOPE...
...AND WEDGE IT IN HIS SHOP DOOR.
Dear Mr. Shu Seto,
Hello, this is Komomo.
I will be holding a dinner party to make up for being unable to give you the sand
promised
...GIVE ONE LAST PRESENT...
...TO MY FIRST LOVE.

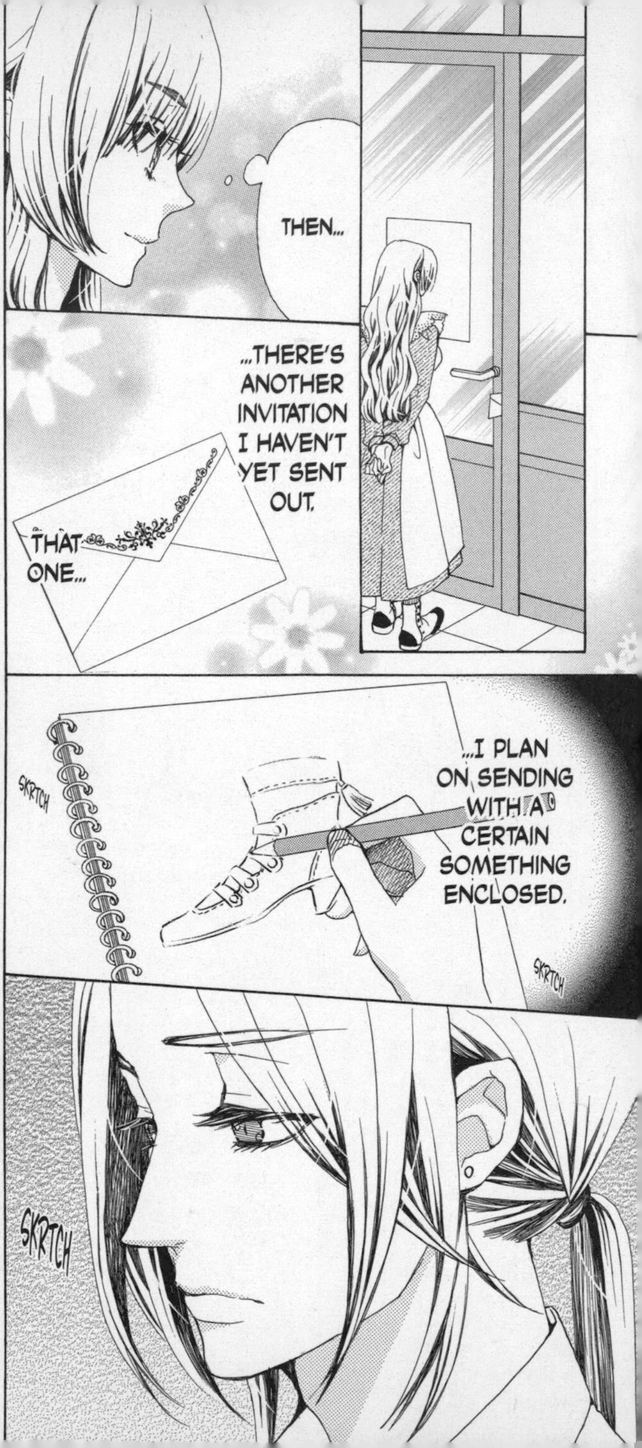
THEN...
...THERE'S ANOTHER INVITATION I HAVEN'T YET SENT OUT.
THAT ONE...
SKRTCH
...I PLAN ON SENDING WITH A CERTAIN SOMETHING ENCLOSED.
SKRTCH
SKRTCH

• Komomo Doll •

My friend made me this for my birthday! She painted on Komomo's face and shaped the hair to be like Komomo's!

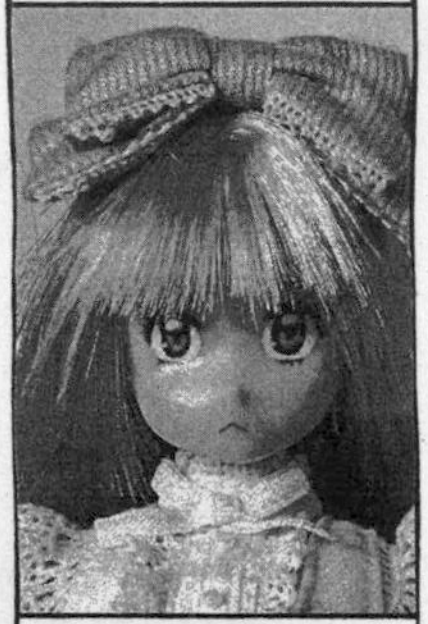

From the front

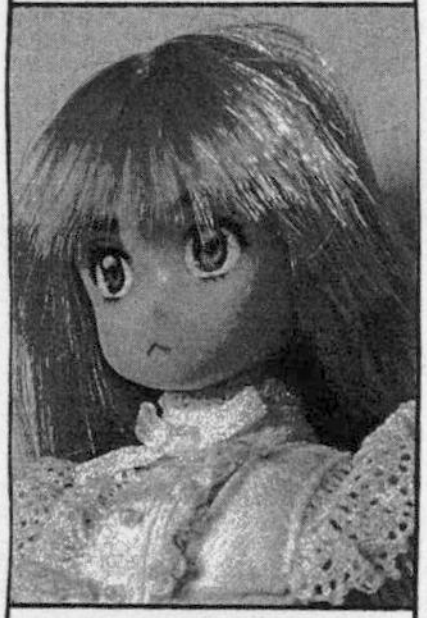

Thick eyebrows!

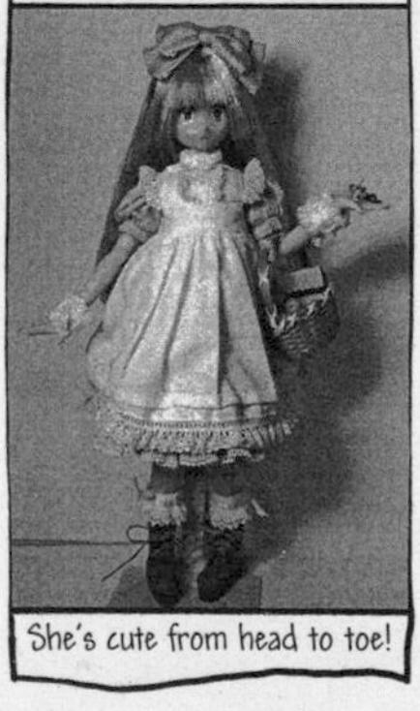

She's cute from head to toe!

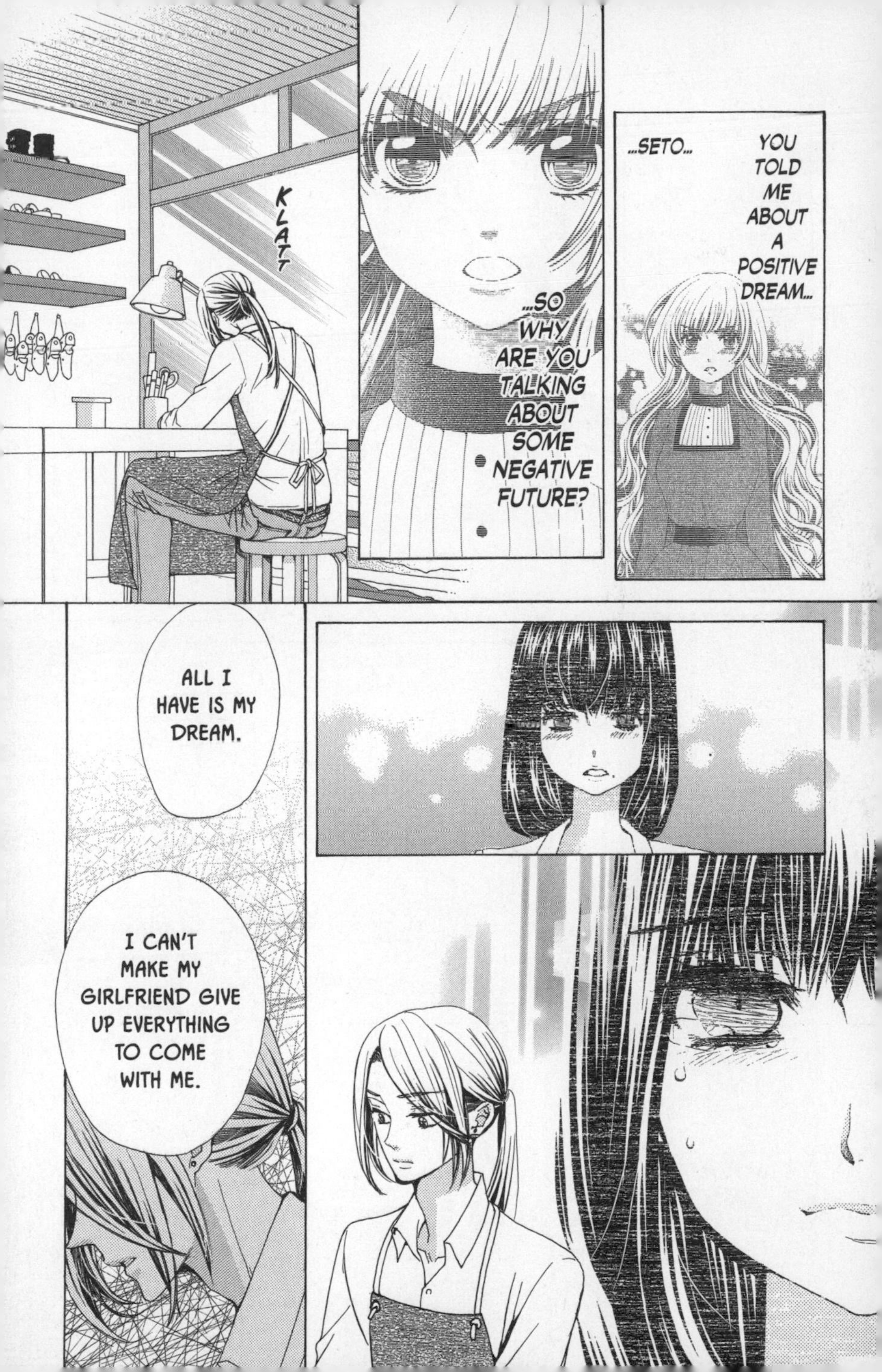
...SETO...
YOU TOLD ME ABOUT A POSITIVE DREAM...
...SO WHY ARE YOU TALKING ABOUT SOME NEGATIVE FUTURE?
KLATT
ALL I HAVE IS MY DREAM.
I CAN'T MAKE MY GIRLFRIEND GIVE UP EVERYTHING TO COME WITH ME.

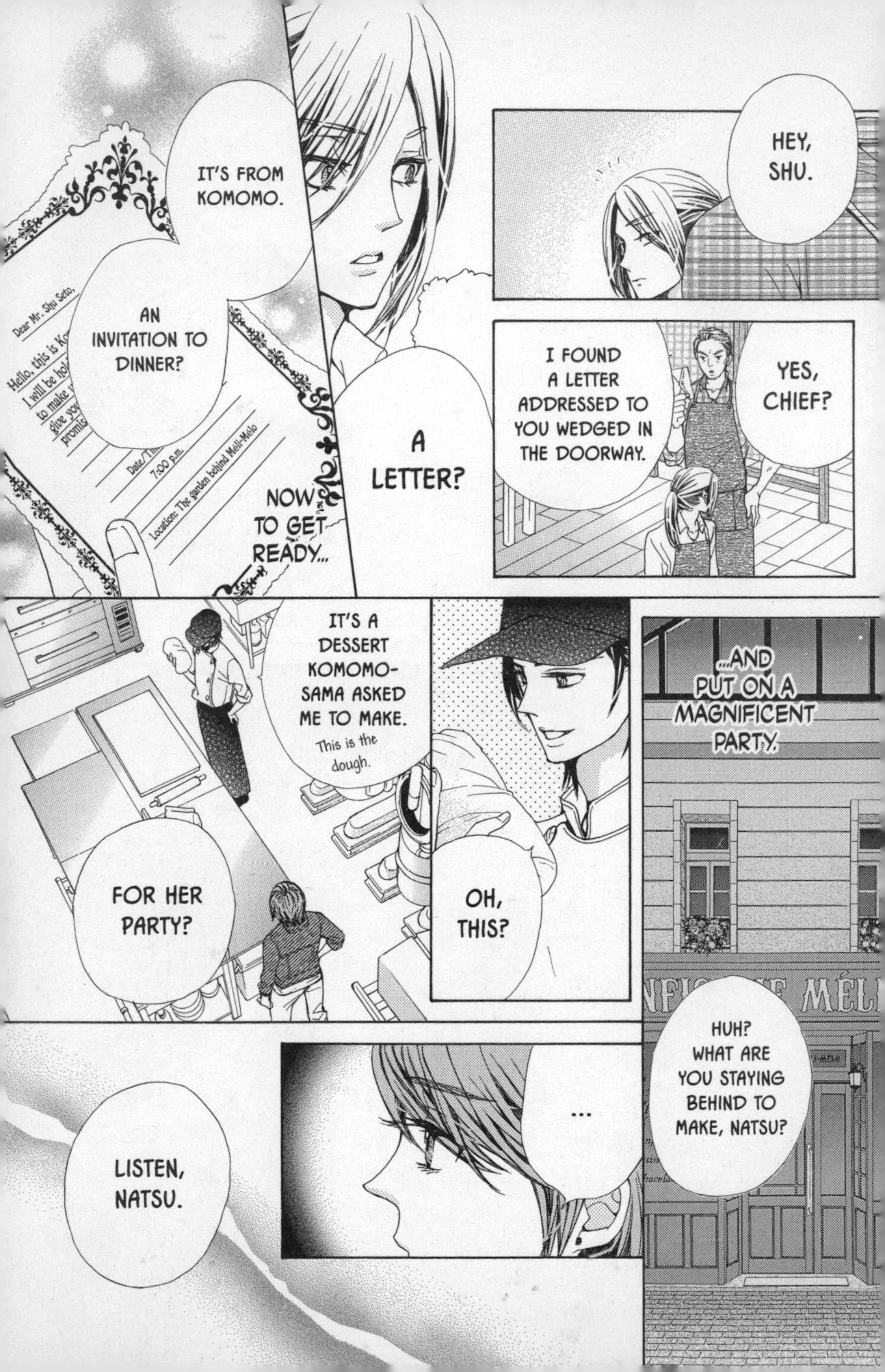
HEY, SHU.
YES, CHIEF?
I FOUND A LETTER ADDRESSED TO YOU WEDGED IN THE DOORWAY.
A LETTER?
IT'S FROM KOMOMO.
AN INVITATION TO DINNER?
Dear Mr. Shu Seto,
7:00 p.m.
Location: The garden behind Meli-Melo
NOW TO GET READY...
...AND PUT ON A MAGNIFICENT PARTY.
HUH? WHAT ARE YOU STAYING BEHIND TO MAKE, NATSU?
OH, THIS?
IT'S A DESSERT KOMOMO-SAMA ASKED ME TO MAKE.
This is the dough.
FOR HER PARTY?
...
LISTEN, NATSU.

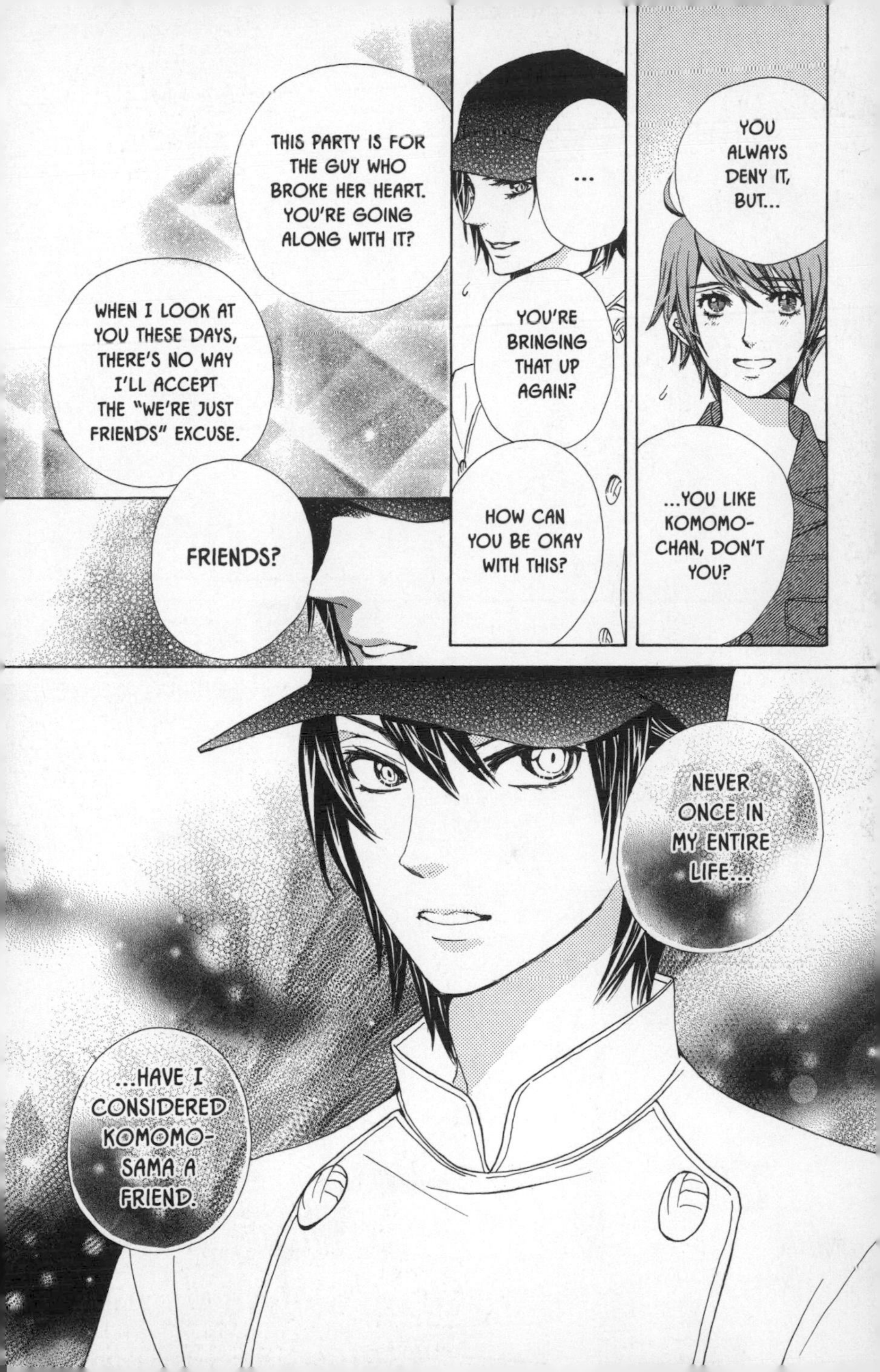
YOU ALWAYS DENY IT, BUT...
...YOU LIKE KOMOMO-CHAN, DON'T YOU?
...
YOU'RE BRINGING THAT UP AGAIN?
HOW CAN YOU BE OKAY WITH THIS?
THIS PARTY IS FOR THE GUY WHO BROKE HER HEART. YOU'RE GOING ALONG WITH IT?
WHEN I LOOK AT YOU THESE DAYS, THERE'S NO WAY I'LL ACCEPT THE "WE'RE JUST FRIENDS" EXCUSE.
FRIENDS?
NEVER ONCE IN MY ENTIRE LIFE...
...HAVE I CONSIDERED KOMOMO-SAMA A FRIEND.

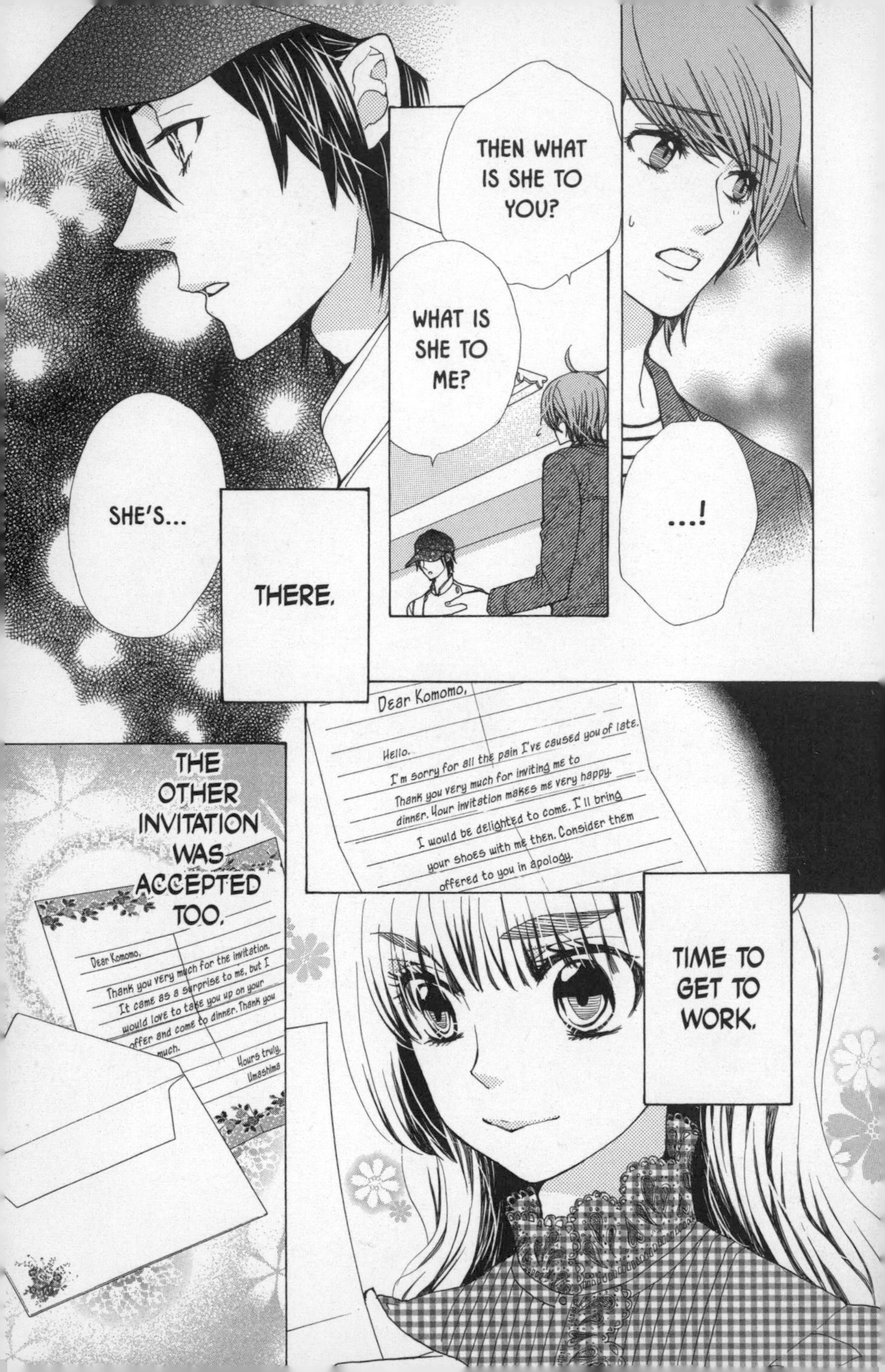
THEN WHAT IS SHE TO YOU?
...!
WHAT IS SHE TO ME?
SHE'S...
THERE.
Dear Komomo,
Hello.
I'm sorry for all the pain I've caused you of late.
Thank you very much for inviting me to dinner. Your invitation makes me very happy.
I would be delighted to come. I'll bring your shoes with me then. Consider them offered to you in apology.
TIME TO GET TO WORK.
THE OTHER INVITATION WAS ACCEPTED TOO.
Dear Komomo,
Thank you very much for the invitation. It came as a surprise to me, but I would love to take you up on your offer and come to dinner. Thank you much.
Yours truly,
Umashima

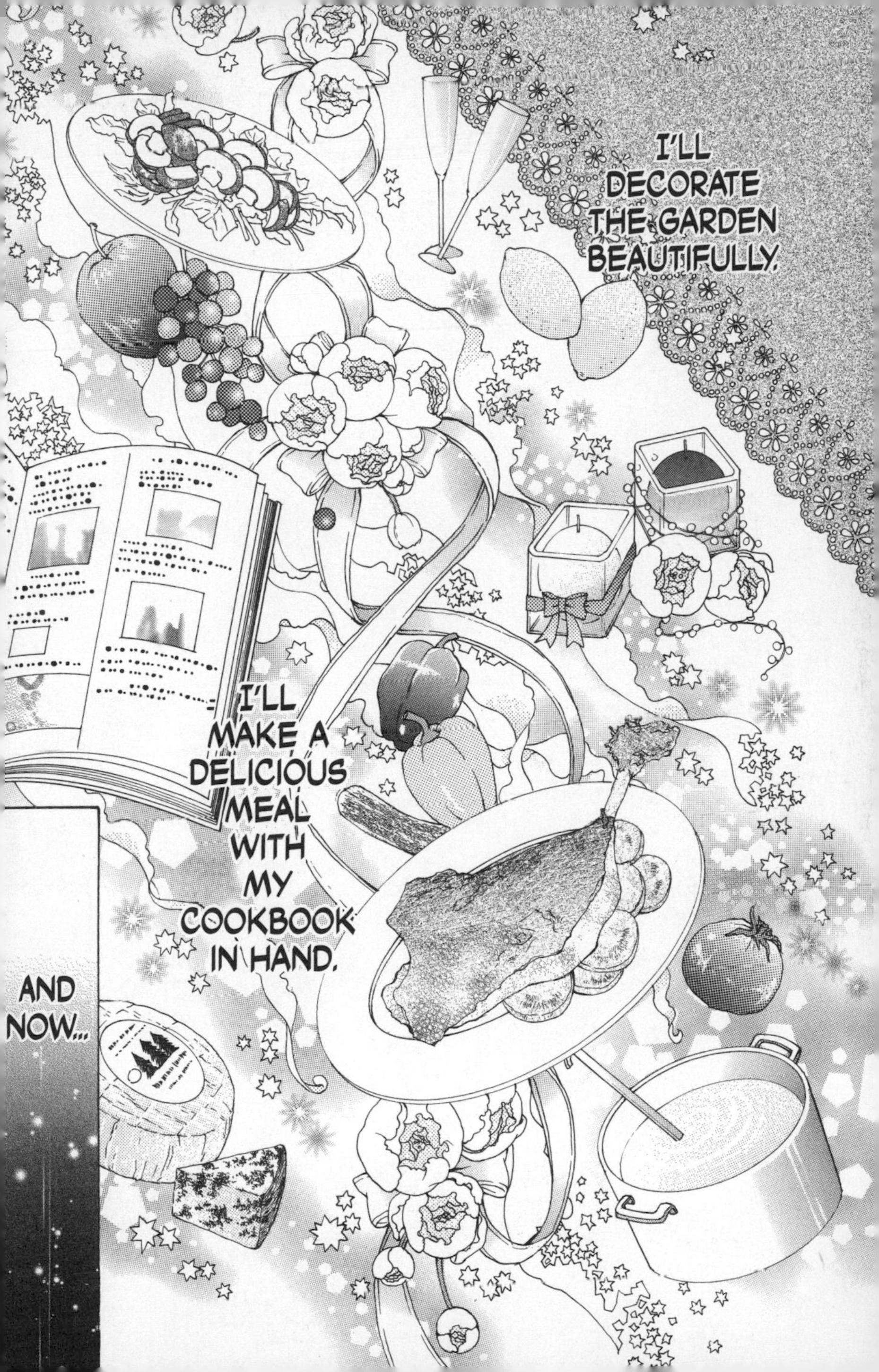
I'LL DECORATE THE GARDEN BEAUTIFULLY.
I'LL MAKE A DELICIOUS MEAL WITH MY COOKBOOK IN HAND.
AND NOW...

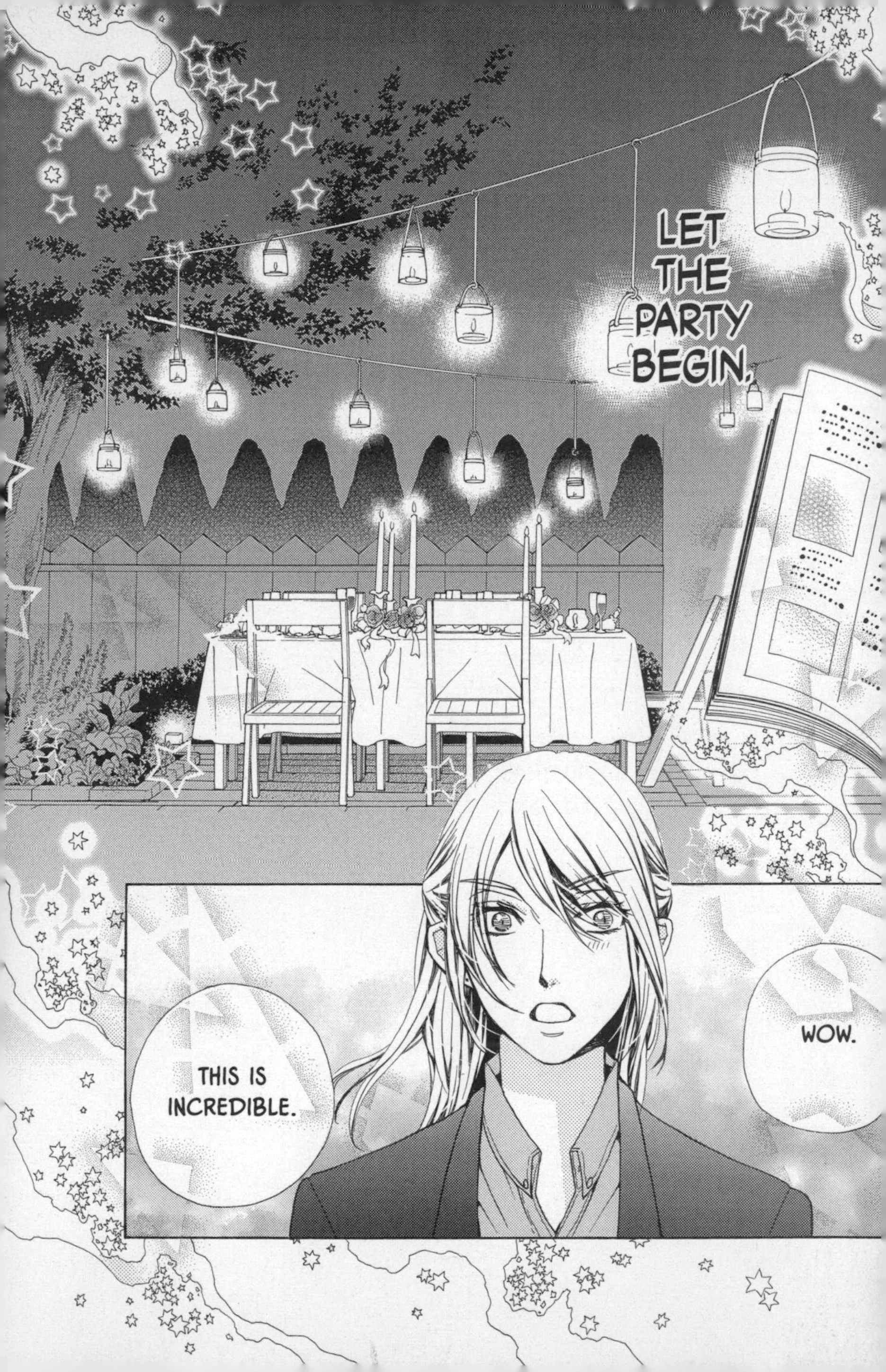
LET THE PARTY BEGIN.
WOW.
THIS IS INCREDIBLE.

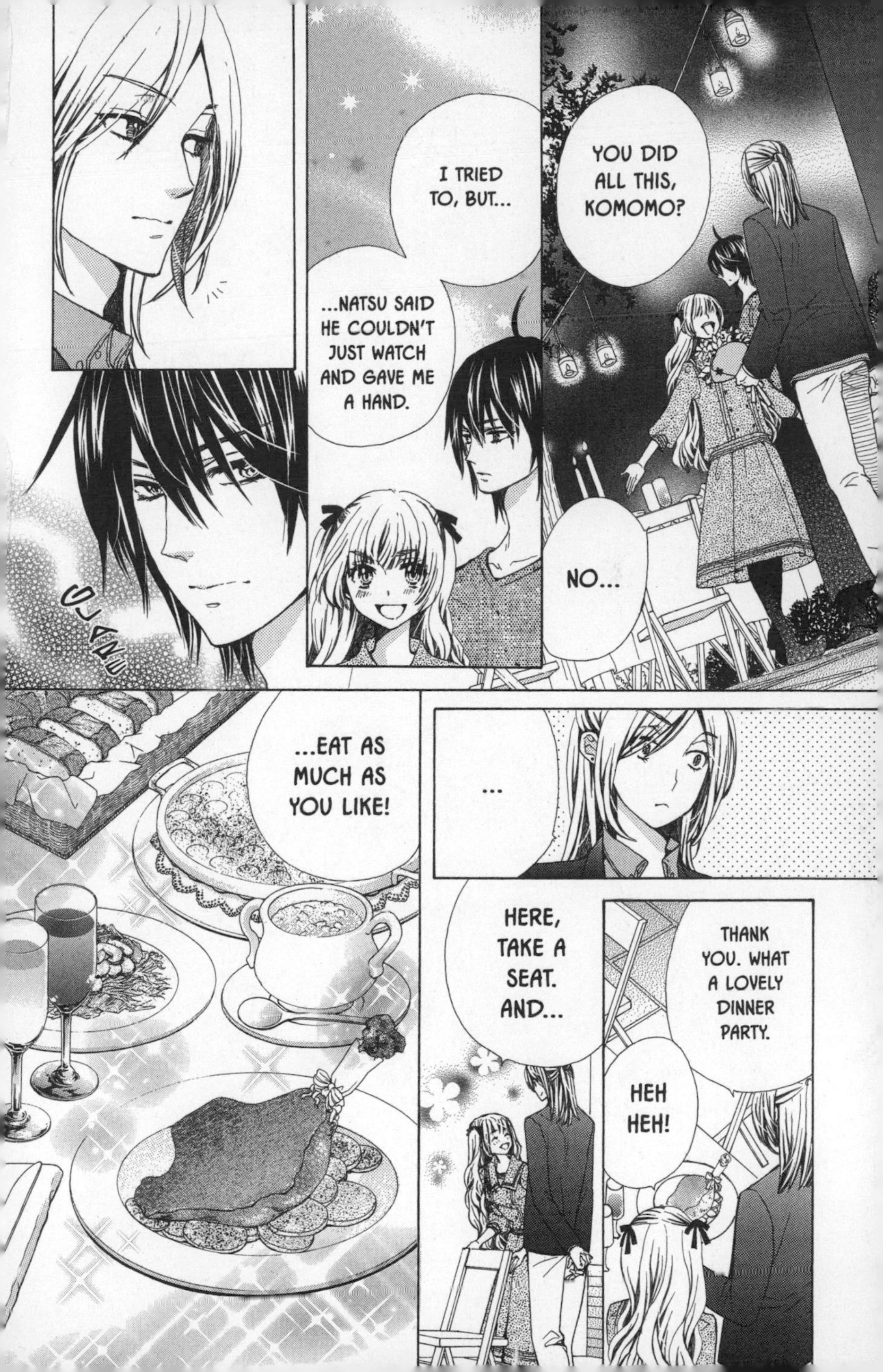
YOU DID ALL THIS, KOMOMO?
NO...
I TRIED TO, BUT...
...NATSU SAID HE COULDN'T JUST WATCH AND GAVE ME A HAND.
...
THANK YOU. WHAT A LOVELY DINNER PARTY.
HEH HEH!
HERE, TAKE A SEAT. AND...
...EAT AS MUCH AS YOU LIKE!

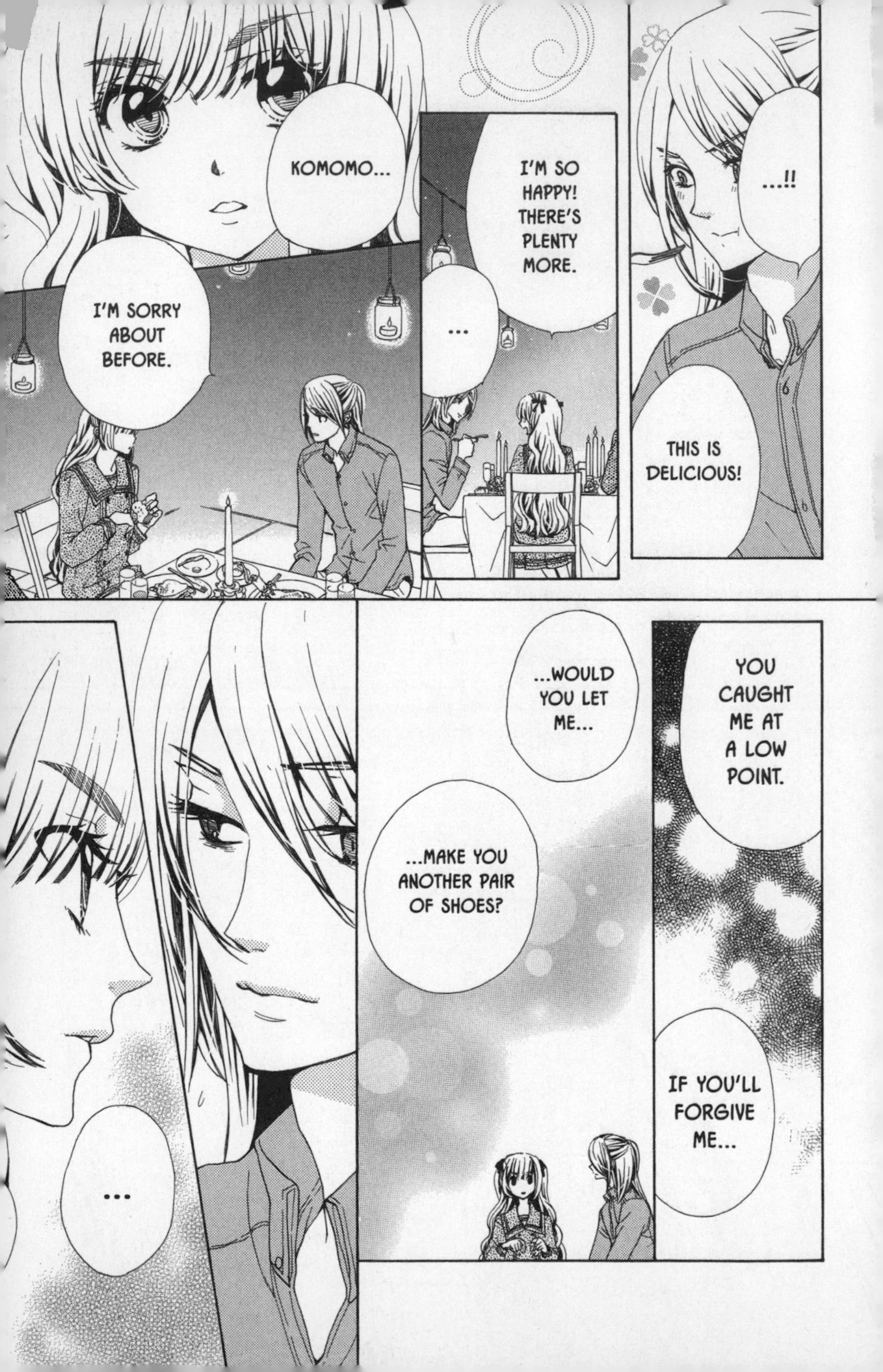
...!!
THIS IS DELICIOUS!
I'M SO HAPPY! THERE'S PLENTY MORE.
...
KOMOMO...
I'M SORRY ABOUT BEFORE.
YOU CAUGHT ME AT A LOW POINT.
IF YOU'LL FORGIVE ME...
...WOULD YOU LET ME...
...MAKE YOU ANOTHER PAIR OF SHOES?
...

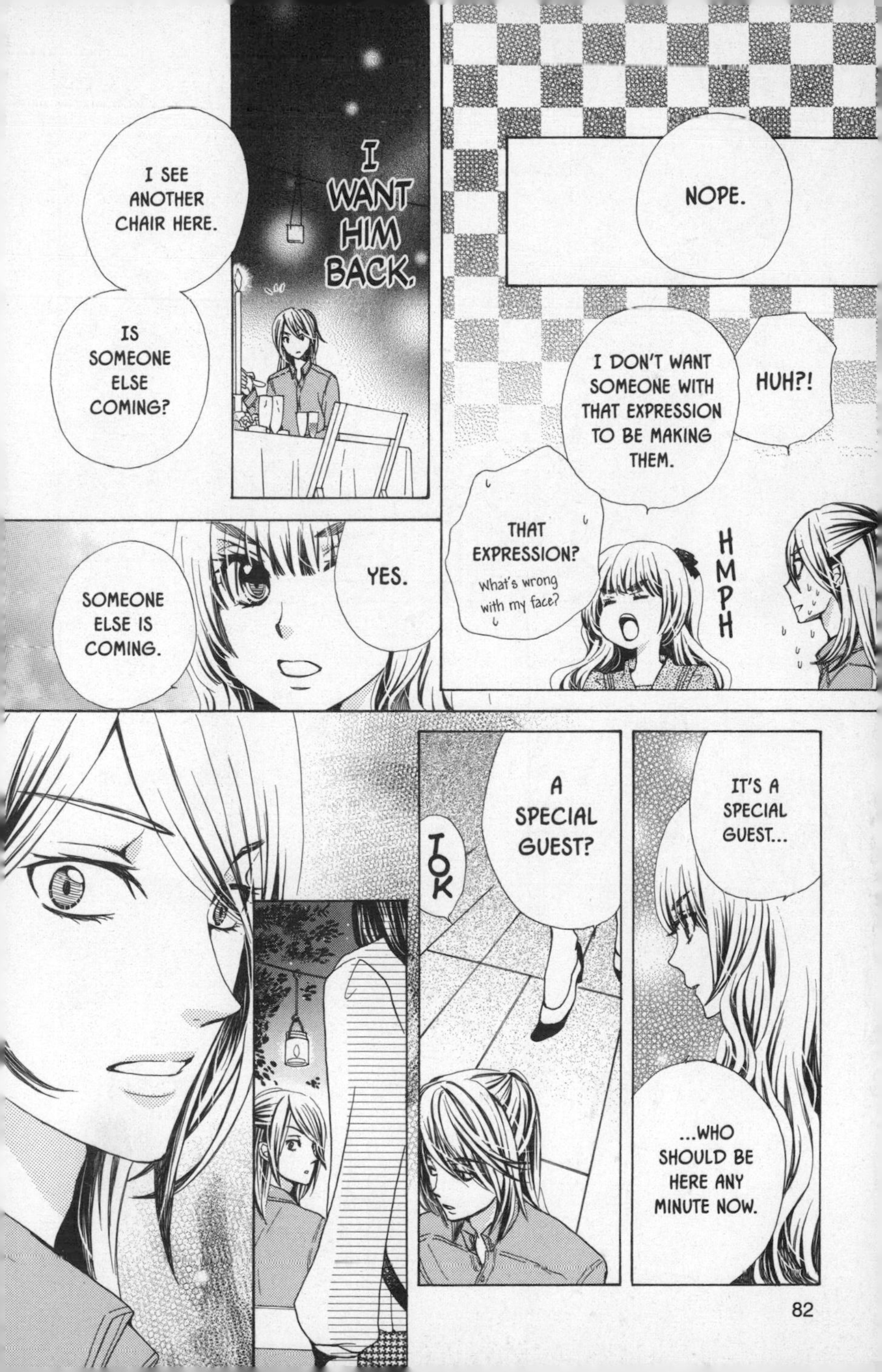
NOPE.
HUH?!
I DON'T WANT SOMEONE WITH THAT EXPRESSION TO BE MAKING THEM.
THAT EXPRESSION?
What's wrong with my face?
HMPH
I WANT HIM BACK.
I SEE ANOTHER CHAIR HERE.
IS SOMEONE ELSE COMING?
YES.
SOMEONE ELSE IS COMING.
IT'S A SPECIAL GUEST...
...WHO SHOULD BE HERE ANY MINUTE NOW.
A SPECIAL GUEST?
TOK

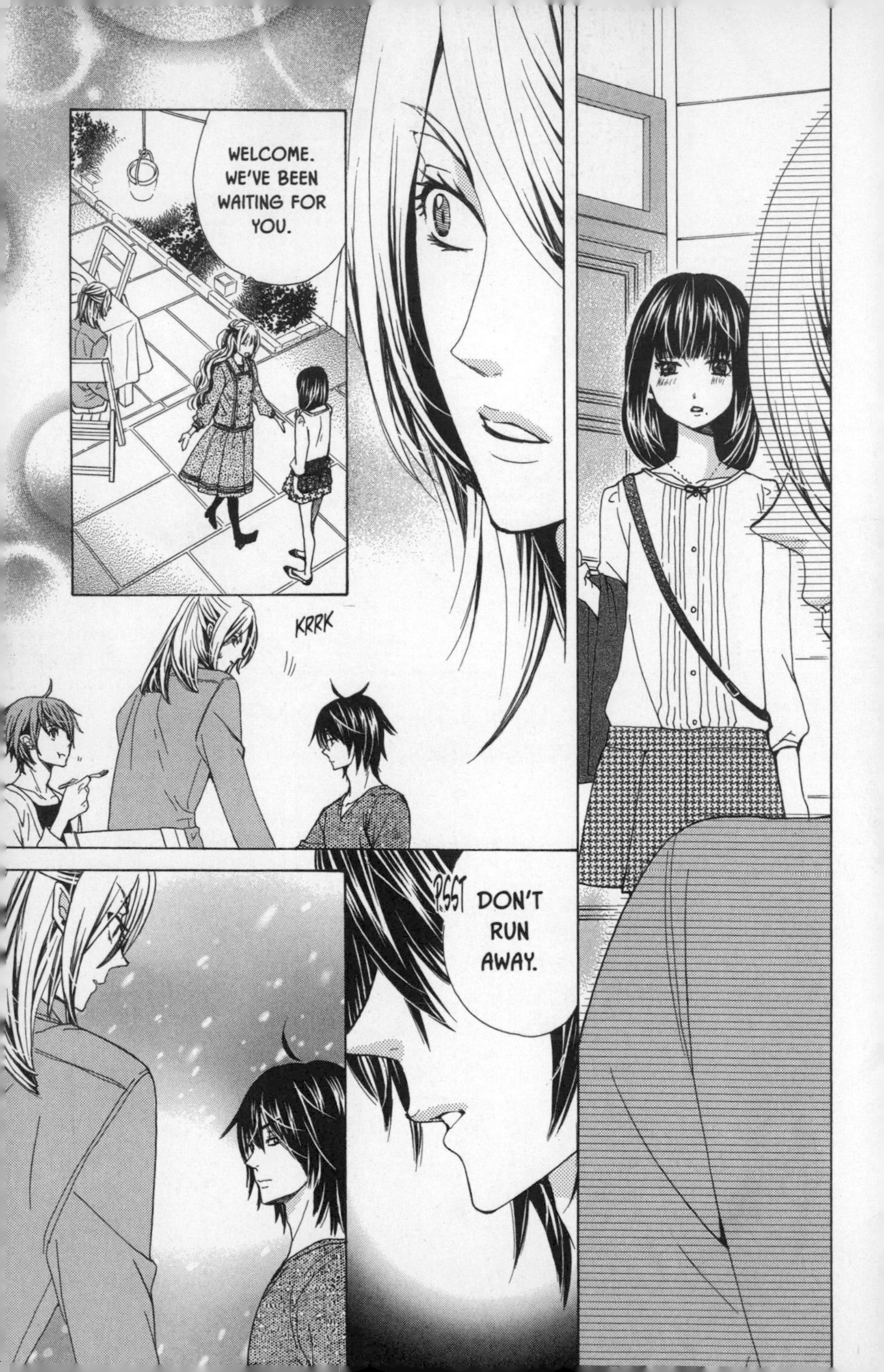
WELCOME. WE'VE BEEN WAITING FOR YOU.
KRRK
PSST
DON'T RUN AWAY.

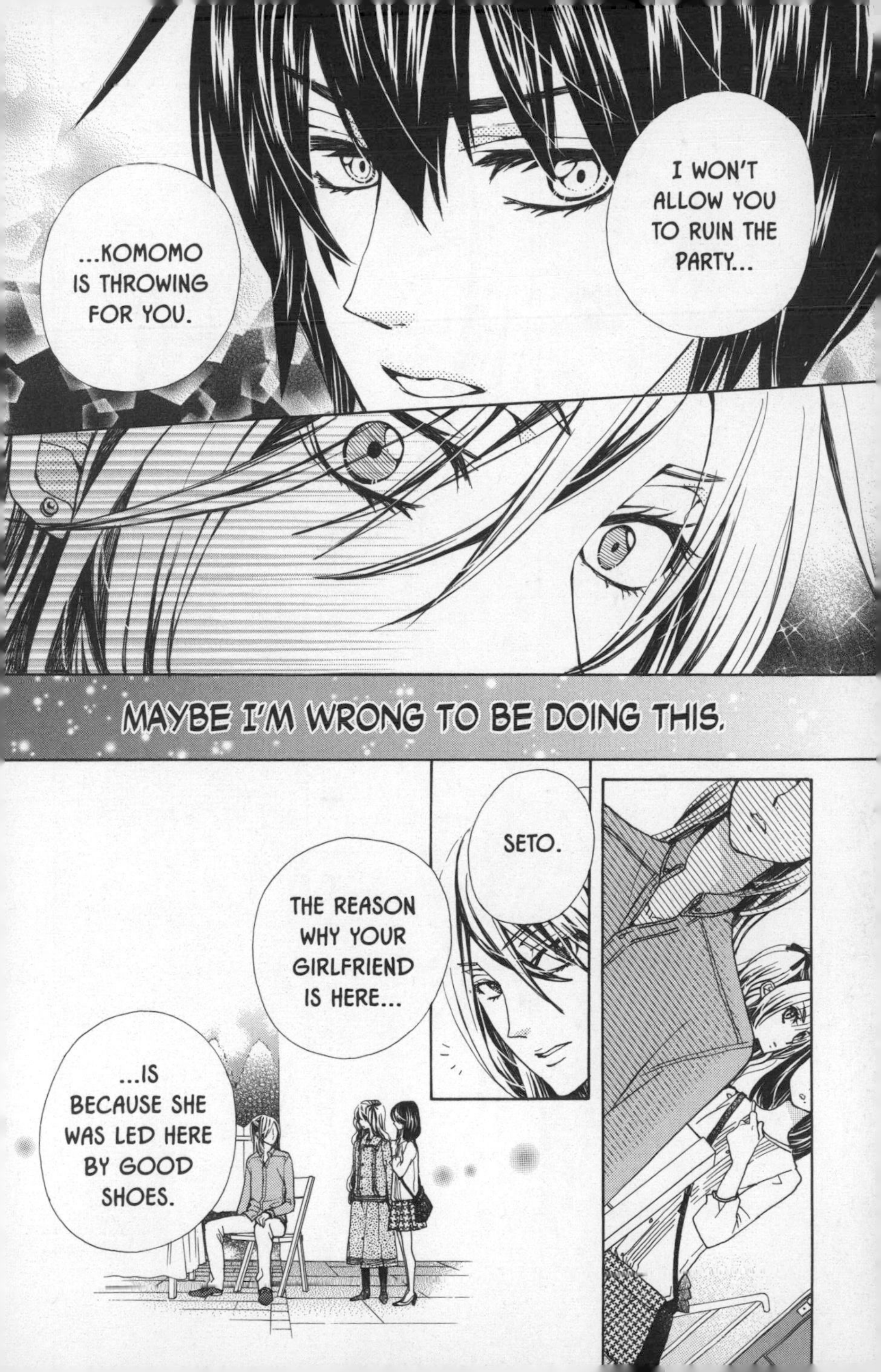
I WON'T ALLOW YOU TO RUIN THE PARTY...
...KOMOMO IS THROWING FOR YOU.
MAYBE I'M WRONG TO BE DOING THIS.
SETO.
THE REASON WHY YOUR GIRLFRIEND IS HERE...
...IS BECAUSE SHE WAS LED HERE BY GOOD SHOES.

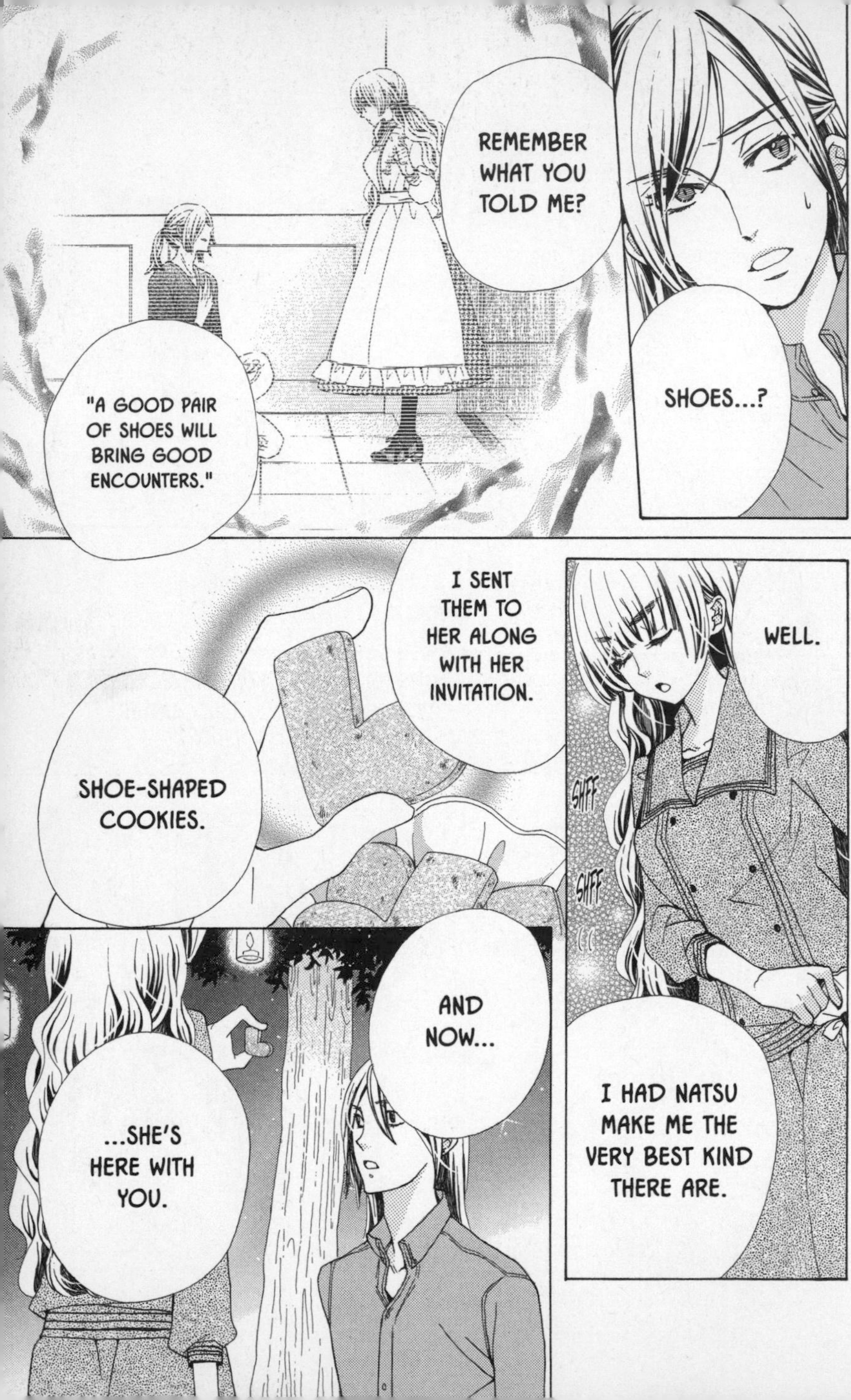
SHOES...?
REMEMBER WHAT YOU TOLD ME?
"A GOOD PAIR OF SHOES WILL BRING GOOD ENCOUNTERS."
WELL.
SHFF
SHFF
I HAD NATSU MAKE ME THE VERY BEST KIND THERE ARE.
I SENT THEM TO HER ALONG WITH HER INVITATION.
SHOE-SHAPED COOKIES.
AND NOW...
...SHE'S HERE WITH YOU.

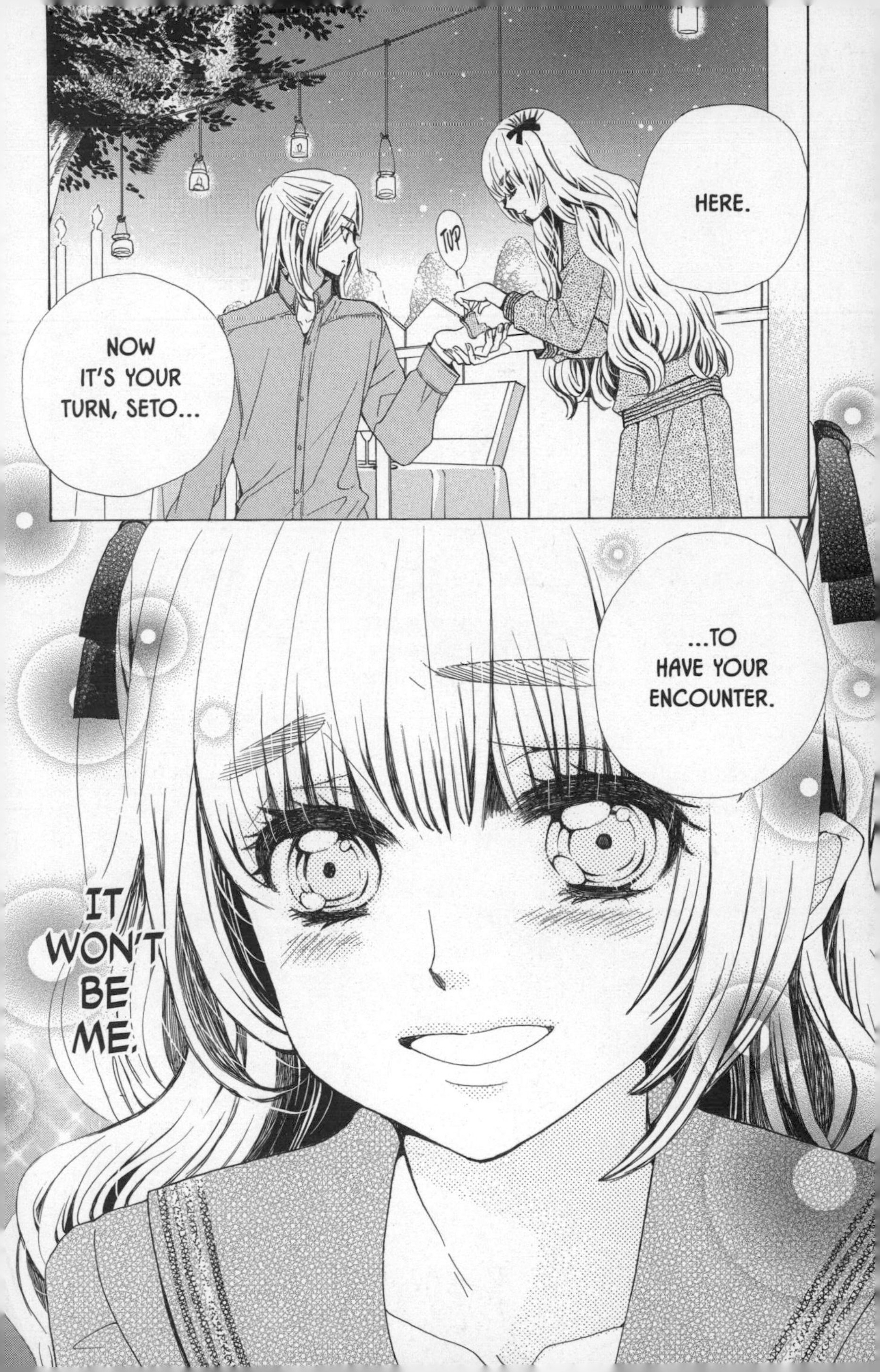
HERE.
TUP
NOW IT'S YOUR TURN, SETO...
...TO HAVE YOUR ENCOUNTER.
IT WON'T BE ME.

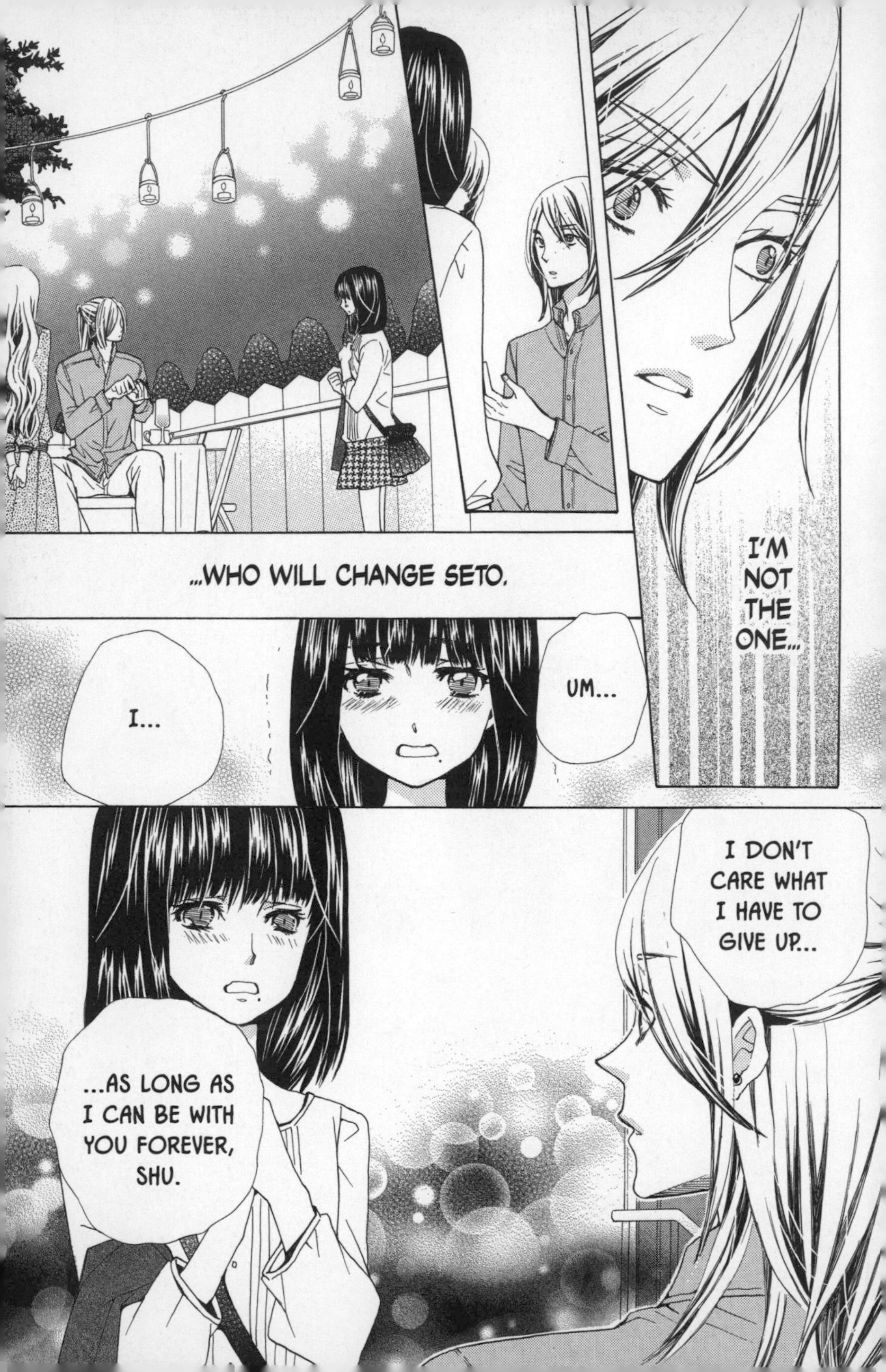
I'M NOT THE ONE...
...WHO WILL CHANGE SETO.
UM...
I...
I DON'T CARE WHAT I HAVE TO GIVE UP...
...AS LONG AS I CAN BE WITH YOU FOREVER, SHU.

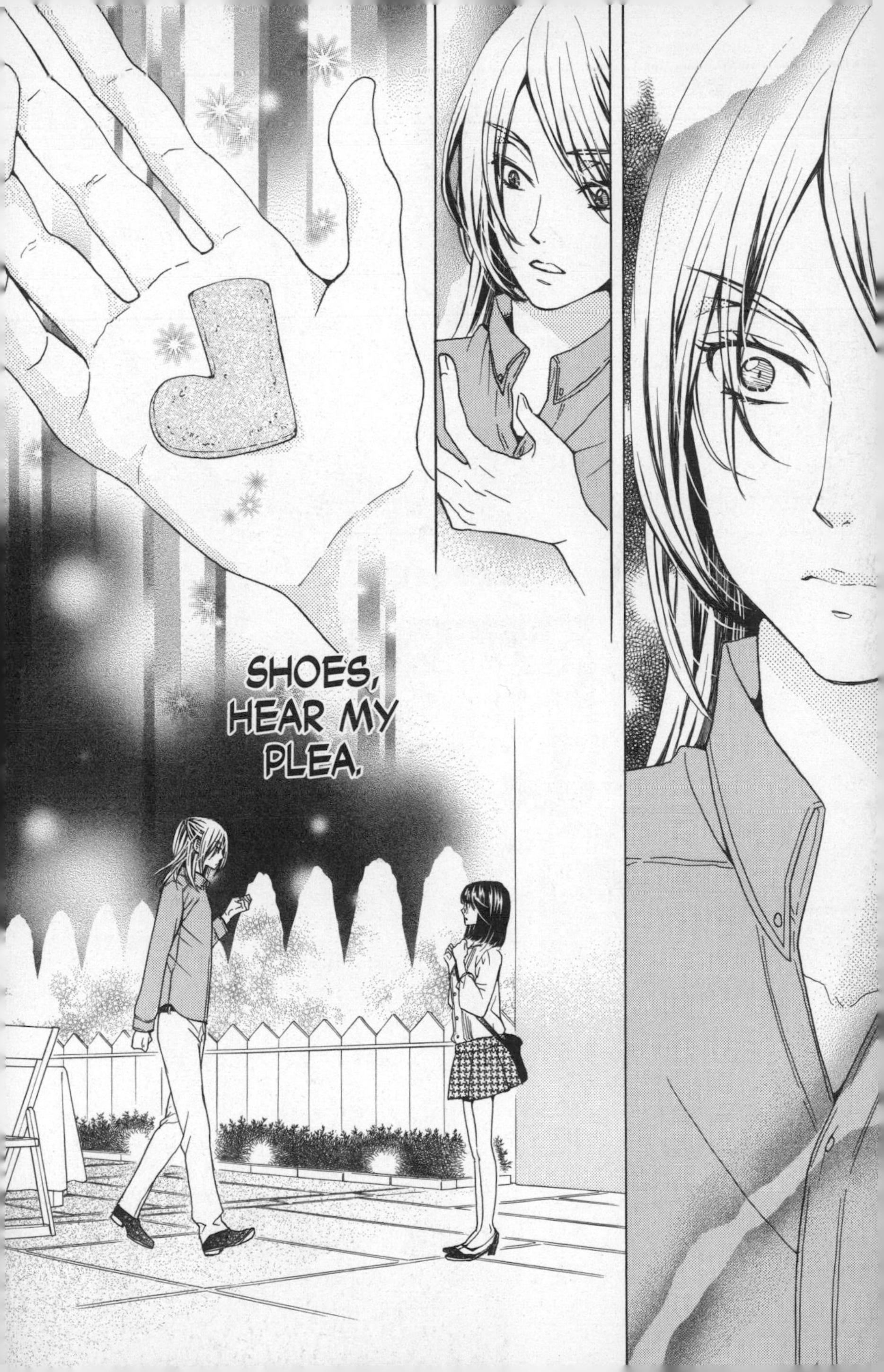
SHOES, HEAR MY PLEA.

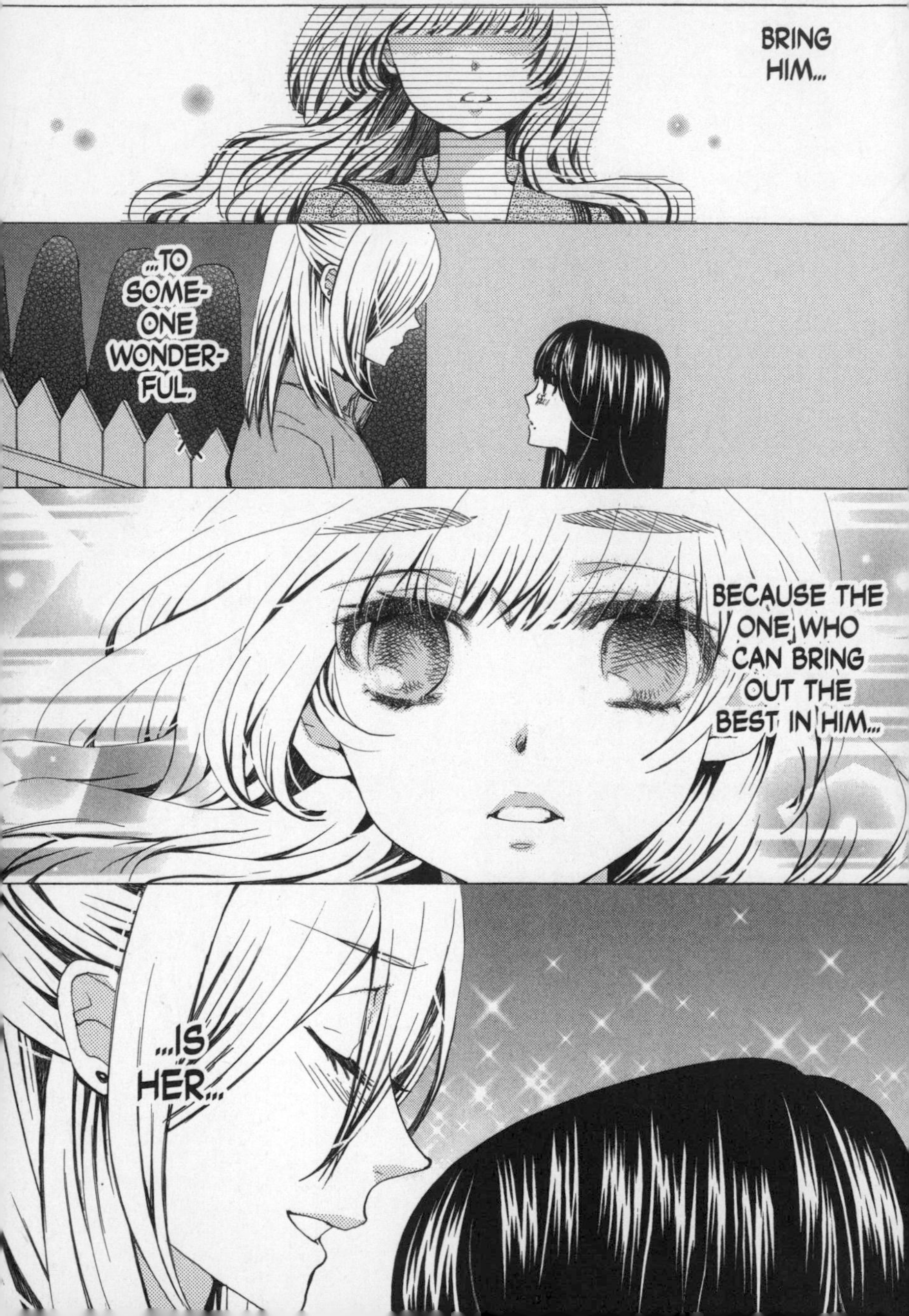
BRING HIM...
...TO SOME-ONE WONDER-FUL.
BECAUSE THE ONE WHO CAN BRING OUT THE BEST IN HIM...
...IS HER...

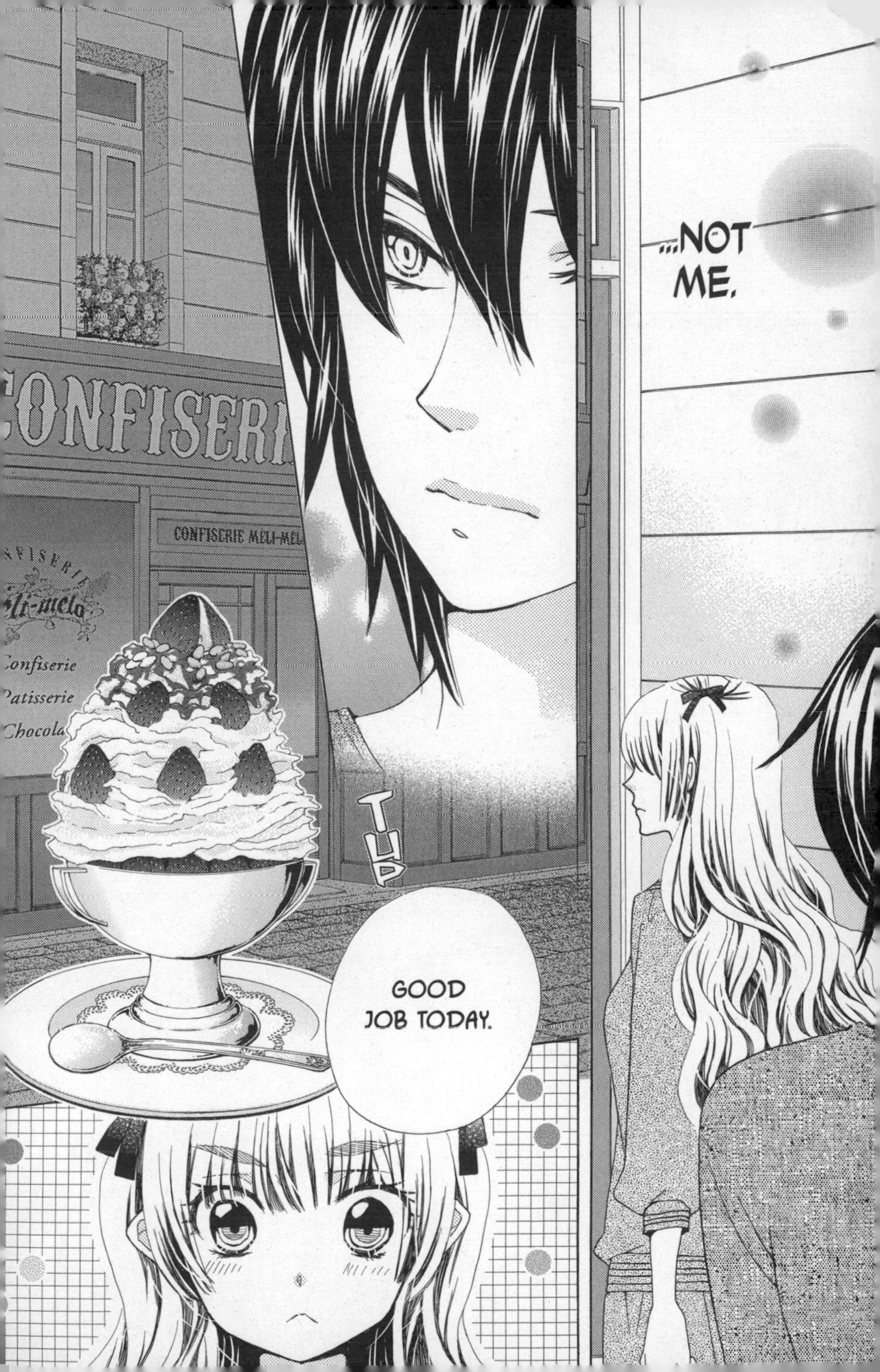
...NOT ME.
TUP
GOOD JOB TODAY.
CONFISERIE MELI-MEL
Confiserie
Patisserie

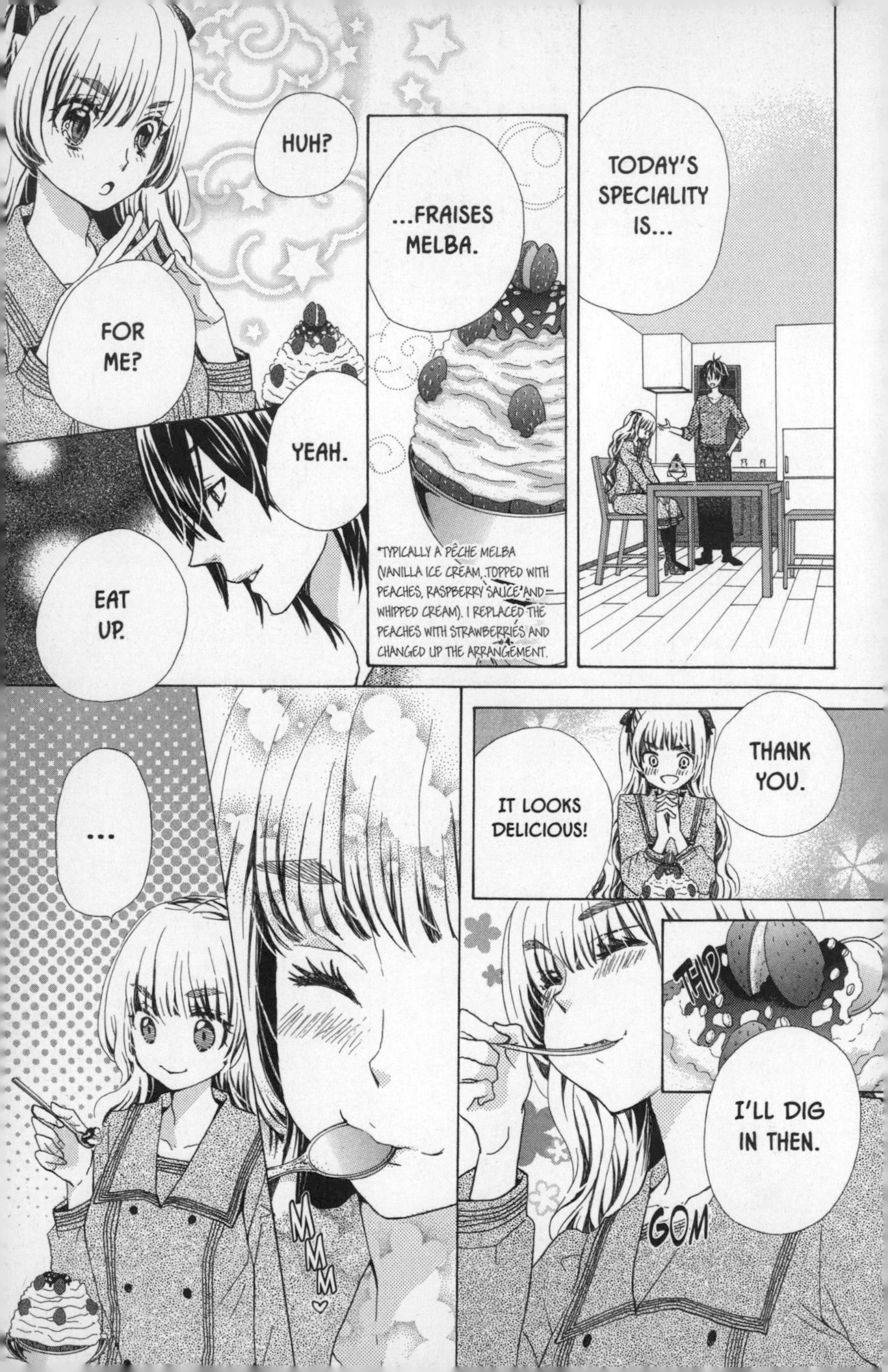
TODAY'S SPECIALITY IS...
...FRAISES MELBA.
*TYPICALLY A PÊCHE MELBA (VANILLA ICE CREAM, TOPPED WITH PEACHES, RASPBERRY SAUCE AND WHIPPED CREAM). I REPLACED THE PEACHES WITH STRAWBERRIES AND CHANGED UP THE ARRANGEMENT.
HUH?
FOR ME?
YEAH.
EAT UP.
THANK YOU.
IT LOOKS DELICIOUS!
THP
I'LL DIG IN THEN.
GOM
MMM♡
...

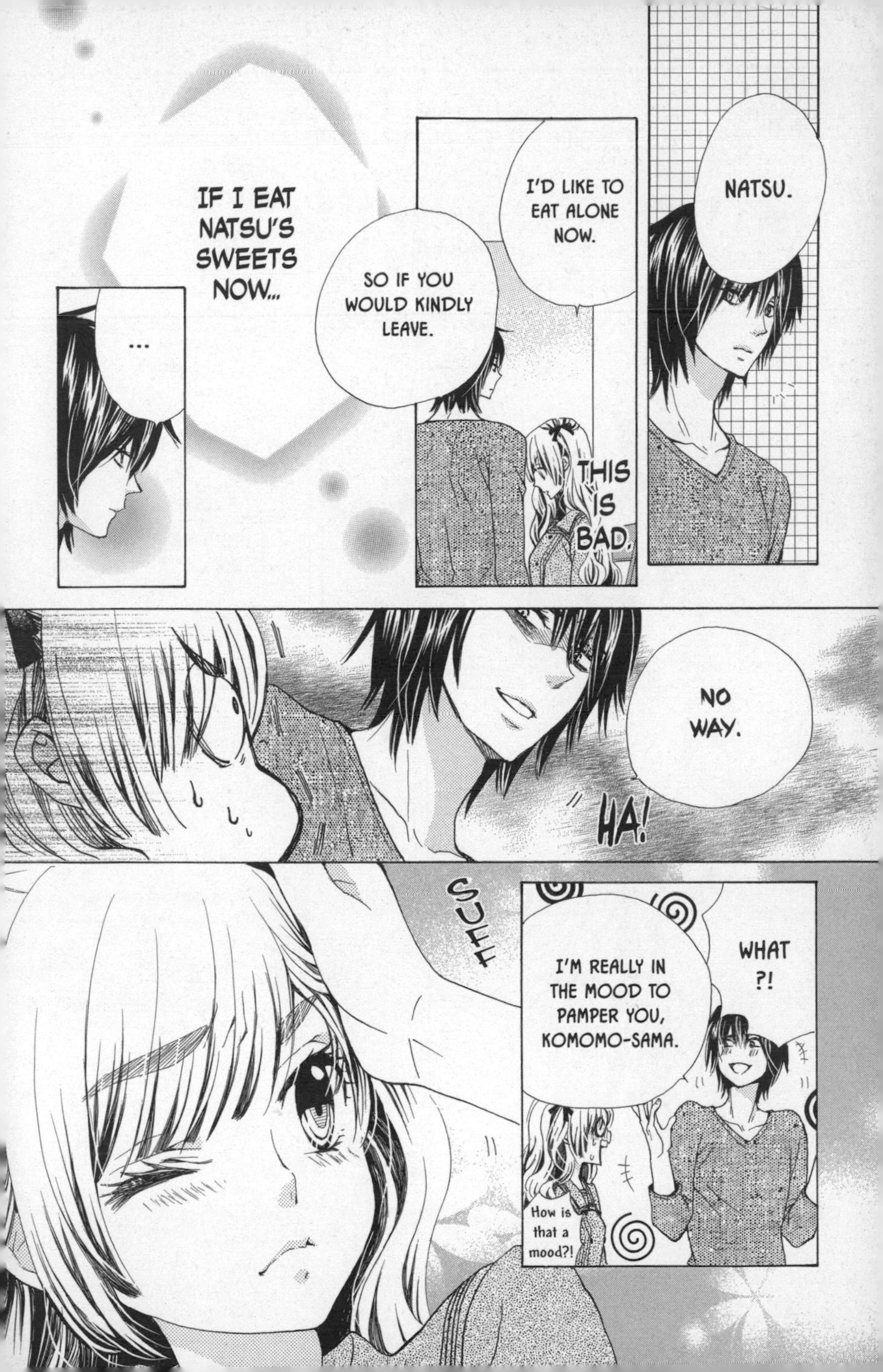
NATSU.
I'D LIKE TO EAT ALONE NOW.
SO IF YOU WOULD KINDLY LEAVE.
THIS IS BAD.
IF I EAT NATSU'S SWEETS NOW...
...
NO WAY.
HA!
WHAT ?!
I'M REALLY IN THE MOOD TO PAMPER YOU, KOMOMO-SAMA.
How is that a mood?!
SUFF

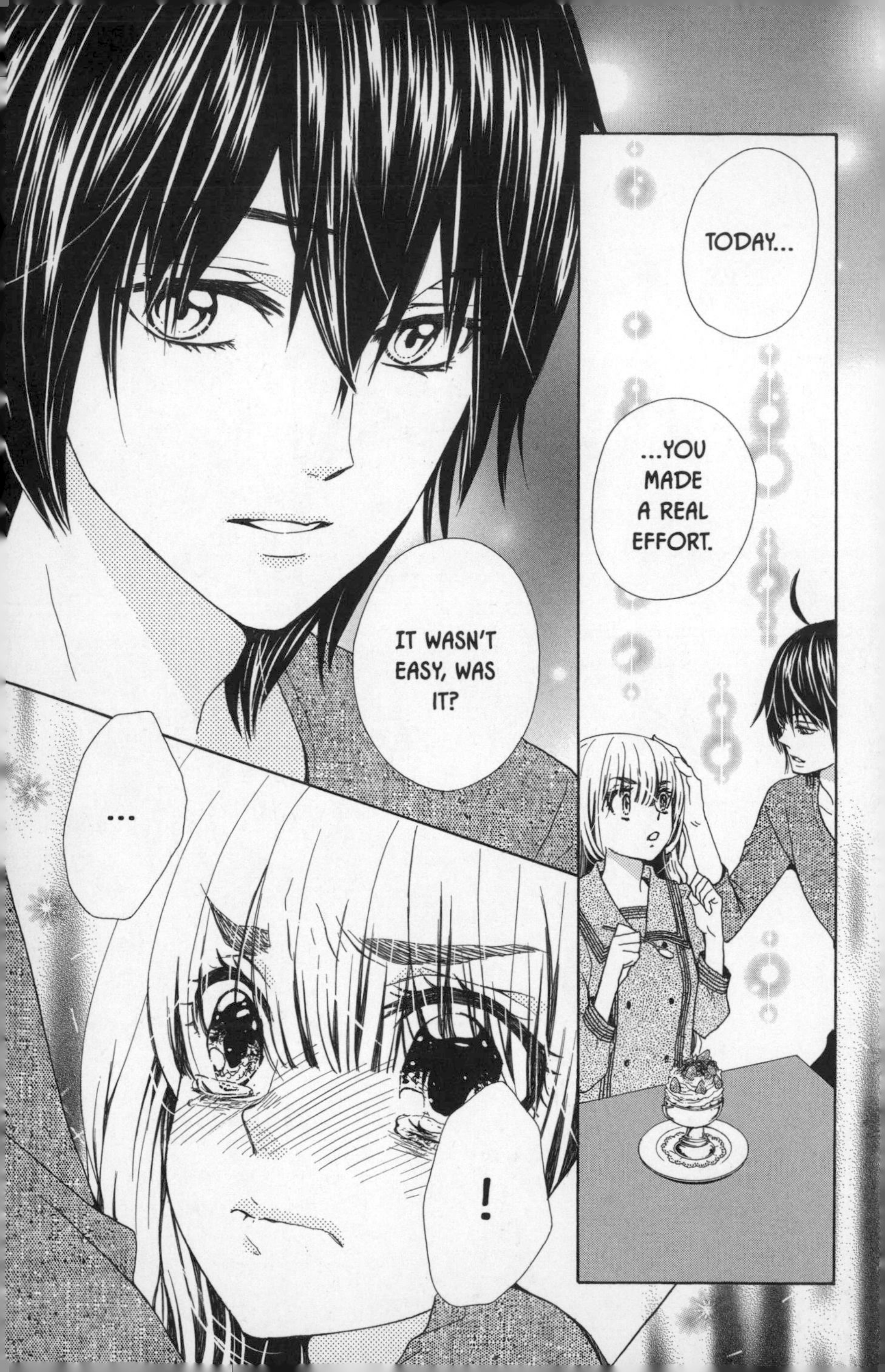
TODAY...
...YOU MADE A REAL EFFORT.
IT WASN'T EASY, WAS IT?
...
!

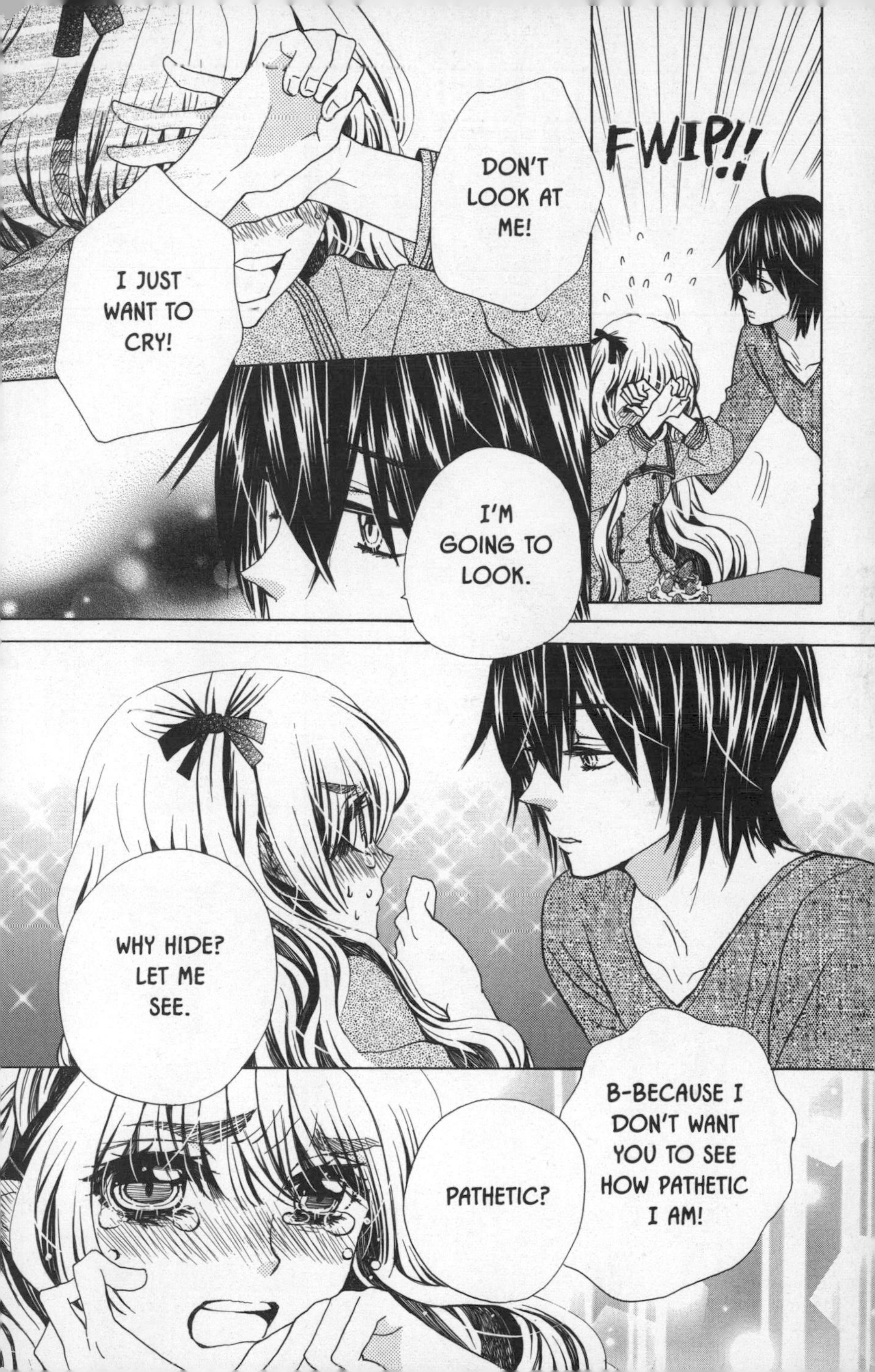
FWIP!!
DON'T LOOK AT ME!
I JUST WANT TO CRY!
I'M GOING TO LOOK.
WHY HIDE? LET ME SEE.
B-BECAUSE I DON'T WANT YOU TO SEE HOW PATHETIC I AM!
PATHETIC?

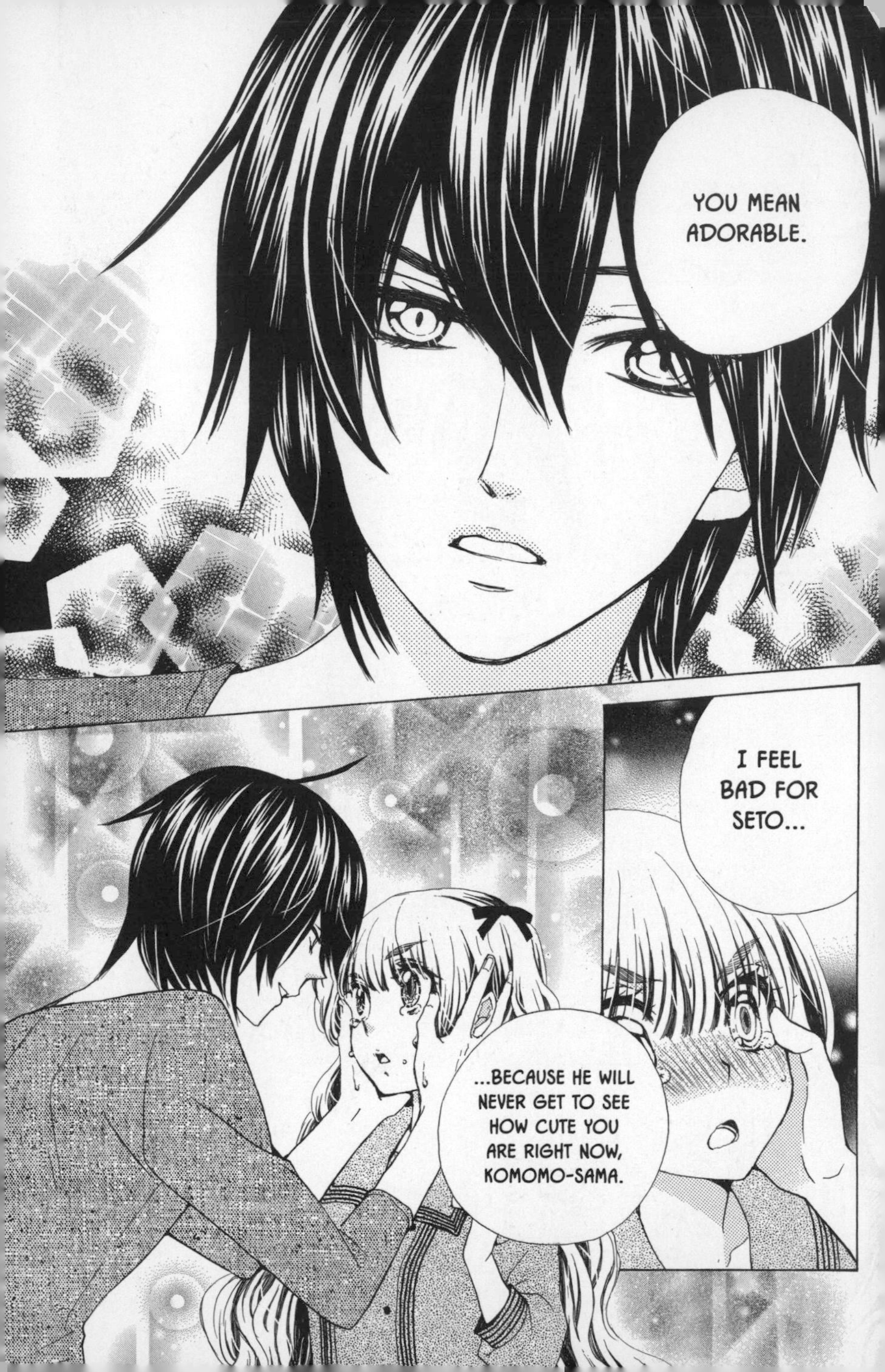
YOU MEAN ADORABLE.
I FEEL BAD FOR SETO...
...BECAUSE HE WILL NEVER GET TO SEE HOW CUTE YOU ARE RIGHT NOW, KOMOMO-SAMA.

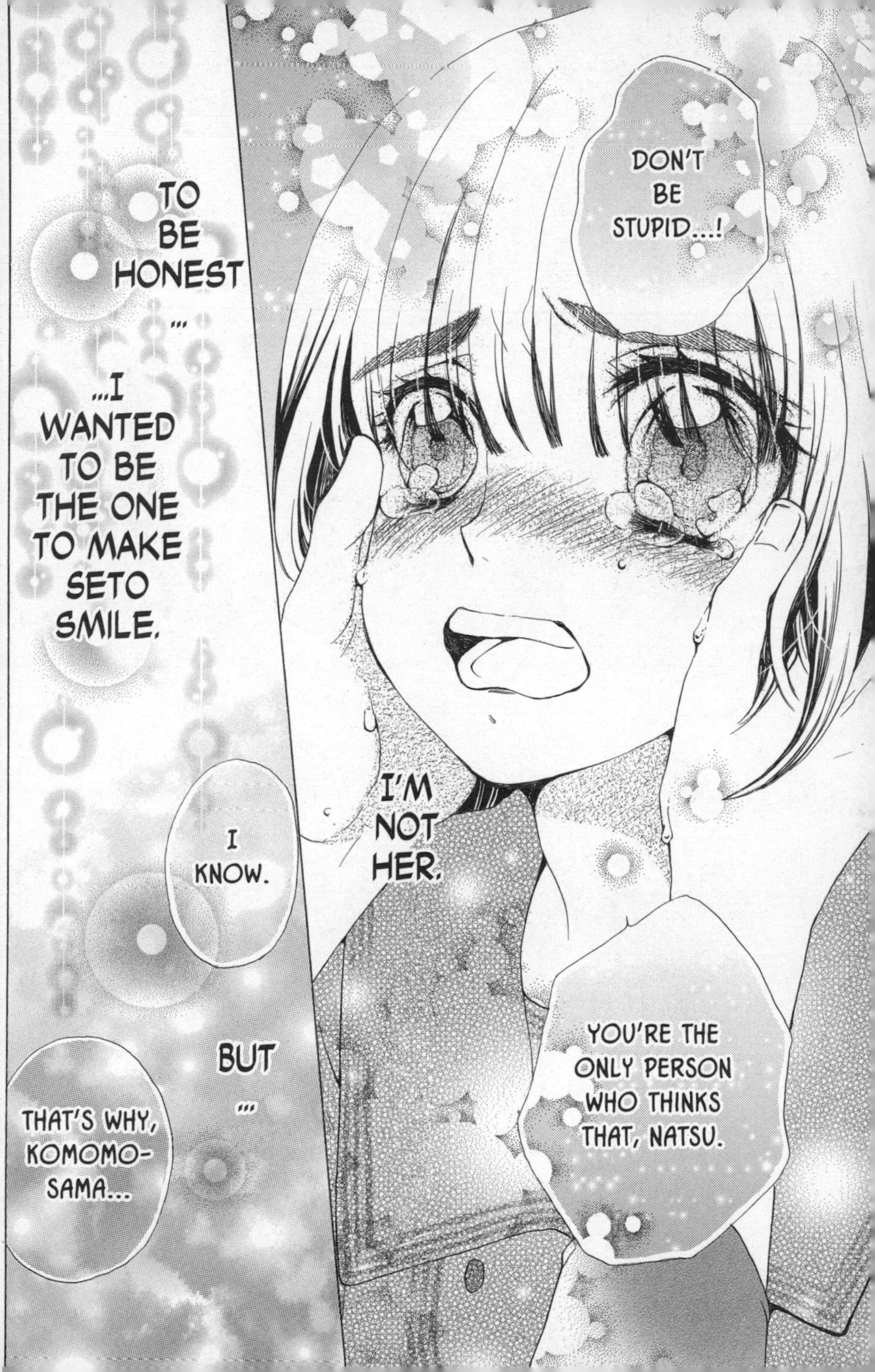
DON'T BE STUPID...!
I'M NOT HER.
YOU'RE THE ONLY PERSON WHO THINKS THAT, NATSU.
TO BE HONEST...
...I WANTED TO BE THE ONE TO MAKE SETO SMILE.
I KNOW.
BUT...
THAT'S WHY, KOMOMO-SAMA...

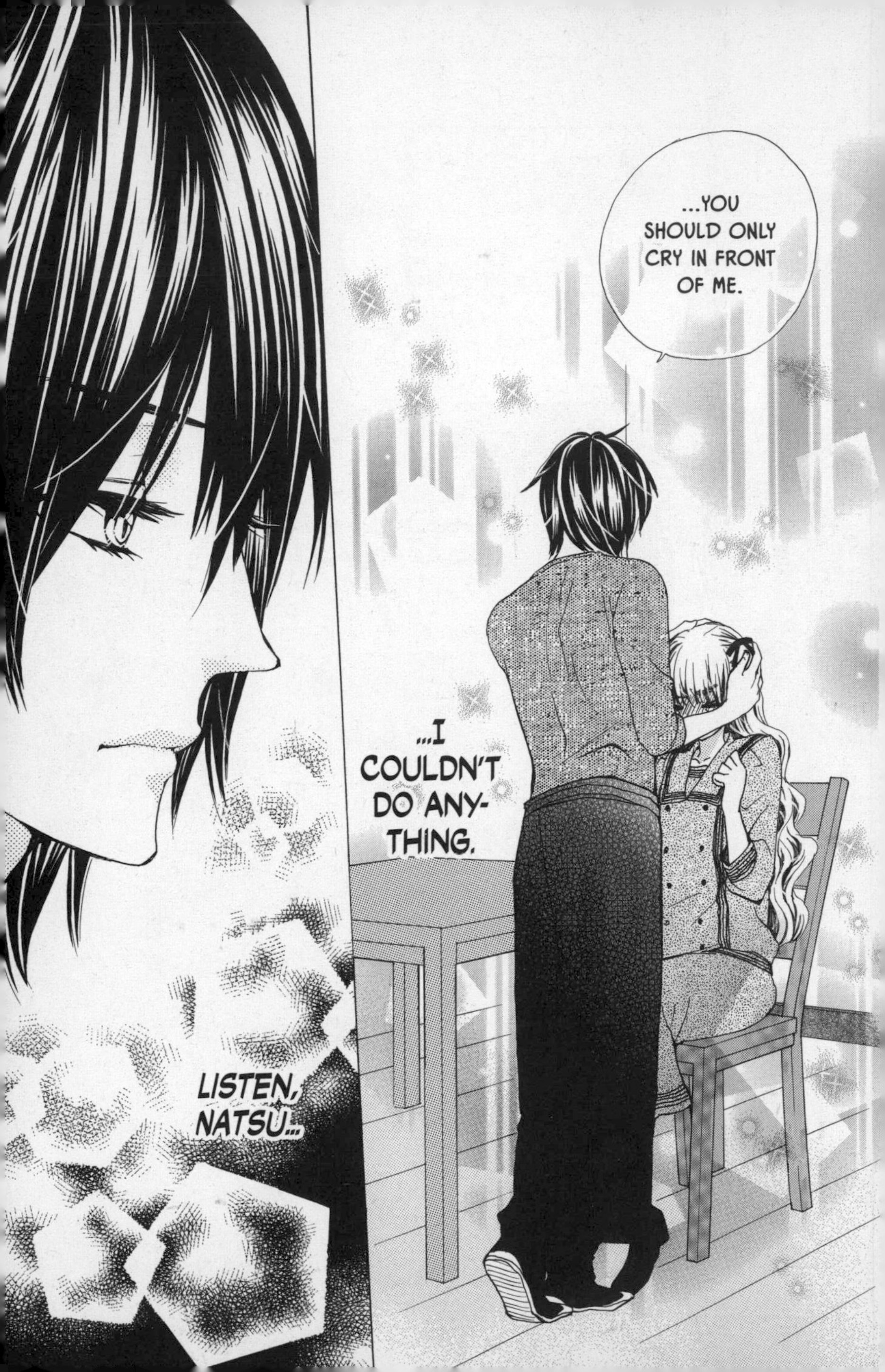
...YOU SHOULD ONLY CRY IN FRONT OF ME.
...I COULDN'T DO ANYTHING.
LISTEN, NATSU...

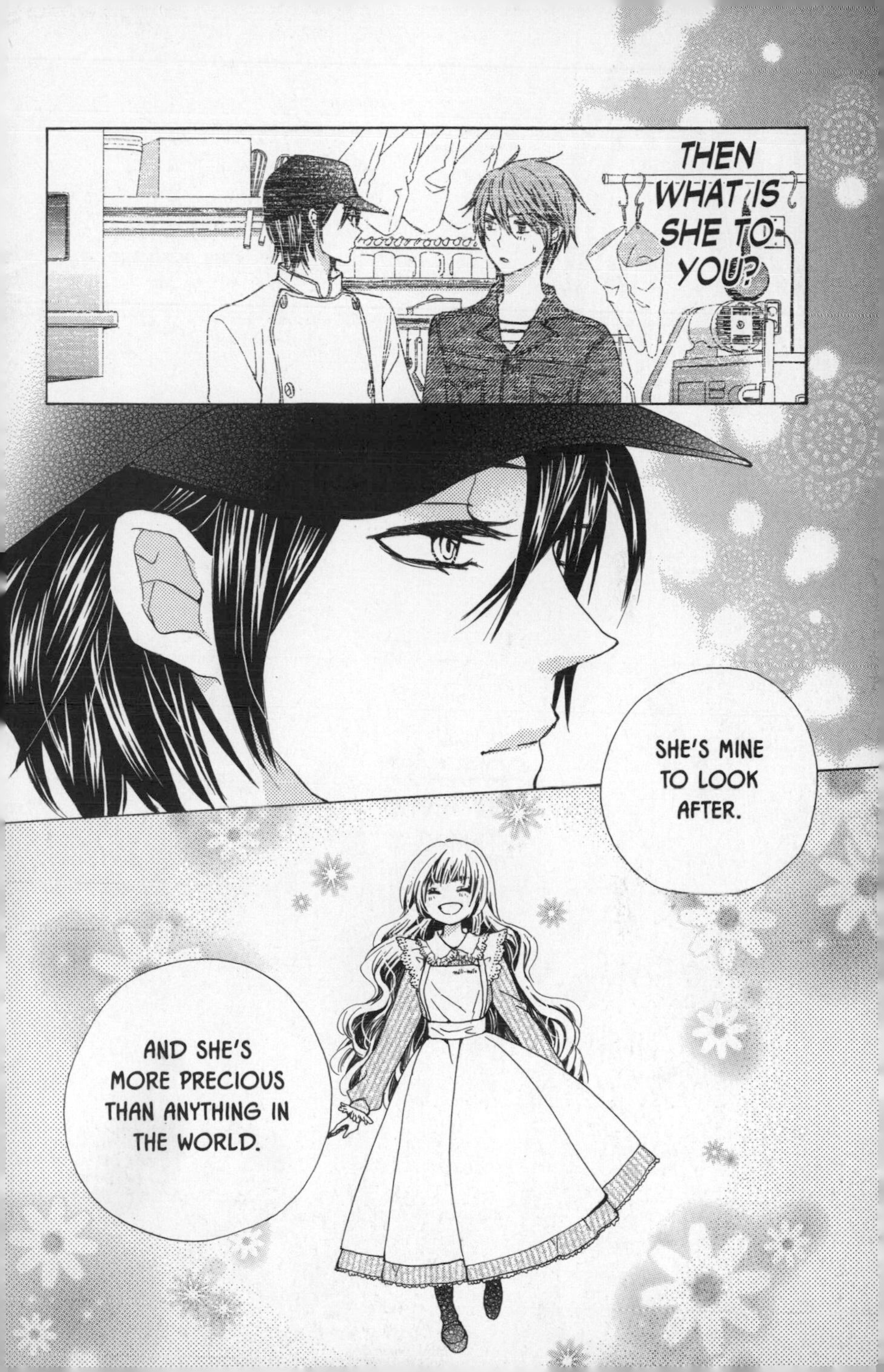
THEN WHAT IS SHE TO YOU?
SHE'S MINE TO LOOK AFTER.
AND SHE'S MORE PRECIOUS THAN ANYTHING IN THE WORLD.

CHAPTER 15

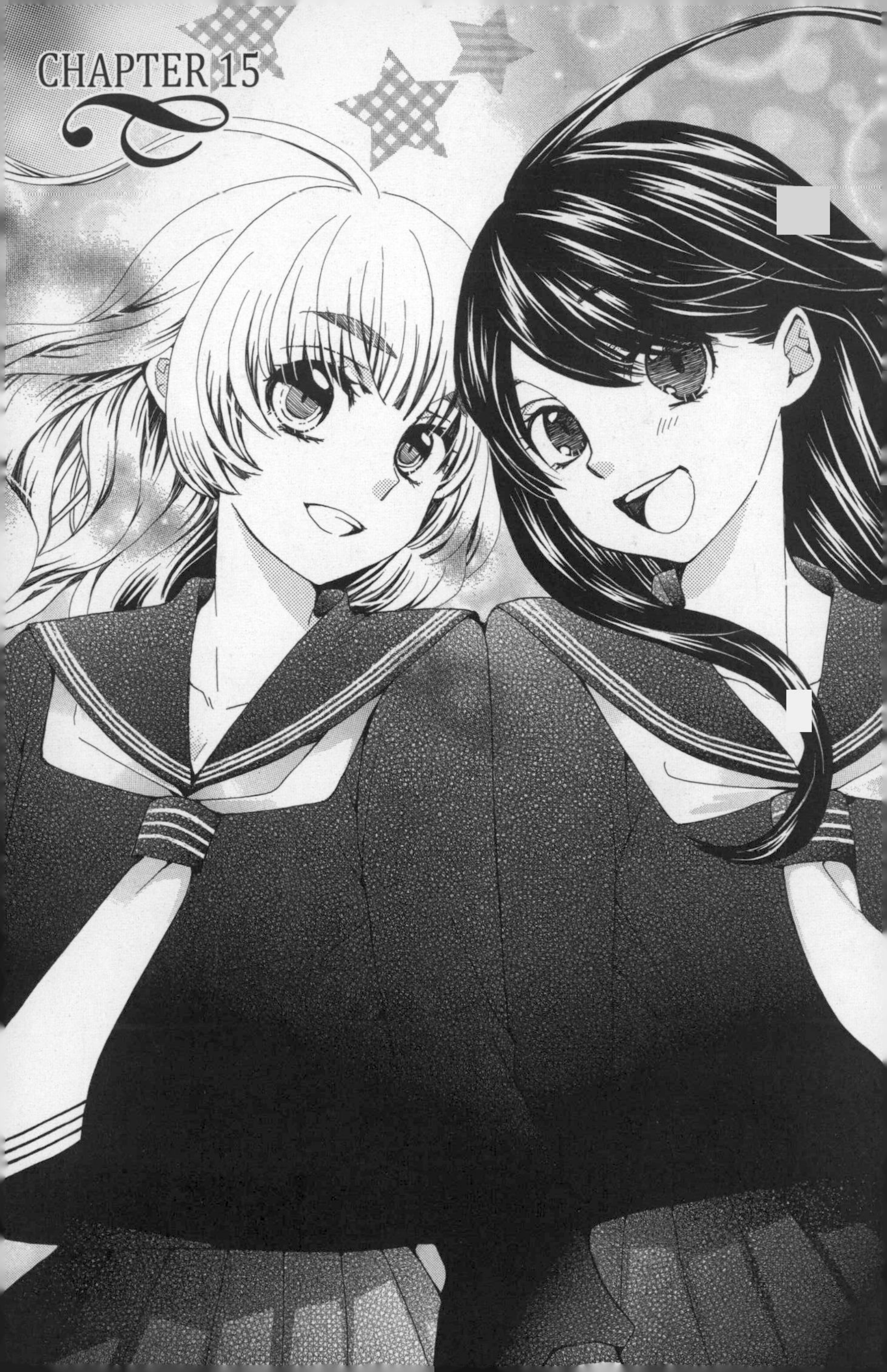

WE REALLY OWE YOU GUYS SO MUCH.

MÉLI-MELO

Confiserie
méli-melo
Traiteur
Épicerie
Spécialités

WELL.

méli-melo

THANK YOU.

• Exploring Different Hairstyles •

☆ Rise   ☆ Short Bob

④

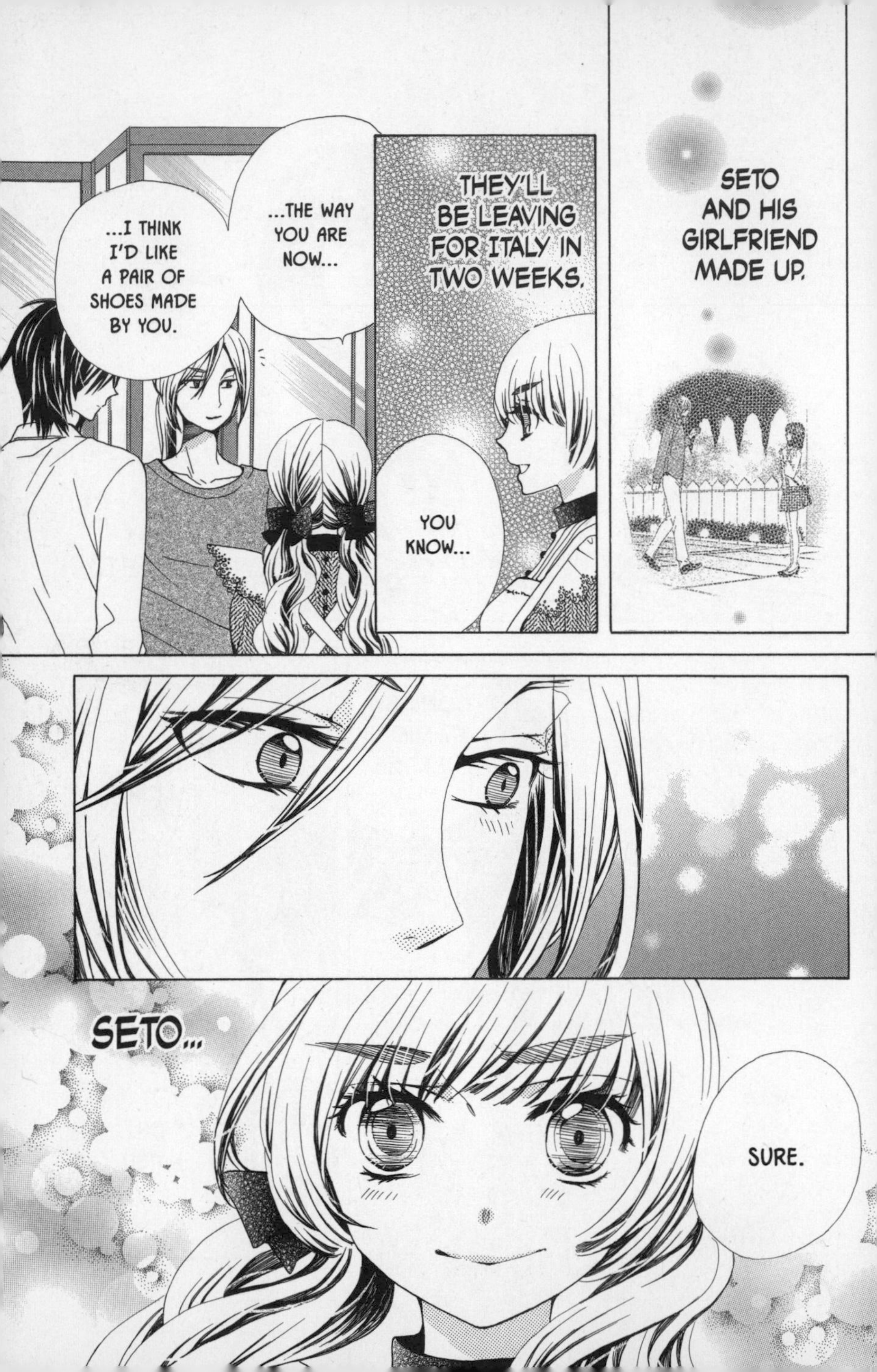
SETO AND HIS GIRLFRIEND MADE UP.
THEY'LL BE LEAVING FOR ITALY IN TWO WEEKS.
YOU KNOW...
...THE WAY YOU ARE NOW...
...I THINK I'D LIKE A PAIR OF SHOES MADE BY YOU.
SETO...
SURE.

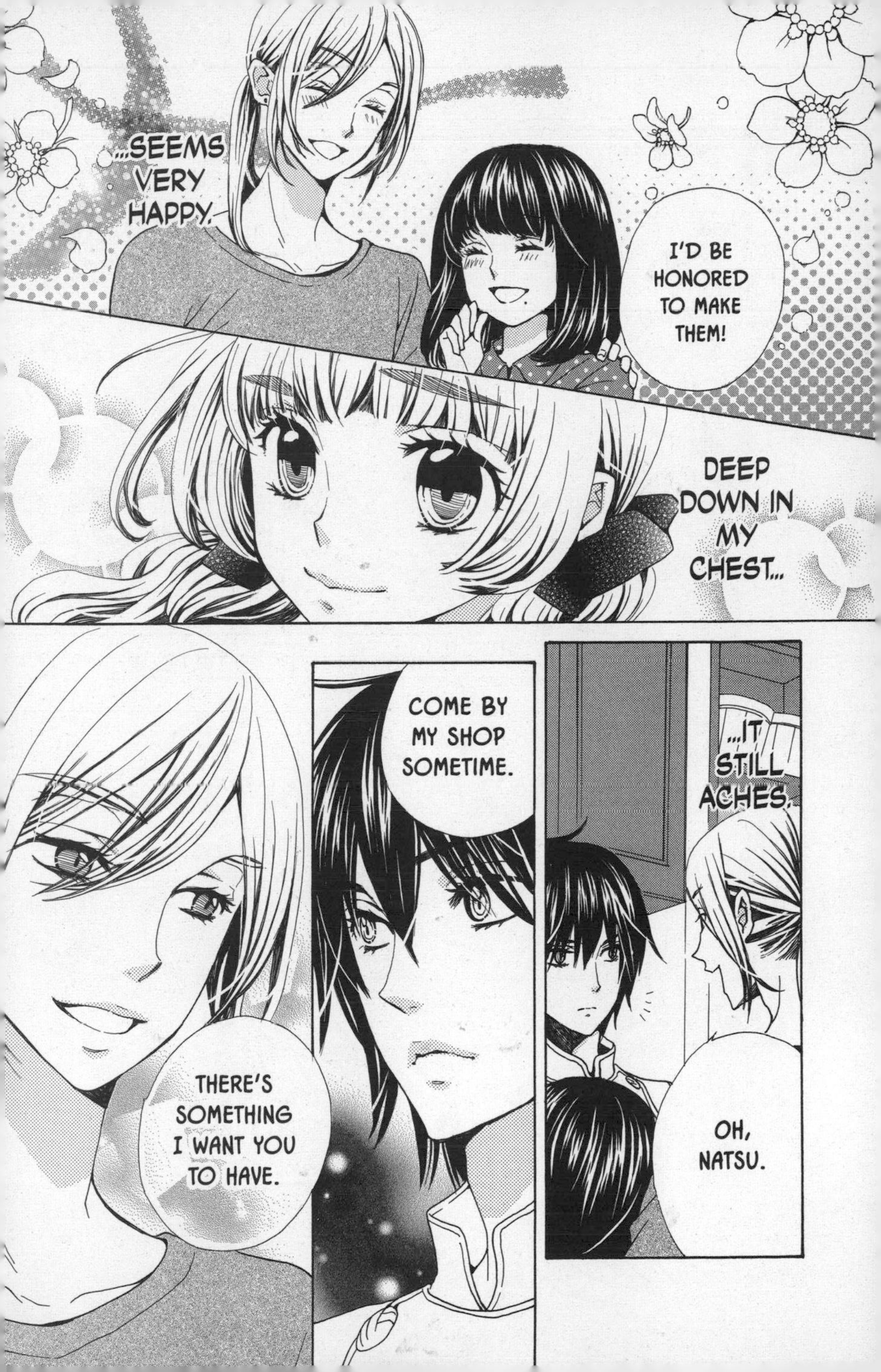
...SEEMS VERY HAPPY.
I'D BE HONORED TO MAKE THEM!
DEEP DOWN IN MY CHEST...
...IT STILL ACHES.
OH, NATSU.
COME BY MY SHOP SOMETIME.
THERE'S SOMETHING I WANT YOU TO HAVE.

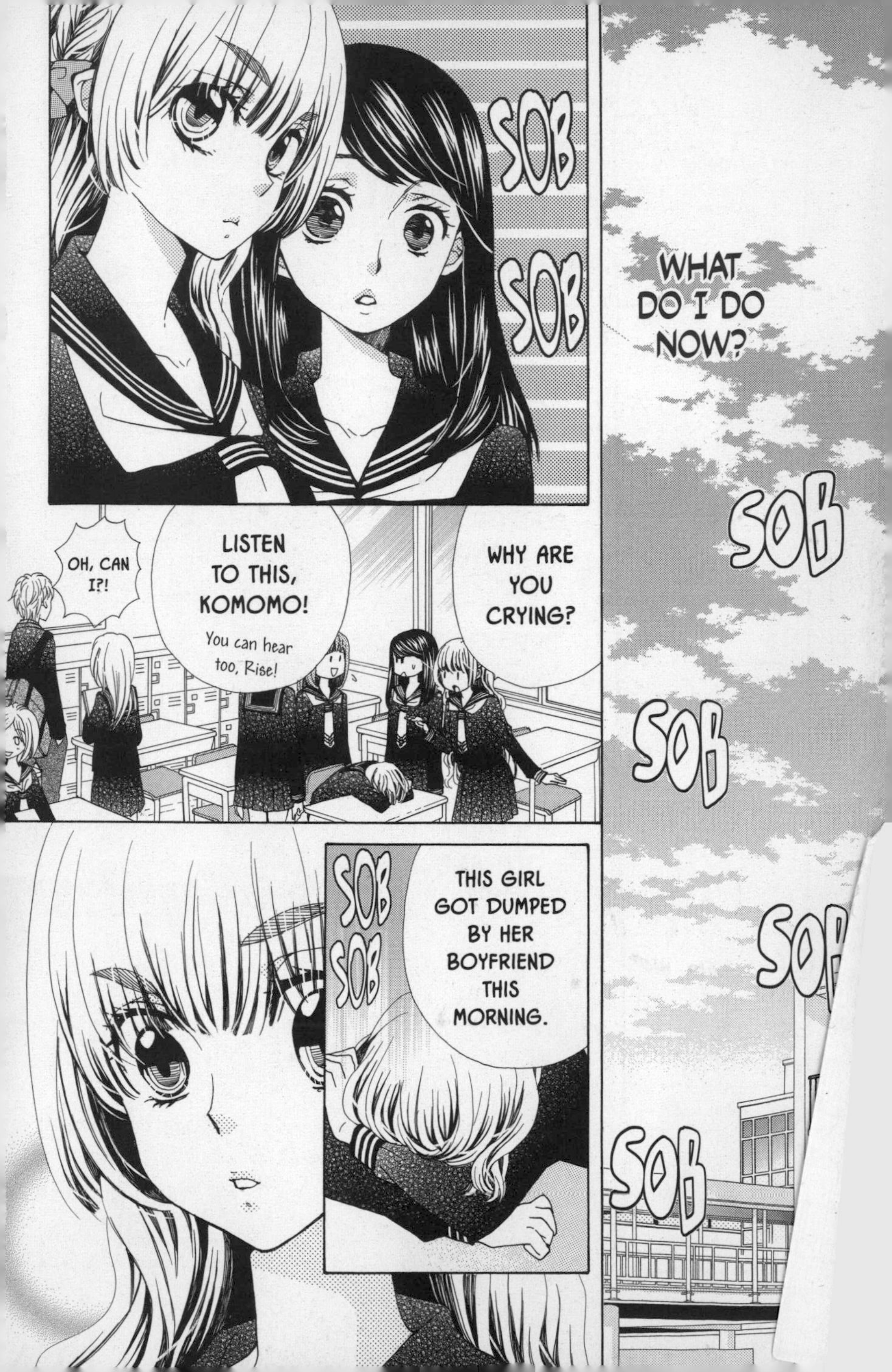
WHAT DO I DO NOW?
SOB
SOB
SOB
SOB
SOB
WHY ARE YOU CRYING?
LISTEN TO THIS, KOMOMO!
You can hear too, Rise!
OH, CAN I?!
SOB SOB
THIS GIRL GOT DUMPED BY HER BOYFRIEND THIS MORNING.

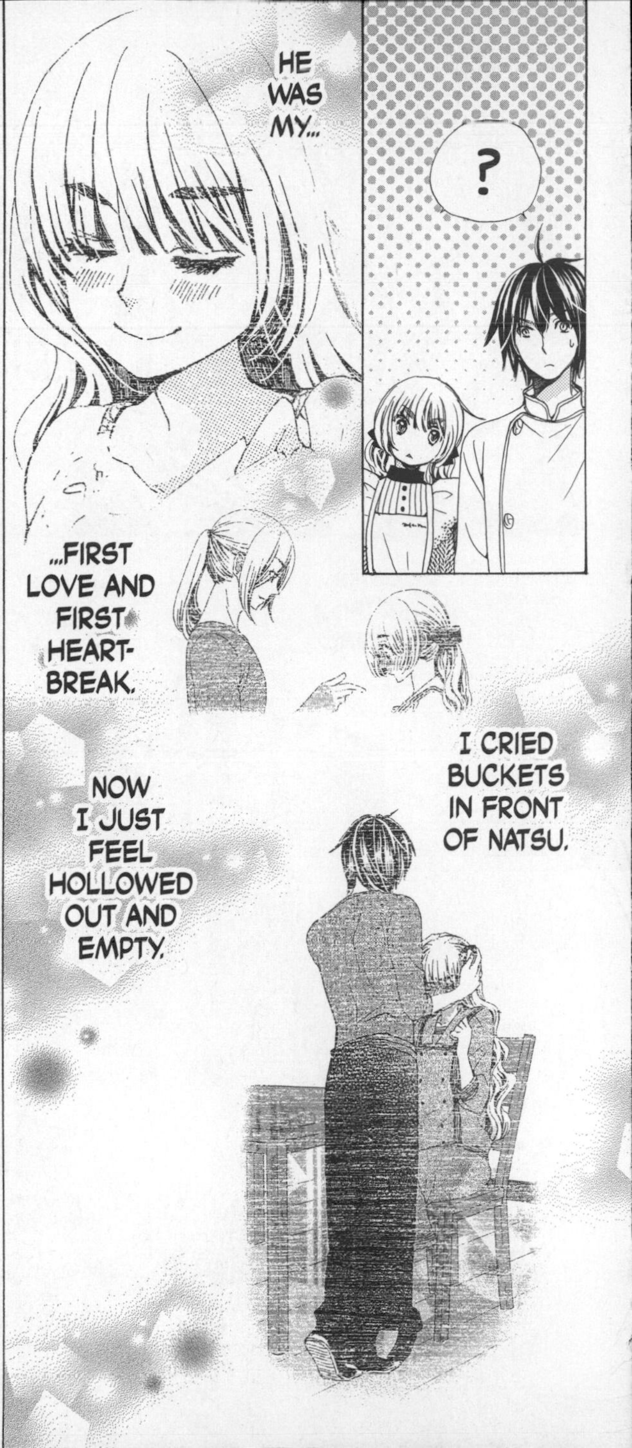
?
HE WAS MY...
...FIRST LOVE AND FIRST HEART-BREAK.
I CRIED BUCKETS IN FRONT OF NATSU.
NOW I JUST FEEL HOLLOWED OUT AND EMPTY.

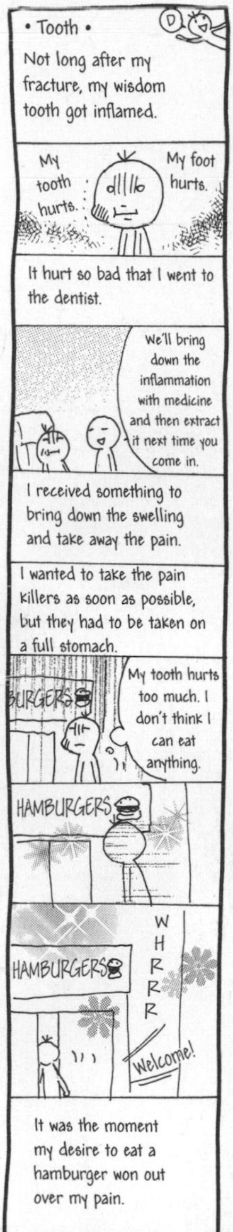
• Tooth •
Not long after my fracture, my wisdom tooth got inflamed.
My tooth hurts.
My foot hurts.
It hurt so bad that I went to the dentist.
We'll bring down the inflammation with medicine and then extract it next time you come in.
I received something to bring down the swelling and take away the pain.
I wanted to take the pain killers as soon as possible, but they had to be taken on a full stomach.
BURGERS
My tooth hurts too much. I don't think I can eat anything.
HAMBURGERS
HAMBURGERS
WHRRR
Welcome!
It was the moment my desire to eat a hamburger won out over my pain.
You can only chew when you're not in pain!

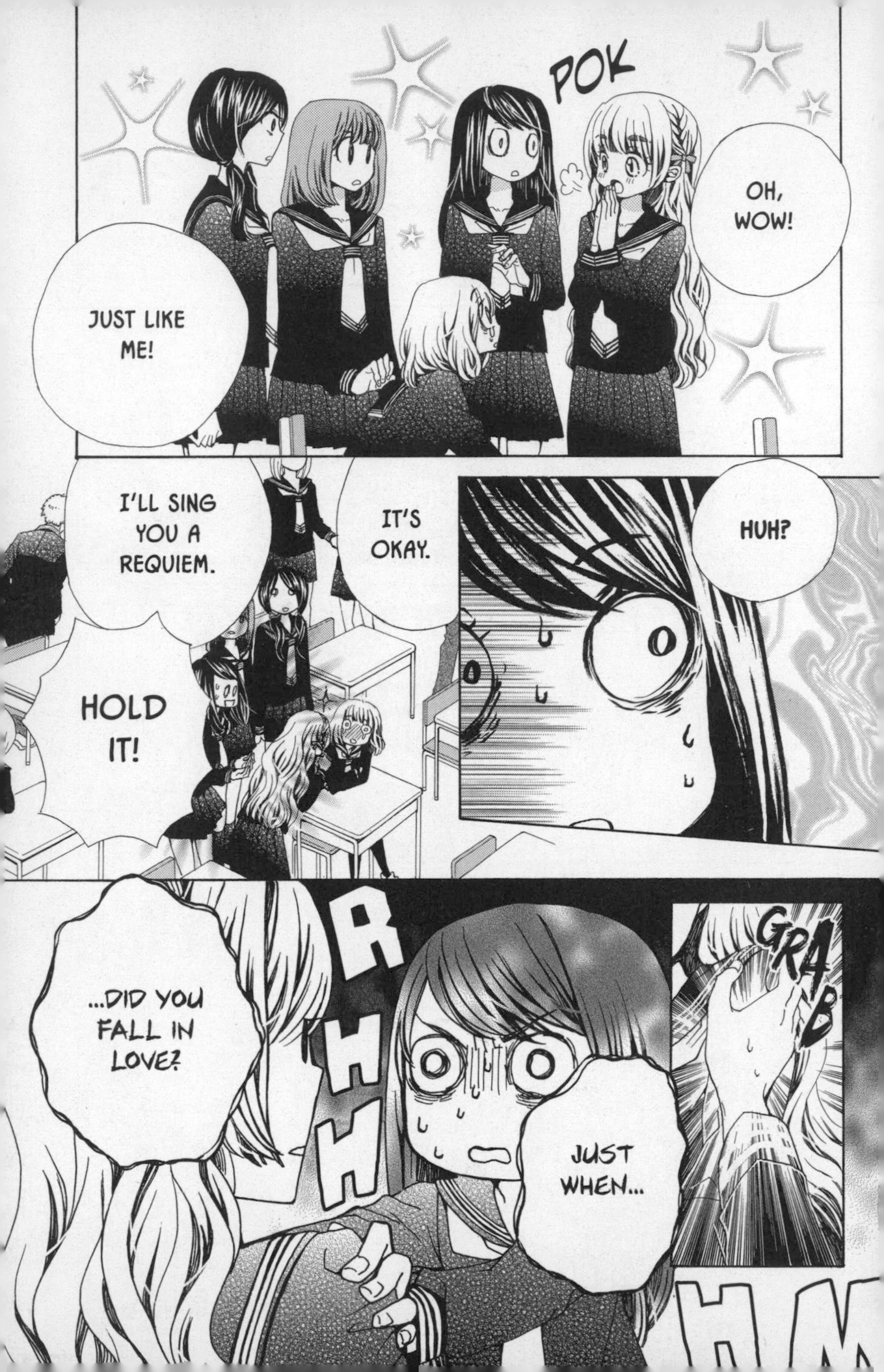

POK
OH, WOW!
JUST LIKE ME!
HUH?
IT'S OKAY.
I'LL SING YOU A REQUIEM.
HOLD IT!
GRAB
RHHH
JUST WHEN...
...DID YOU FALL IN LOVE?
HM

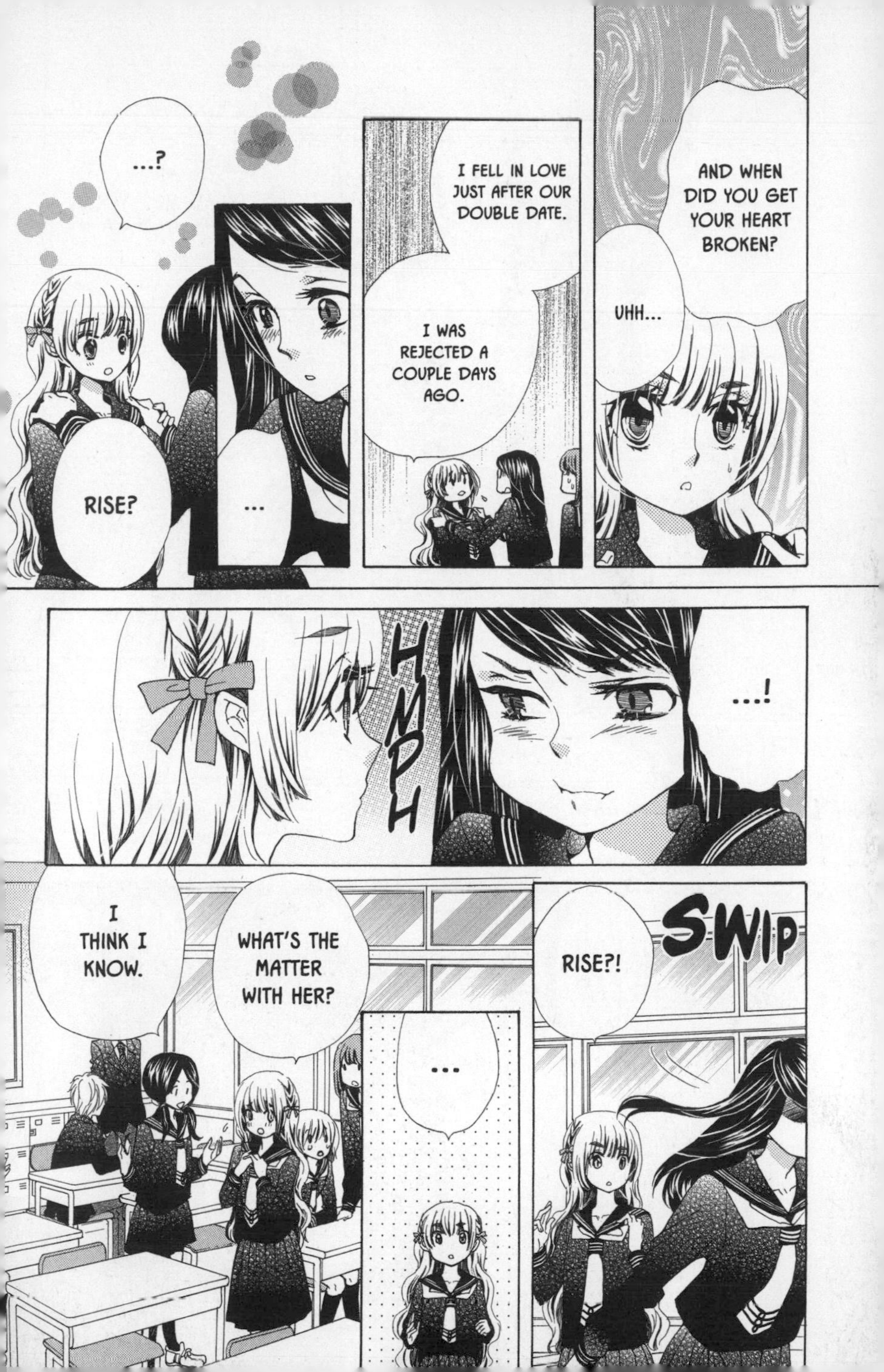
AND WHEN DID YOU GET YOUR HEART BROKEN?
UHH...
I FELL IN LOVE JUST AFTER OUR DOUBLE DATE.
I WAS REJECTED A COUPLE DAYS AGO.
...?
...
RISE?
...!
HMPH
SWIP
RISE?!
...
WHAT'S THE MATTER WITH HER?
I THINK I KNOW.

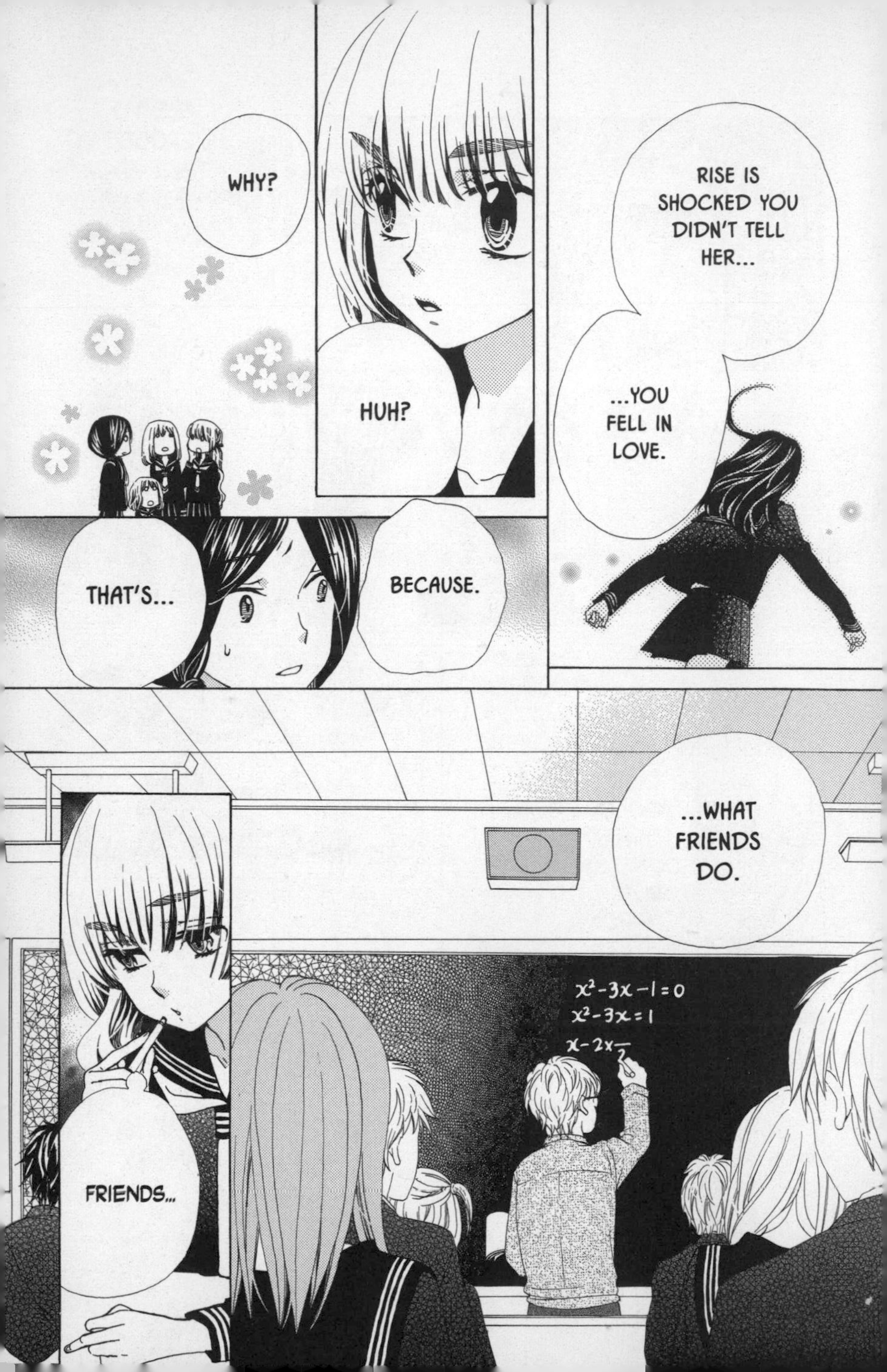
RISE IS SHOCKED YOU DIDN'T TELL HER...
...YOU FELL IN LOVE.
HUH?
WHY?
BECAUSE.
THAT'S...
...WHAT FRIENDS DO.
$x^2-3x-1=0$
$x^2-3x=1$
FRIENDS...

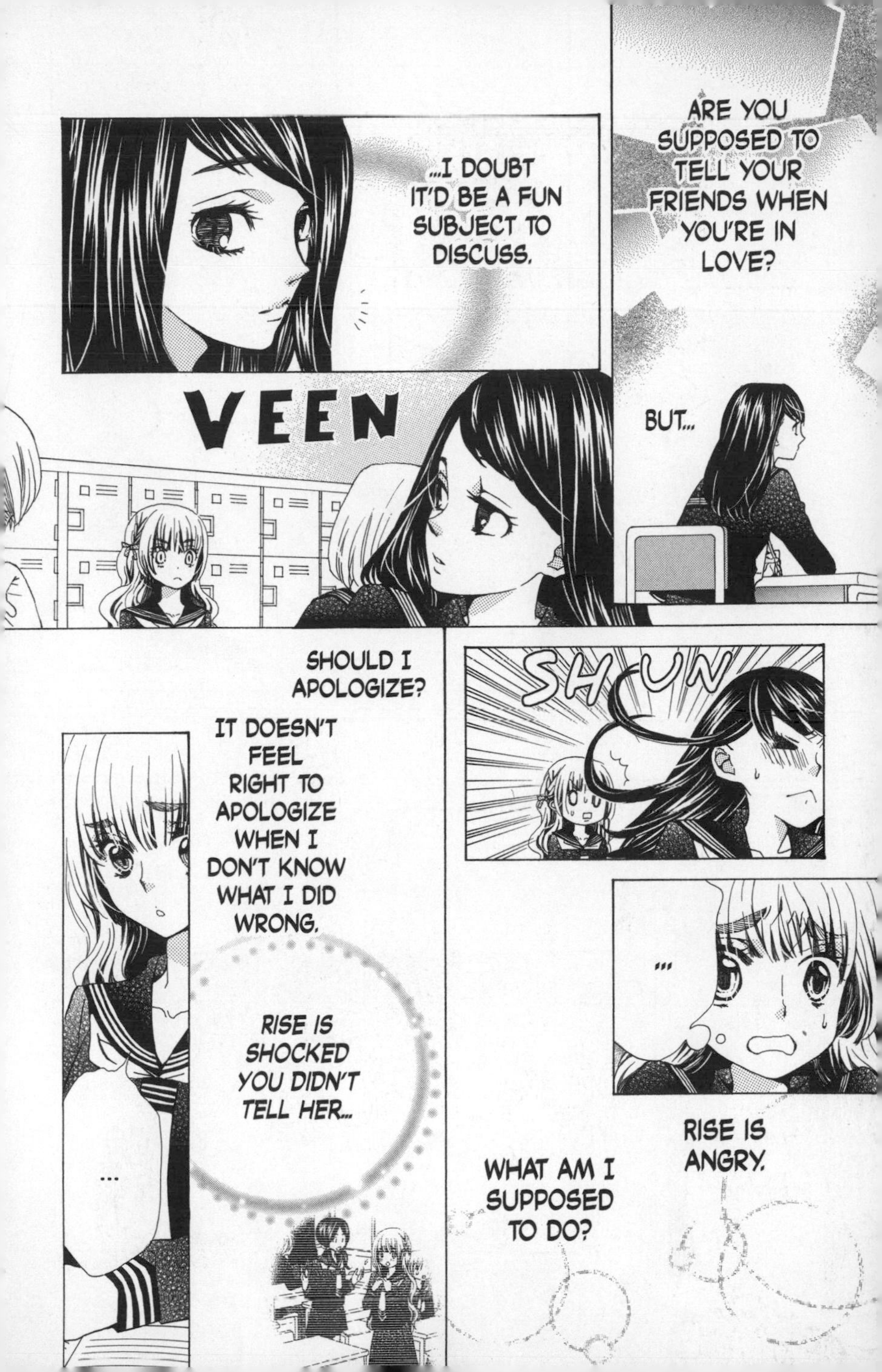
ARE YOU SUPPOSED TO TELL YOUR FRIENDS WHEN YOU'RE IN LOVE?
BUT...
...I DOUBT IT'D BE A FUN SUBJECT TO DISCUSS.
VEEN
SHUN
...
RISE IS ANGRY.
WHAT AM I SUPPOSED TO DO?
SHOULD I APOLOGIZE?
IT DOESN'T FEEL RIGHT TO APOLOGIZE WHEN I DON'T KNOW WHAT I DID WRONG.
RISE IS SHOCKED YOU DIDN'T TELL HER...
...

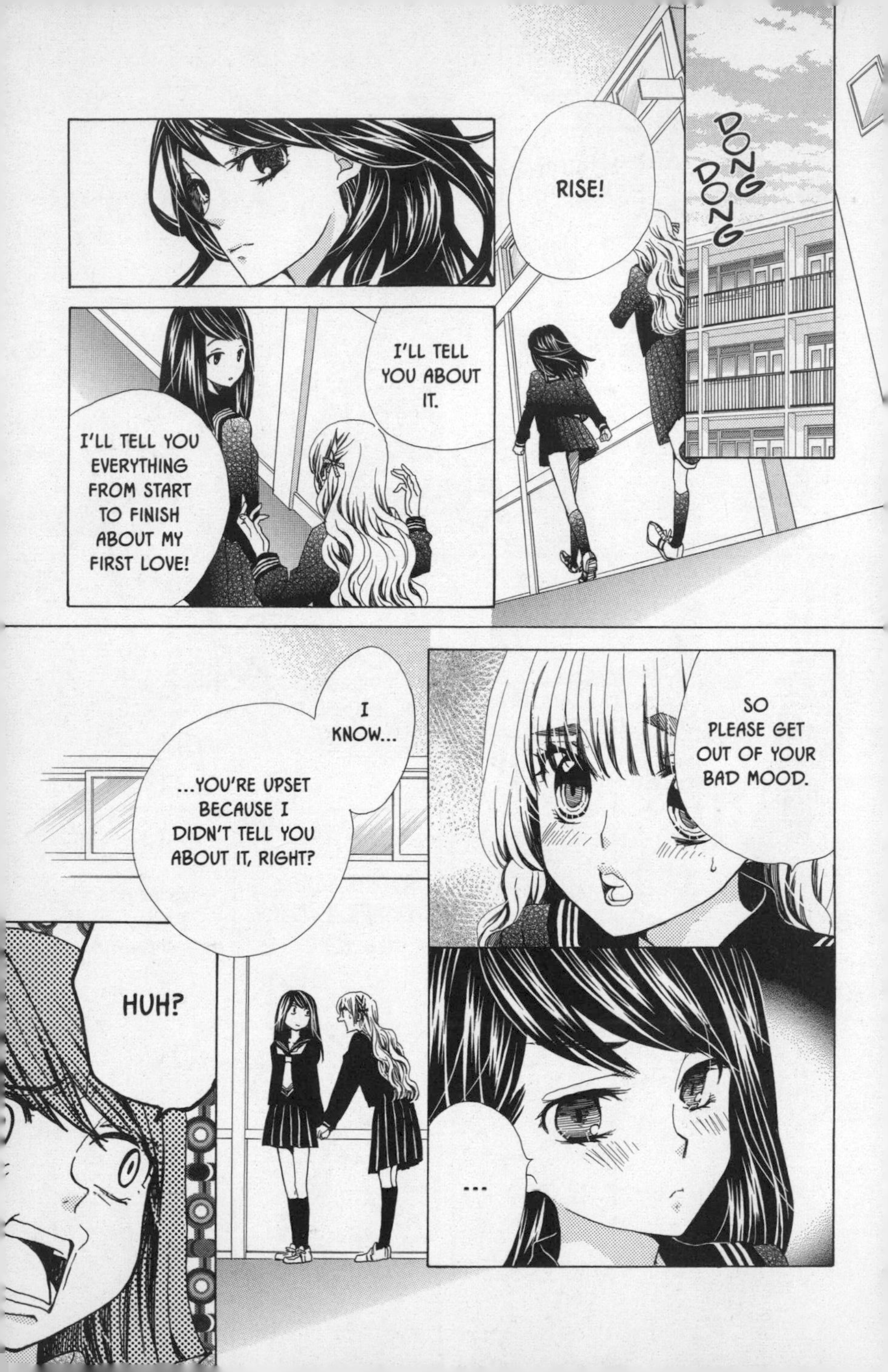
DONG DONG
RISE!
I'LL TELL YOU ABOUT IT.
I'LL TELL YOU EVERYTHING FROM START TO FINISH ABOUT MY FIRST LOVE!
SO PLEASE GET OUT OF YOUR BAD MOOD.
...
I KNOW...
...YOU'RE UPSET BECAUSE I DIDN'T TELL YOU ABOUT IT, RIGHT?
HUH?

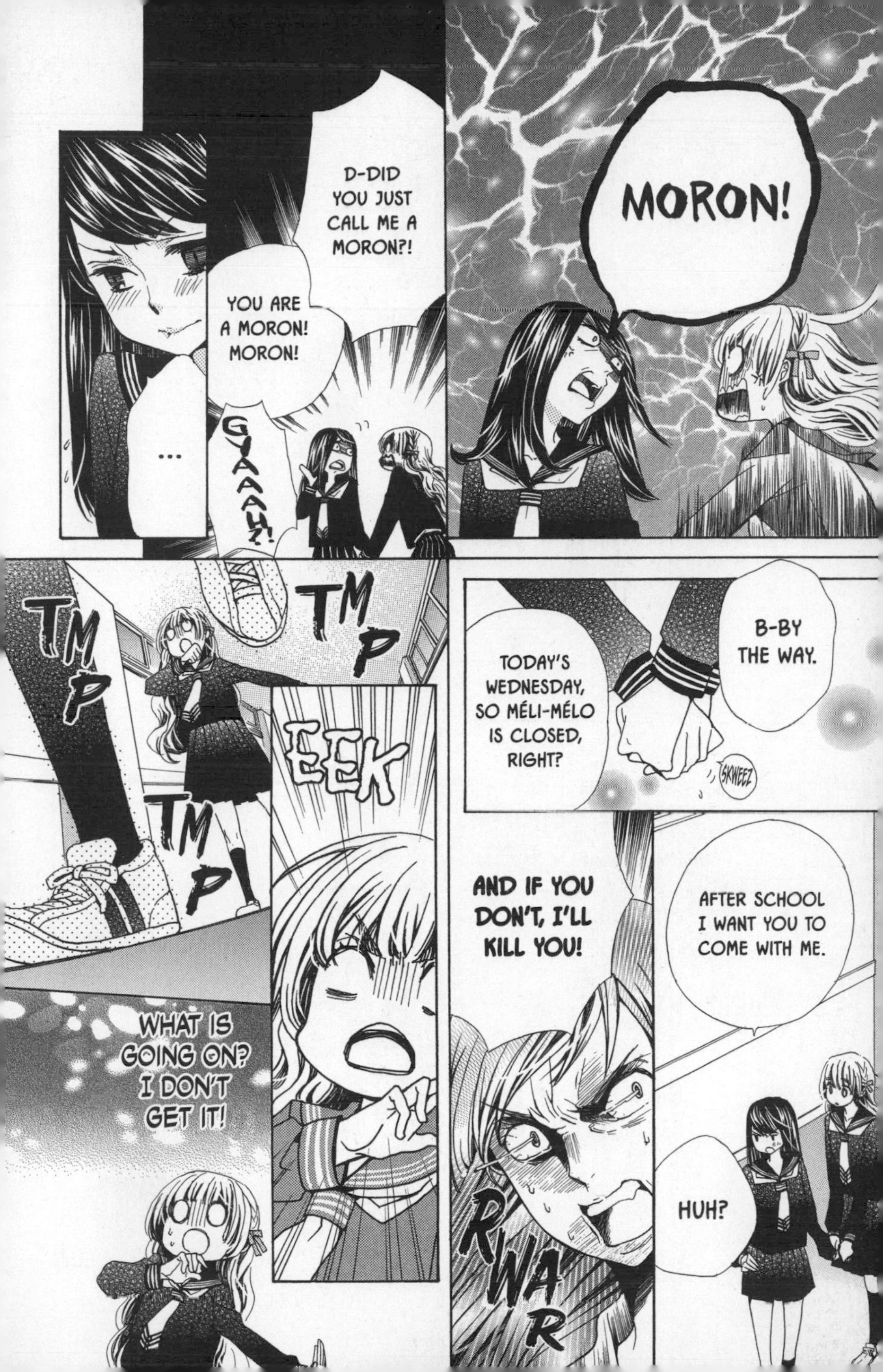
MORON!
D-DID YOU JUST CALL ME A MORON?!
YOU ARE A MORON! MORON!
GYAAAAH?!
...
B-BY THE WAY.
TODAY'S WEDNESDAY, SO MÉLI-MÉLO IS CLOSED, RIGHT?
SKWEEZ
AFTER SCHOOL I WANT YOU TO COME WITH ME.
HUH?
AND IF YOU DON'T, I'LL KILL YOU!
RWAR
TMP
TMP
EEK
TMP
WHAT IS GOING ON? I DON'T GET IT!

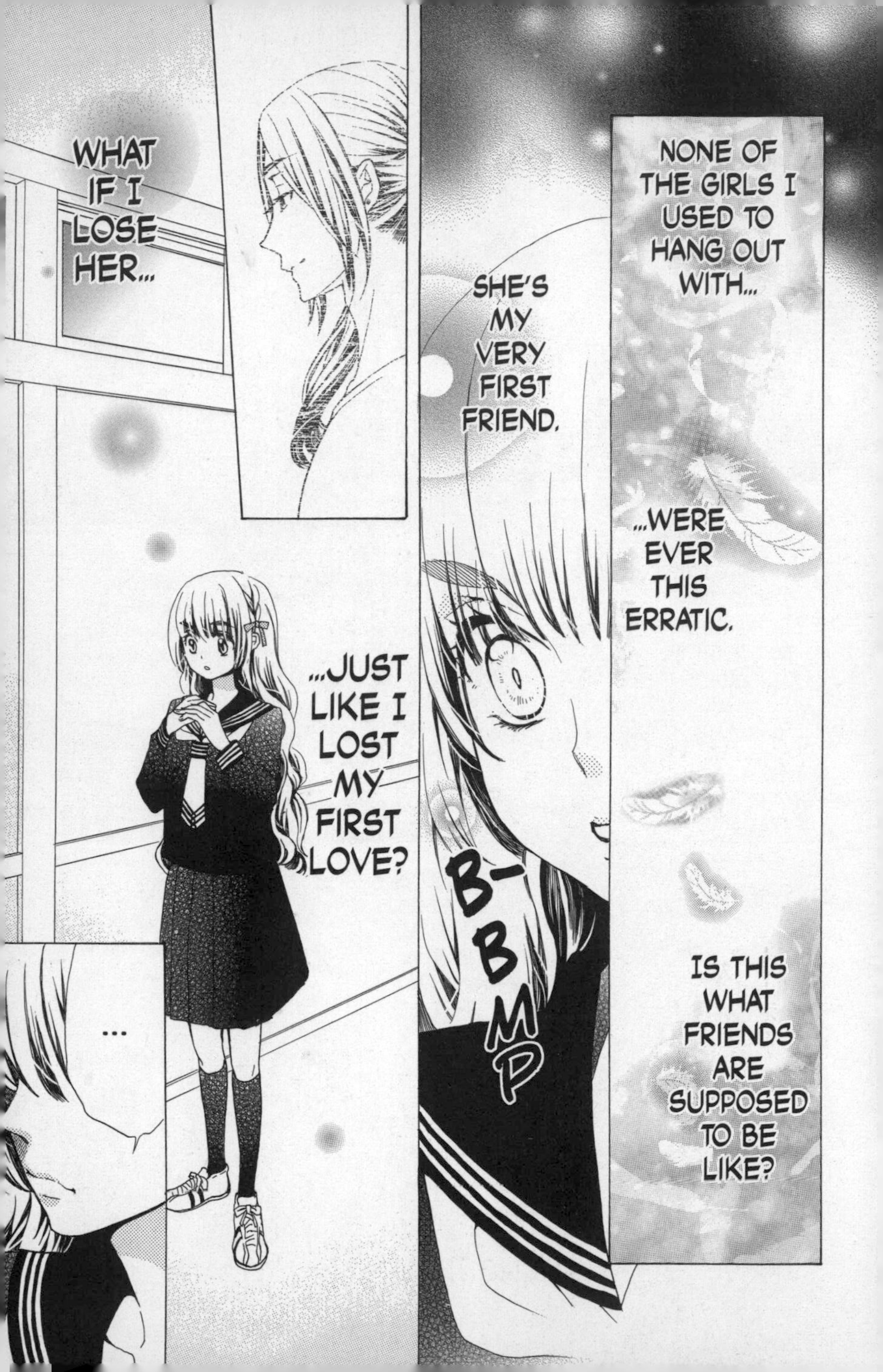
NONE OF THE GIRLS I USED TO HANG OUT WITH...
SHE'S MY VERY FIRST FRIEND.
...WERE EVER THIS ERRATIC.
B-BMP
IS THIS WHAT FRIENDS ARE SUPPOSED TO BE LIKE?
WHAT IF I LOSE HER...
...JUST LIKE I LOST MY FIRST LOVE?
...

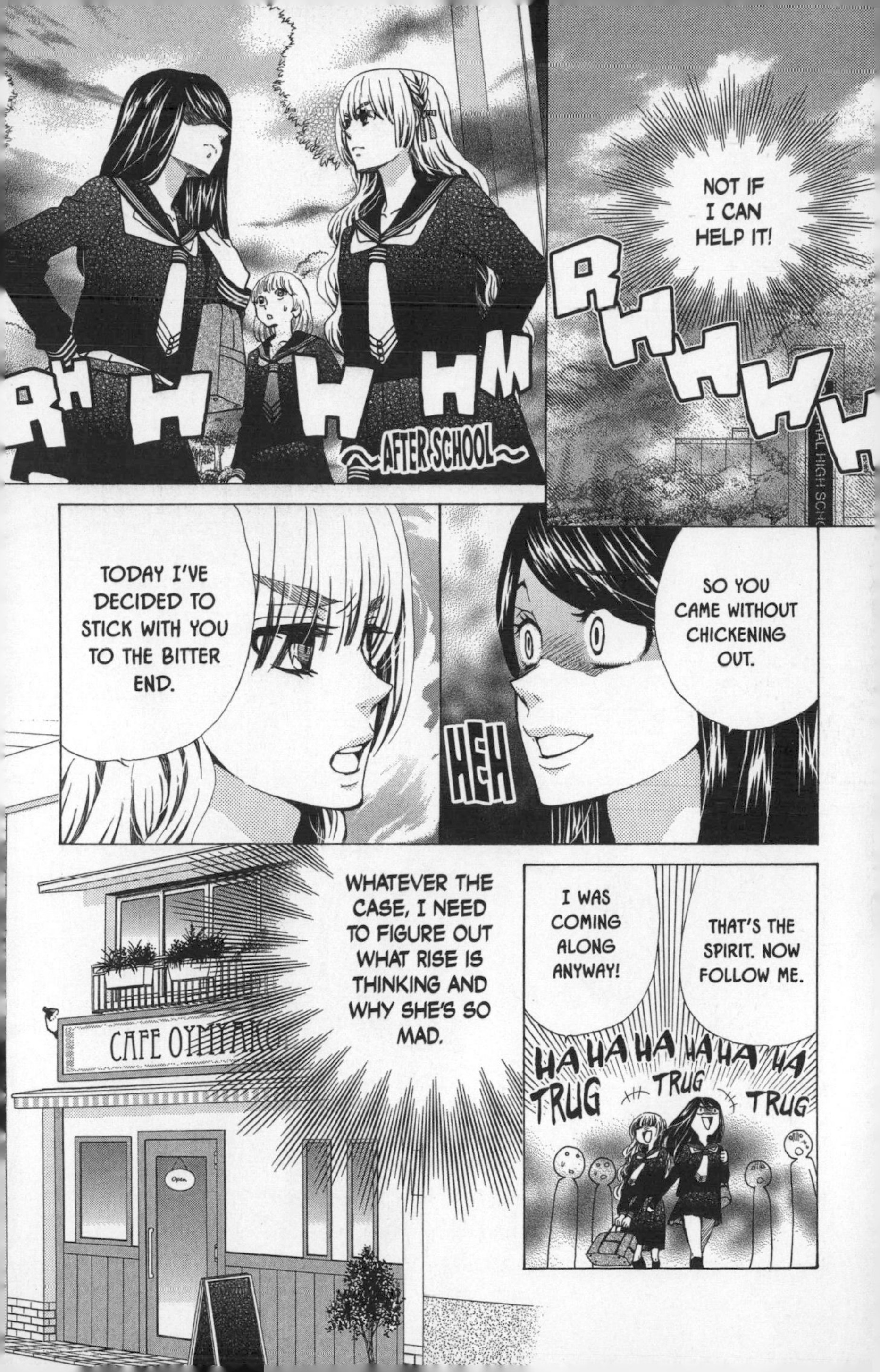
NOT IF I CAN HELP IT!
RHHHHH
RHHHHM
~AFTER SCHOOL~
SO YOU CAME WITHOUT CHICKENING OUT.
HEH
TODAY I'VE DECIDED TO STICK WITH YOU TO THE BITTER END.
THAT'S THE SPIRIT. NOW FOLLOW ME.
I WAS COMING ALONG ANYWAY!
HA HA HA HA HA HA HA
TRUG TRUG TRUG
WHATEVER THE CASE, I NEED TO FIGURE OUT WHAT RISE IS THINKING AND WHY SHE'S SO MAD.

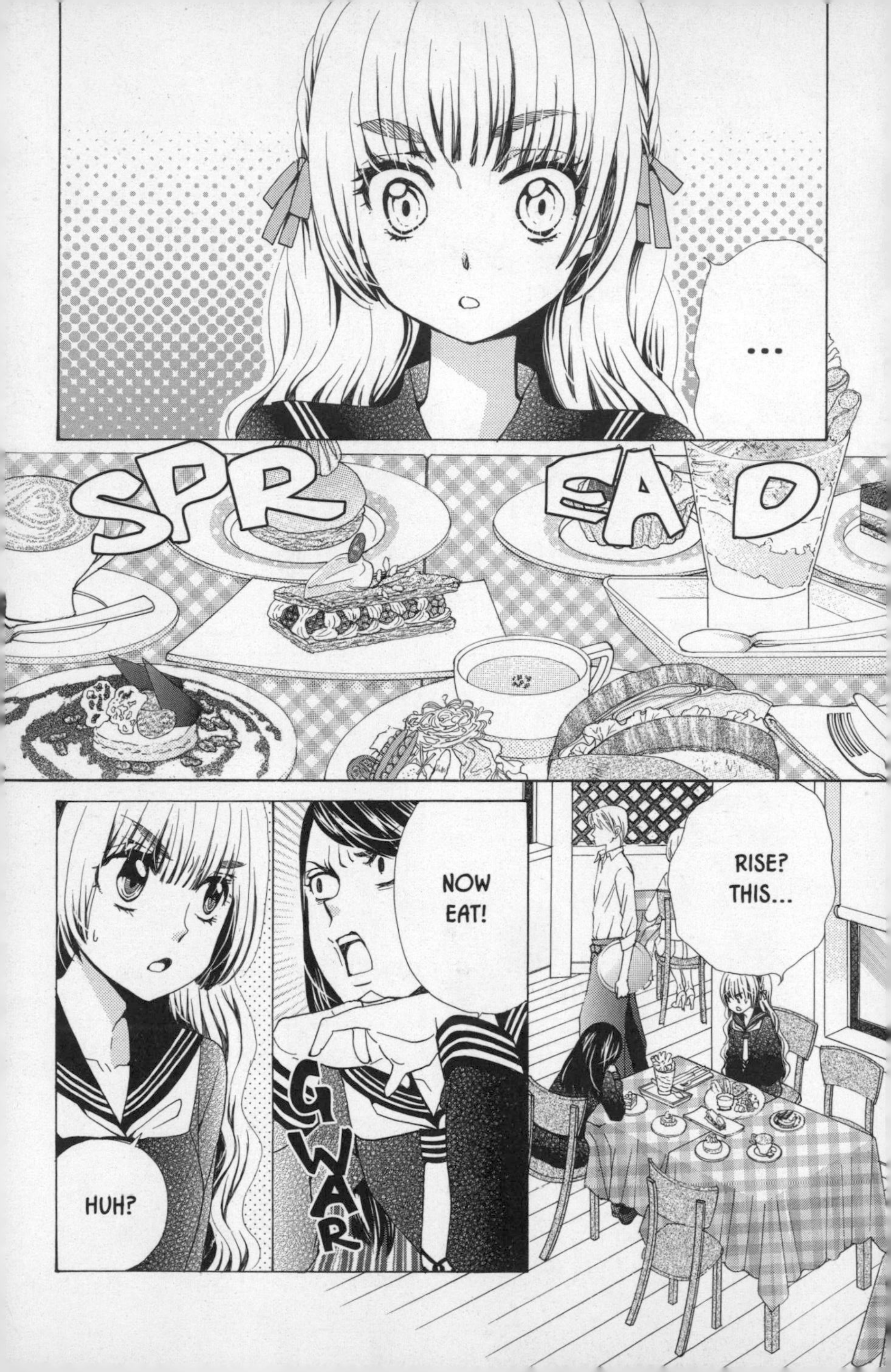
...
SPREAD
RISE? THIS...
NOW EAT!
GWAR
HUH?

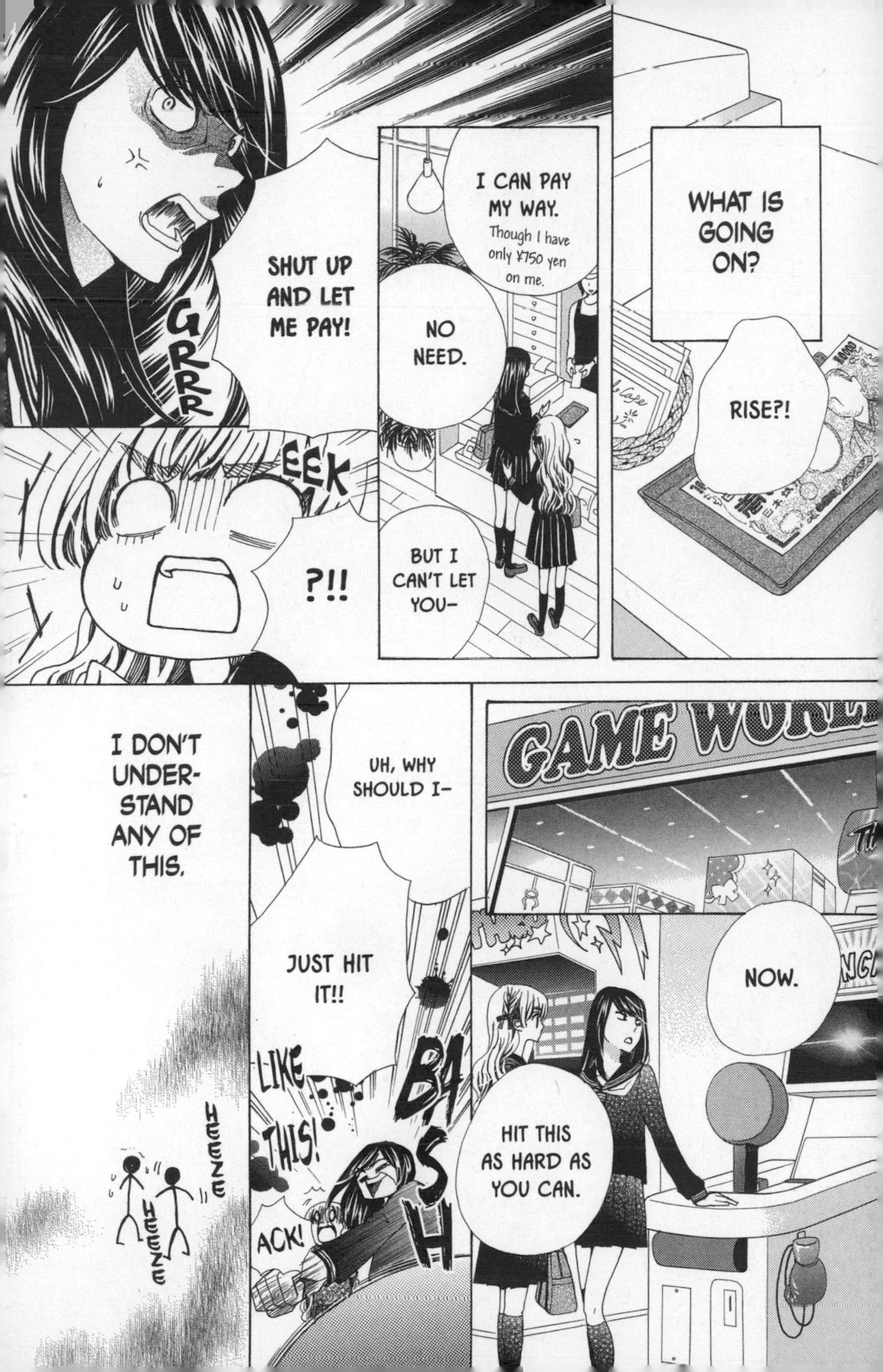
WHAT IS GOING ON?
RISE?!
I CAN PAY MY WAY.
Though I have only ¥750 yen on me.
NO NEED.
BUT I CAN'T LET YOU–
SHUT UP AND LET ME PAY!
GRRR
EEK
?!!
GAME WORL
NOW.
HIT THIS AS HARD AS YOU CAN.
UH, WHY SHOULD I–
JUST HIT IT!!
LIKE THIS!
BASH
ACK!
I DON'T UNDER-STAND ANY OF THIS.
HEEZE
HEEZE

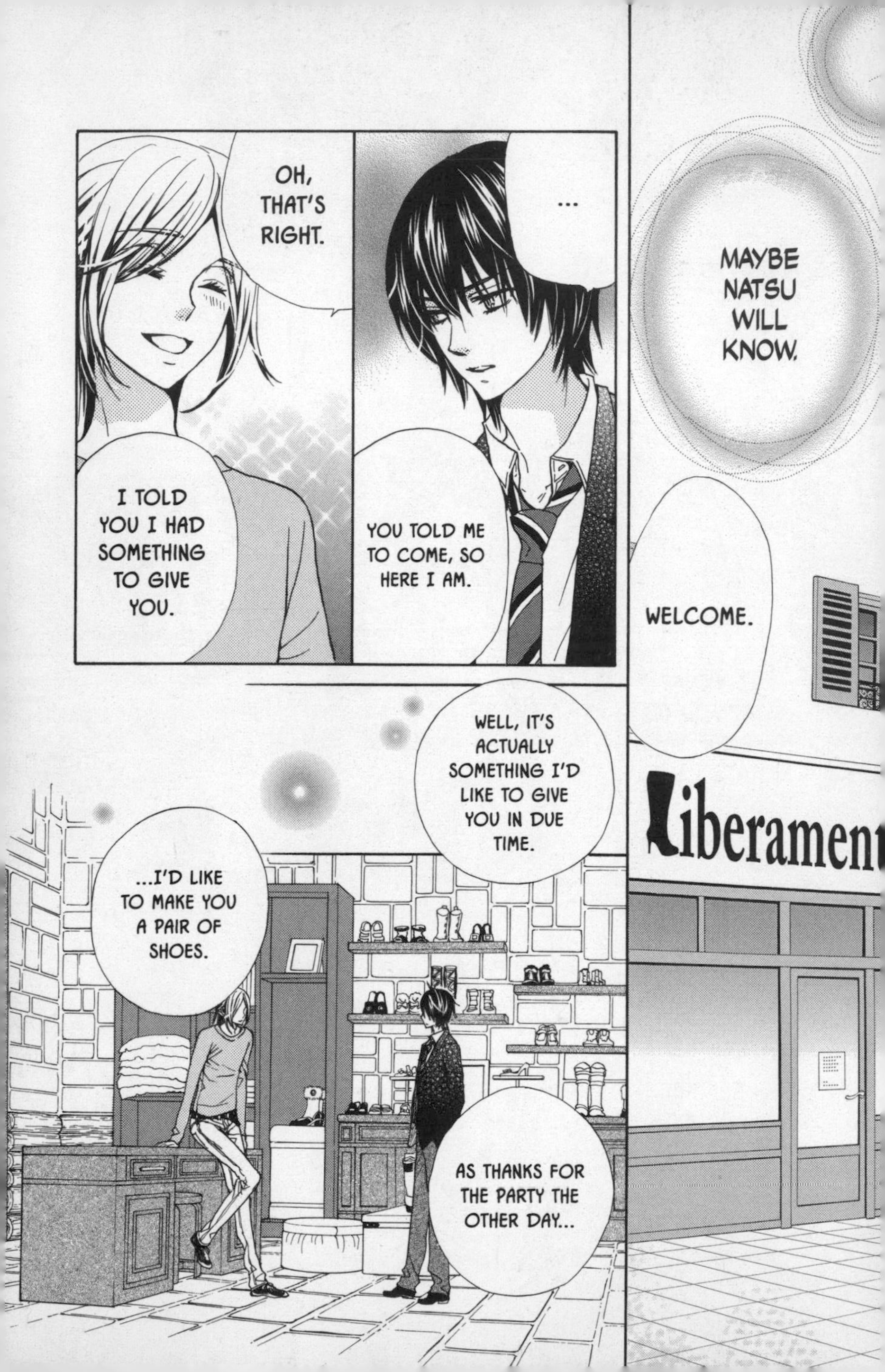
MAYBE NATSU WILL KNOW.
WELCOME.
Liberament
...
YOU TOLD ME TO COME, SO HERE I AM.
OH, THAT'S RIGHT.
I TOLD YOU I HAD SOMETHING TO GIVE YOU.
WELL, IT'S ACTUALLY SOMETHING I'D LIKE TO GIVE YOU IN DUE TIME.
AS THANKS FOR THE PARTY THE OTHER DAY...
...I'D LIKE TO MAKE YOU A PAIR OF SHOES.

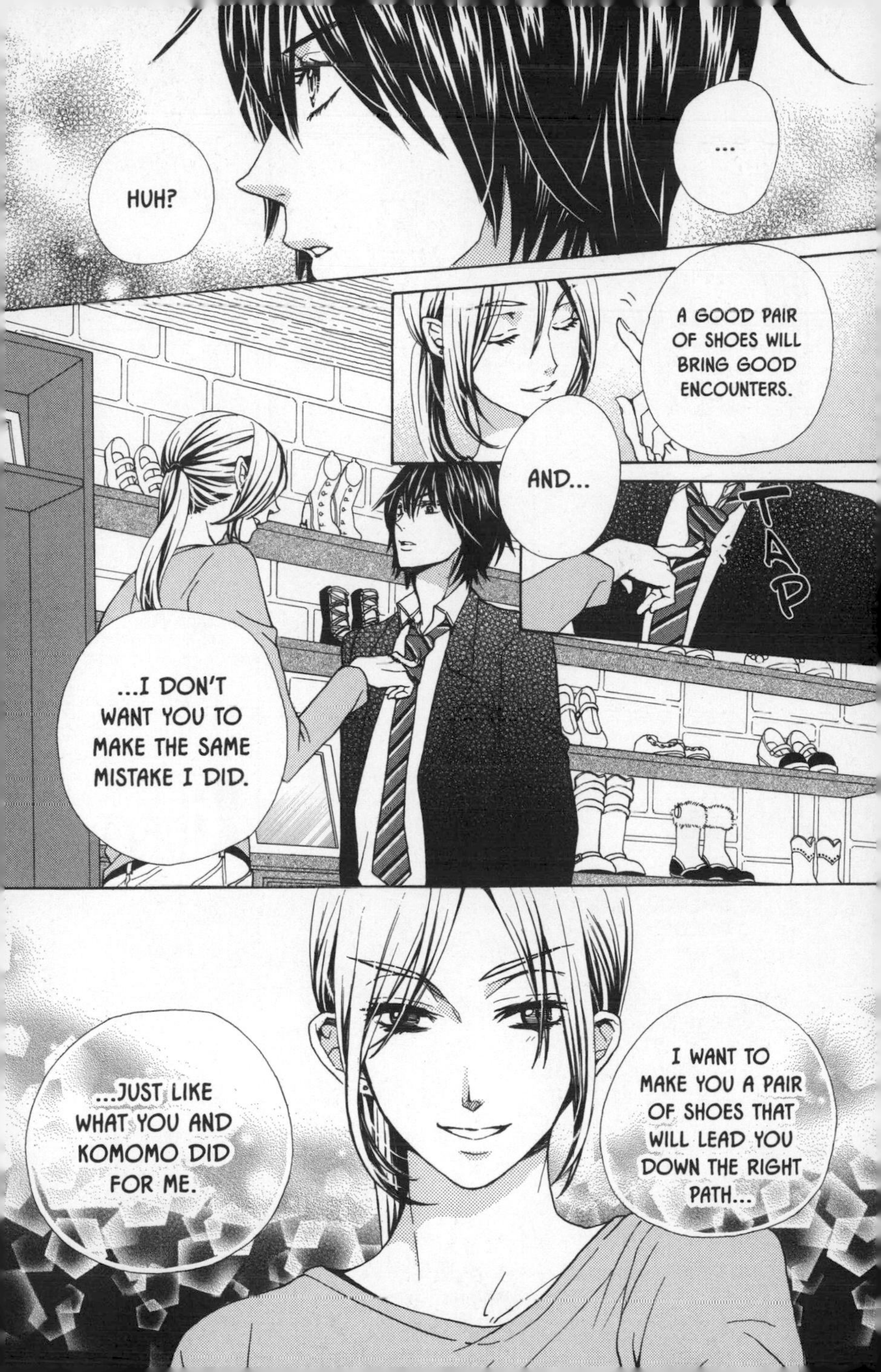
...
HUH?
A GOOD PAIR OF SHOES WILL BRING GOOD ENCOUNTERS.
AND...
TAP
...I DON'T WANT YOU TO MAKE THE SAME MISTAKE I DID.
I WANT TO MAKE YOU A PAIR OF SHOES THAT WILL LEAD YOU DOWN THE RIGHT PATH...
...JUST LIKE WHAT YOU AND KOMOMO DID FOR ME.

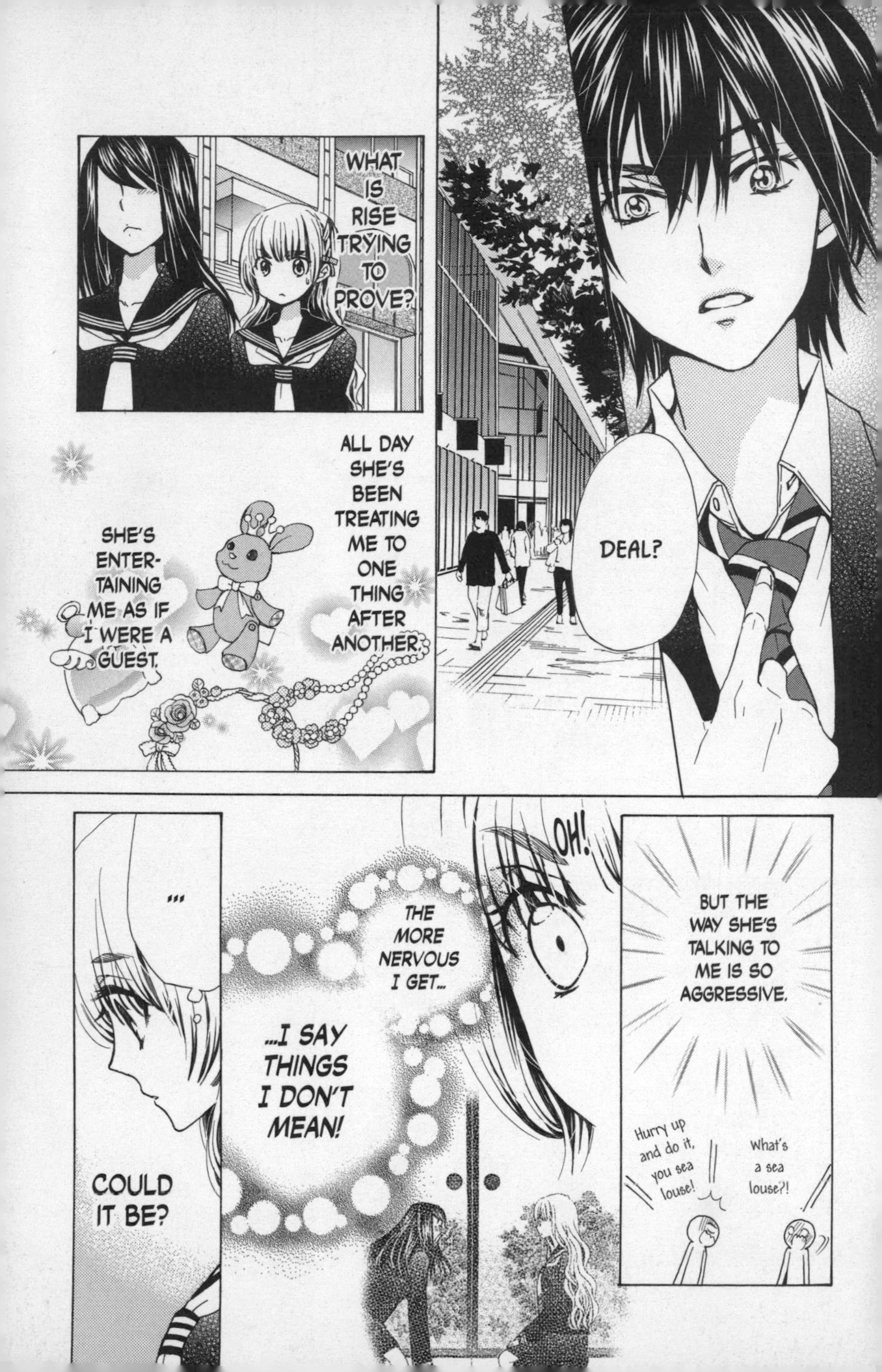
DEAL?
WHAT IS RISE TRYING TO PROVE?
ALL DAY SHE'S BEEN TREATING ME TO ONE THING AFTER ANOTHER.
SHE'S ENTER-TAINING ME AS IF I WERE A GUEST.
BUT THE WAY SHE'S TALKING TO ME IS SO AGGRESSIVE.
Hurry up and do it, you sea louse!
What's a sea louse?!
OH!
THE MORE NERVOUS I GET...
...I SAY THINGS I DON'T MEAN!
...
COULD IT BE?

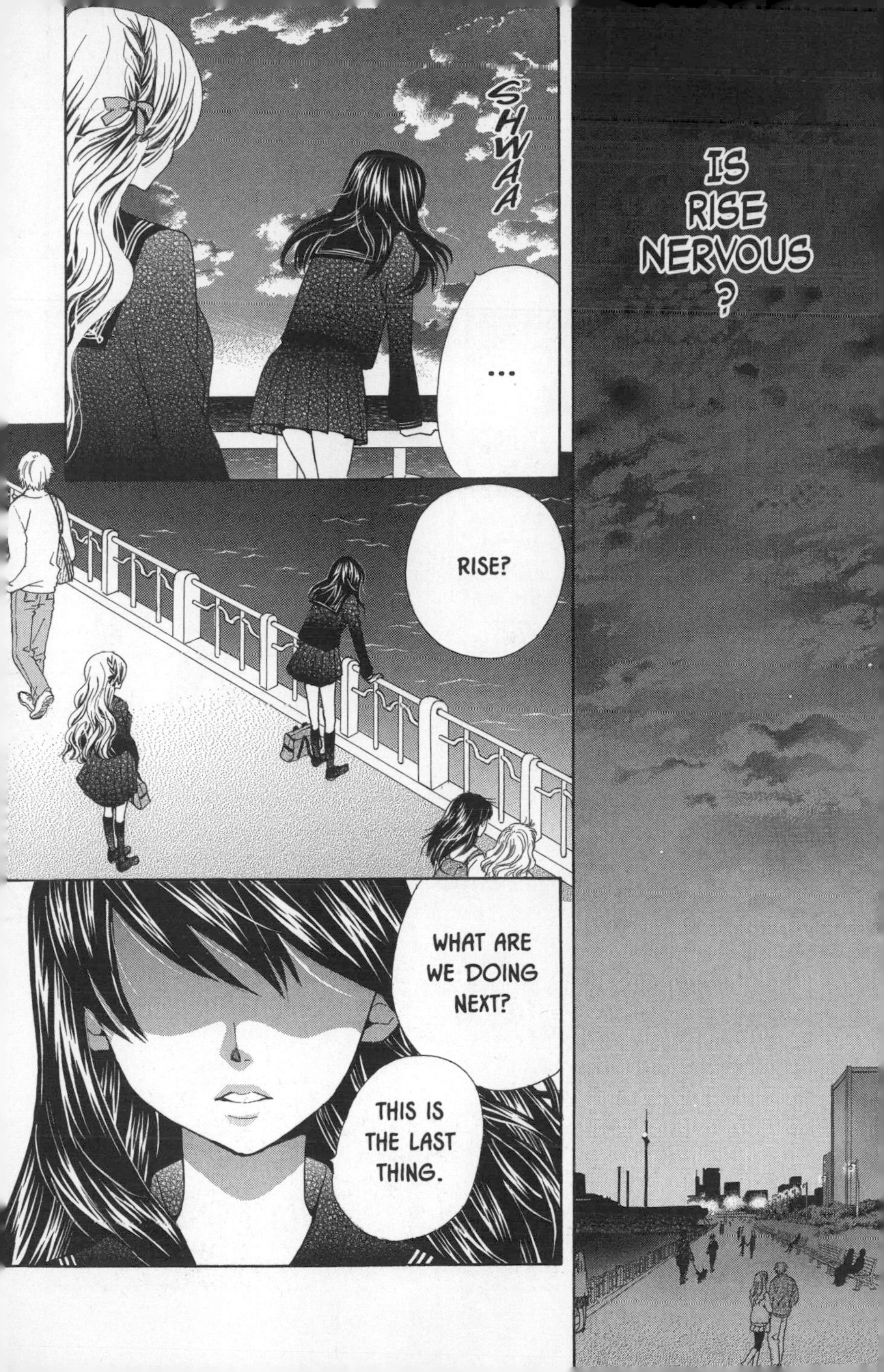
IS RISE NERVOUS ?
SHWAA
...
RISE?
WHAT ARE WE DOING NEXT?
THIS IS THE LAST THING.

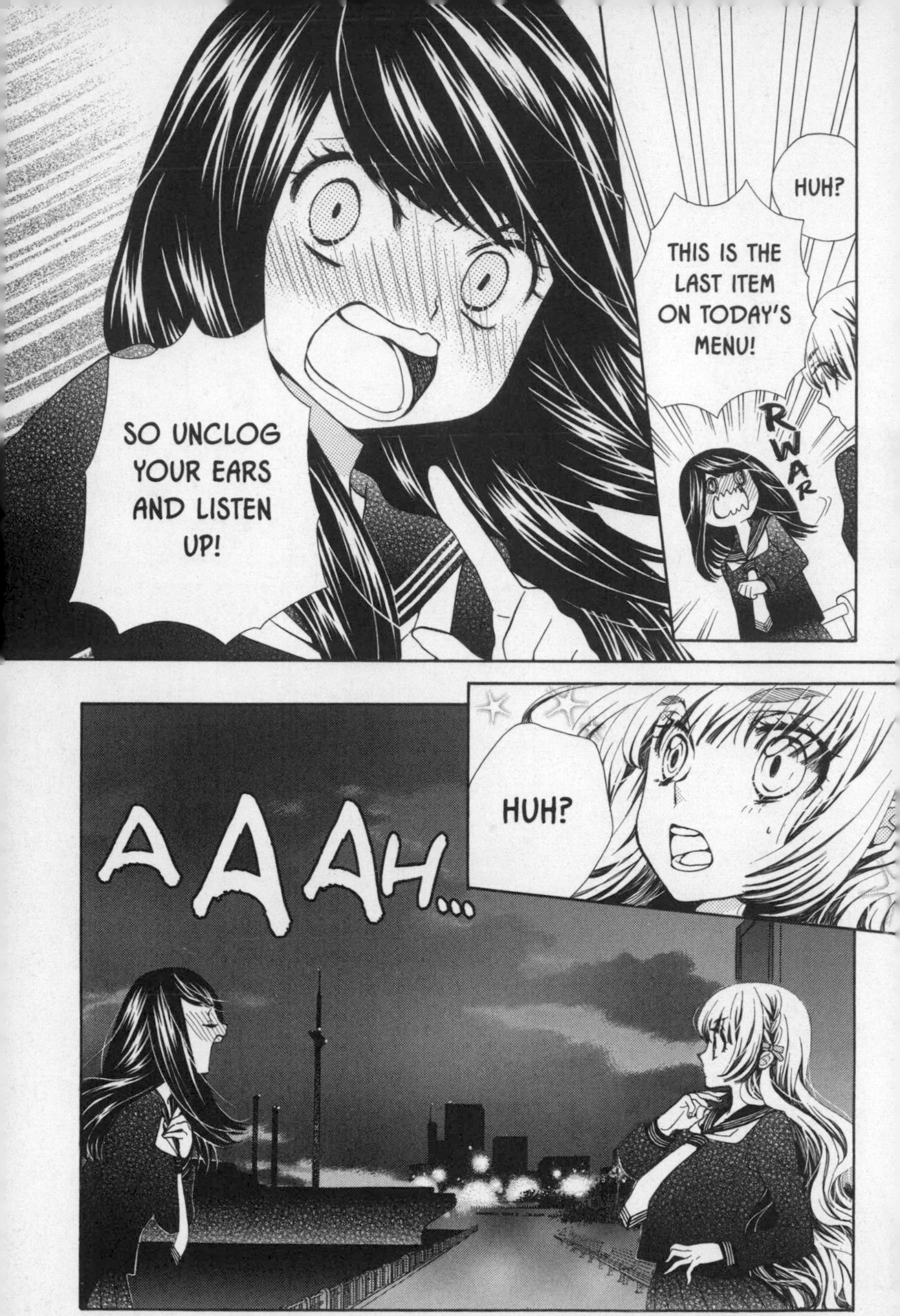
HUH?
THIS IS THE LAST ITEM ON TODAY'S MENU!
RWAR
SO UNCLOG YOUR EARS AND LISTEN UP!
HUH?
AAAH...

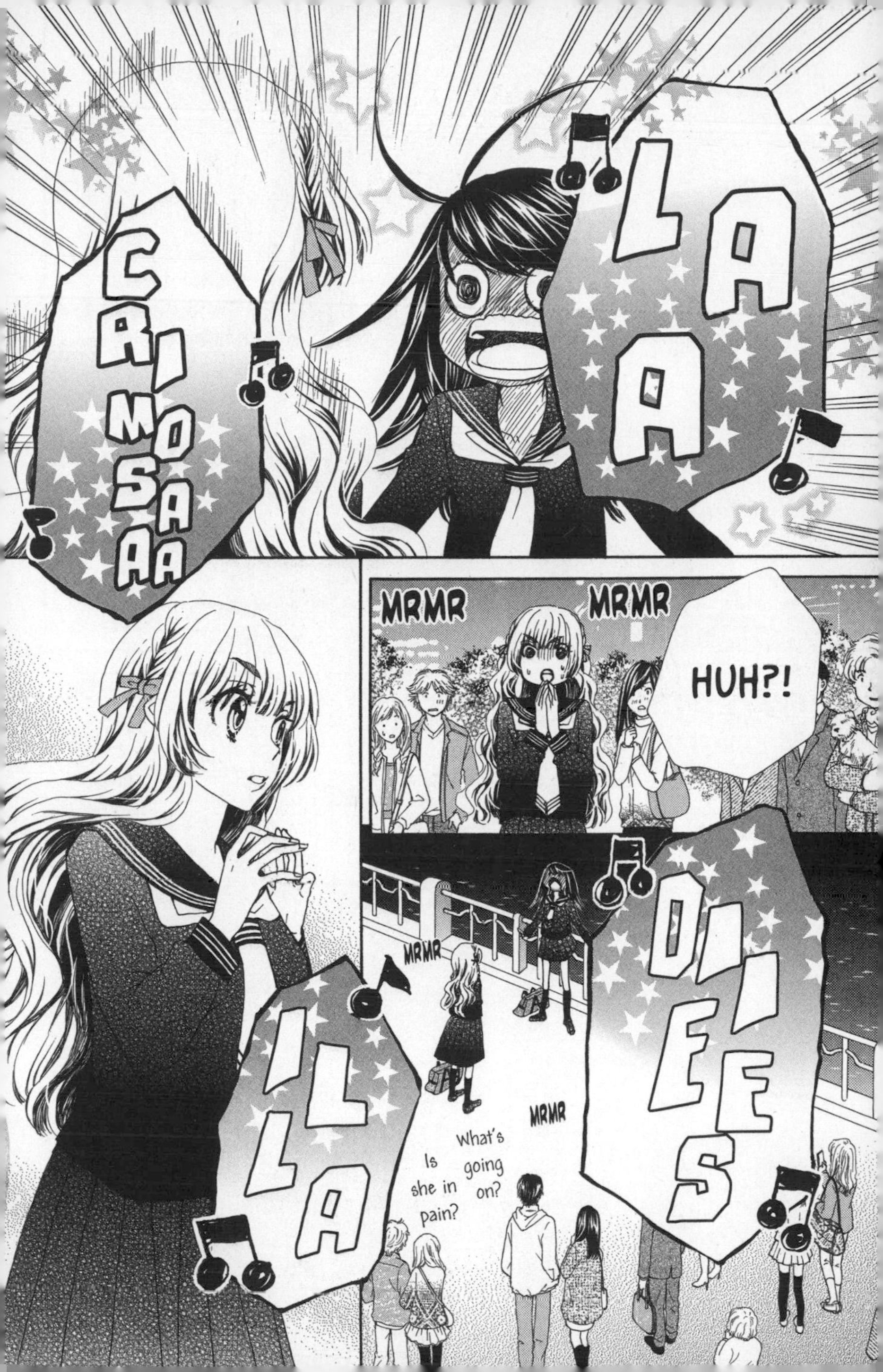
LAAA
CRIMOSAAAA
HUH?!
MRMR
MRMR
DIIEES
MRMR
What's going on?
Is she in pain?
MRMR
ILLA

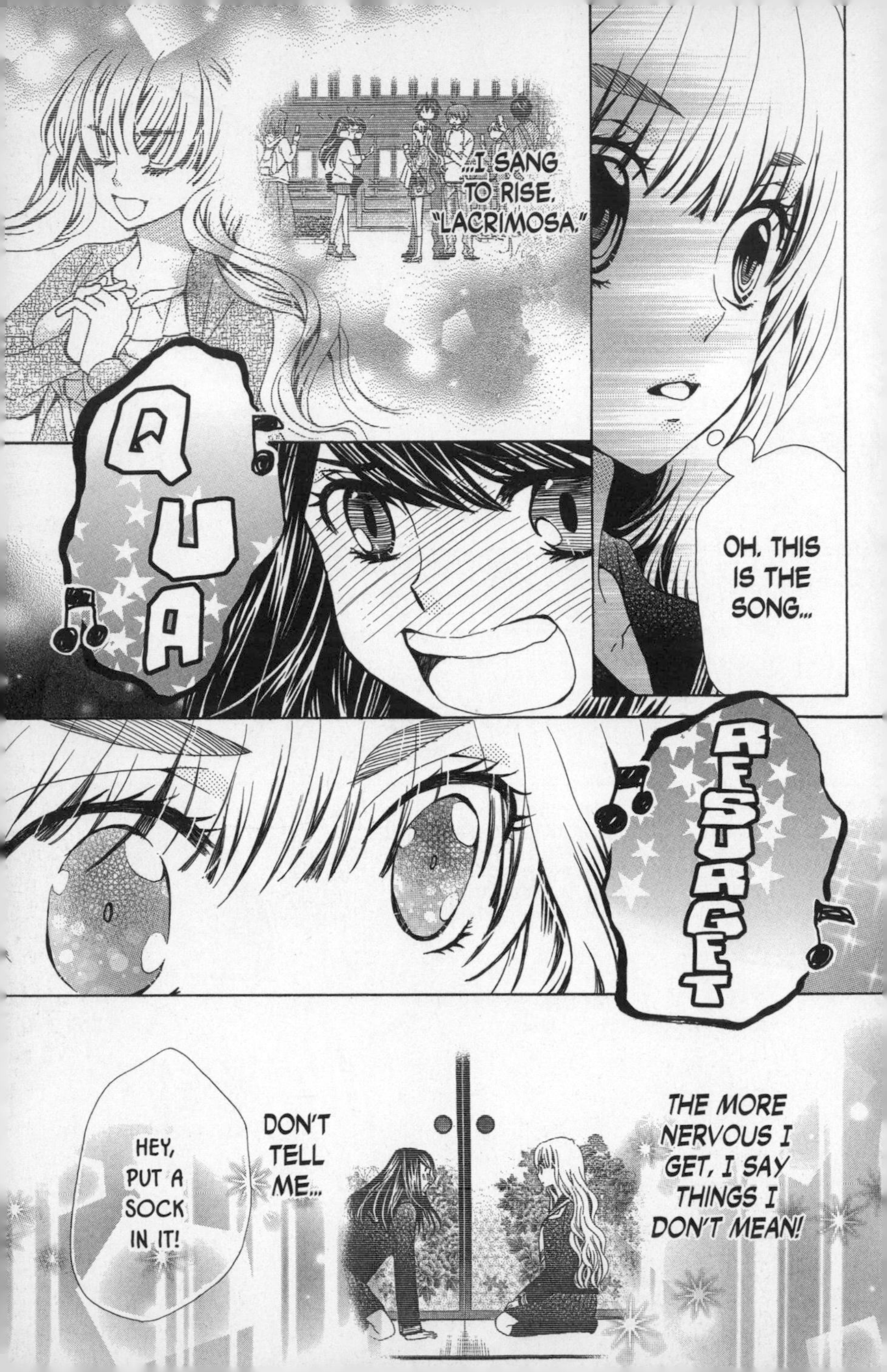

OH, THIS IS THE SONG...
...I SANG TO RISE. "LACRIMOSA."
QUA
RESURGET
THE MORE NERVOUS I GET, I SAY THINGS I DON'T MEAN!
DON'T TELL ME...
HEY, PUT A SOCK IN IT!

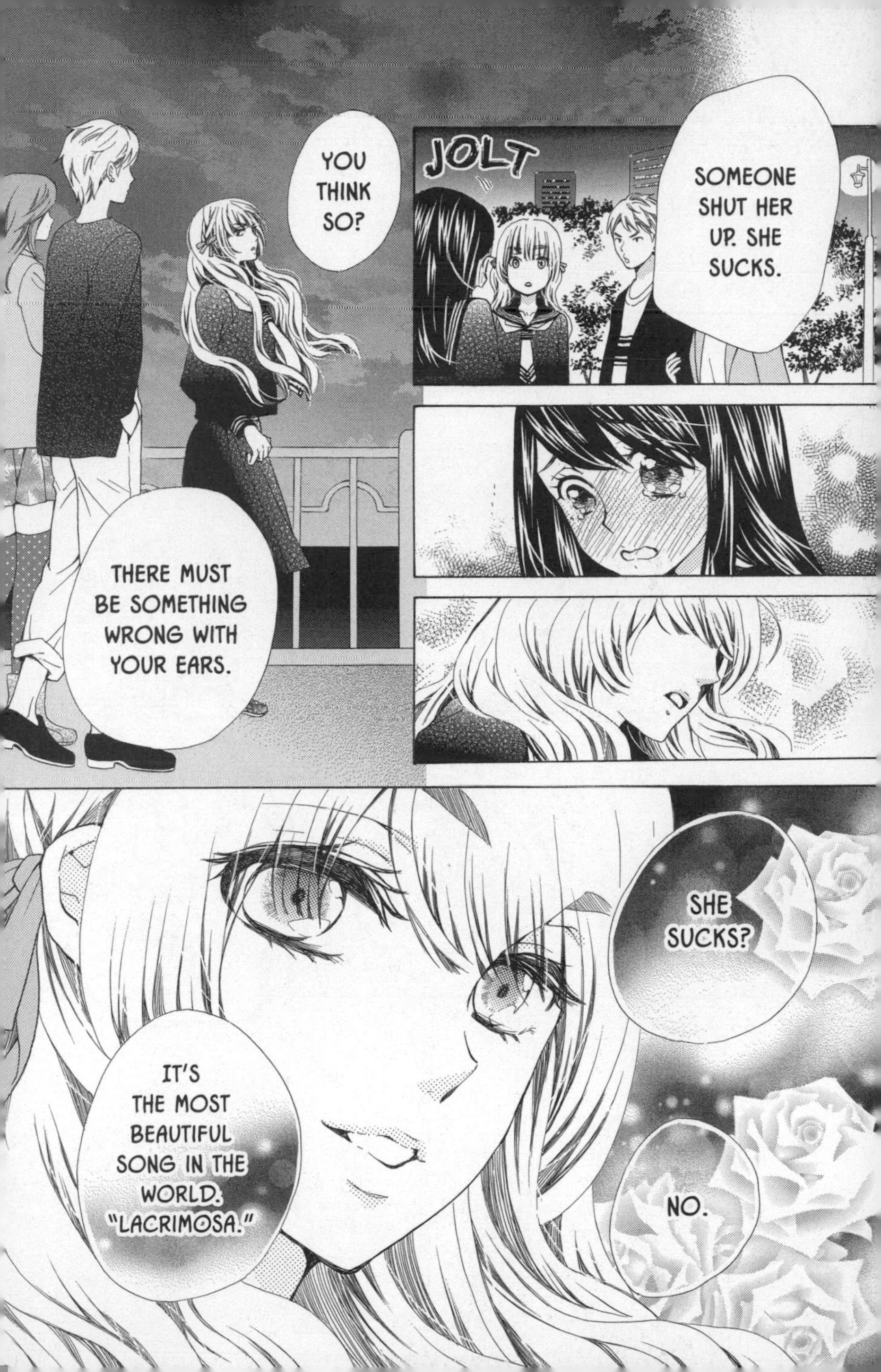
SOMEONE SHUT HER UP. SHE SUCKS.
JOLT
YOU THINK SO?
THERE MUST BE SOMETHING WRONG WITH YOUR EARS.
SHE SUCKS?
NO.
IT'S THE MOST BEAUTIFUL SONG IN THE WORLD. "LACRIMOSA."

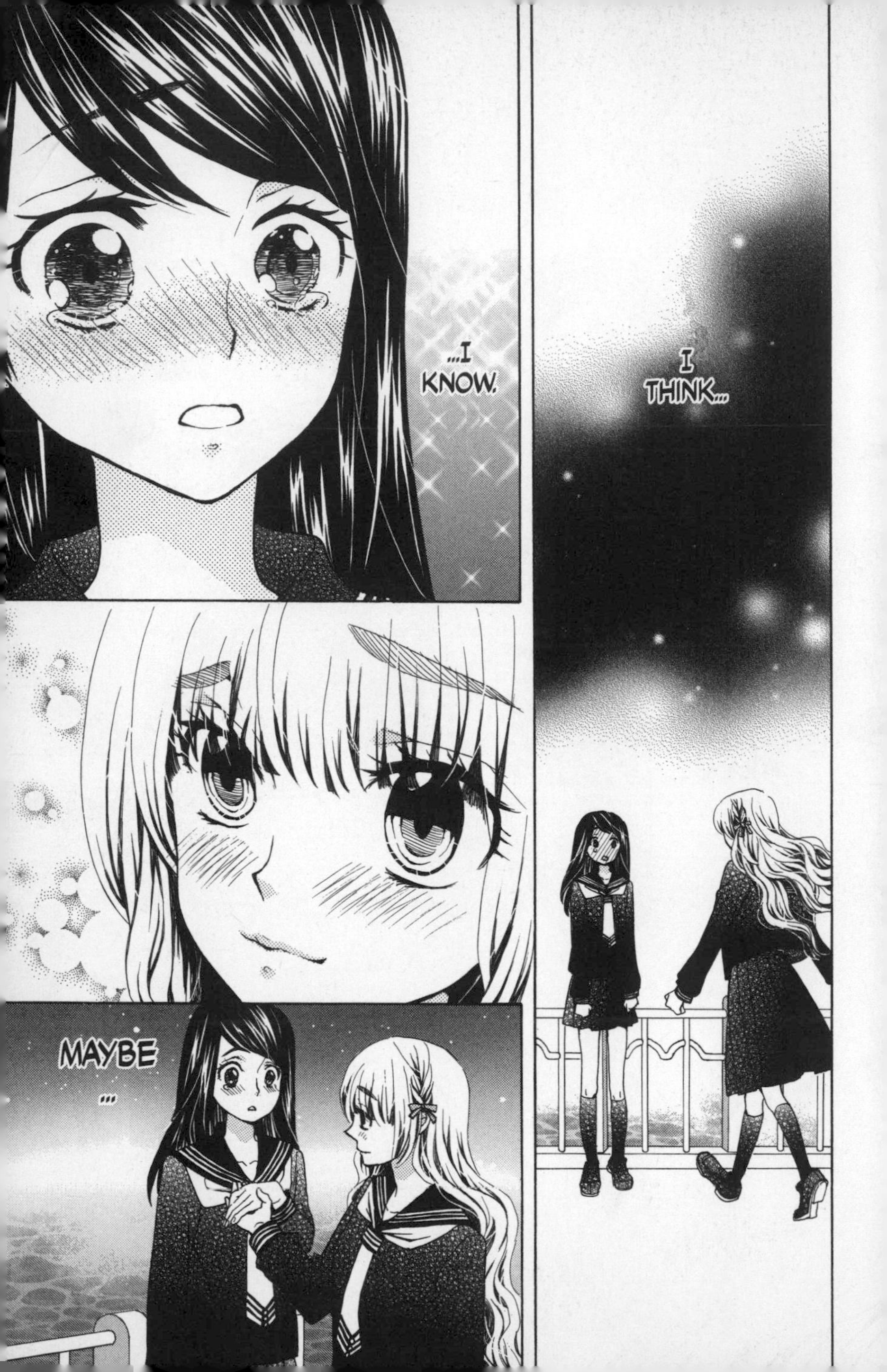
I THINK...
...I KNOW.
MAYBE ...

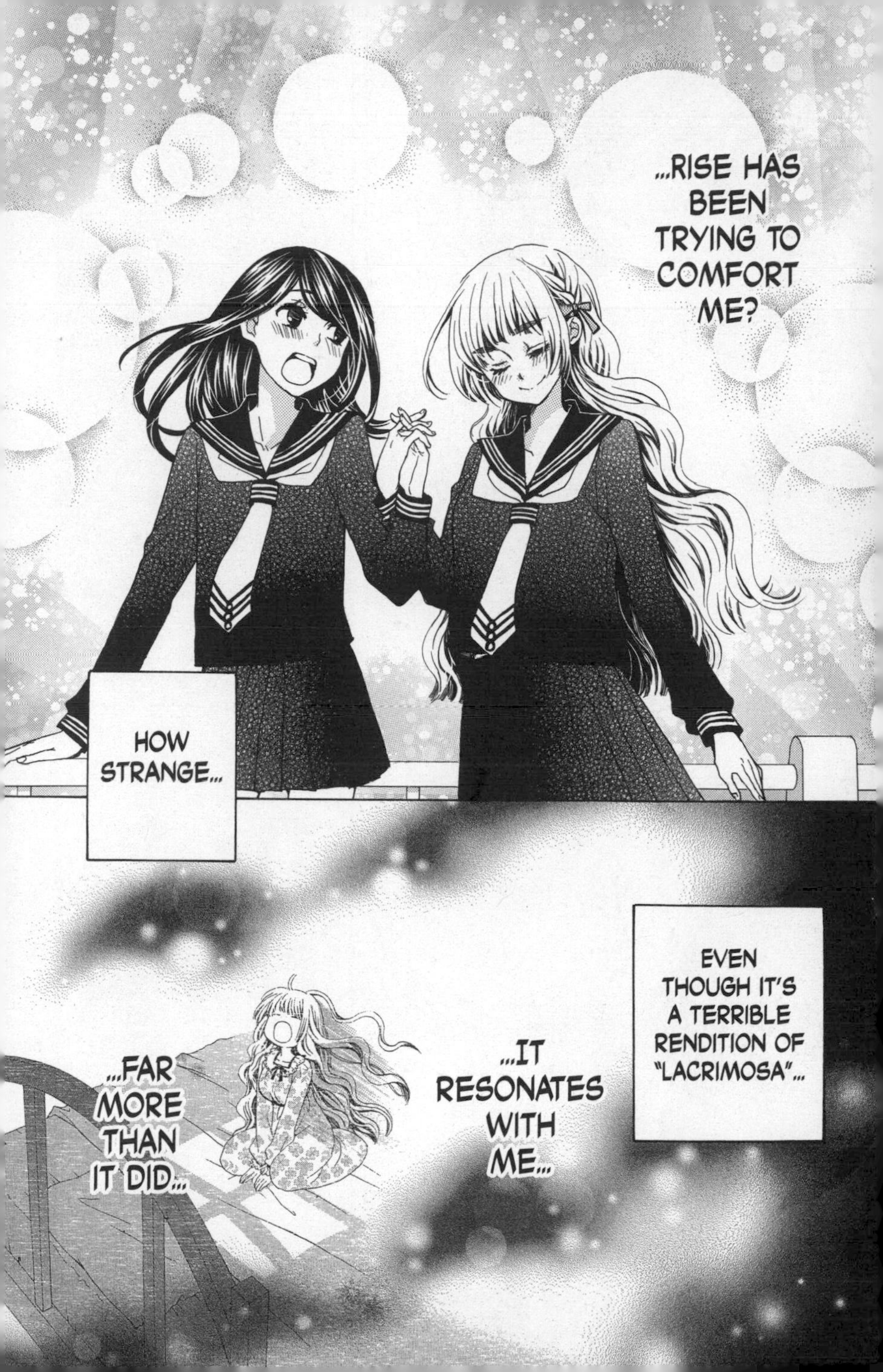
...RISE HAS BEEN TRYING TO COMFORT ME?
HOW STRANGE...
EVEN THOUGH IT'S A TERRIBLE RENDITION OF "LACRIMOSA"...
...IT RESONATES WITH ME...
...FAR MORE THAN IT DID...

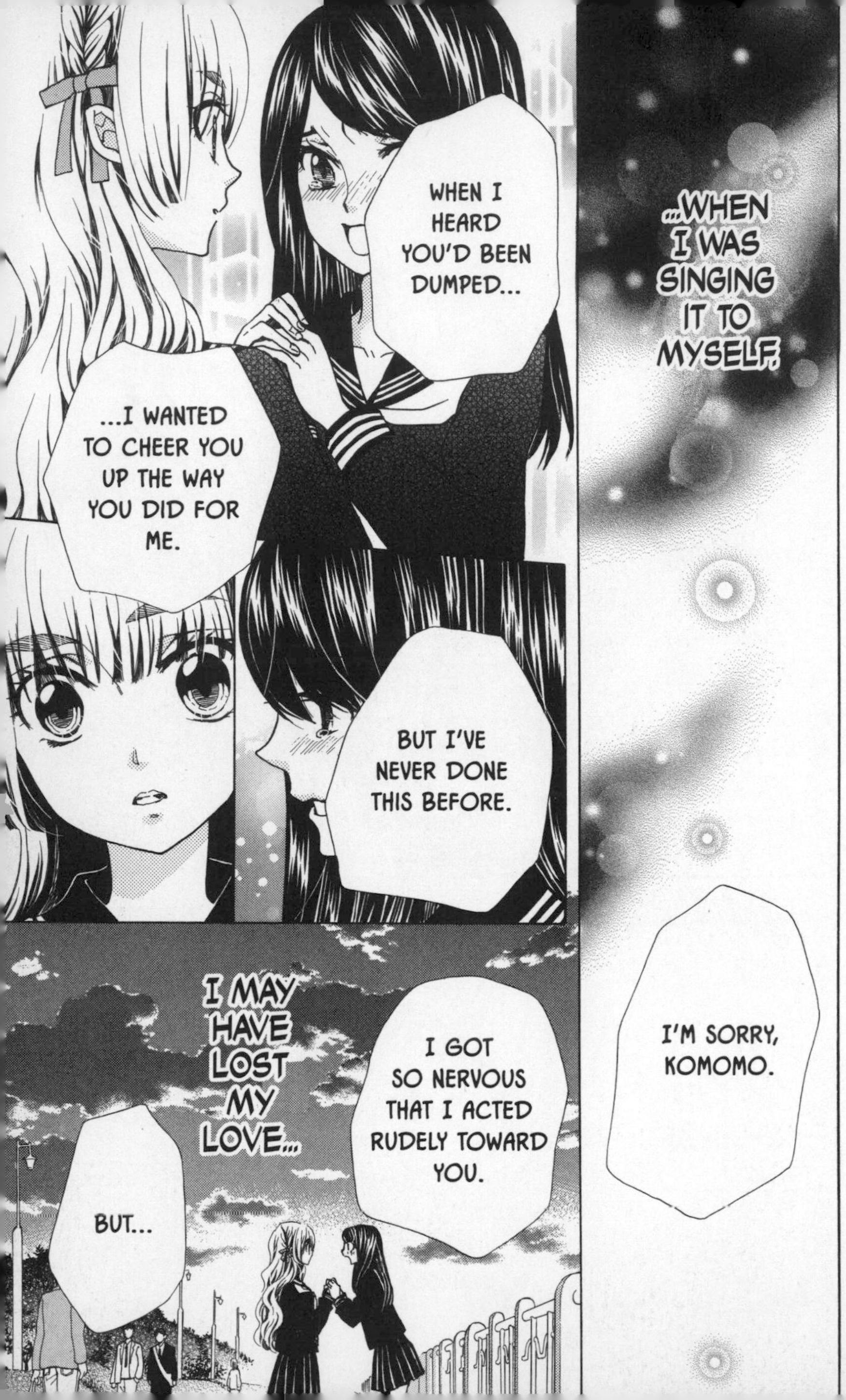
...WHEN I WAS SINGING IT TO MYSELF.
I'M SORRY, KOMOMO.
WHEN I HEARD YOU'D BEEN DUMPED...
...I WANTED TO CHEER YOU UP THE WAY YOU DID FOR ME.
BUT I'VE NEVER DONE THIS BEFORE.
I GOT SO NERVOUS THAT I ACTED RUDELY TOWARD YOU.
I MAY HAVE LOST MY LOVE...
BUT...

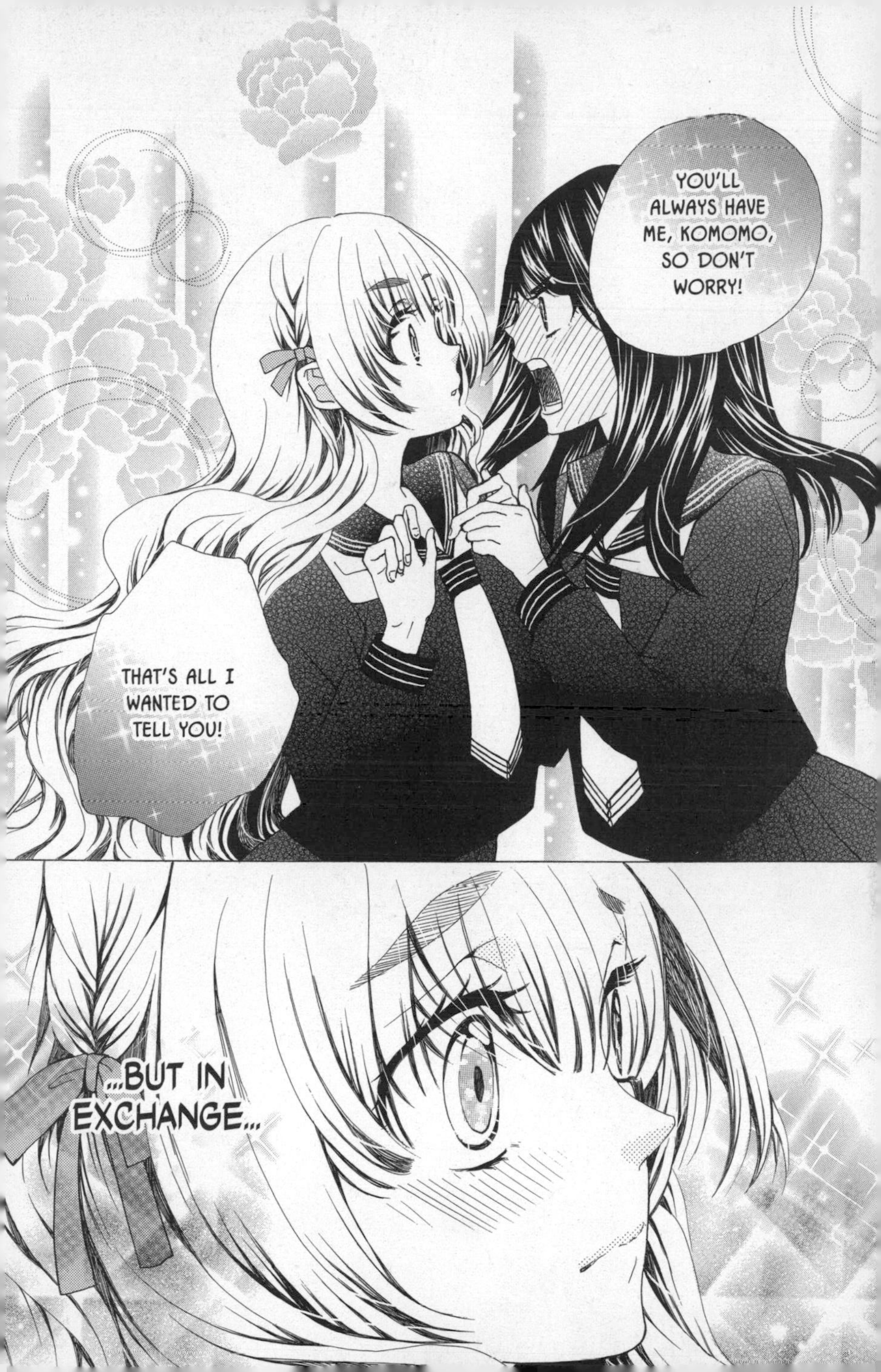
YOU'LL ALWAYS HAVE ME, KOMOMO, SO DON'T WORRY!
THAT'S ALL I WANTED TO TELL YOU!
...BUT IN EXCHANGE...

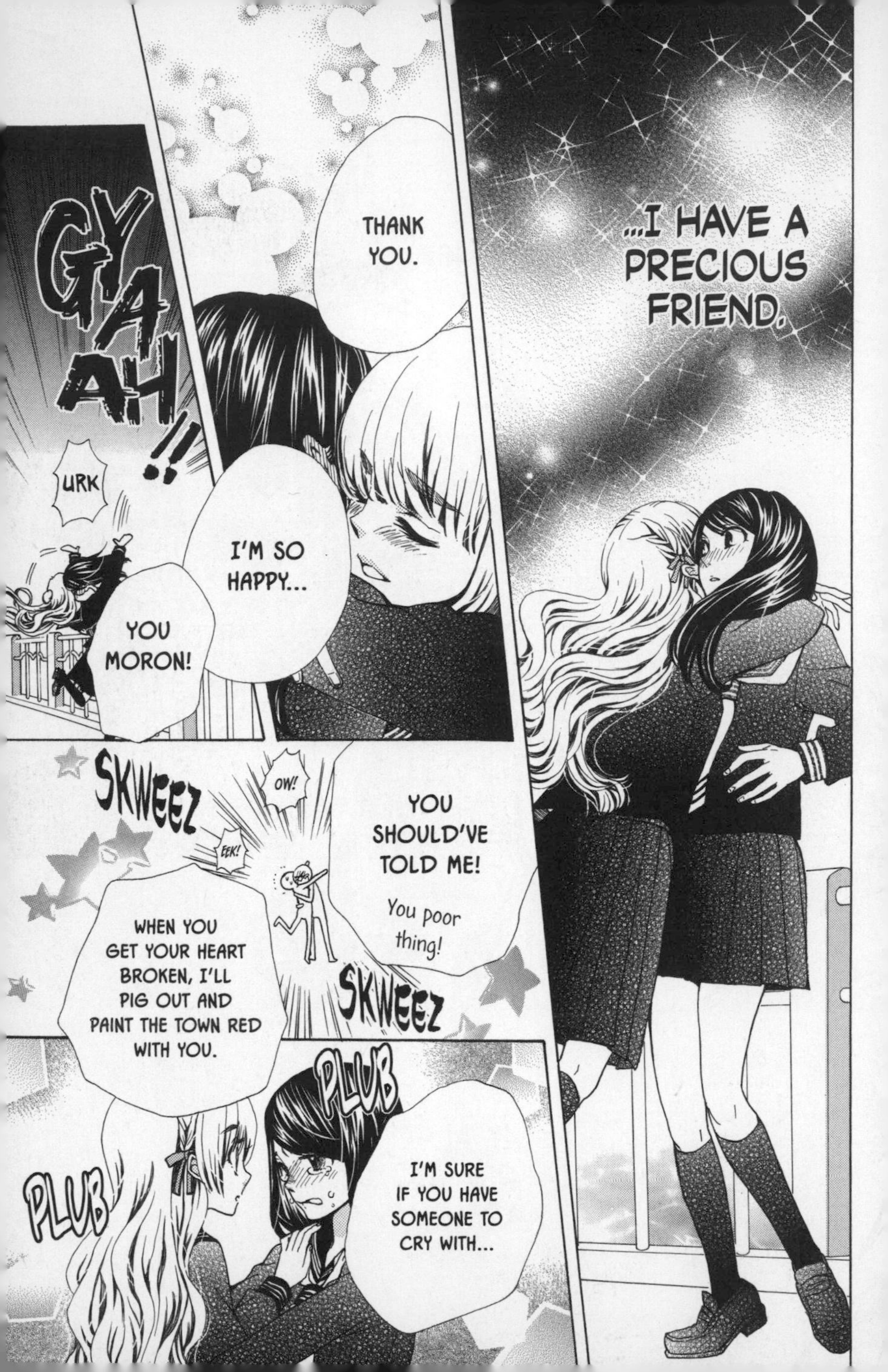
...I HAVE A PRECIOUS FRIEND.
THANK YOU.
I'M SO HAPPY...
GYAAH!!
URK
YOU MORON!
SKWEEZ
OW!
EEK!
YOU SHOULD'VE TOLD ME!
You poor thing!
WHEN YOU GET YOUR HEART BROKEN, I'LL PIG OUT AND PAINT THE TOWN RED WITH YOU.
SKWEEZ
PLUB
I'M SURE IF YOU HAVE SOMEONE TO CRY WITH...
PLUB

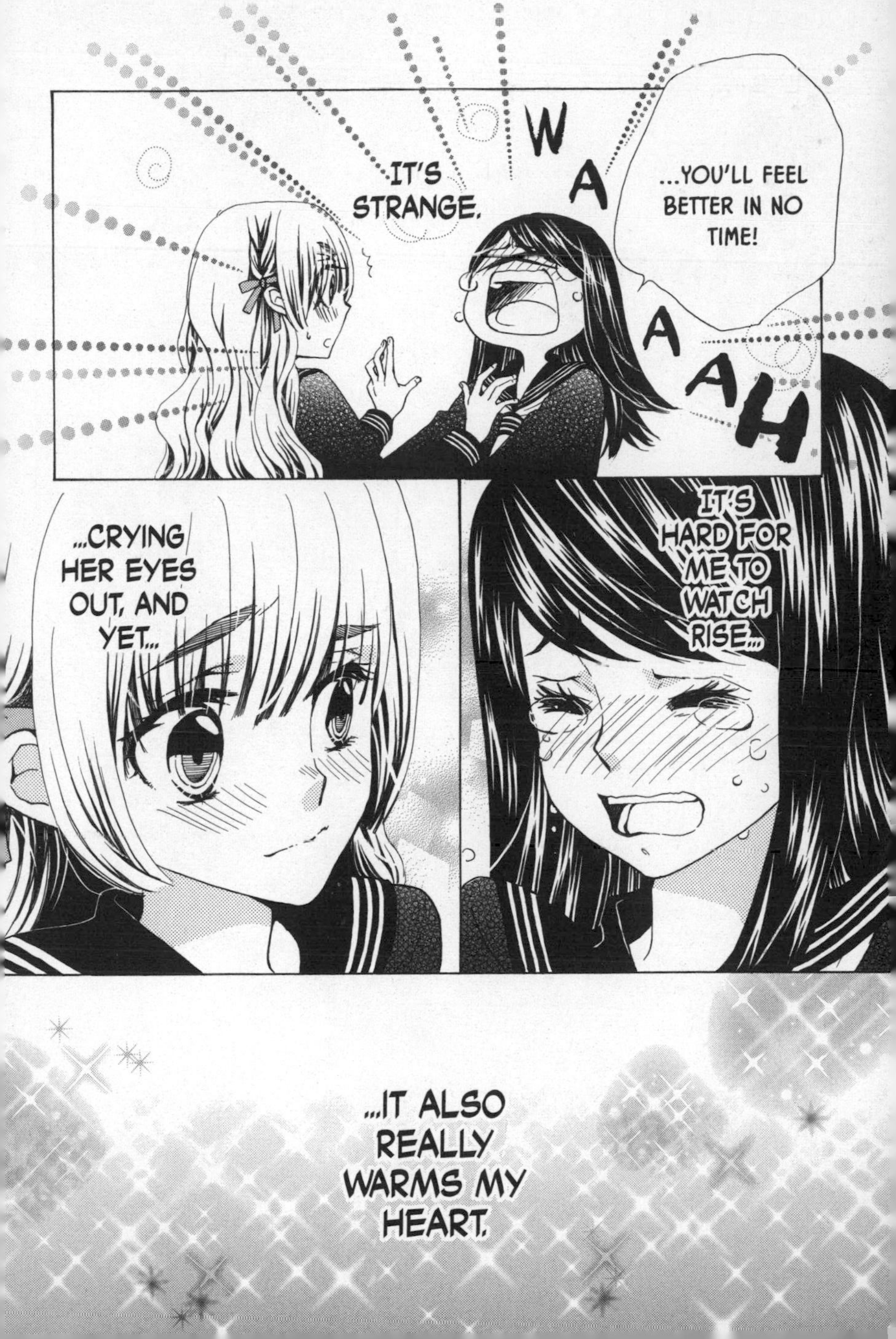
...YOU'LL FEEL BETTER IN NO TIME!
WAAAH
IT'S STRANGE.
IT'S HARD FOR ME TO WATCH RISE...
...CRYING HER EYES OUT, AND YET...
...IT ALSO REALLY WARMS MY HEART.

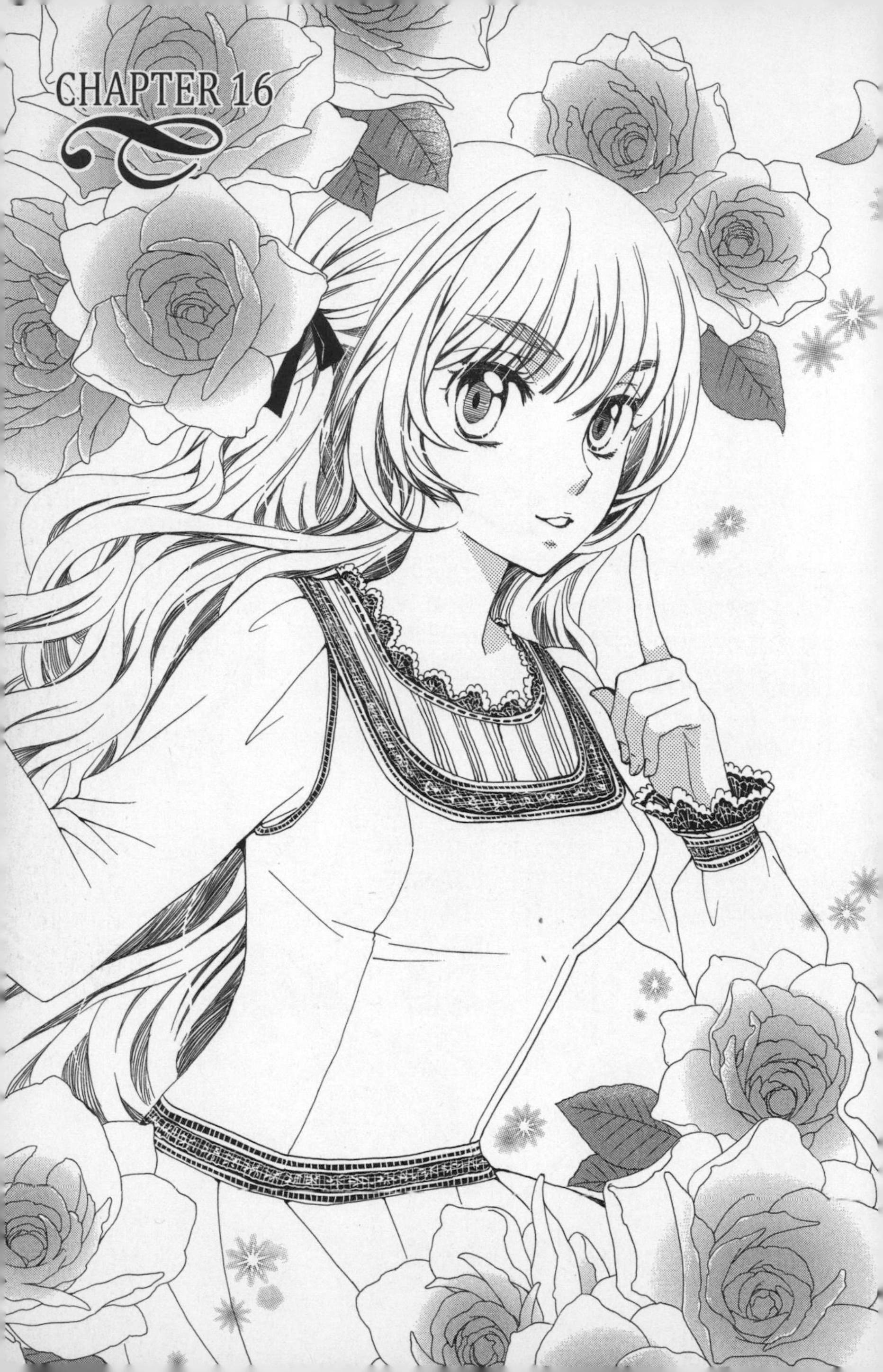
CHAPTER 16

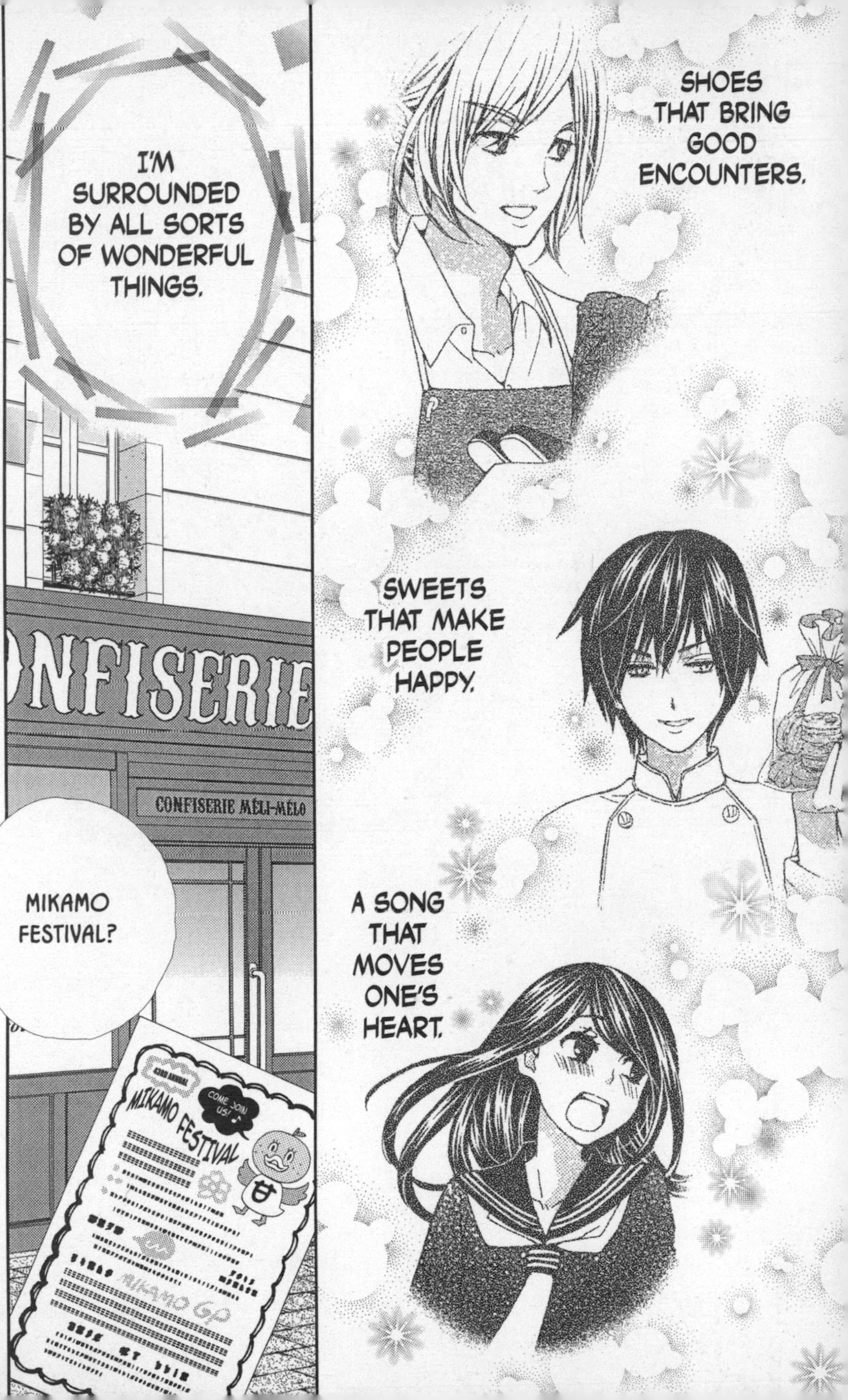
SHOES THAT BRING GOOD ENCOUNTERS.
SWEETS THAT MAKE PEOPLE HAPPY.
A SONG THAT MOVES ONE'S HEART.
I'M SURROUNDED BY ALL SORTS OF WONDERFUL THINGS.
ONFISERIE
CONFISERIE MÉLI-MÉLO
MIKAMO FESTIVAL?
MIKAMO FESTIVAL
COME JOIN US!
MIKAMO GP

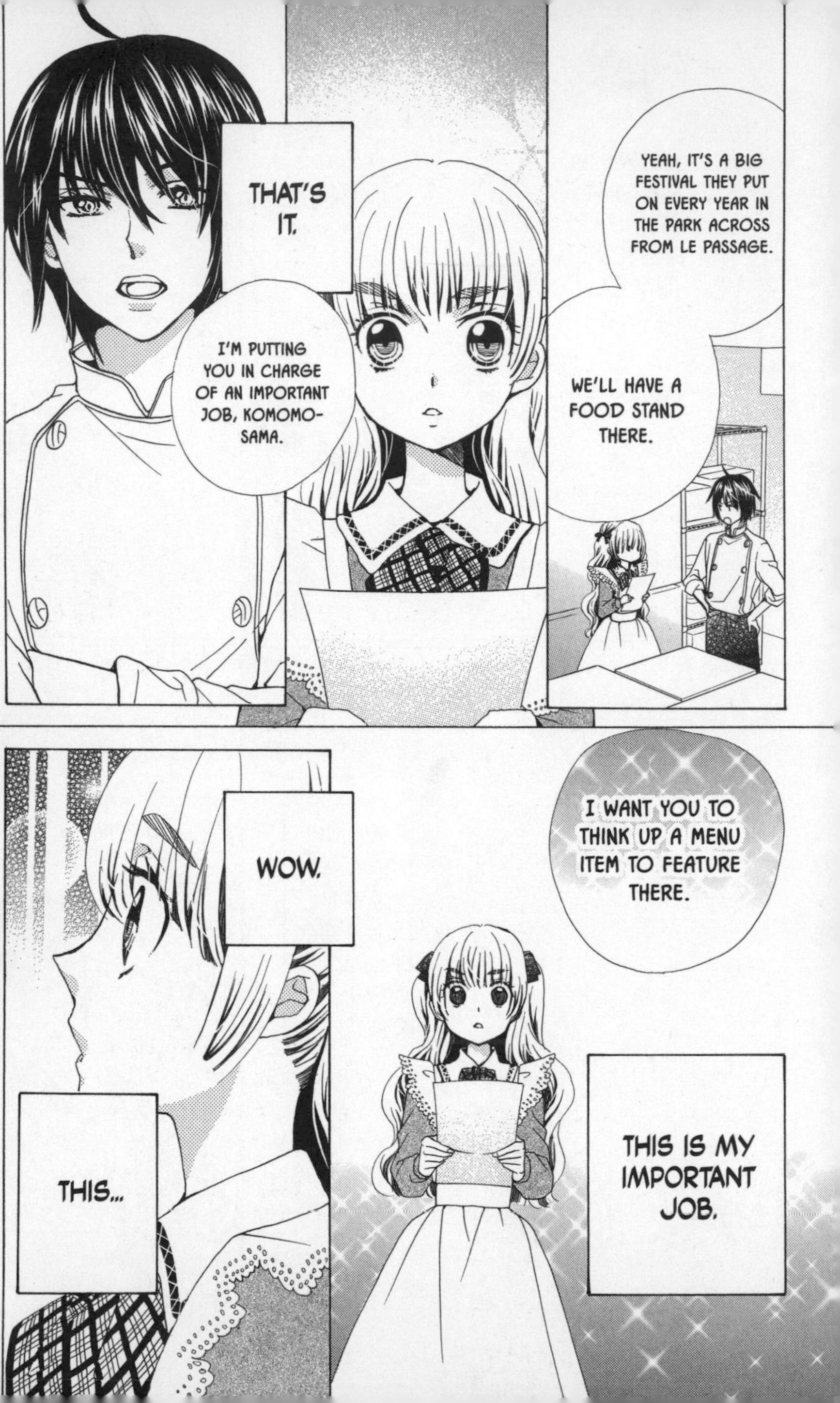
YEAH, IT'S A BIG FESTIVAL THEY PUT ON EVERY YEAR IN THE PARK ACROSS FROM LE PASSAGE.
WE'LL HAVE A FOOD STAND THERE.
I'M PUTTING YOU IN CHARGE OF AN IMPORTANT JOB, KOMOMO-SAMA.
THAT'S IT.
I WANT YOU TO THINK UP A MENU ITEM TO FEATURE THERE.
THIS IS MY IMPORTANT JOB.
WOW.
THIS...

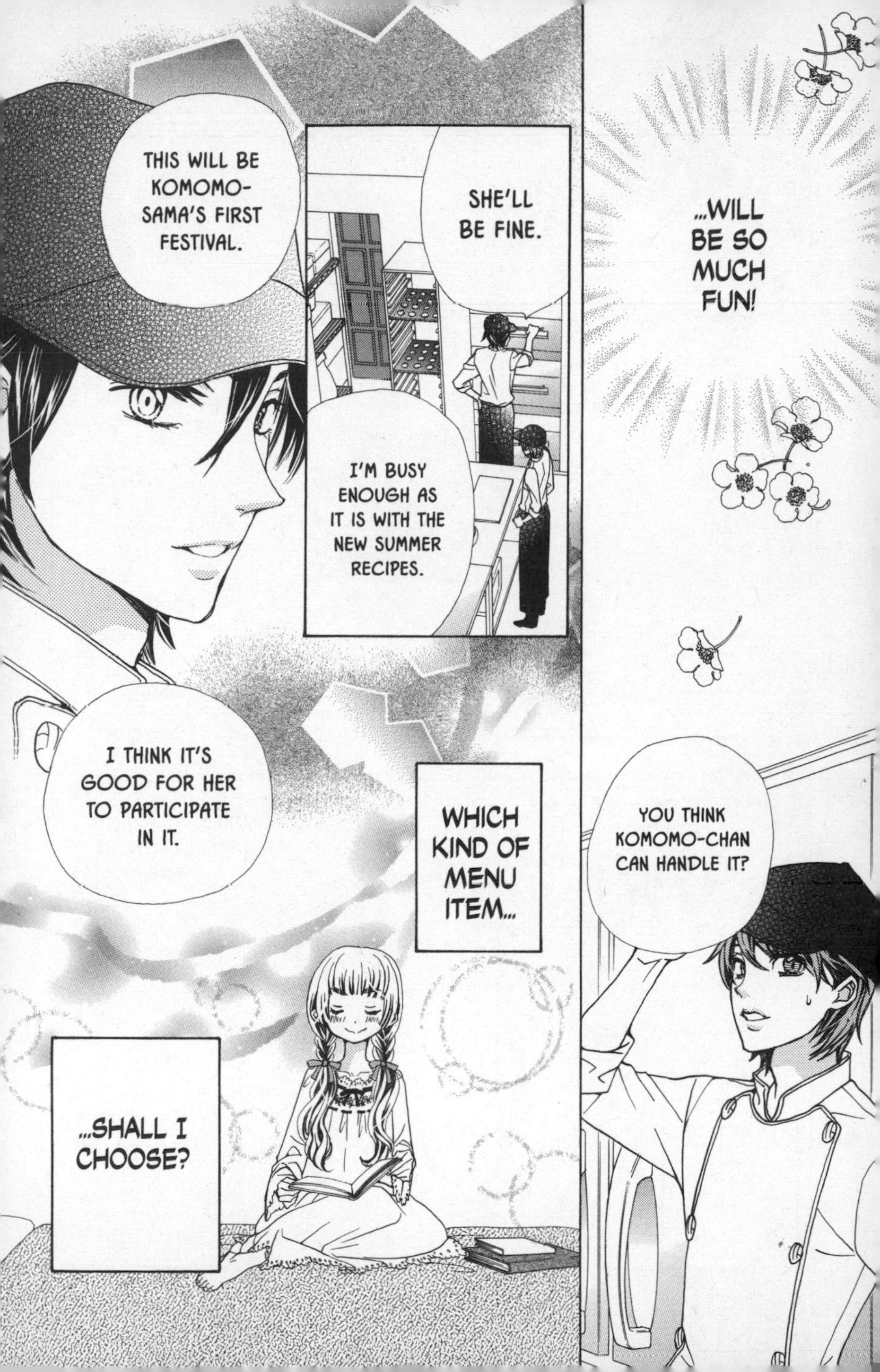
...WILL BE SO MUCH FUN!
YOU THINK KOMOMO-CHAN CAN HANDLE IT?
SHE'LL BE FINE.
I'M BUSY ENOUGH AS IT IS WITH THE NEW SUMMER RECIPES.
THIS WILL BE KOMOMO-SAMA'S FIRST FESTIVAL.
I THINK IT'S GOOD FOR HER TO PARTICIPATE IN IT.
WHICH KIND OF MENU ITEM...
...SHALL I CHOOSE?

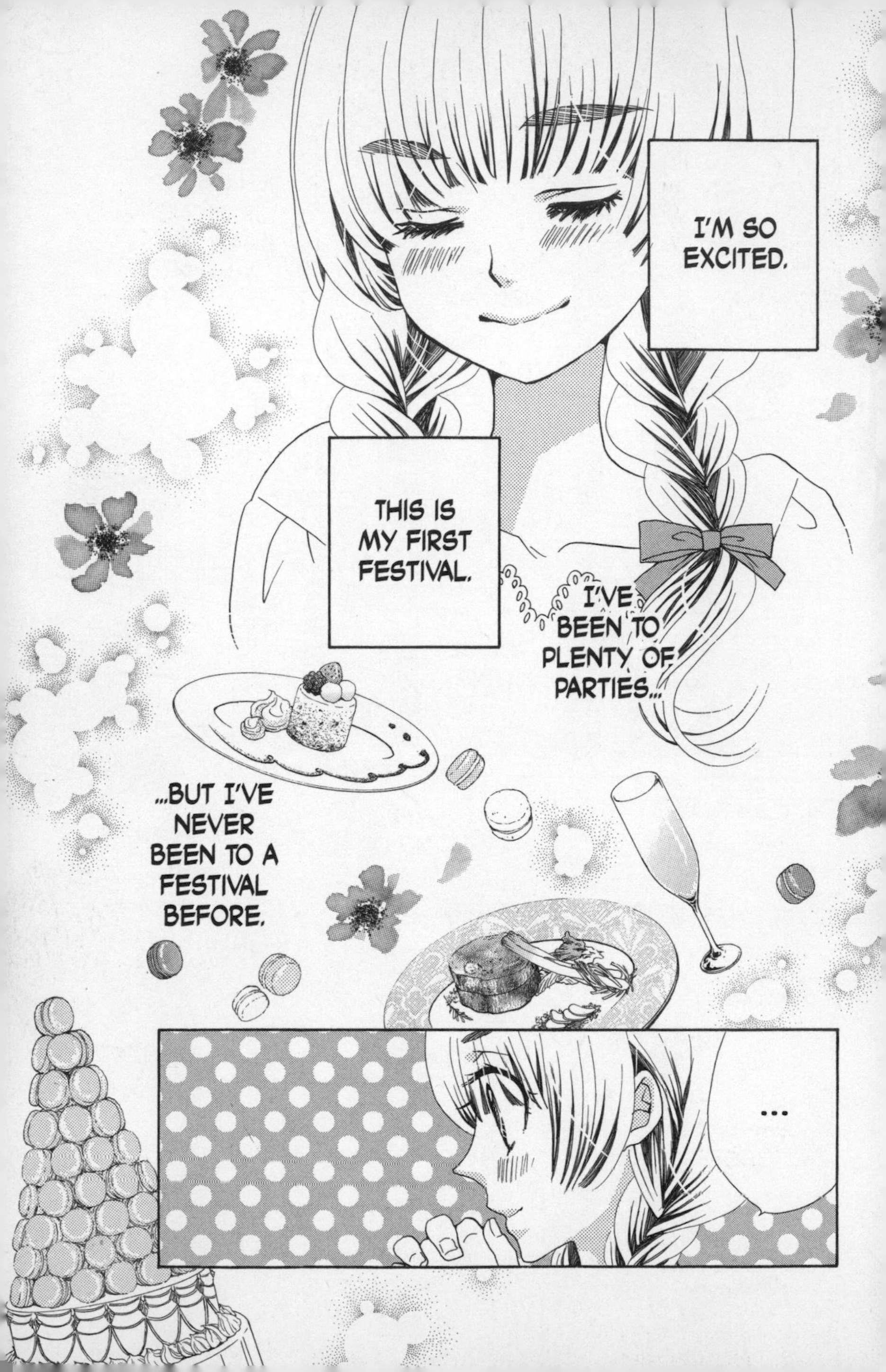
I'M SO EXCITED.
THIS IS MY FIRST FESTIVAL.
I'VE BEEN TO PLENTY OF PARTIES...
...BUT I'VE NEVER BEEN TO A FESTIVAL BEFORE.
...

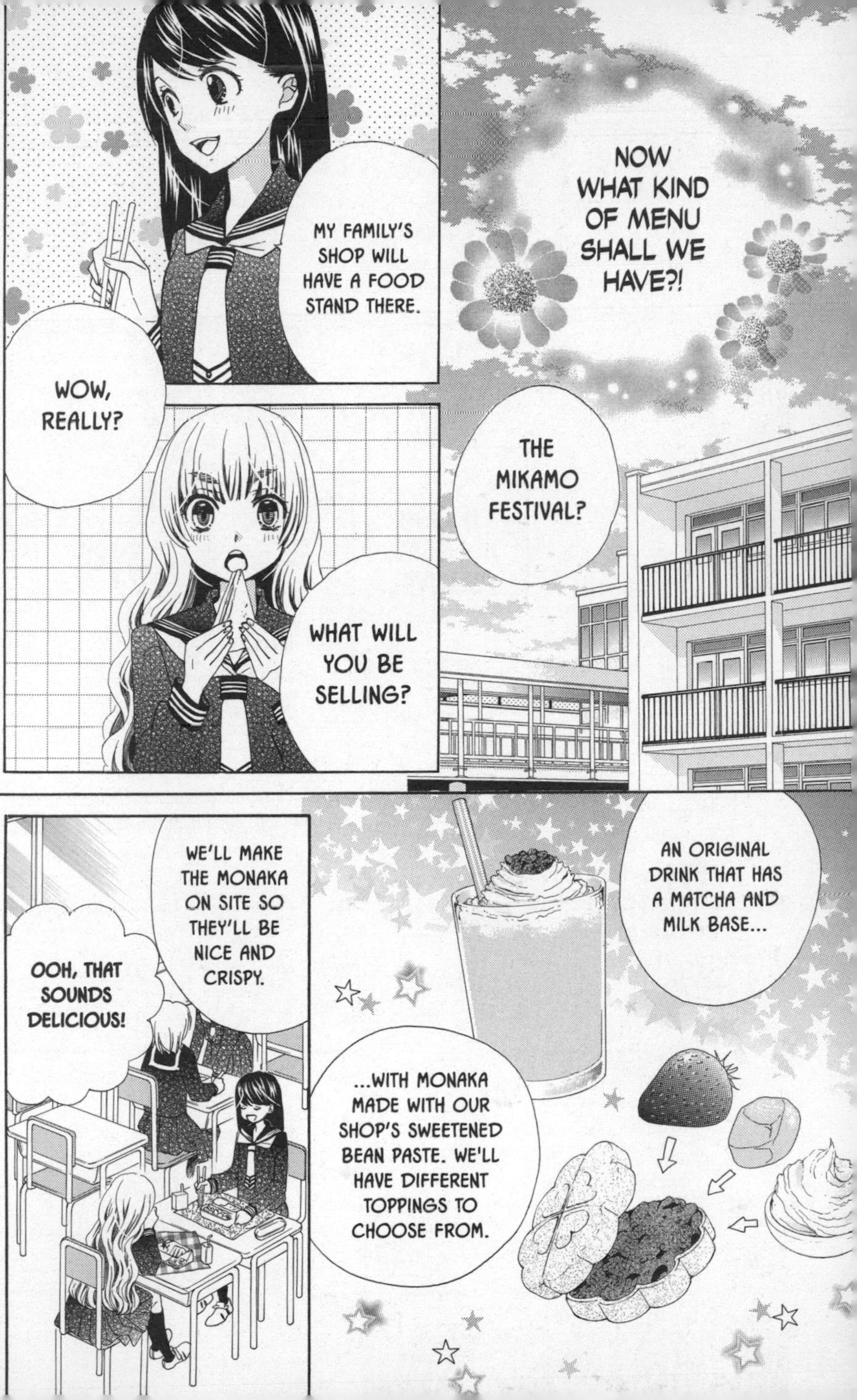
NOW WHAT KIND OF MENU SHALL WE HAVE?!
THE MIKAMO FESTIVAL?
MY FAMILY'S SHOP WILL HAVE A FOOD STAND THERE.
WOW, REALLY?
WHAT WILL YOU BE SELLING?
AN ORIGINAL DRINK THAT HAS A MATCHA AND MILK BASE...
...WITH MONAKA MADE WITH OUR SHOP'S SWEETENED BEAN PASTE. WE'LL HAVE DIFFERENT TOPPINGS TO CHOOSE FROM.
WE'LL MAKE THE MONAKA ON SITE SO THEY'LL BE NICE AND CRISPY.
OOH, THAT SOUNDS DELICIOUS!

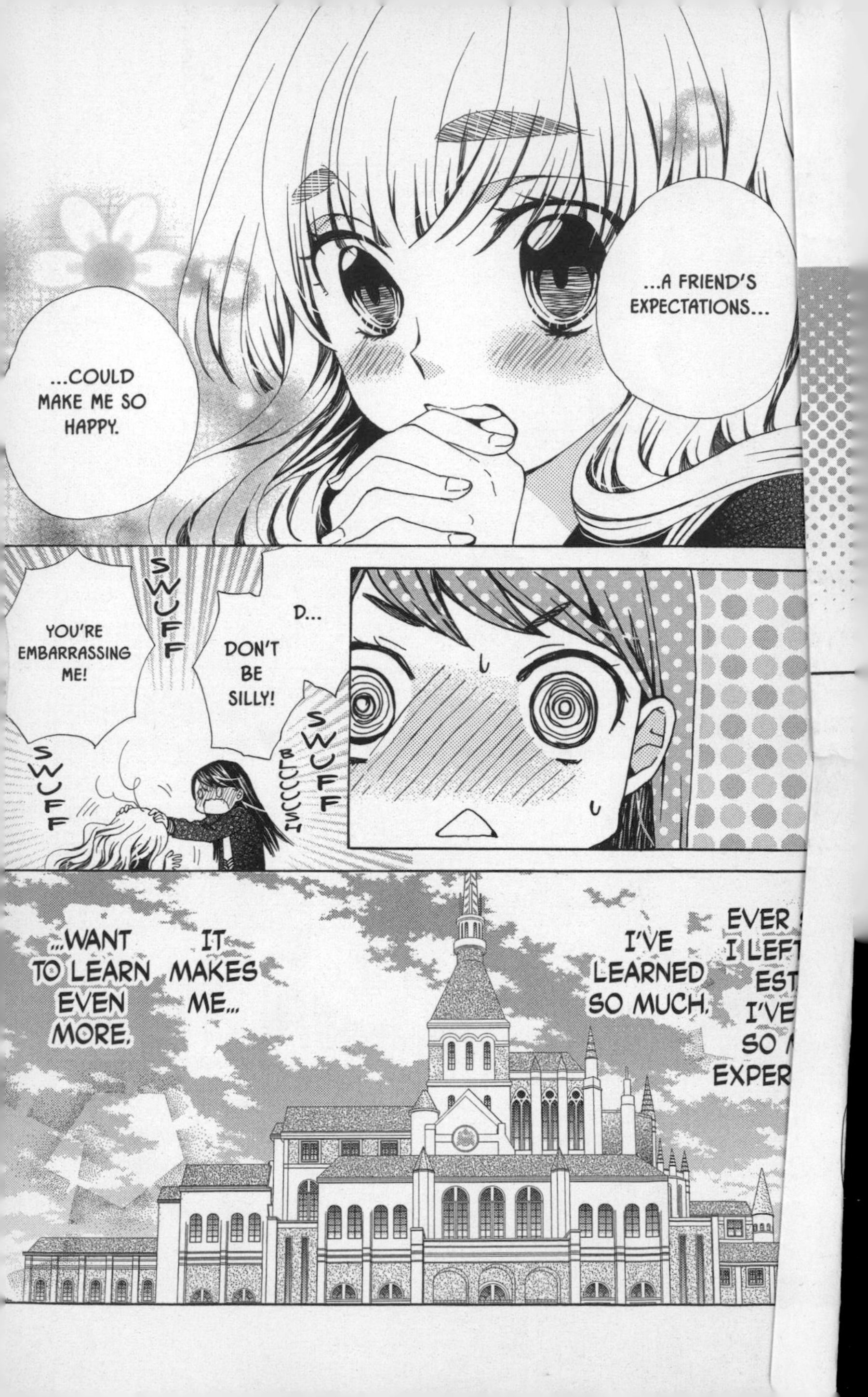
...A FRIEND'S EXPECTATIONS...
...COULD MAKE ME SO HAPPY.
D...
DON'T BE SILLY!
SWUFF
BLUUUUSH
SWUFF
YOU'RE EMBARRASSING ME!
SWUFF
EVER
I LEFT
EST
I'VE
SO
EXPER
I'VE LEARNED SO MUCH.
IT MAKES ME...
...WANT TO LEARN EVEN MORE.

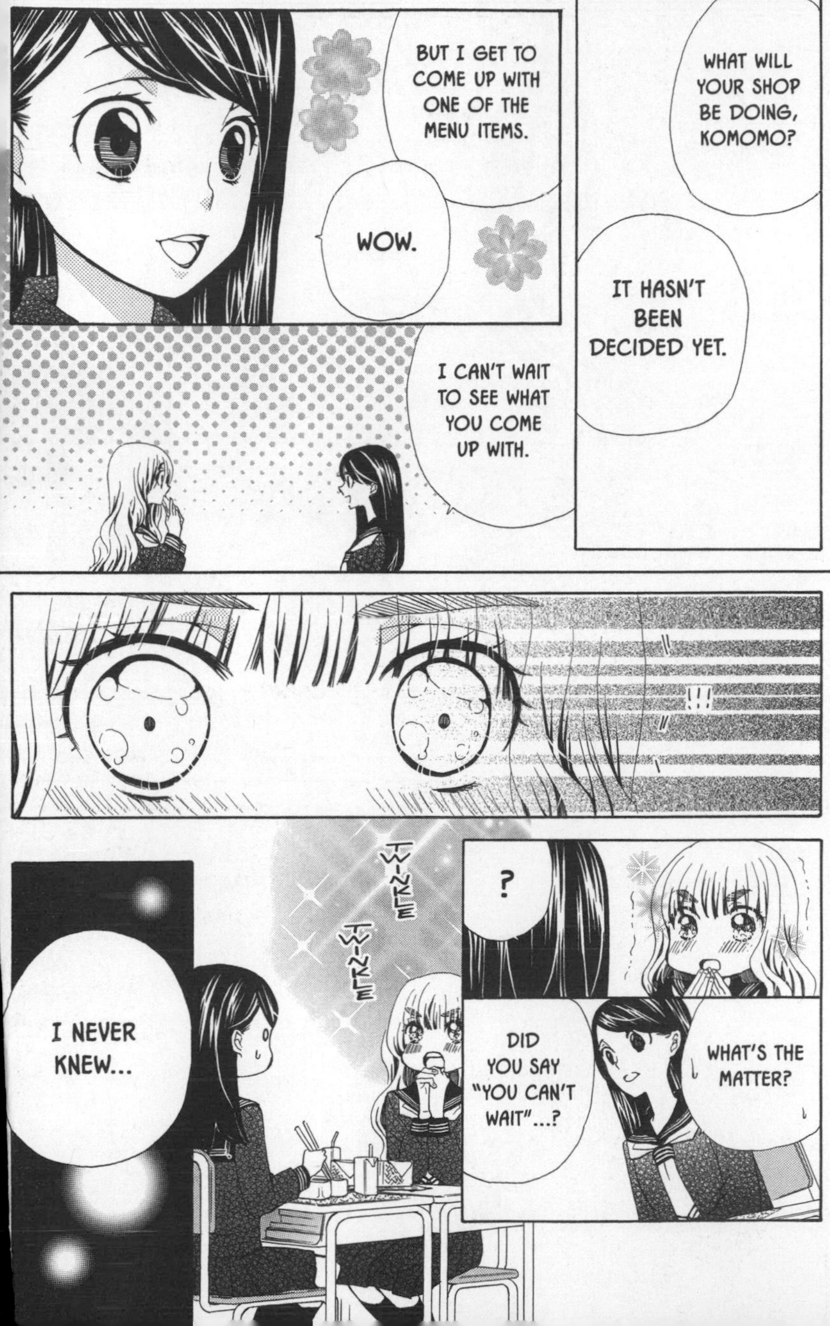
WHAT WILL YOUR SHOP BE DOING, KOMOMO?
IT HASN'T BEEN DECIDED YET.
BUT I GET TO COME UP WITH ONE OF THE MENU ITEMS.
WOW.
I CAN'T WAIT TO SEE WHAT YOU COME UP WITH.
!!
?
WHAT'S THE MATTER?
DID YOU SAY "YOU CAN'T WAIT"...?
TWINKLE
TWINKLE
I NEVER KNEW...

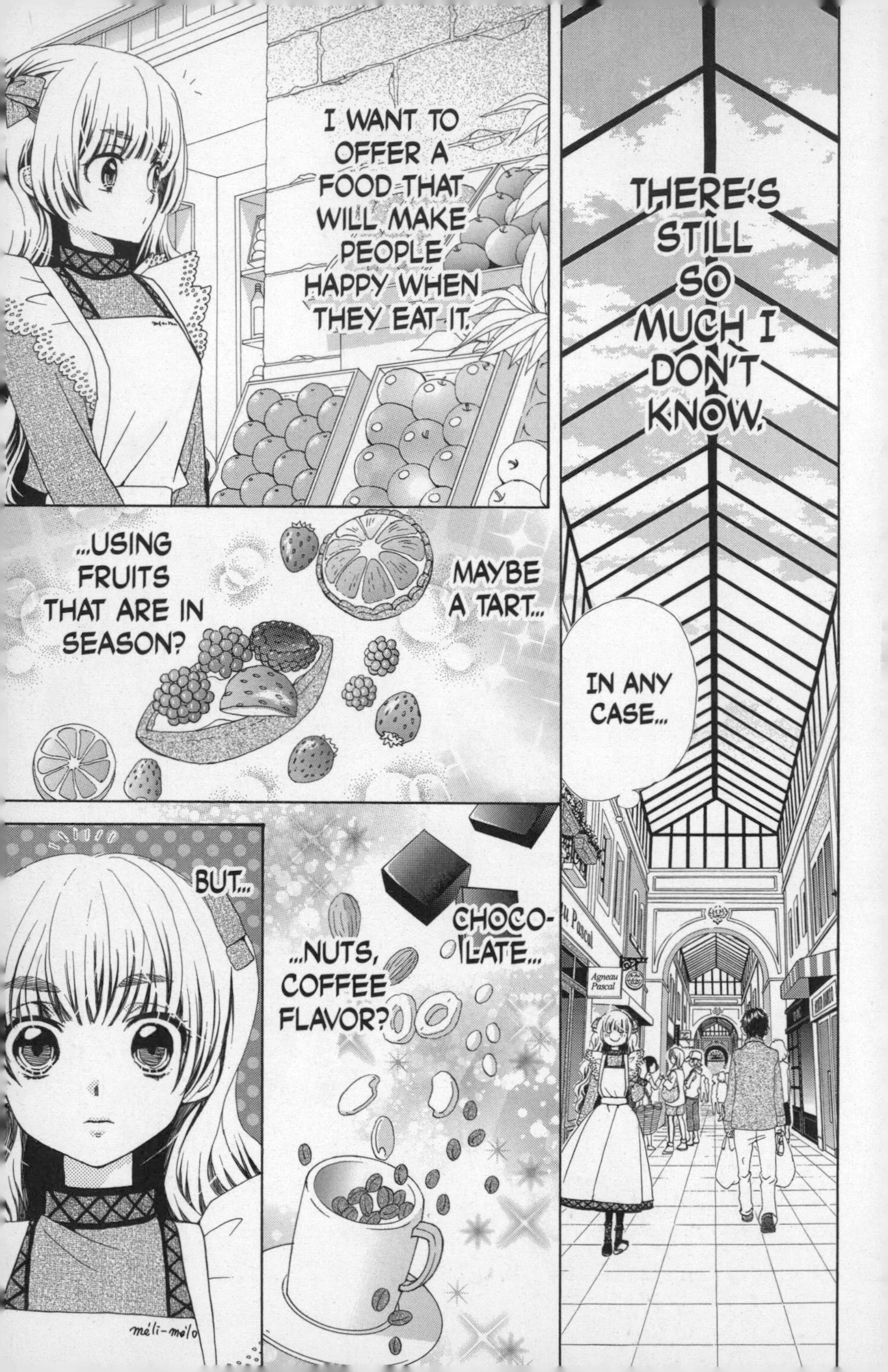
THERE'S STILL SO MUCH I DON'T KNOW.
IN ANY CASE...
Agneau Pascal
I WANT TO OFFER A FOOD THAT WILL MAKE PEOPLE HAPPY WHEN THEY EAT IT.
MAYBE A TART...
...USING FRUITS THAT ARE IN SEASON?
CHOCO-LATE...
...NUTS, COFFEE FLAVOR?
BUT...
méli-mélo

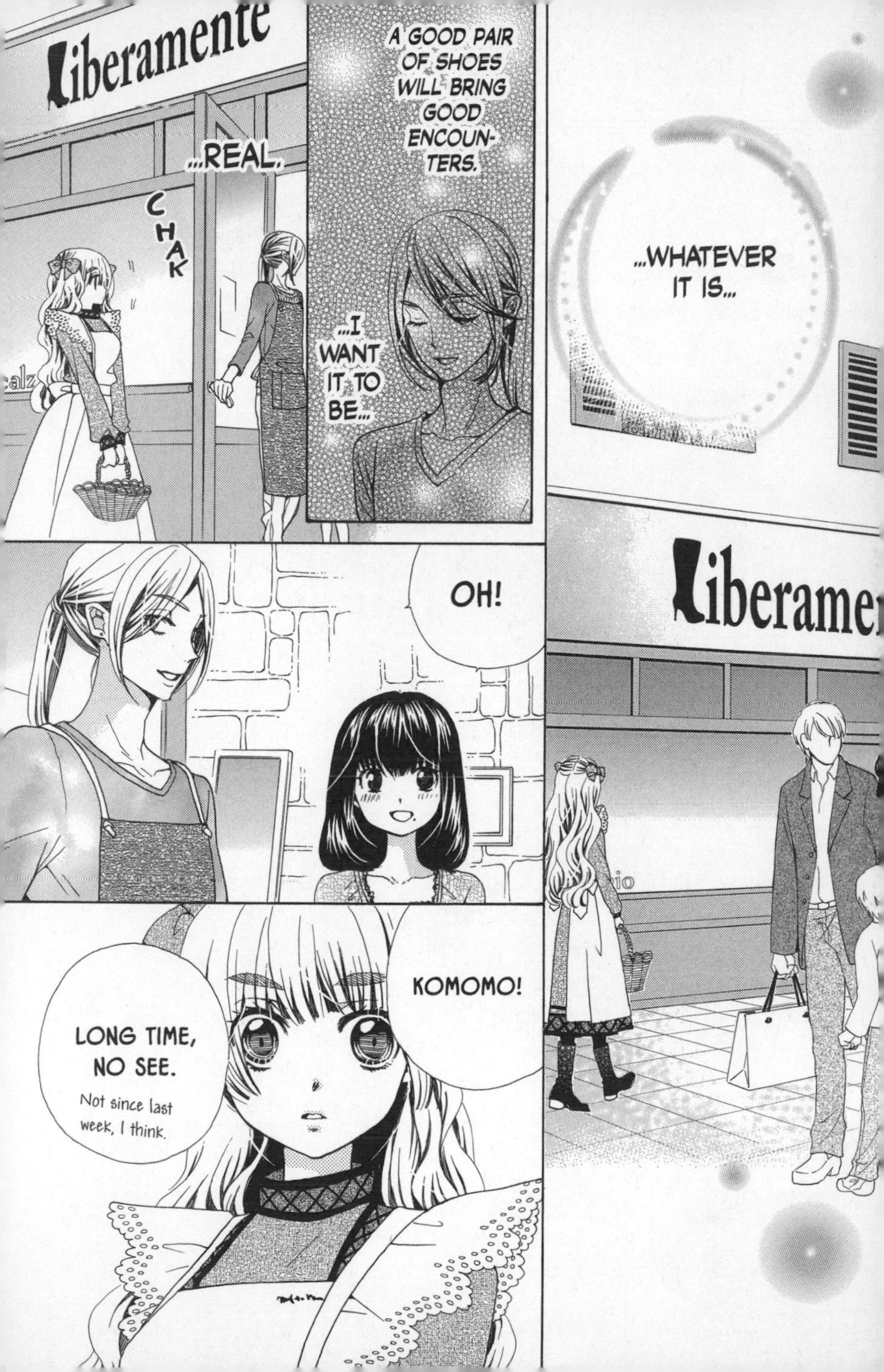
...WHATEVER IT IS...
Liberamen
A GOOD PAIR OF SHOES WILL BRING GOOD ENCOUN-TERS.
...I WANT IT TO BE...
...REAL.
CHAK
Liberamente
OH!
KOMOMO!
LONG TIME, NO SEE.
Not since last week, I think.

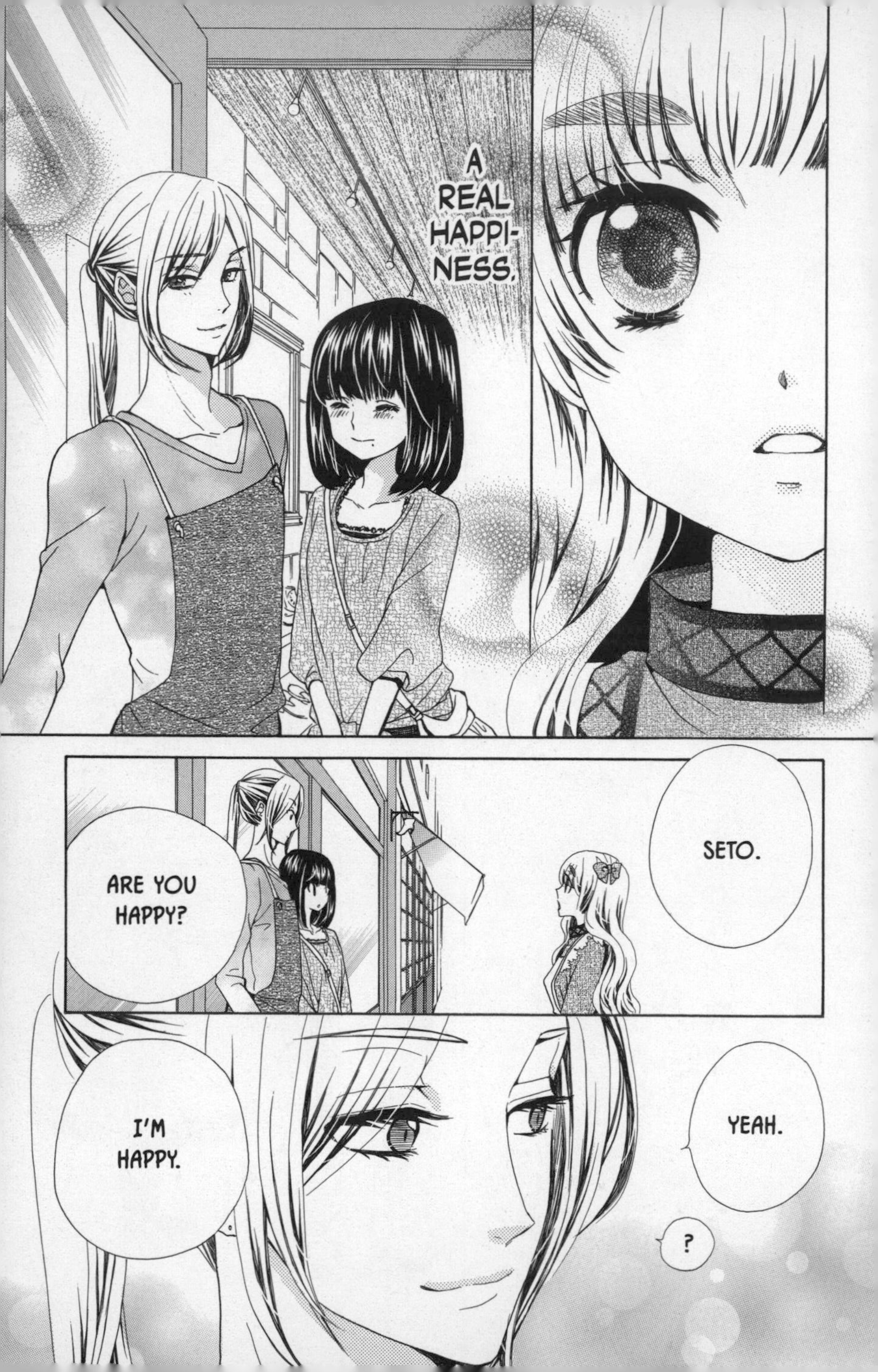
A REAL HAPPI-NESS.
SETO.
ARE YOU HAPPY?
YEAH.
?
I'M HAPPY.

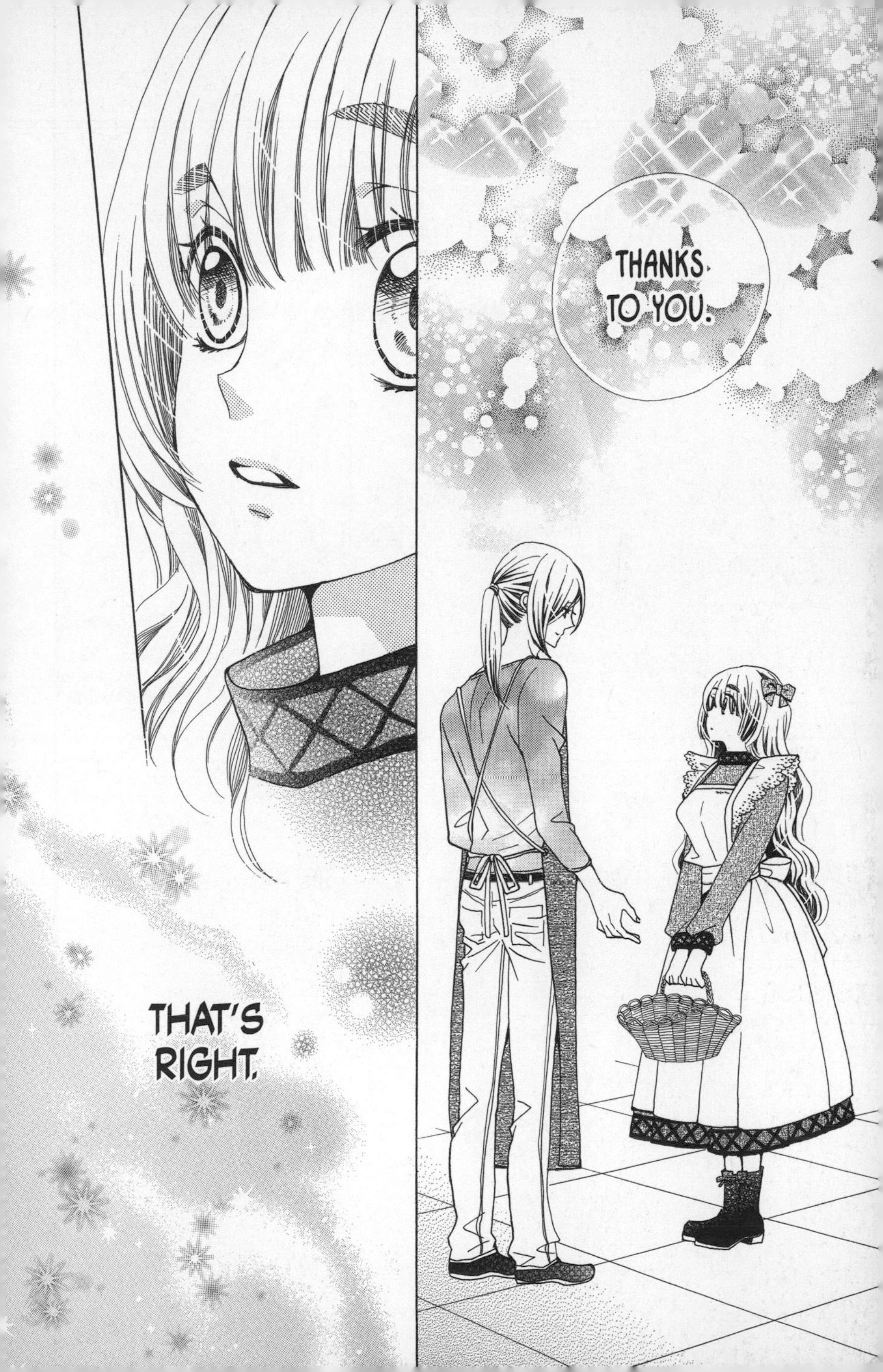
THANKS TO YOU.
THAT'S RIGHT.

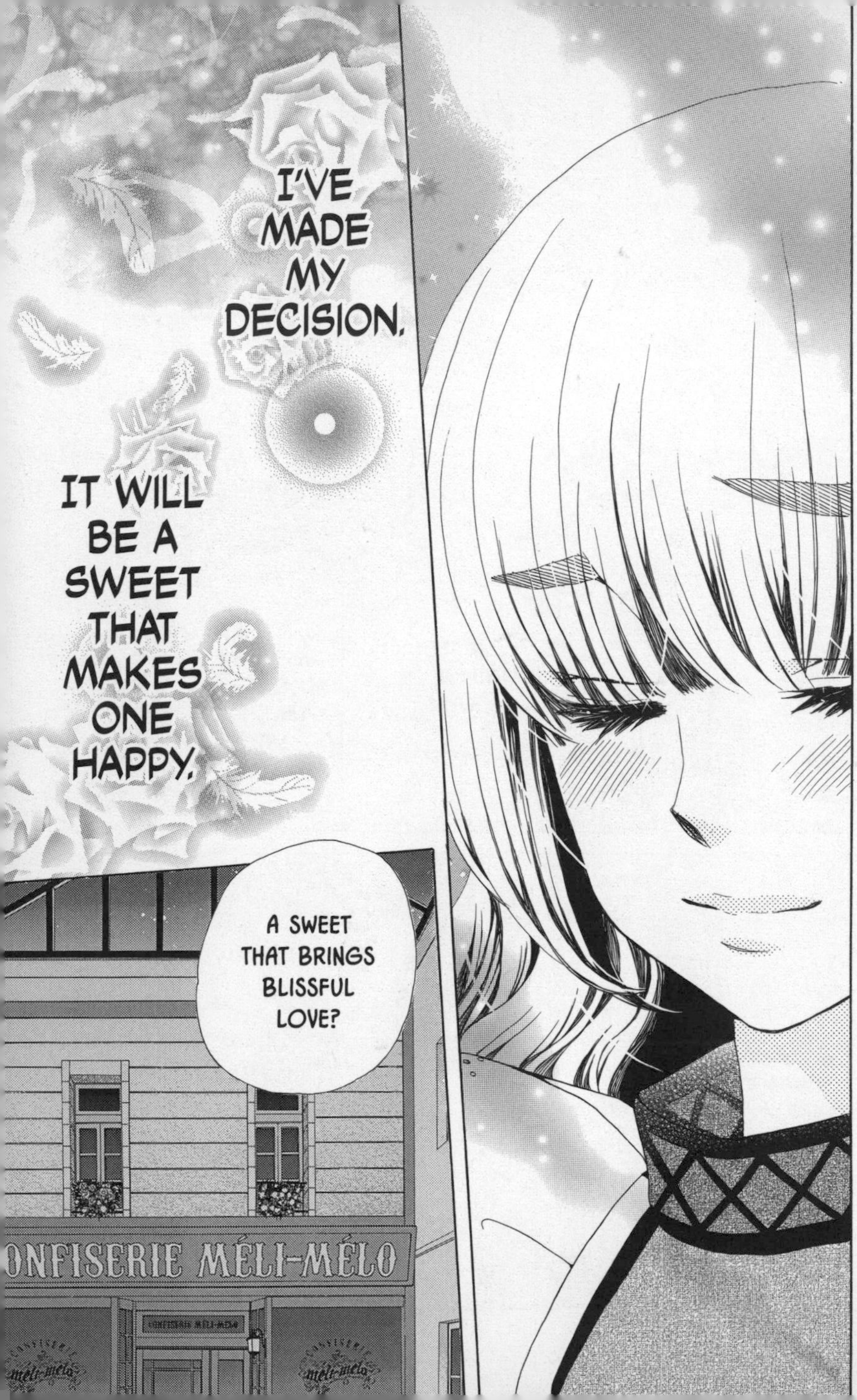
I'VE MADE MY DECISION.
IT WILL BE A SWEET THAT MAKES ONE HAPPY.
A SWEET THAT BRINGS BLISSFUL LOVE?
ONFISERIE MÉLI-MÉLO

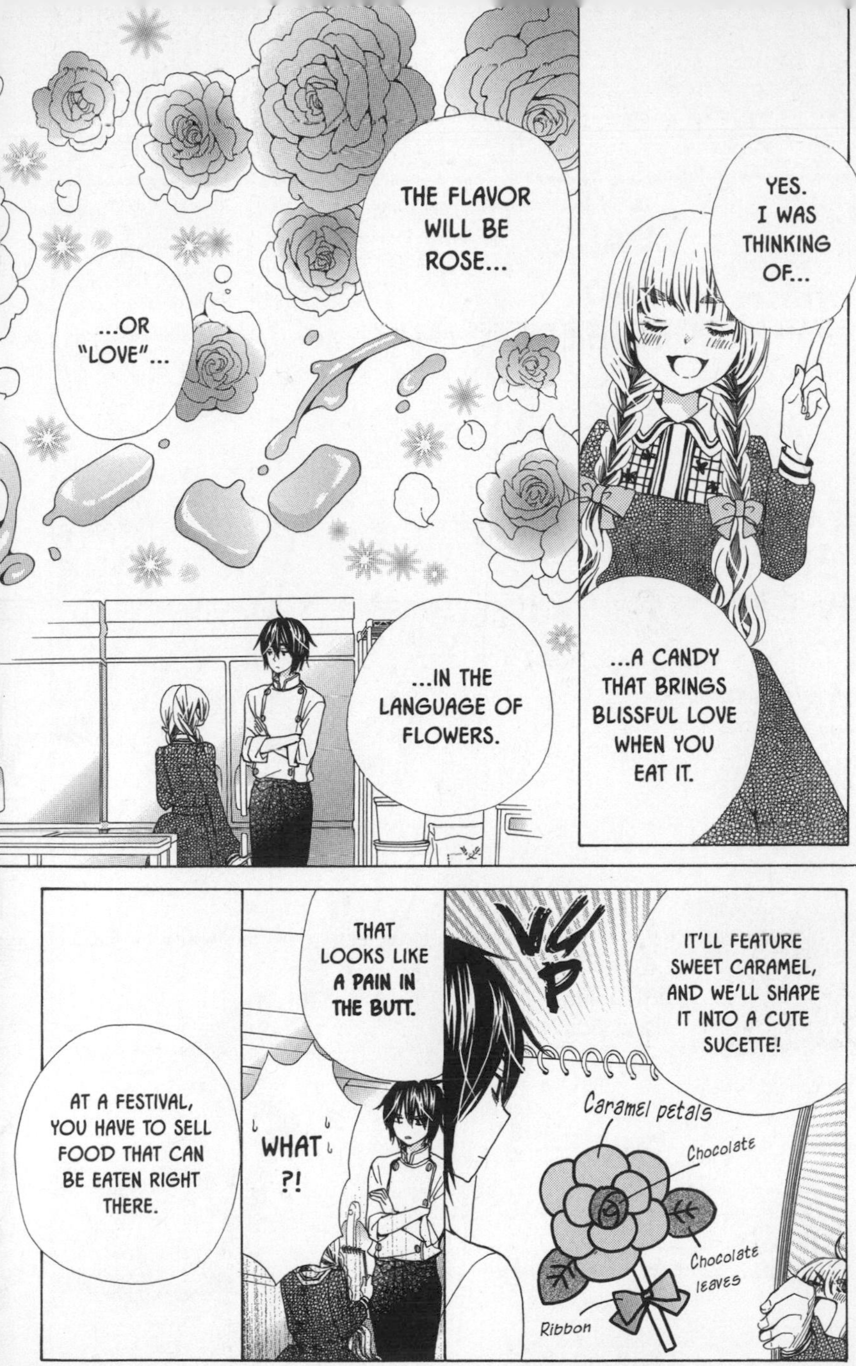
YES. I WAS THINKING OF...
...A CANDY THAT BRINGS BLISSFUL LOVE WHEN YOU EAT IT.
THE FLAVOR WILL BE ROSE...
...OR "LOVE"...
...IN THE LANGUAGE OF FLOWERS.
VUP
IT'LL FEATURE SWEET CARAMEL, AND WE'LL SHAPE IT INTO A CUTE SUCETTE!
Caramel petals
Chocolate
Chocolate leaves
Ribbon
THAT LOOKS LIKE A PAIN IN THE BUTT.
WHAT?!
AT A FESTIVAL, YOU HAVE TO SELL FOOD THAT CAN BE EATEN RIGHT THERE.

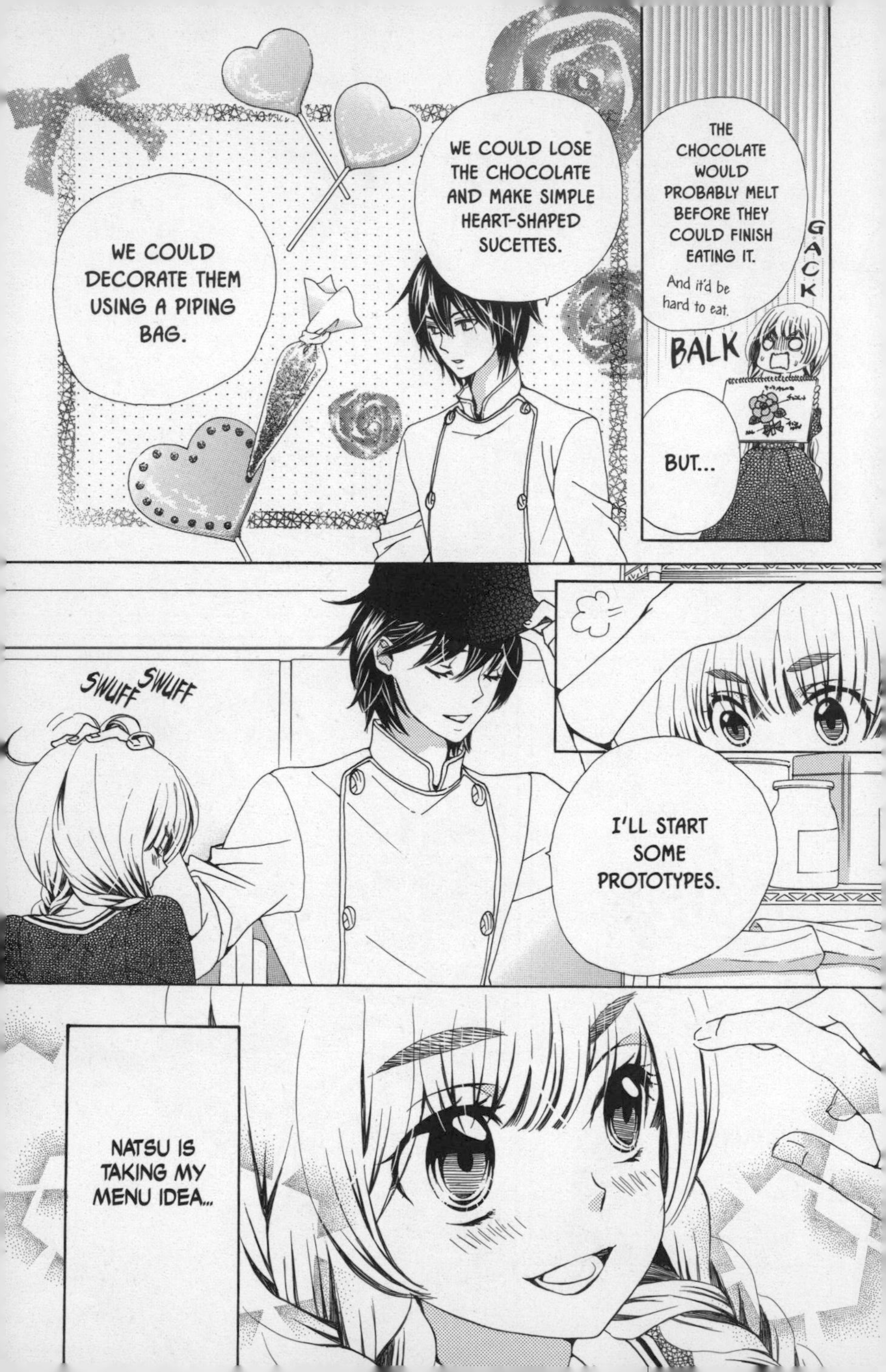
THE CHOCOLATE WOULD PROBABLY MELT BEFORE THEY COULD FINISH EATING IT.
And it'd be hard to eat.
GACK
BALK
BUT...
WE COULD LOSE THE CHOCOLATE AND MAKE SIMPLE HEART-SHAPED SUCETTES.
WE COULD DECORATE THEM USING A PIPING BAG.
I'LL START SOME PROTOTYPES.
SWUFF SWUFF
NATSU IS TAKING MY MENU IDEA...

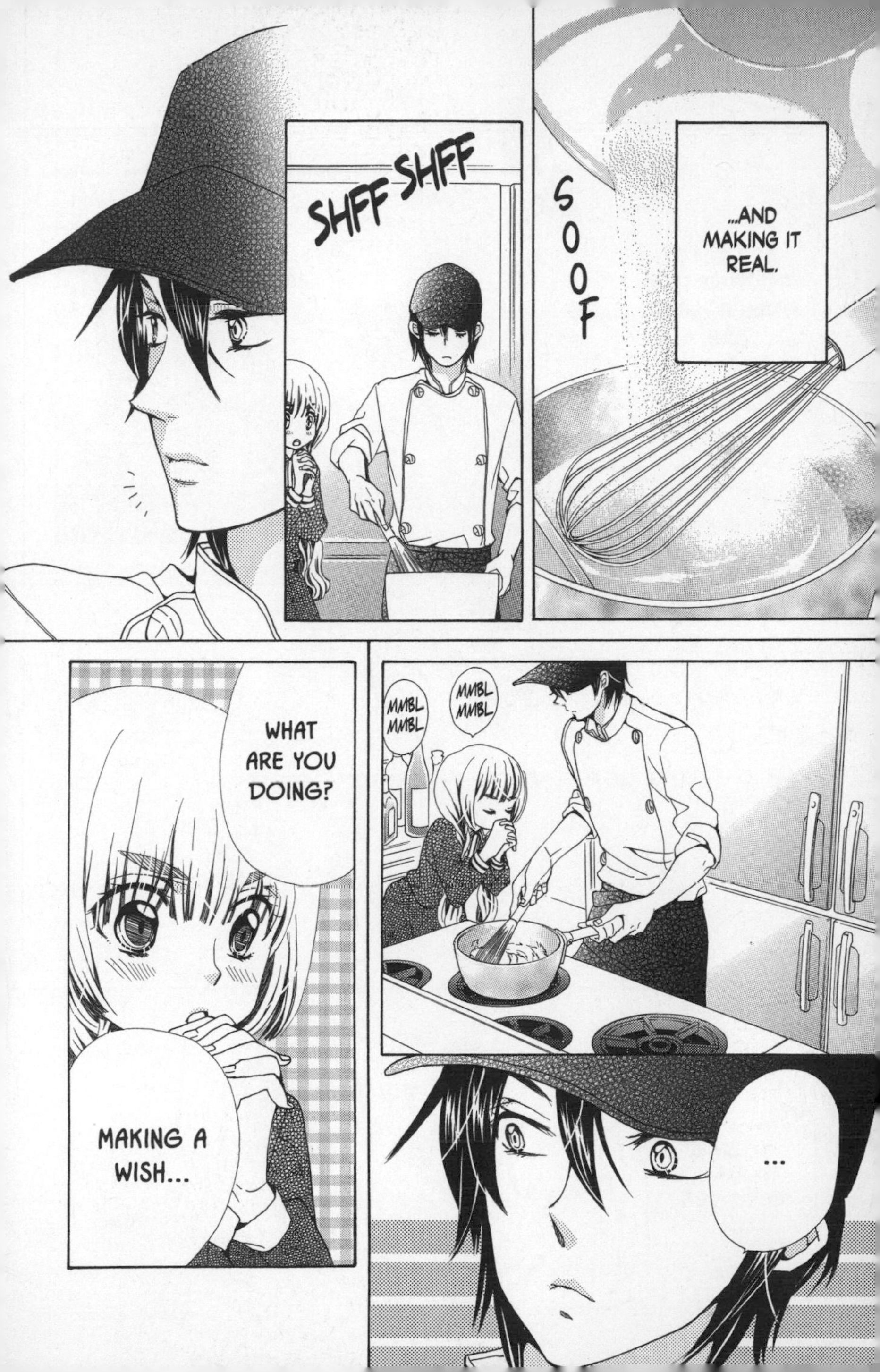
...AND MAKING IT REAL.
SOOF
SHFF SHFF
MMBL MMBL
MMBL MMBL
...
WHAT ARE YOU DOING?
MAKING A WISH...

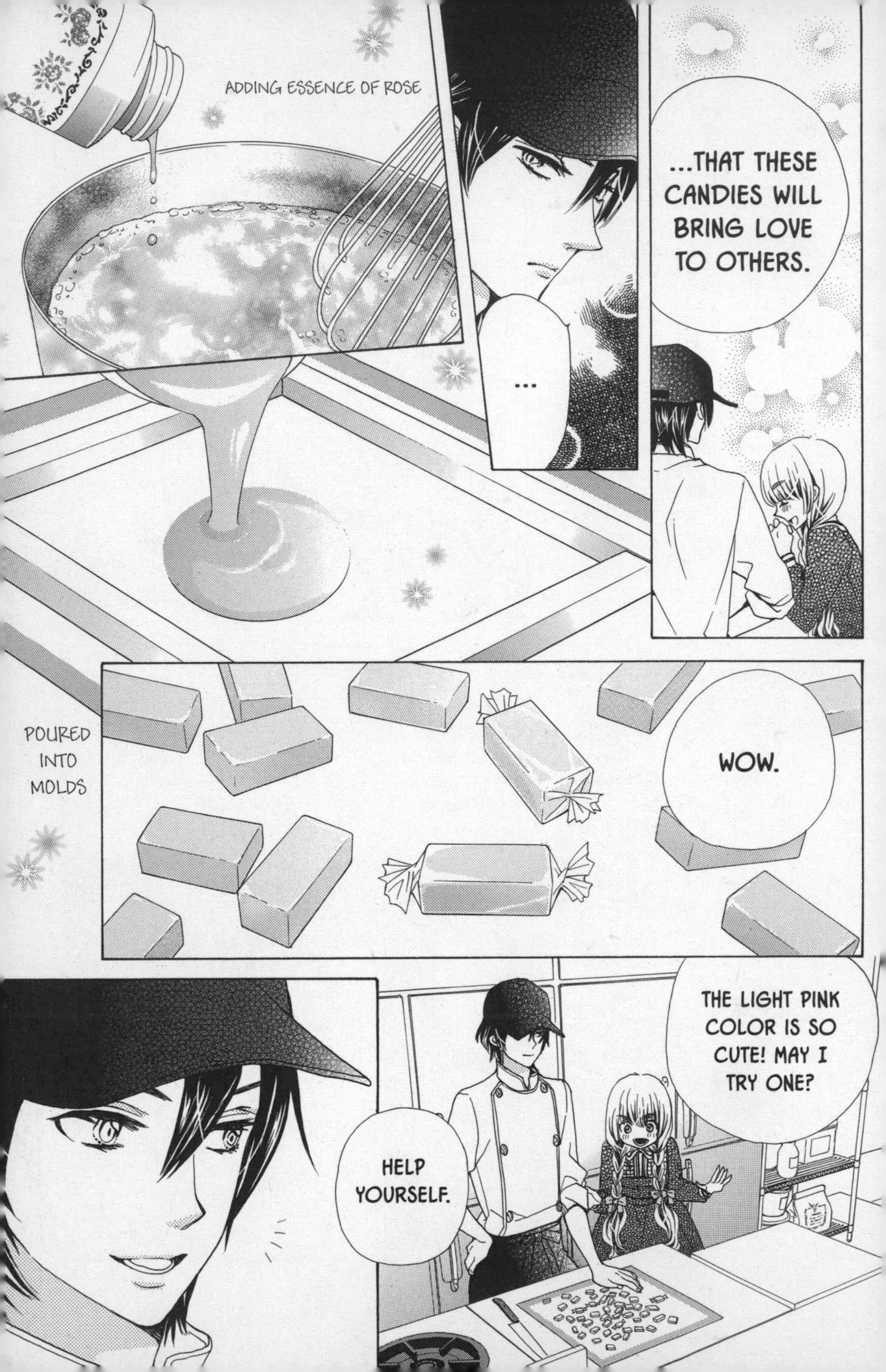
...THAT THESE CANDIES WILL BRING LOVE TO OTHERS.
...
ADDING ESSENCE OF ROSE
WOW.
POURED INTO MOLDS
THE LIGHT PINK COLOR IS SO CUTE! MAY I TRY ONE?
HELP YOURSELF.

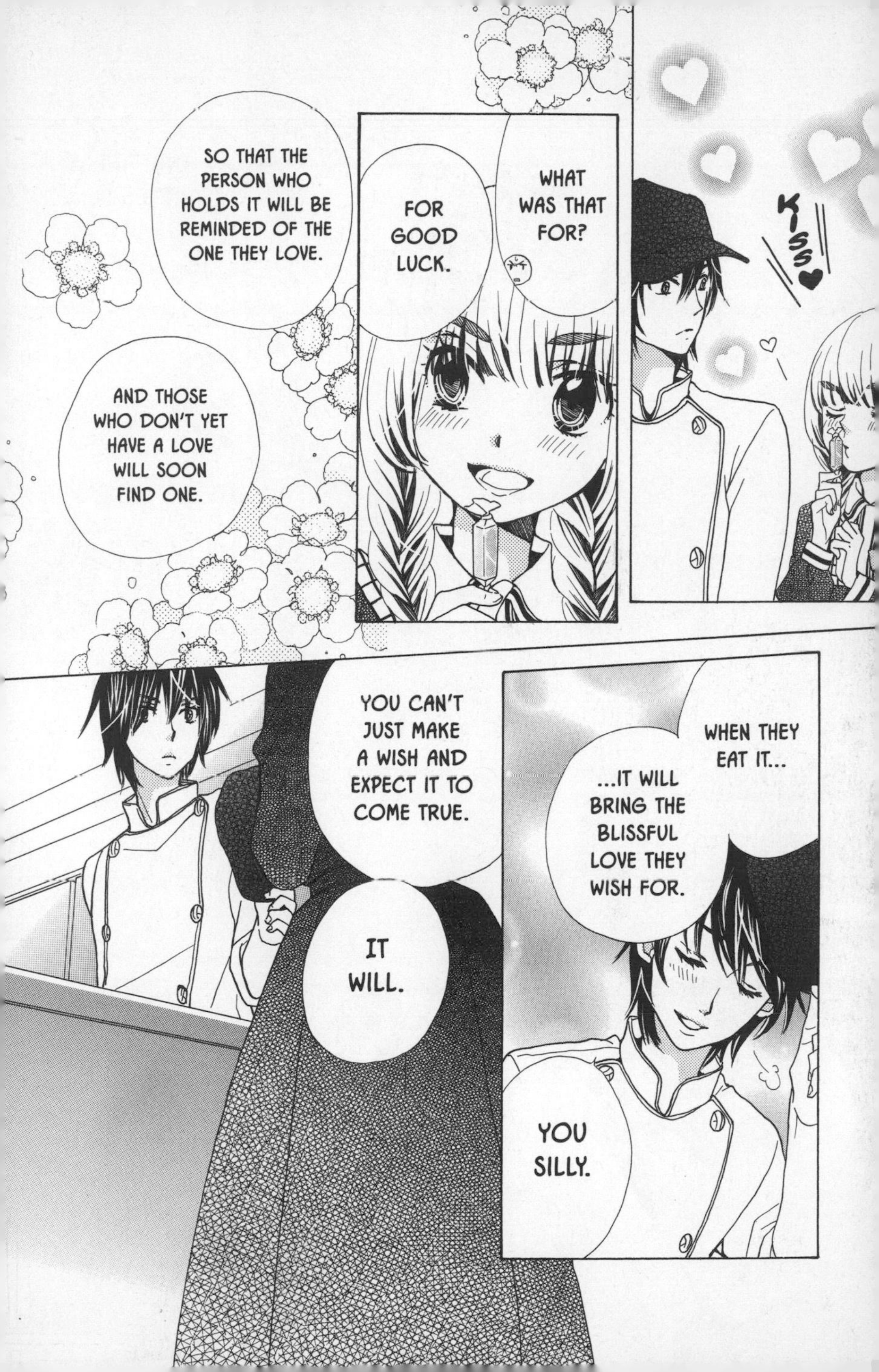
KISS
WHAT WAS THAT FOR?
FOR GOOD LUCK.
SO THAT THE PERSON WHO HOLDS IT WILL BE REMINDED OF THE ONE THEY LOVE.
AND THOSE WHO DON'T YET HAVE A LOVE WILL SOON FIND ONE.
WHEN THEY EAT IT...
...IT WILL BRING THE BLISSFUL LOVE THEY WISH FOR.
YOU SILLY.
YOU CAN'T JUST MAKE A WISH AND EXPECT IT TO COME TRUE.
IT WILL.

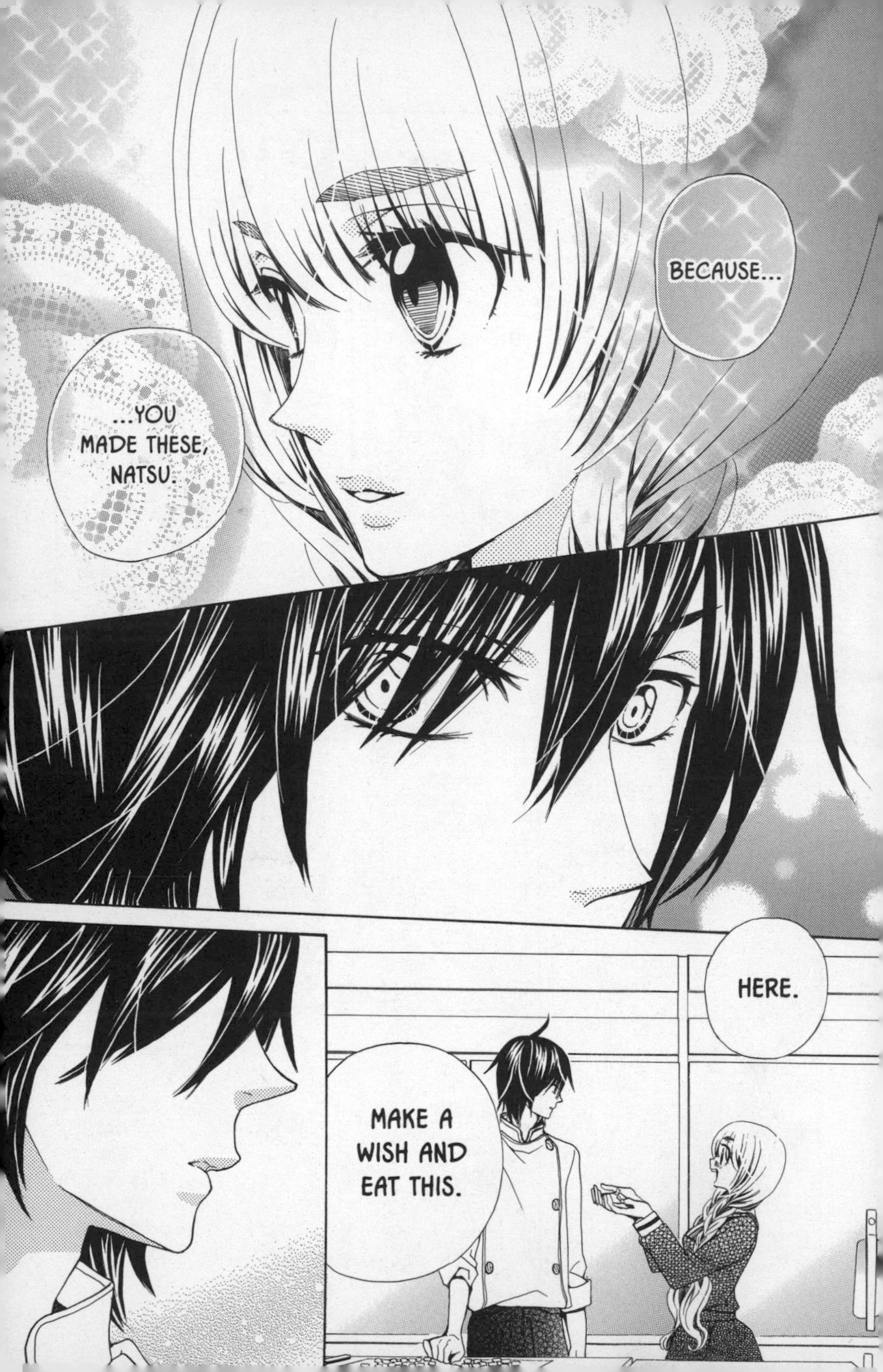
BECAUSE...
...YOU MADE THESE, NATSU.
HERE.
MAKE A WISH AND EAT THIS.

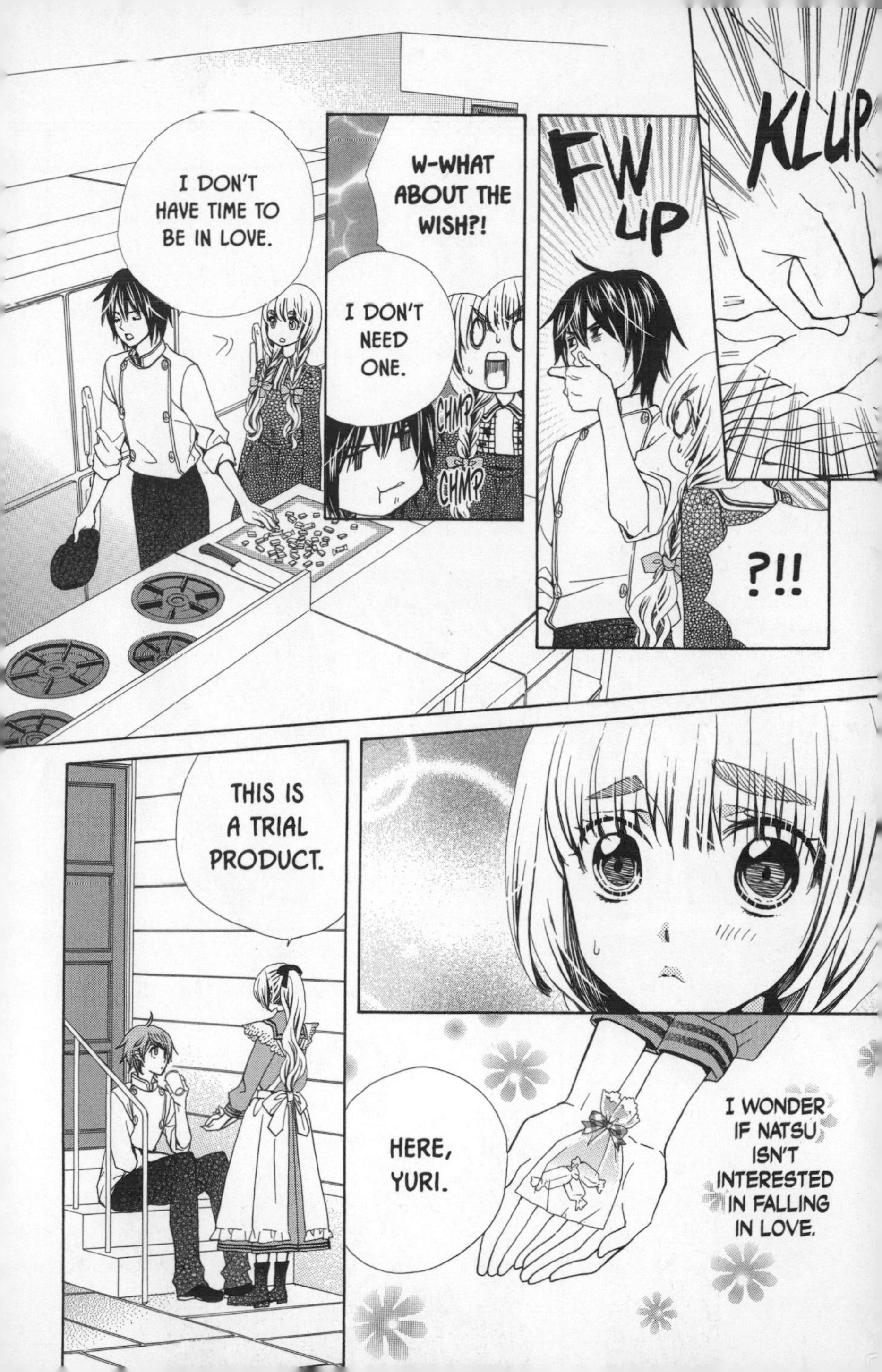
I DON'T HAVE TIME TO BE IN LOVE.
W-WHAT ABOUT THE WISH?!
I DON'T NEED ONE.
CHMP
CHMP
FW UP
?!!
KLUP
THIS IS A TRIAL PRODUCT.
HERE, YURI.
I WONDER IF NATSU ISN'T INTERESTED IN FALLING IN LOVE.

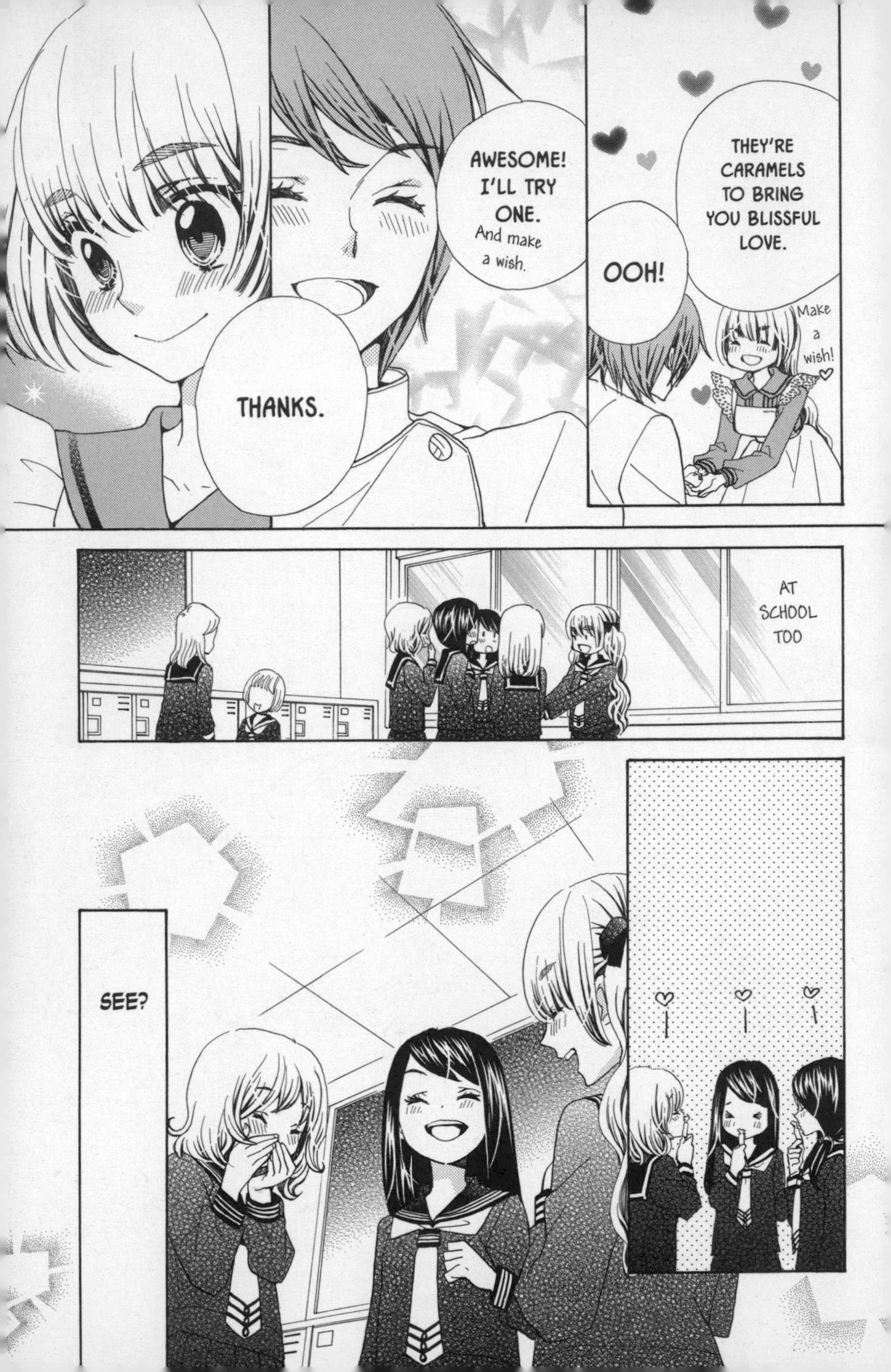
THEY'RE CARAMELS TO BRING YOU BLISSFUL LOVE.
OOH!
Make a wish!
AWESOME! I'LL TRY ONE.
And make a wish.
THANKS.
AT SCHOOL TOO
SEE?

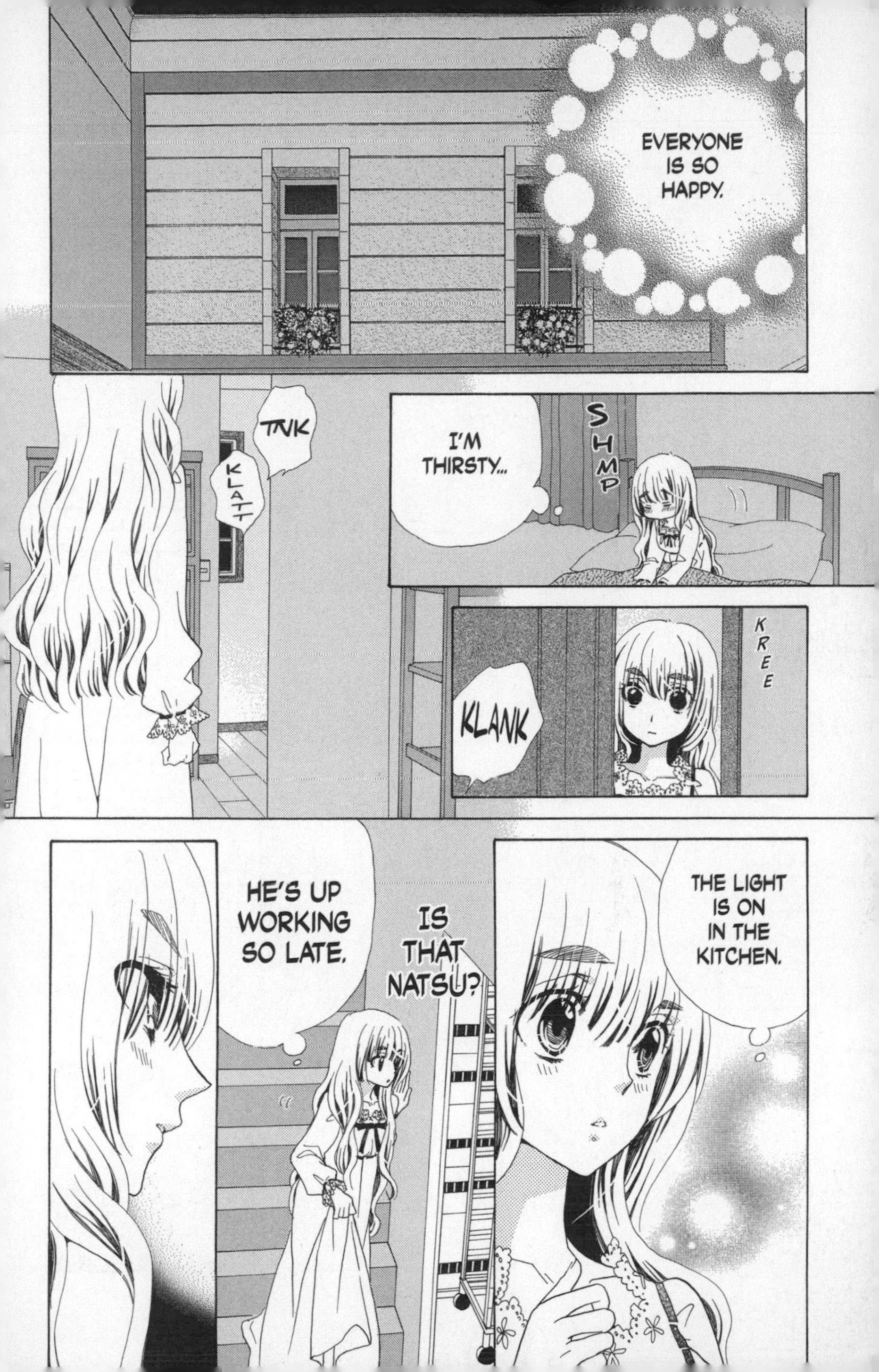
EVERYONE IS SO HAPPY.
I'M THIRSTY...
SHMP
KREE
KLANK
TNK
KLATT
THE LIGHT IS ON IN THE KITCHEN.
IS THAT NATSU?
HE'S UP WORKING SO LATE.

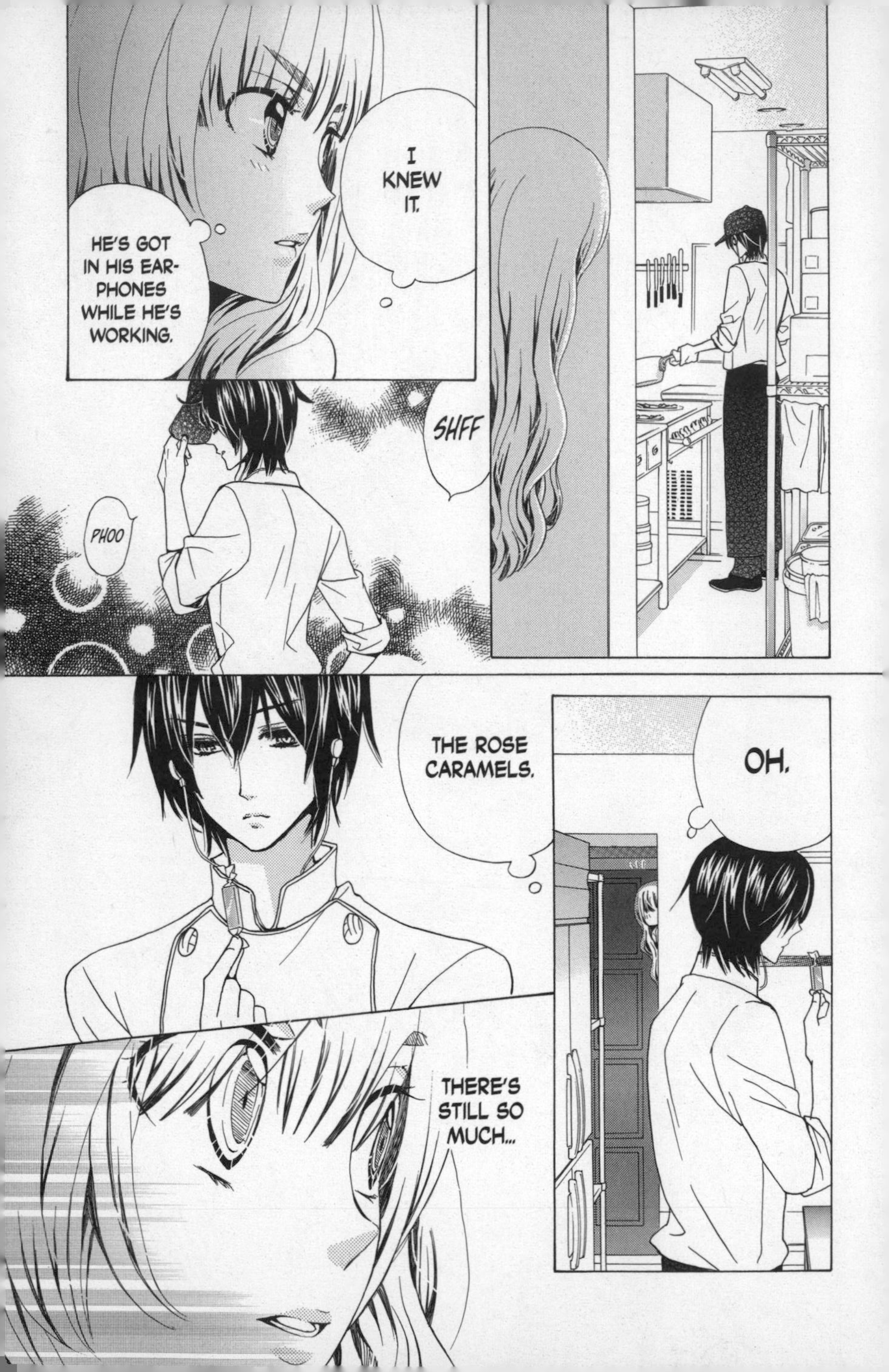
I KNEW IT.
HE'S GOT IN HIS EAR-PHONES WHILE HE'S WORKING.
SHFF
PHOO
OH.
THE ROSE CARAMELS.
THERE'S STILL SO MUCH...

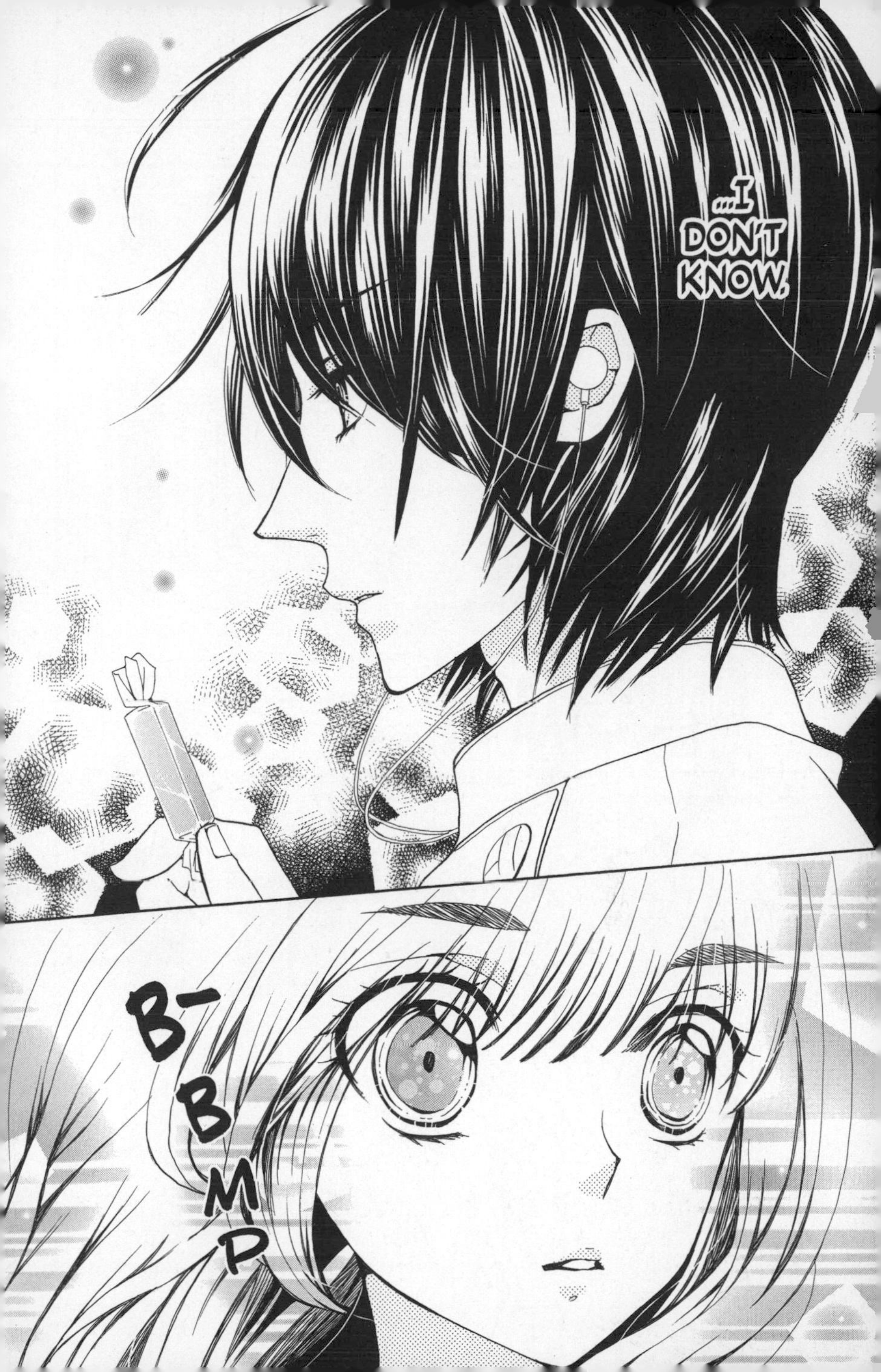
...I DON'T KNOW.
B-BMP

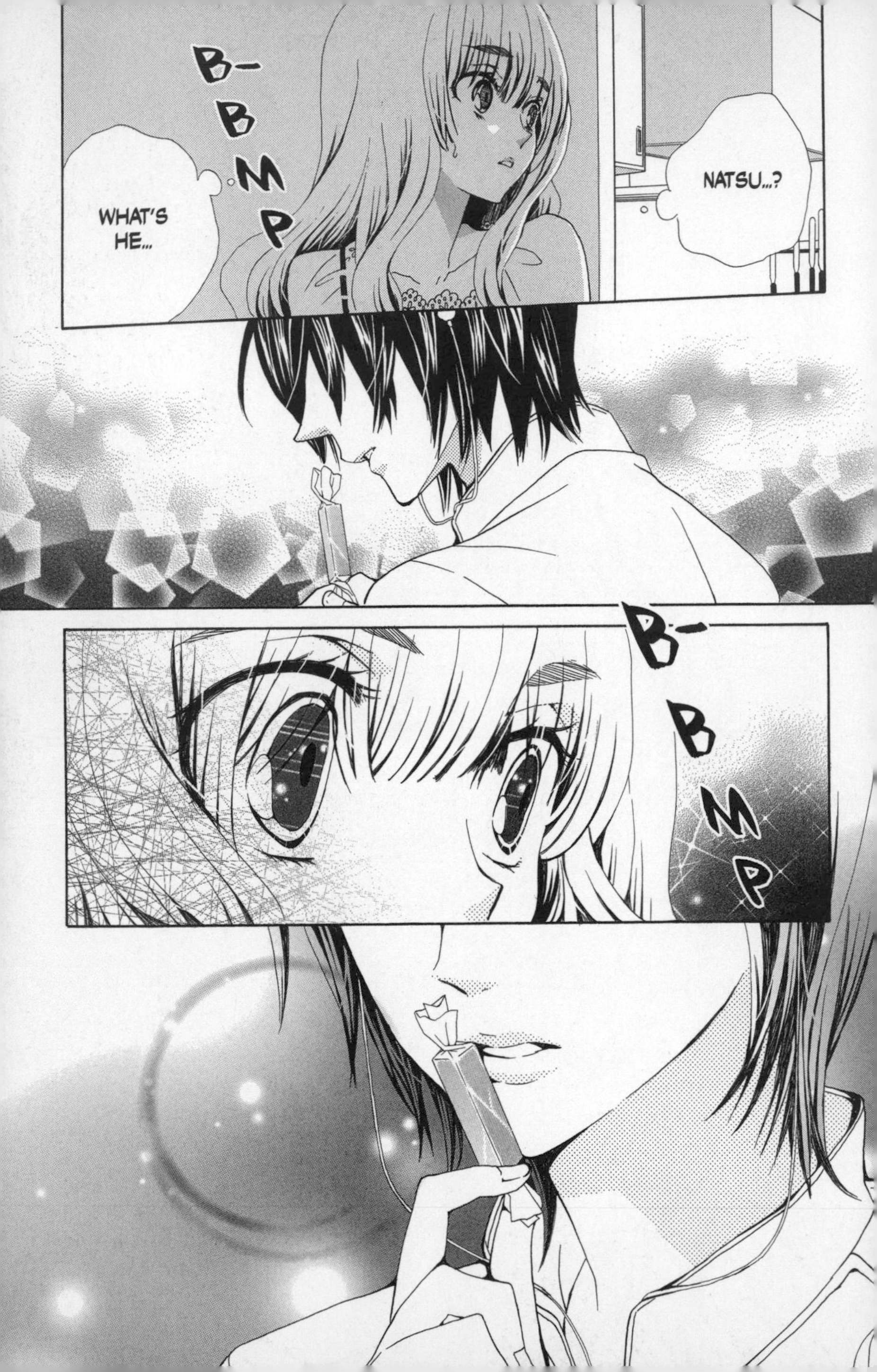
NATSU...?
B-BMP
WHAT'S HE...
B-BMP

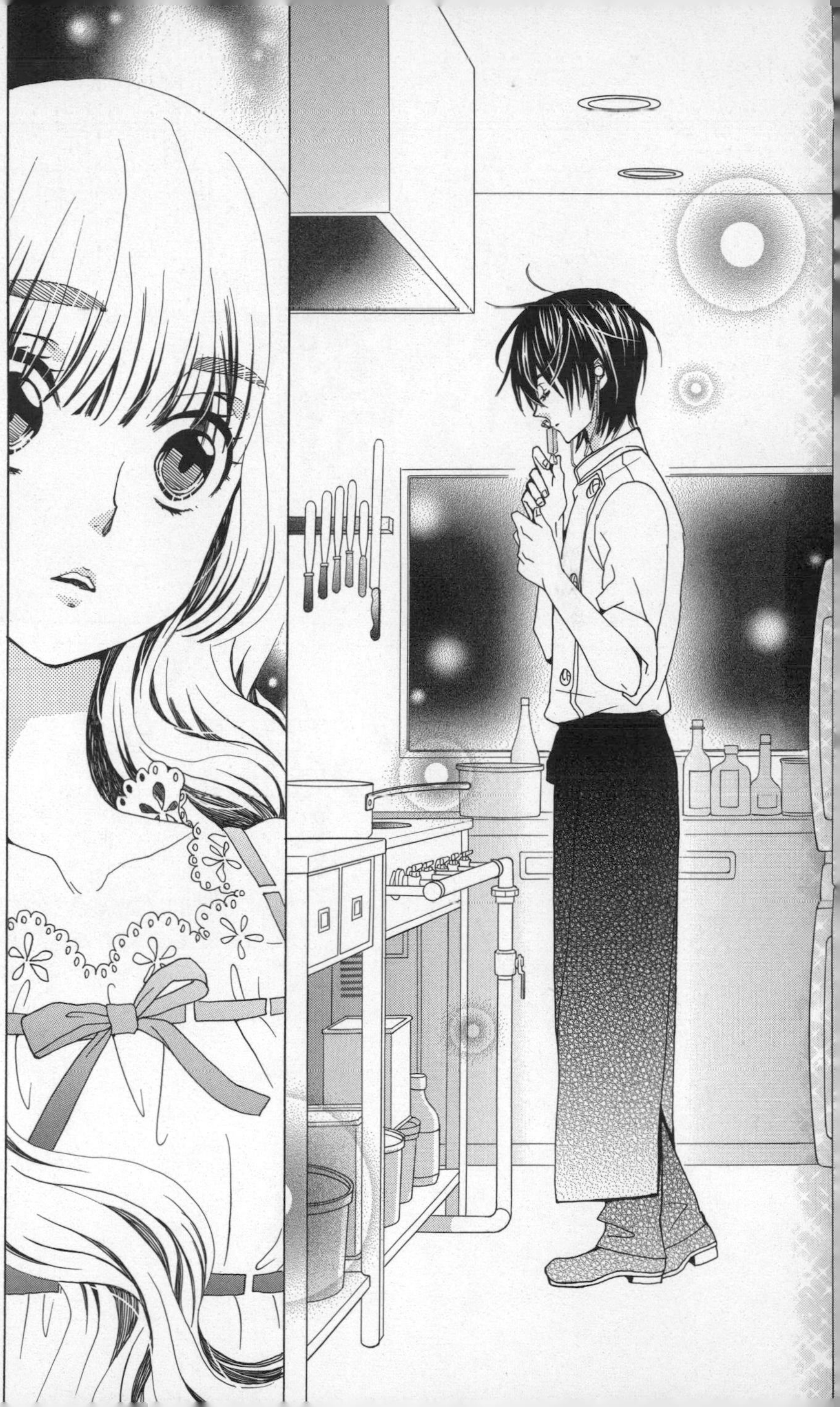

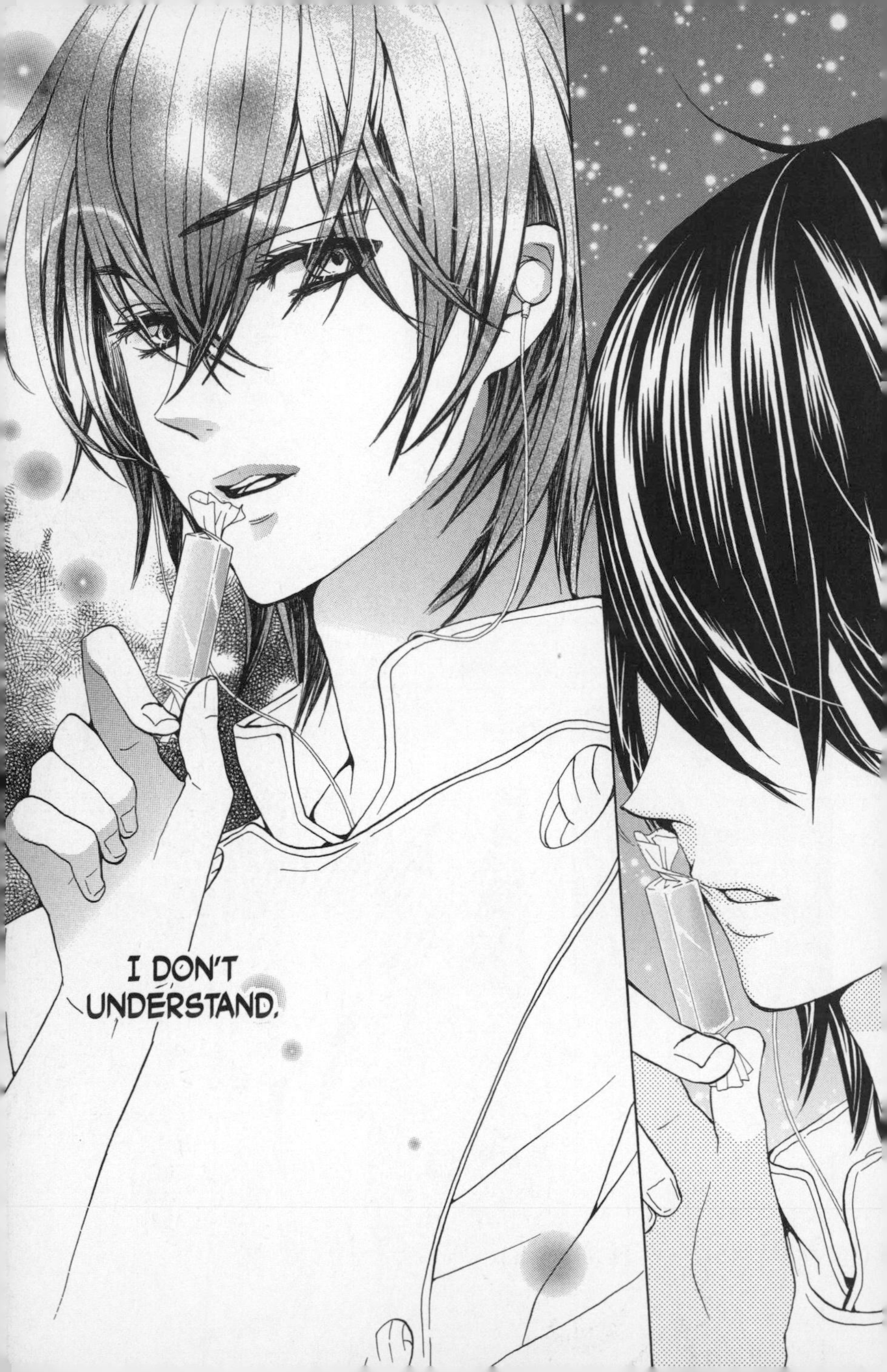
I DON'T UNDERSTAND.

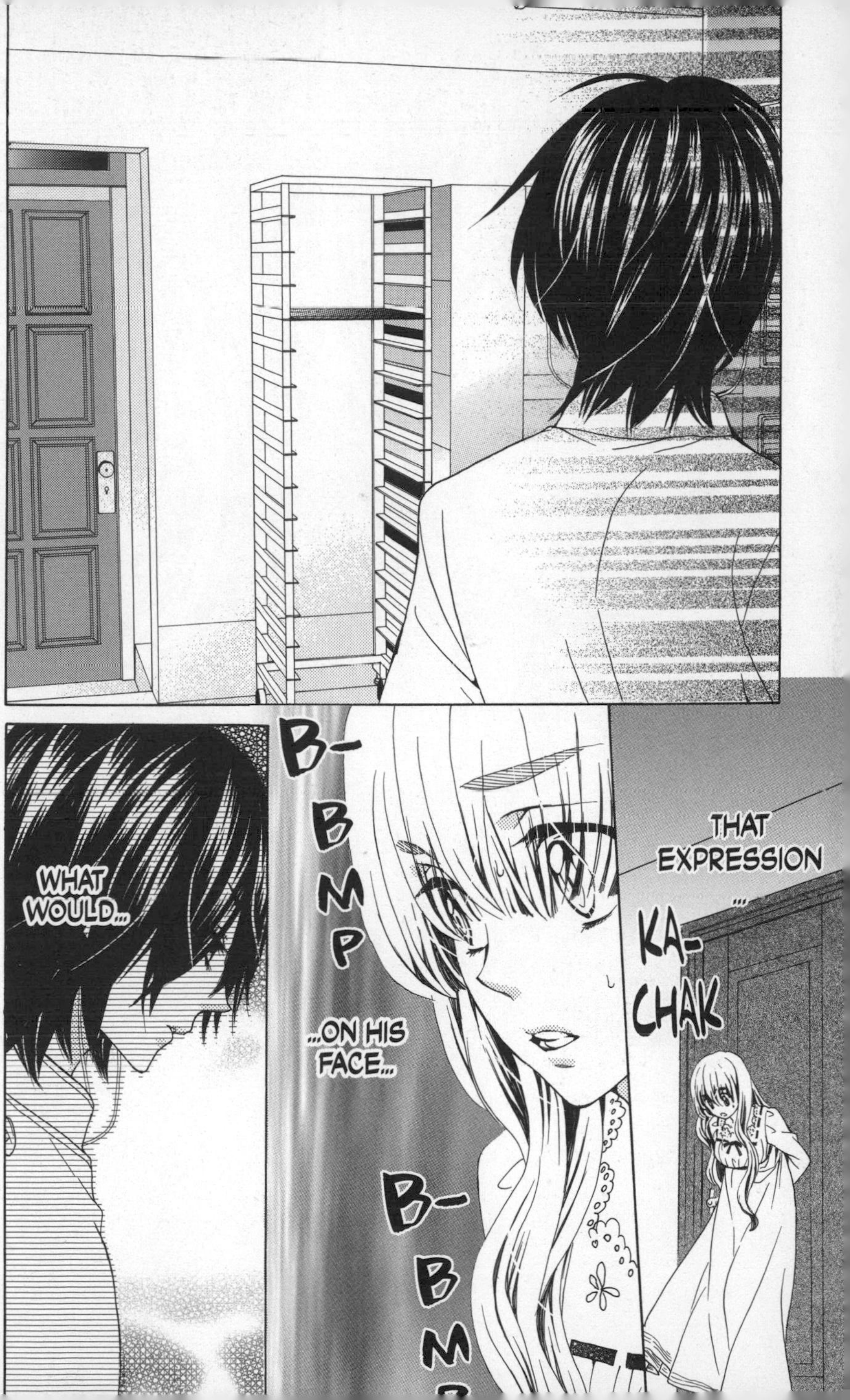
THAT EXPRESSION
...
KA-CHAK
B-BMP
...ON HIS FACE...
B-BM
WHAT WOULD...

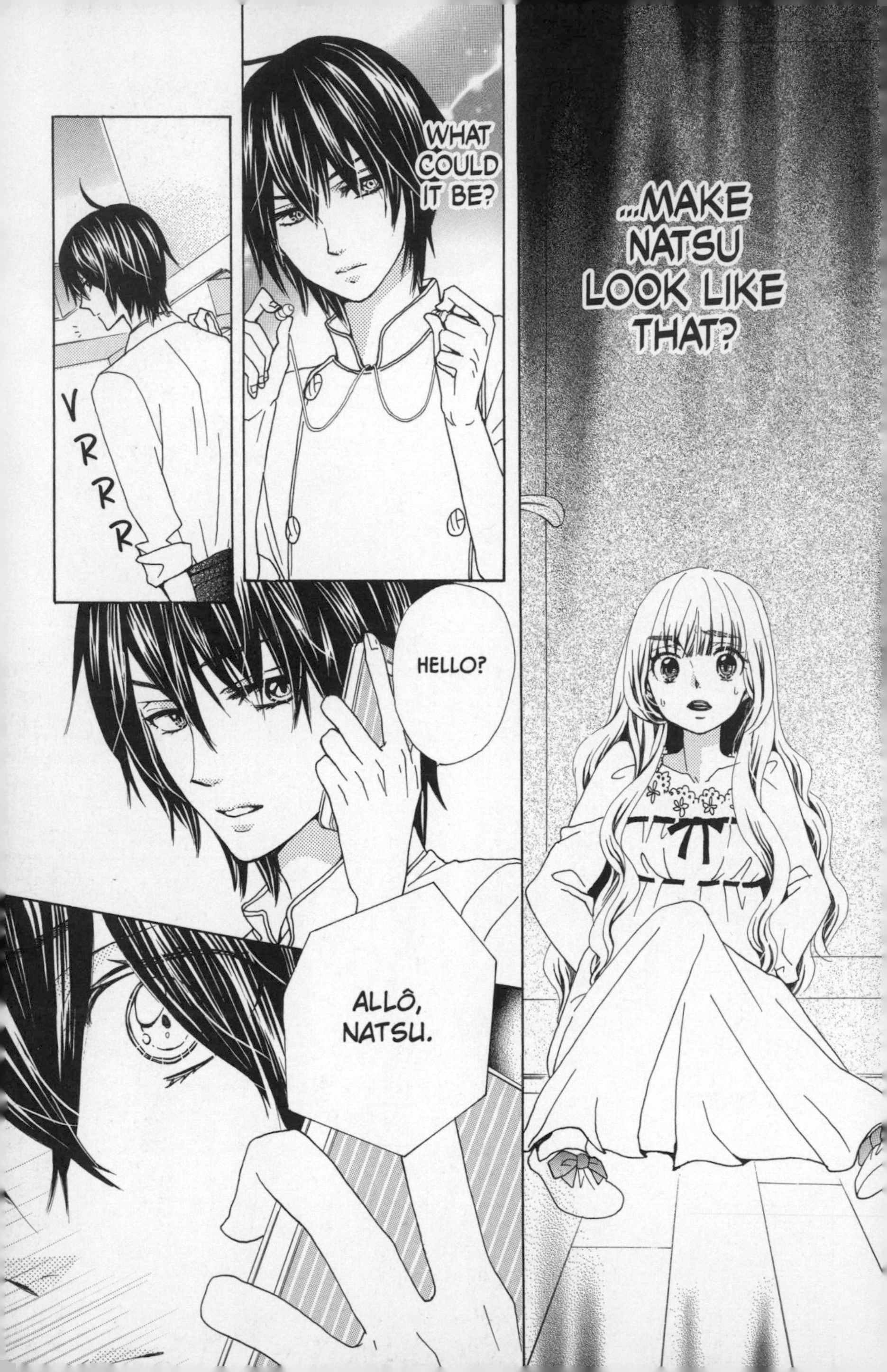
...MAKE NATSU LOOK LIKE THAT?
WHAT COULD IT BE?
VRRRR
HELLO?
ALLÔ, NATSU.

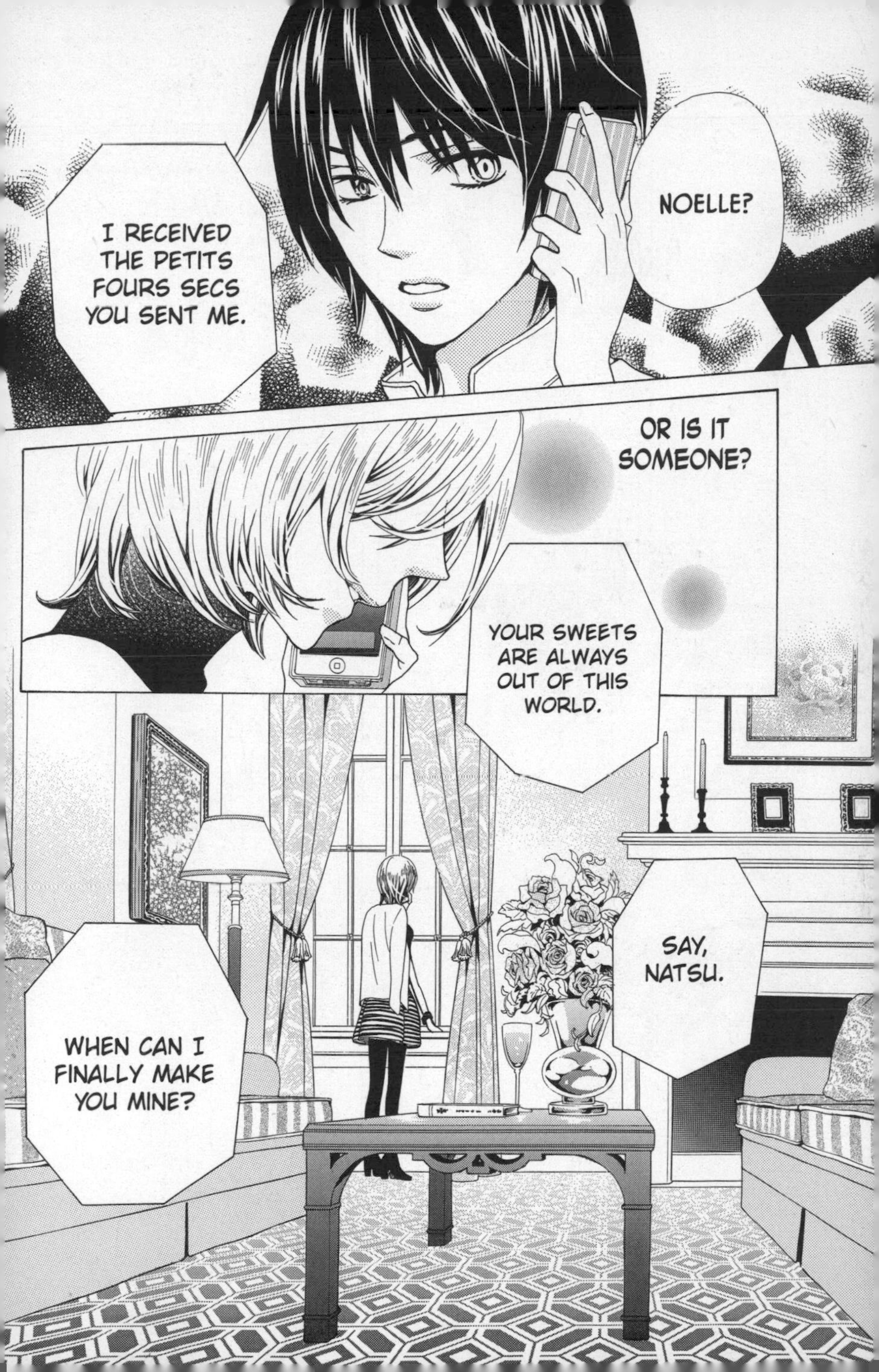
NOELLE?
I RECEIVED THE PETITS FOURS SECS YOU SENT ME.
OR IS IT SOMEONE?
YOUR SWEETS ARE ALWAYS OUT OF THIS WORLD.
SAY, NATSU.
WHEN CAN I FINALLY MAKE YOU MINE?

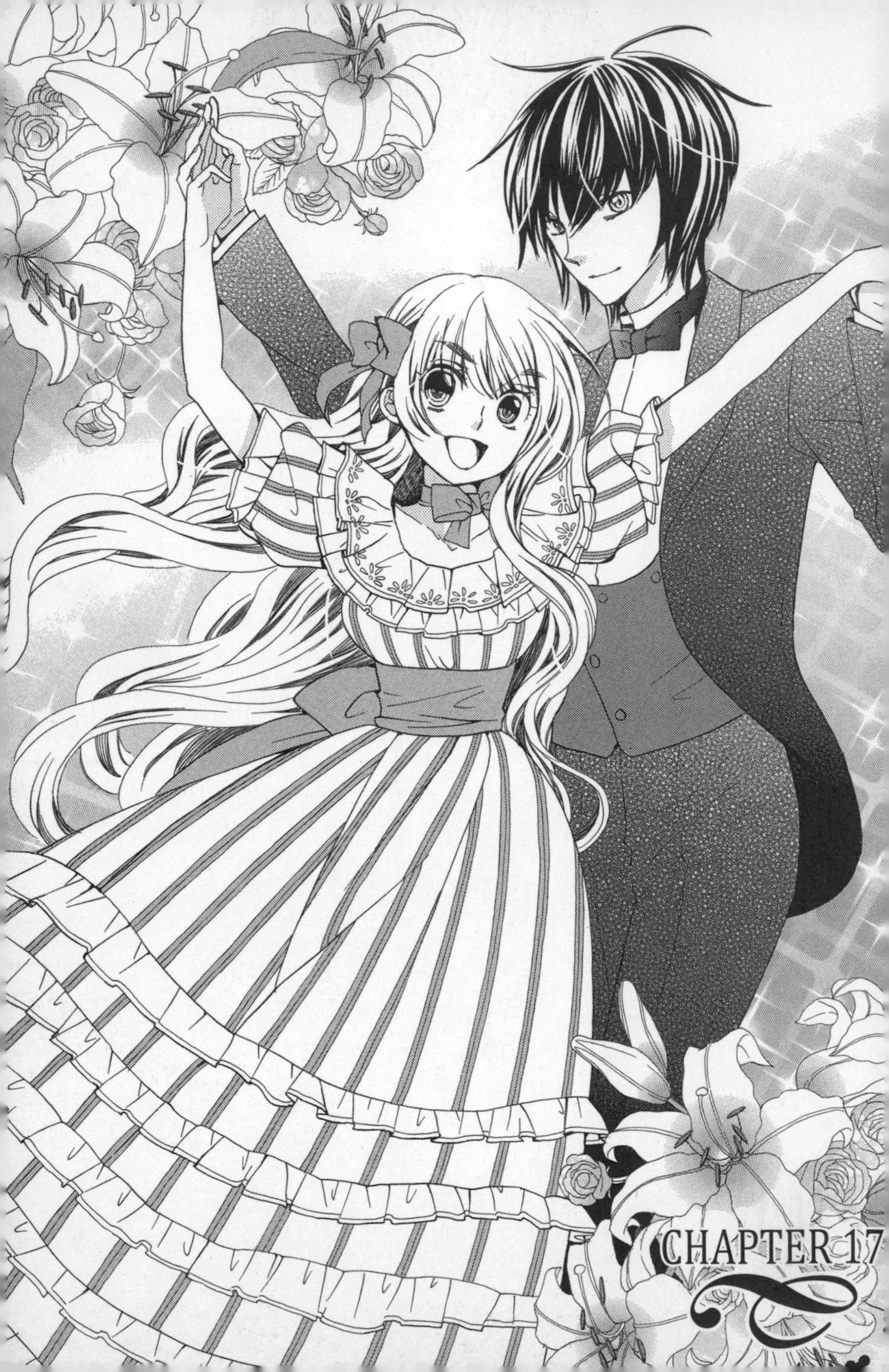
CHAPTER 17

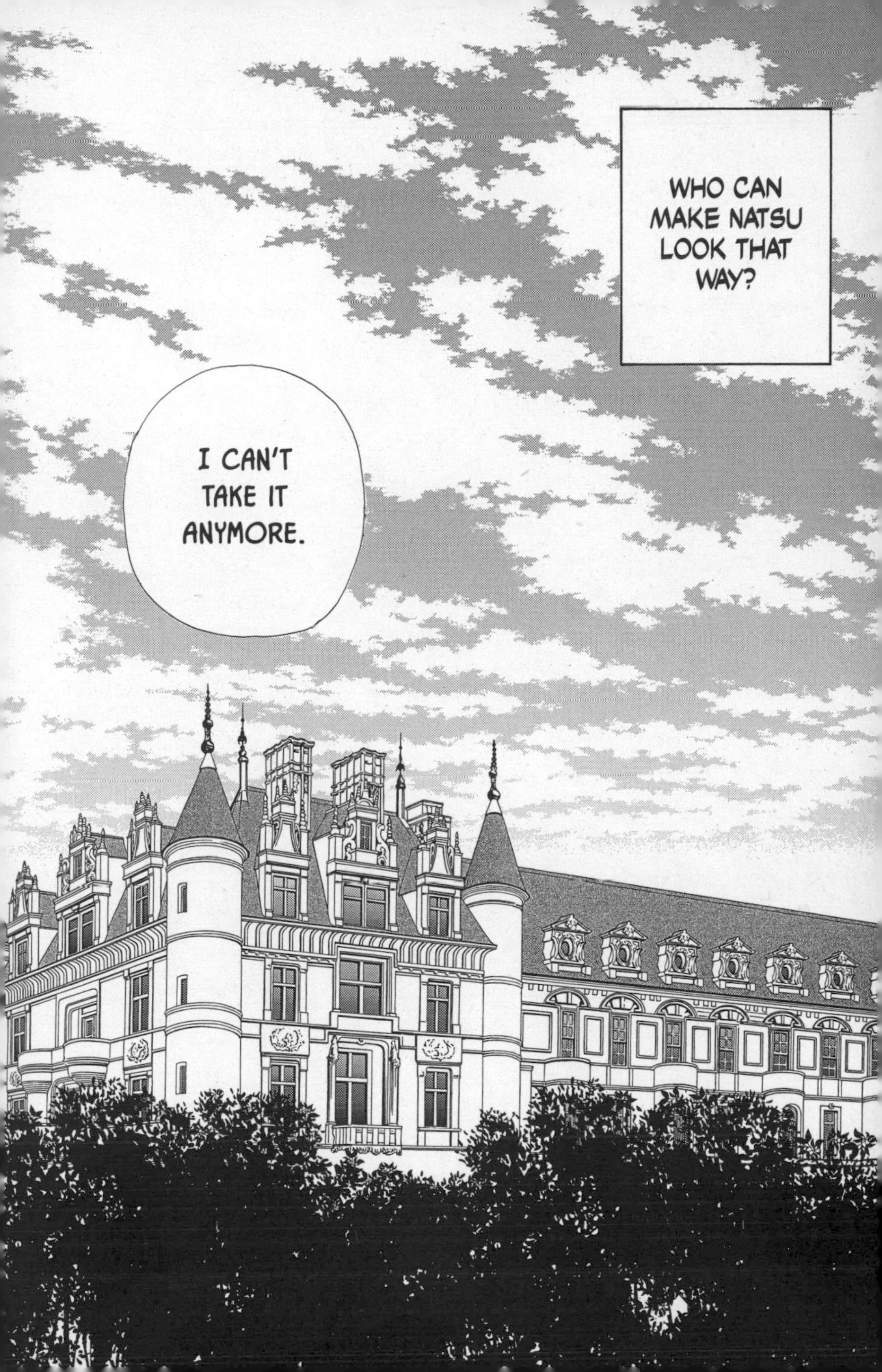
WHO CAN MAKE NATSU LOOK THAT WAY?
I CAN'T TAKE IT ANYMORE.

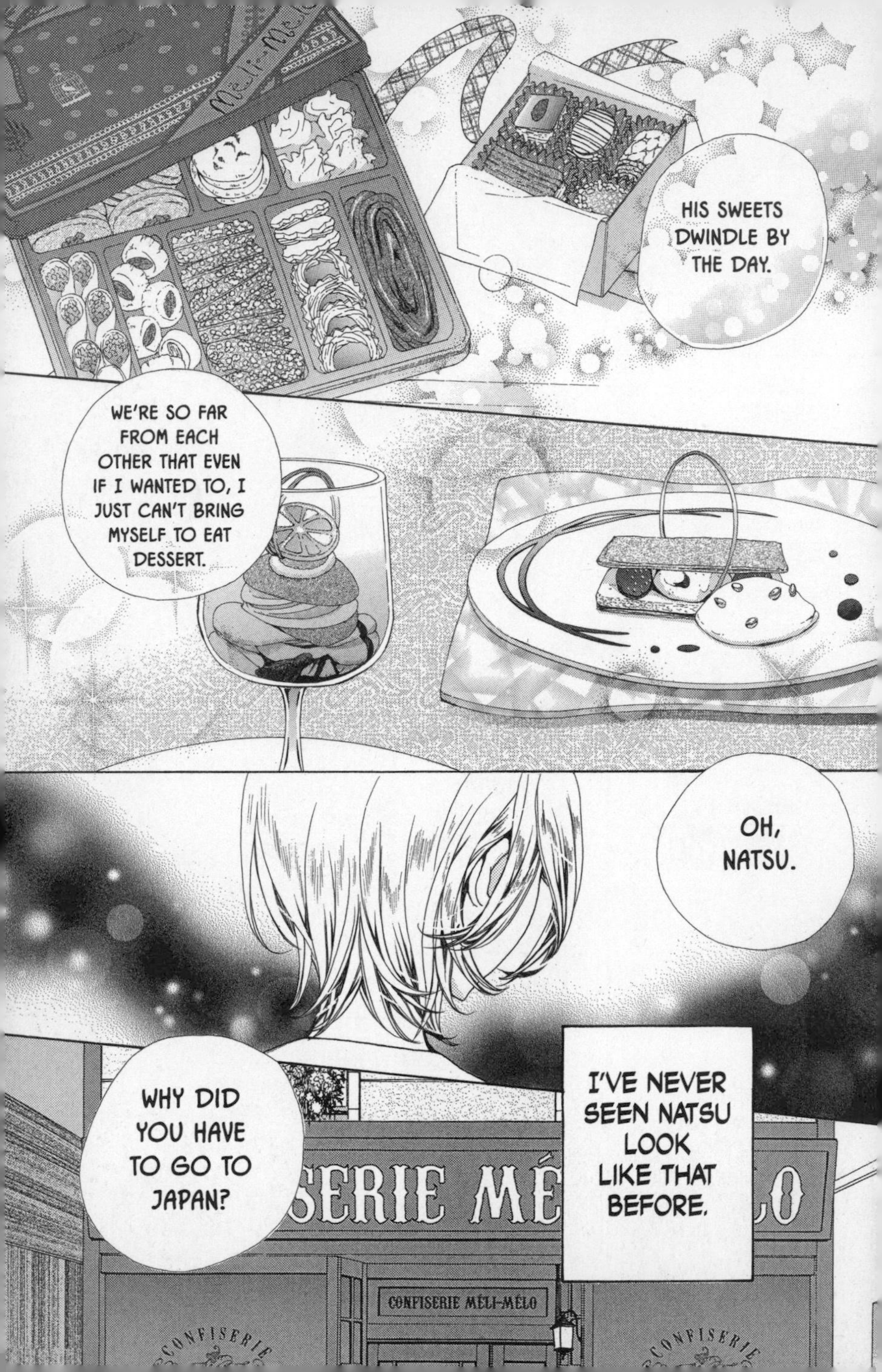
HIS SWEETS DWINDLE BY THE DAY.
WE'RE SO FAR FROM EACH OTHER THAT EVEN IF I WANTED TO, I JUST CAN'T BRING MYSELF TO EAT DESSERT.
OH, NATSU.
I'VE NEVER SEEN NATSU LOOK LIKE THAT BEFORE.
WHY DID YOU HAVE TO GO TO JAPAN?
CONFISERIE MÉLI-MÉLO

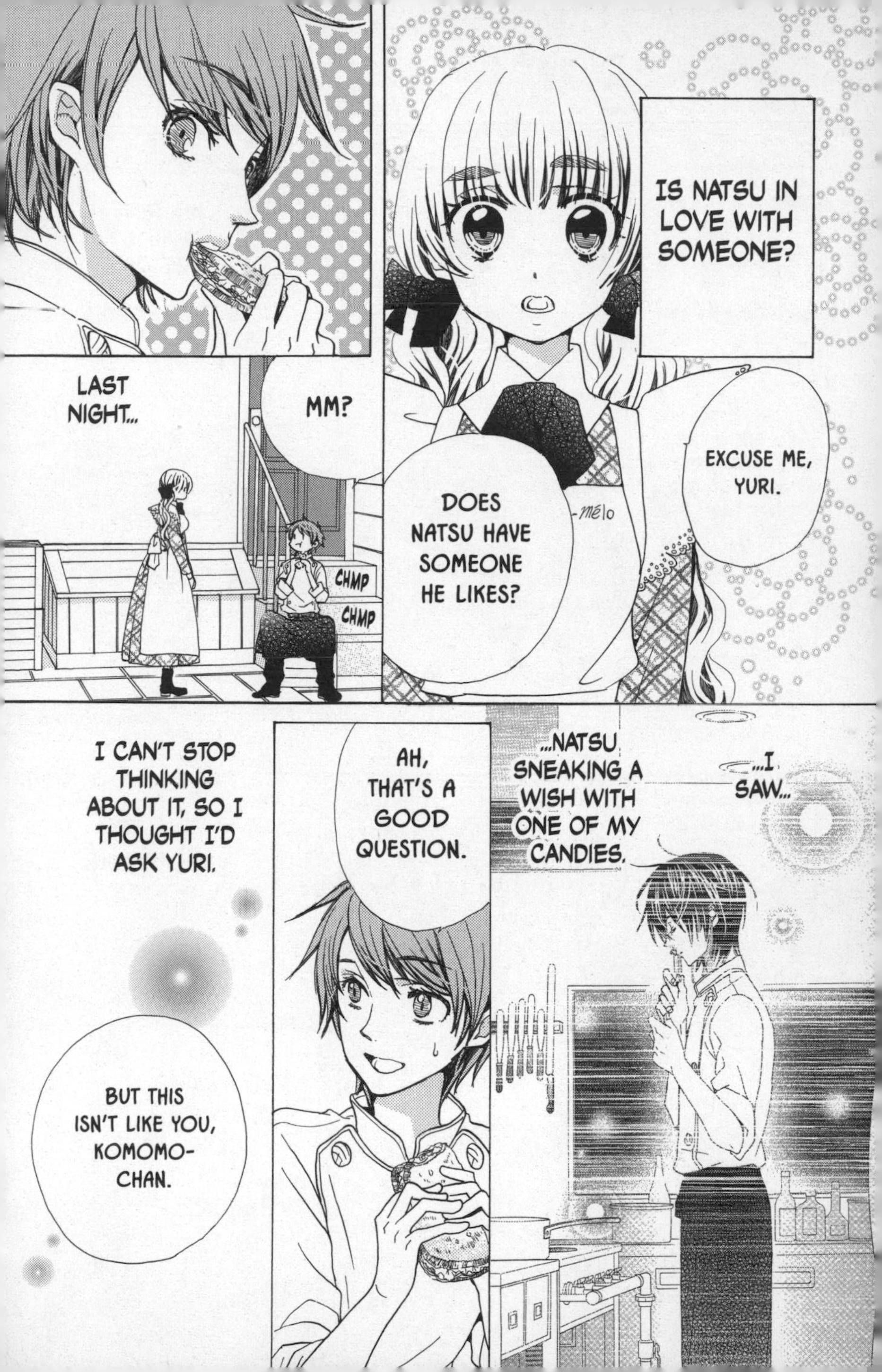
IS NATSU IN LOVE WITH SOMEONE?
EXCUSE ME, YURI.
DOES NATSU HAVE SOMEONE HE LIKES?
-mélo
MM?
LAST NIGHT...
CHMP
CHMP
...I SAW...
...NATSU SNEAKING A WISH WITH ONE OF MY CANDIES.
AH, THAT'S A GOOD QUESTION.
I CAN'T STOP THINKING ABOUT IT, SO I THOUGHT I'D ASK YURI.
BUT THIS ISN'T LIKE YOU, KOMOMO-CHAN.

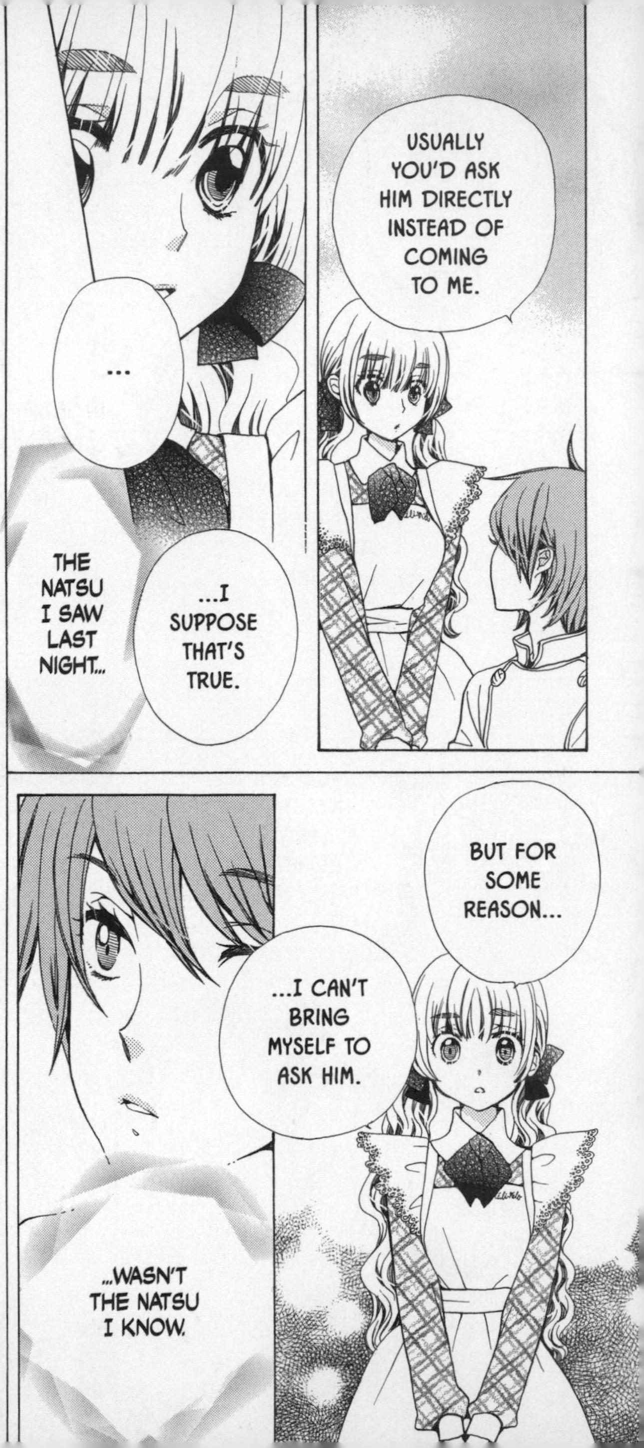
USUALLY YOU'D ASK HIM DIRECTLY INSTEAD OF COMING TO ME.
...
...I SUPPOSE THAT'S TRUE.
THE NATSU I SAW LAST NIGHT...
BUT FOR SOME REASON...
...I CAN'T BRING MYSELF TO ASK HIM.
...WASN'T THE NATSU I KNOW.

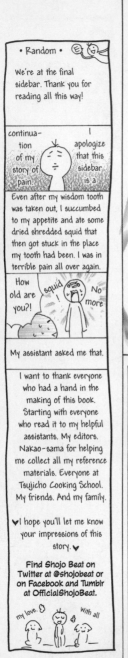

• Random •

We're at the final sidebar. Thank you for reading all this way!

continuation of my story of pain. I apologize that this sidebar is a

Even after my wisdom tooth was taken out, I succumbed to my appetite and ate some dried shredded squid that then got stuck in the place my tooth had been. I was in terrible pain all over again.

How old are you?!

No more squid!

My assistant asked me that.

I want to thank everyone who had a hand in the making of this book. Starting with everyone who read it to my helpful assistants. My editors. Nakao-sama for helping me collect all my reference materials. Everyone at Tsujicho Cooking School. My friends. And my family.

♥I hope you'll let me know your impressions of this story.♥

Find Shojo Beat on Twitter at @shojobeat or on Facebook and Tumblr at OfficialShojoBeat.

With all my love.

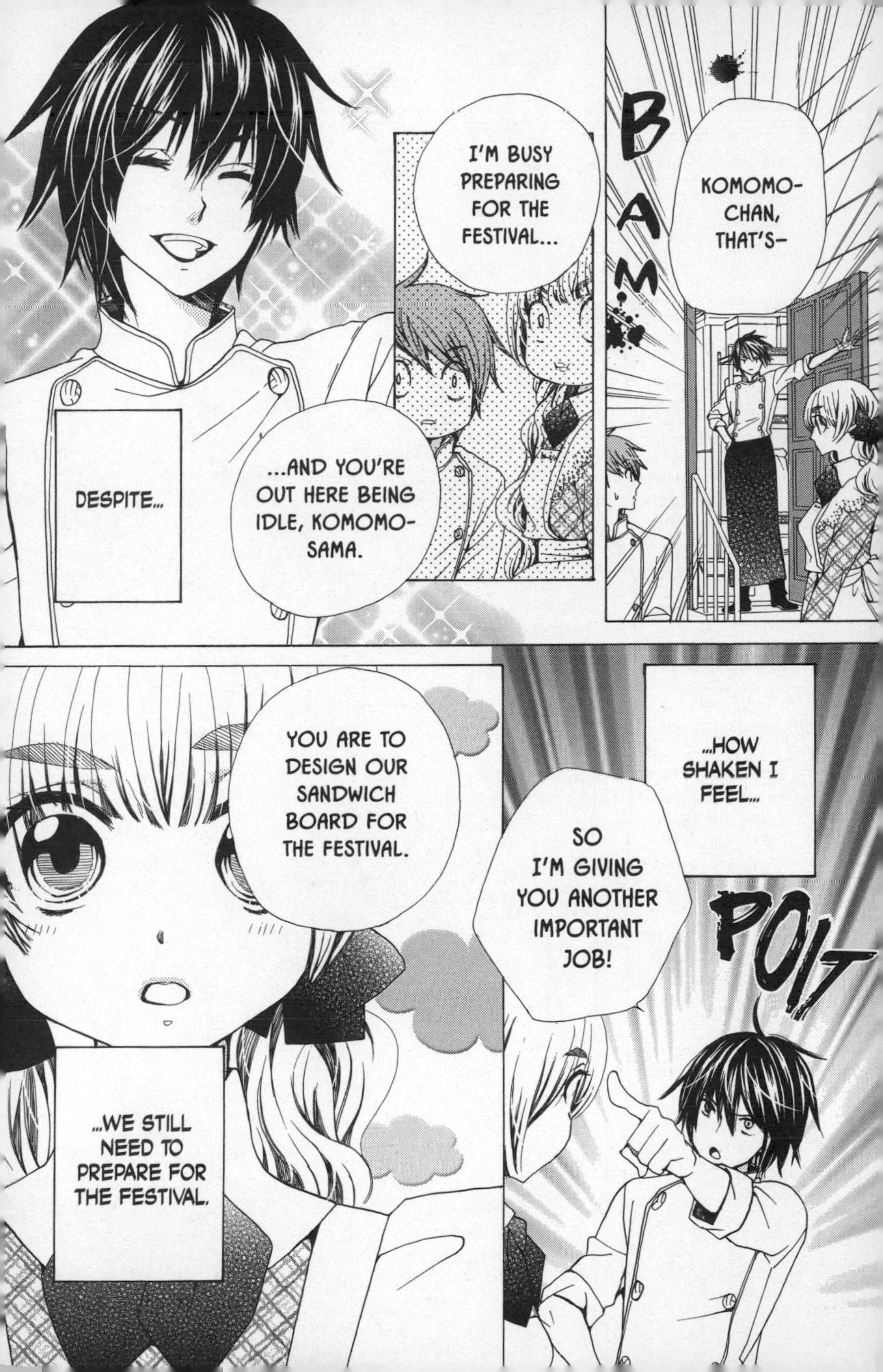
BAM
KOMOMO-CHAN, THAT'S-
I'M BUSY PREPARING FOR THE FESTIVAL...
...AND YOU'RE OUT HERE BEING IDLE, KOMOMO-SAMA.
DESPITE...
...HOW SHAKEN I FEEL...
SO I'M GIVING YOU ANOTHER IMPORTANT JOB!
POIT
YOU ARE TO DESIGN OUR SANDWICH BOARD FOR THE FESTIVAL.
...WE STILL NEED TO PREPARE FOR THE FESTIVAL.

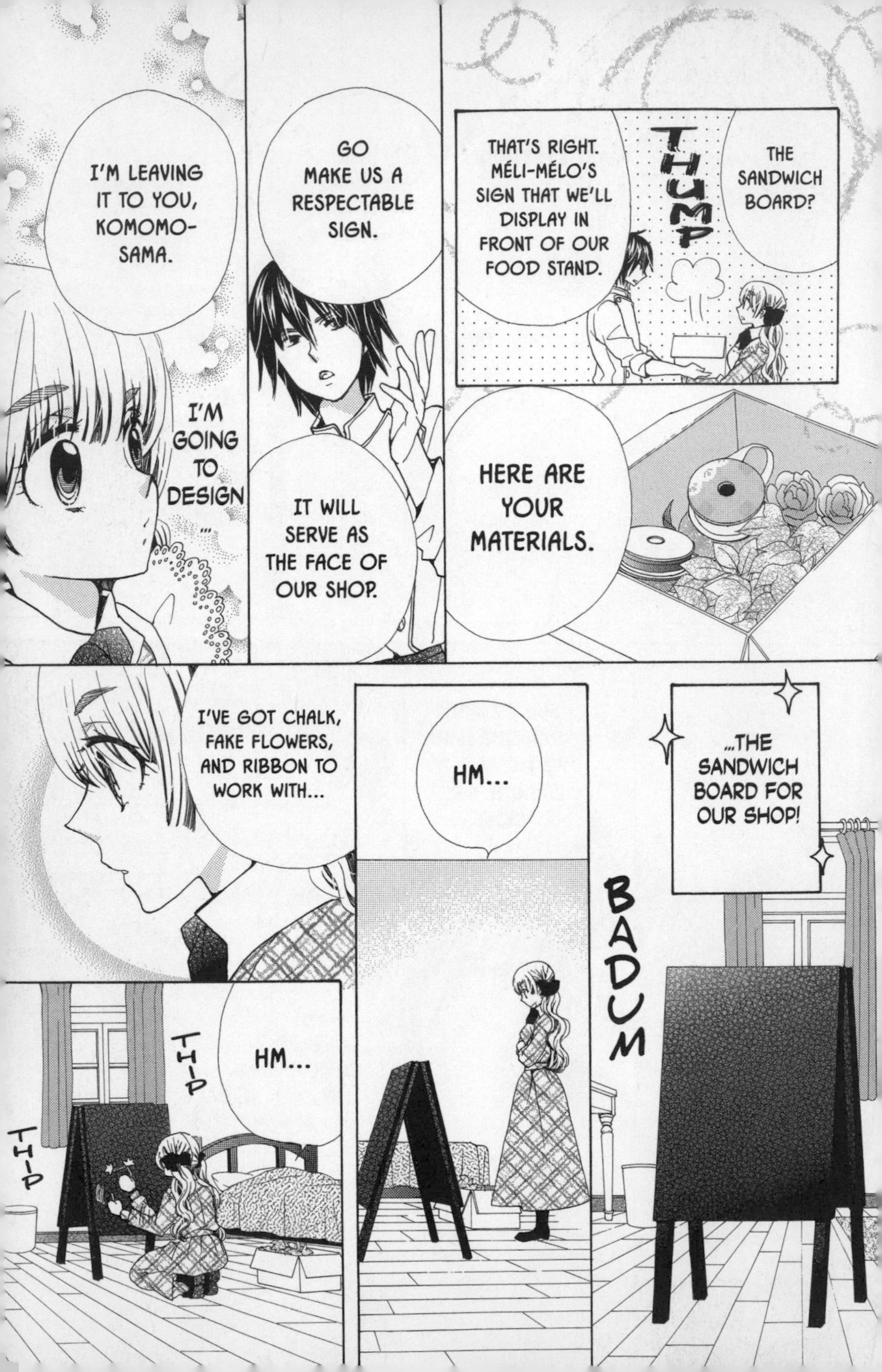
THE SANDWICH BOARD?
THUMP
THAT'S RIGHT. MÉLI-MÉLO'S SIGN THAT WE'LL DISPLAY IN FRONT OF OUR FOOD STAND.
HERE ARE YOUR MATERIALS.
GO MAKE US A RESPECTABLE SIGN.
IT WILL SERVE AS THE FACE OF OUR SHOP.
I'M LEAVING IT TO YOU, KOMOMO-SAMA.
I'M GOING TO DESIGN...
...THE SANDWICH BOARD FOR OUR SHOP!
BADUM
HM...
I'VE GOT CHALK, FAKE FLOWERS, AND RIBBON TO WORK WITH...
HM...
THIP
THIP

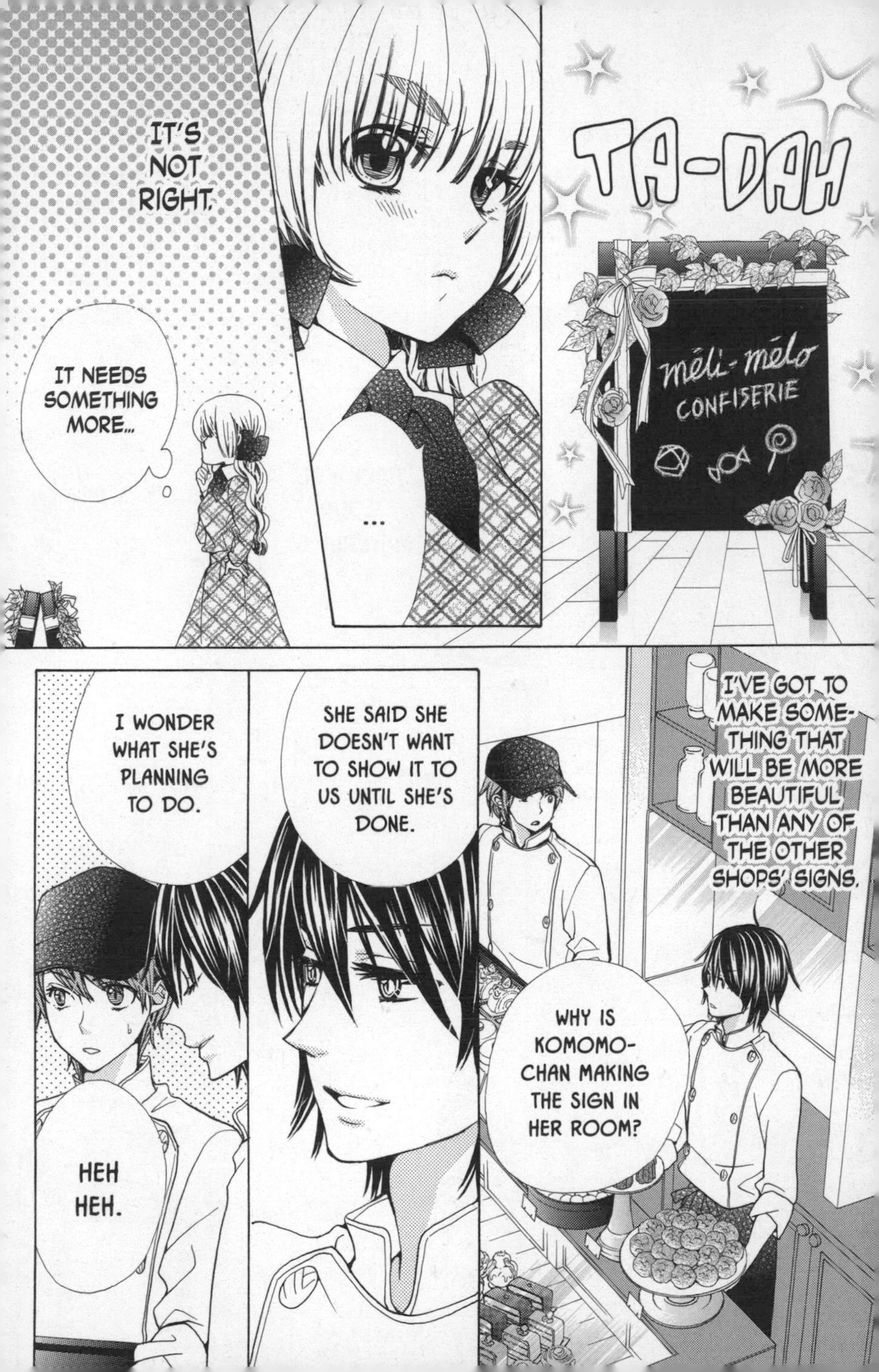
TA-DAH
méli-mélo
CONFISERIE
...
IT'S NOT RIGHT.
IT NEEDS SOMETHING MORE...
I'VE GOT TO MAKE SOME-THING THAT WILL BE MORE BEAUTIFUL THAN ANY OF THE OTHER SHOPS' SIGNS.
WHY IS KOMOMO-CHAN MAKING THE SIGN IN HER ROOM?
SHE SAID SHE DOESN'T WANT TO SHOW IT TO US UNTIL SHE'S DONE.
I WONDER WHAT SHE'S PLANNING TO DO.
HEH HEH.

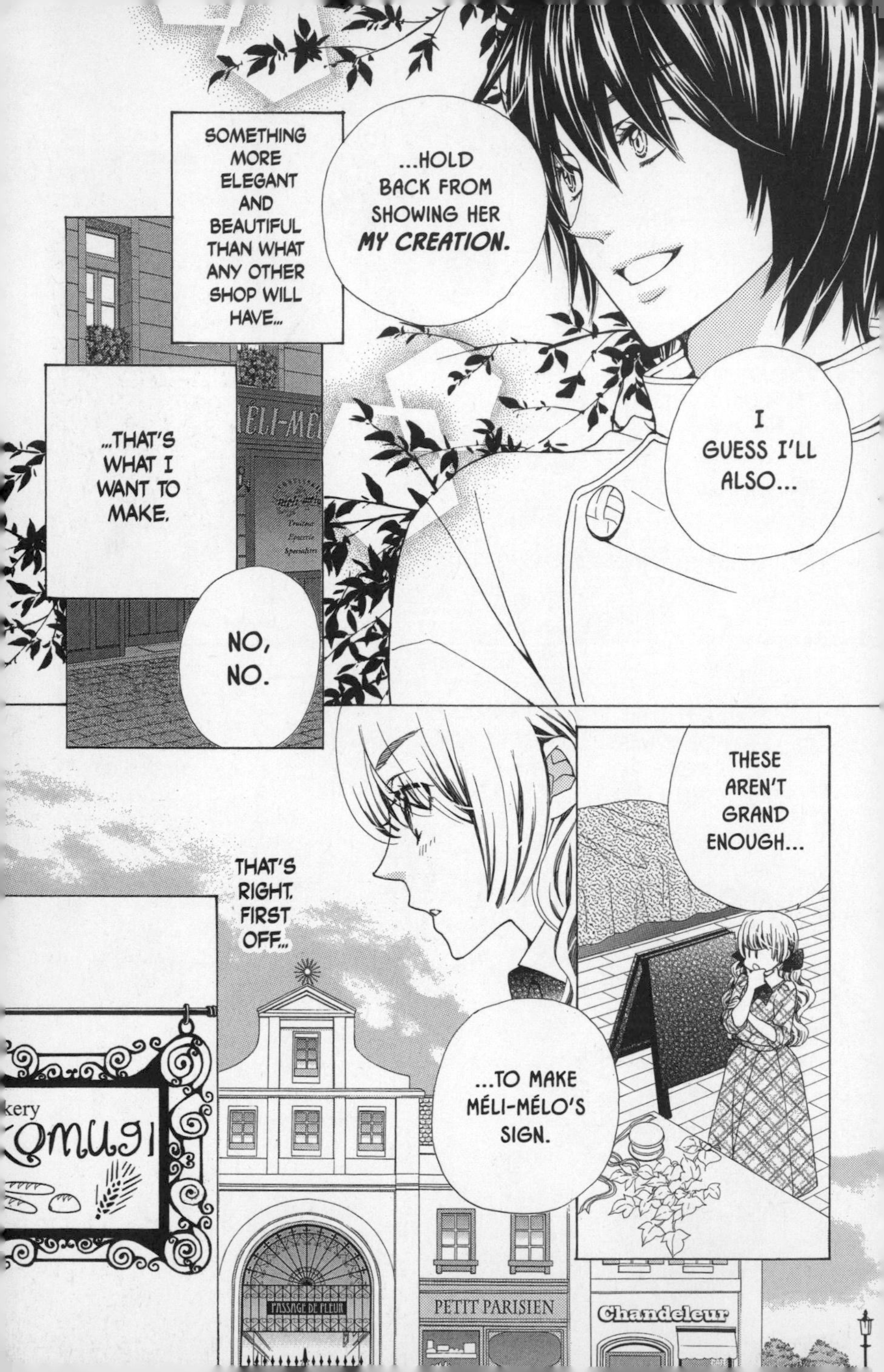
I GUESS I'LL ALSO...
...HOLD BACK FROM SHOWING HER *MY CREATION.*
NO, NO.
SOMETHING MORE ELEGANT AND BEAUTIFUL THAN WHAT ANY OTHER SHOP WILL HAVE...
...THAT'S WHAT I WANT TO MAKE.
THESE AREN'T GRAND ENOUGH...
THAT'S RIGHT. FIRST OFF...
...TO MAKE MÉLI-MÉLO'S SIGN.
Chandeleur
PETIT PARISIEN
PASSAGE DE FLEUR

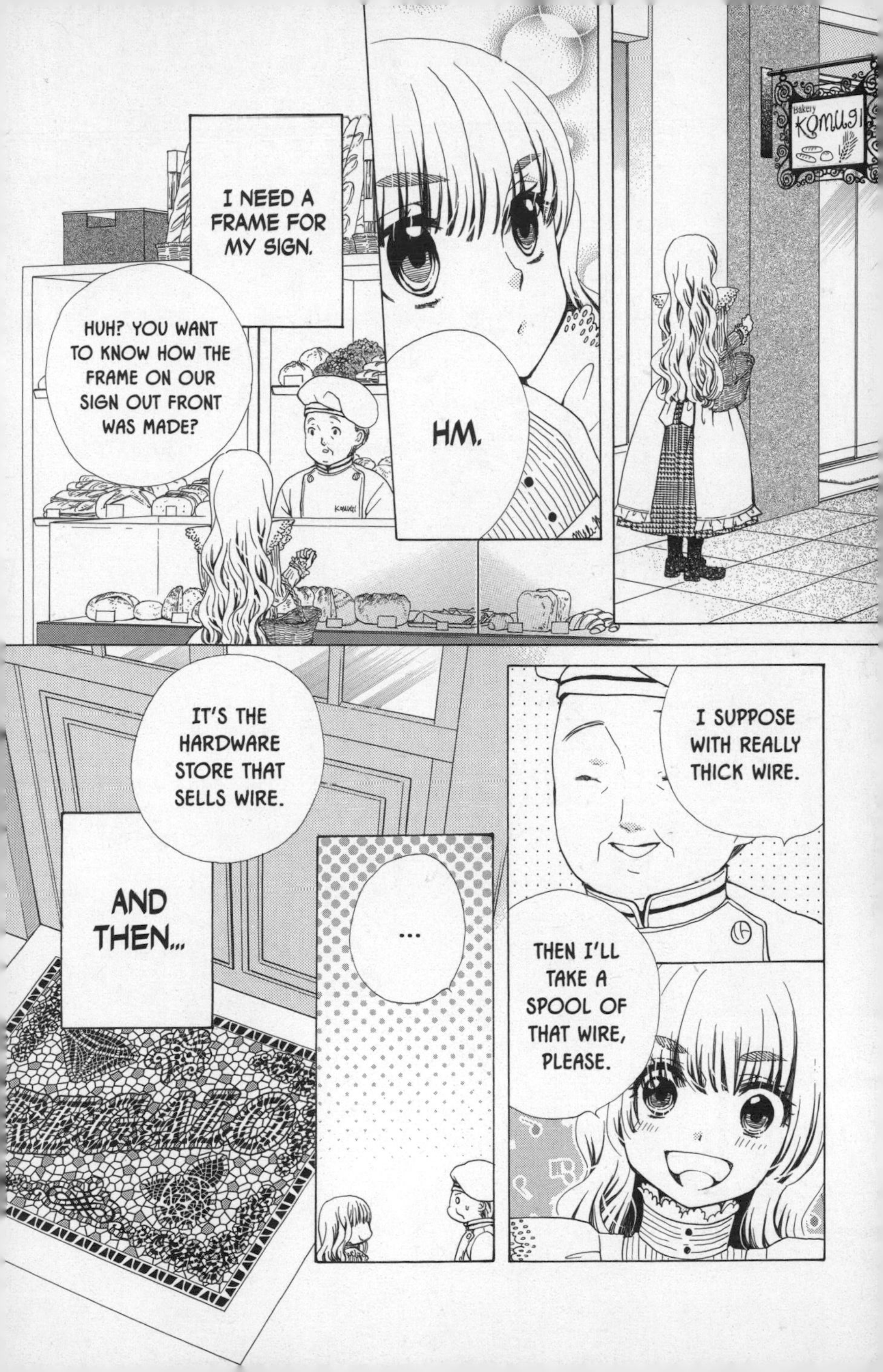
Bakery
KOMUGI
HM.
I NEED A FRAME FOR MY SIGN.
HUH? YOU WANT TO KNOW HOW THE FRAME ON OUR SIGN OUT FRONT WAS MADE?
I SUPPOSE WITH REALLY THICK WIRE.
THEN I'LL TAKE A SPOOL OF THAT WIRE, PLEASE.
...
IT'S THE HARDWARE STORE THAT SELLS WIRE.
AND THEN...

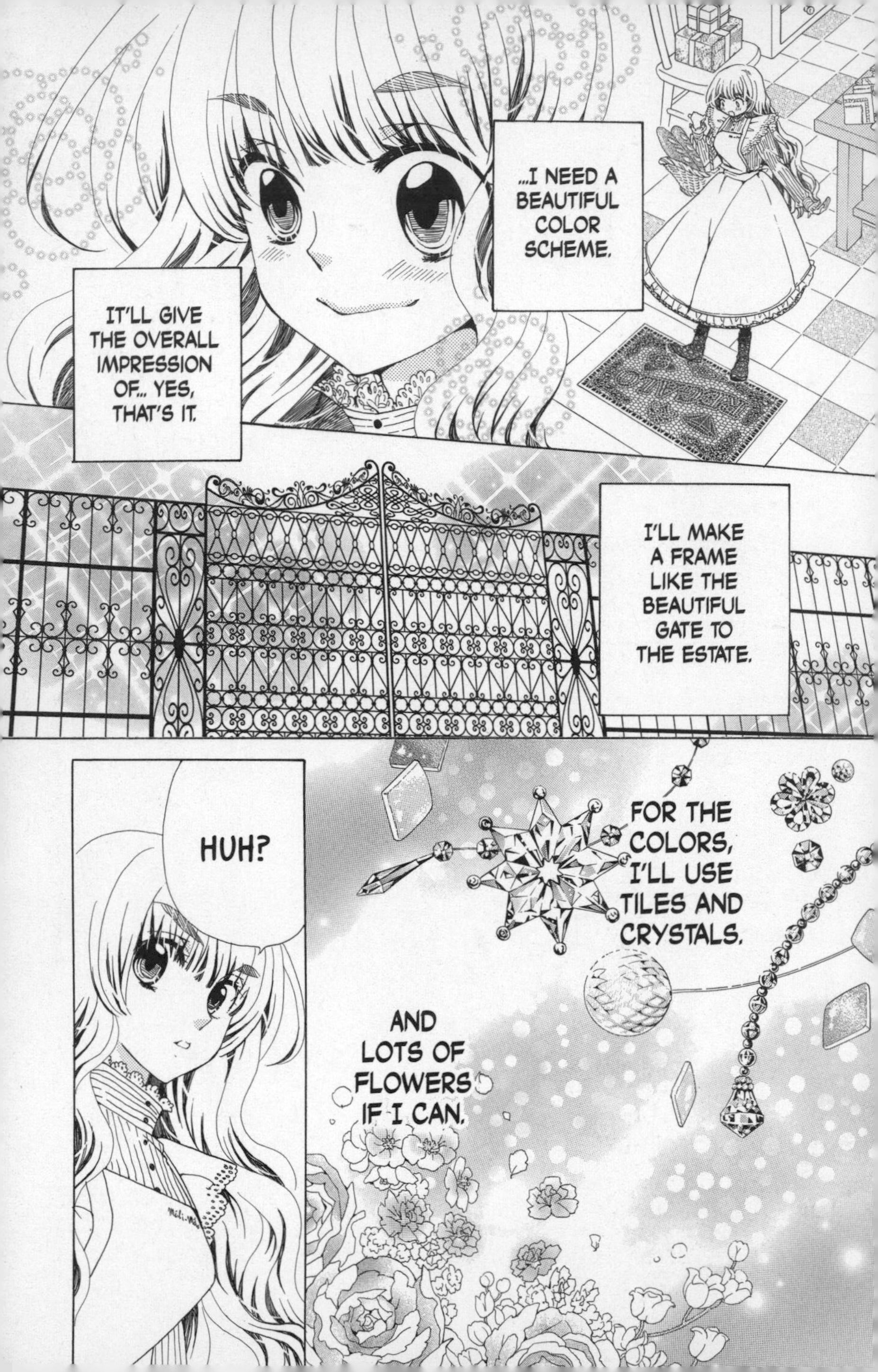
...I NEED A BEAUTIFUL COLOR SCHEME.
IT'LL GIVE THE OVERALL IMPRESSION OF... YES, THAT'S IT.
I'LL MAKE A FRAME LIKE THE BEAUTIFUL GATE TO THE ESTATE.
FOR THE COLORS, I'LL USE TILES AND CRYSTALS.
AND LOTS OF FLOWERS IF I CAN.
HUH?

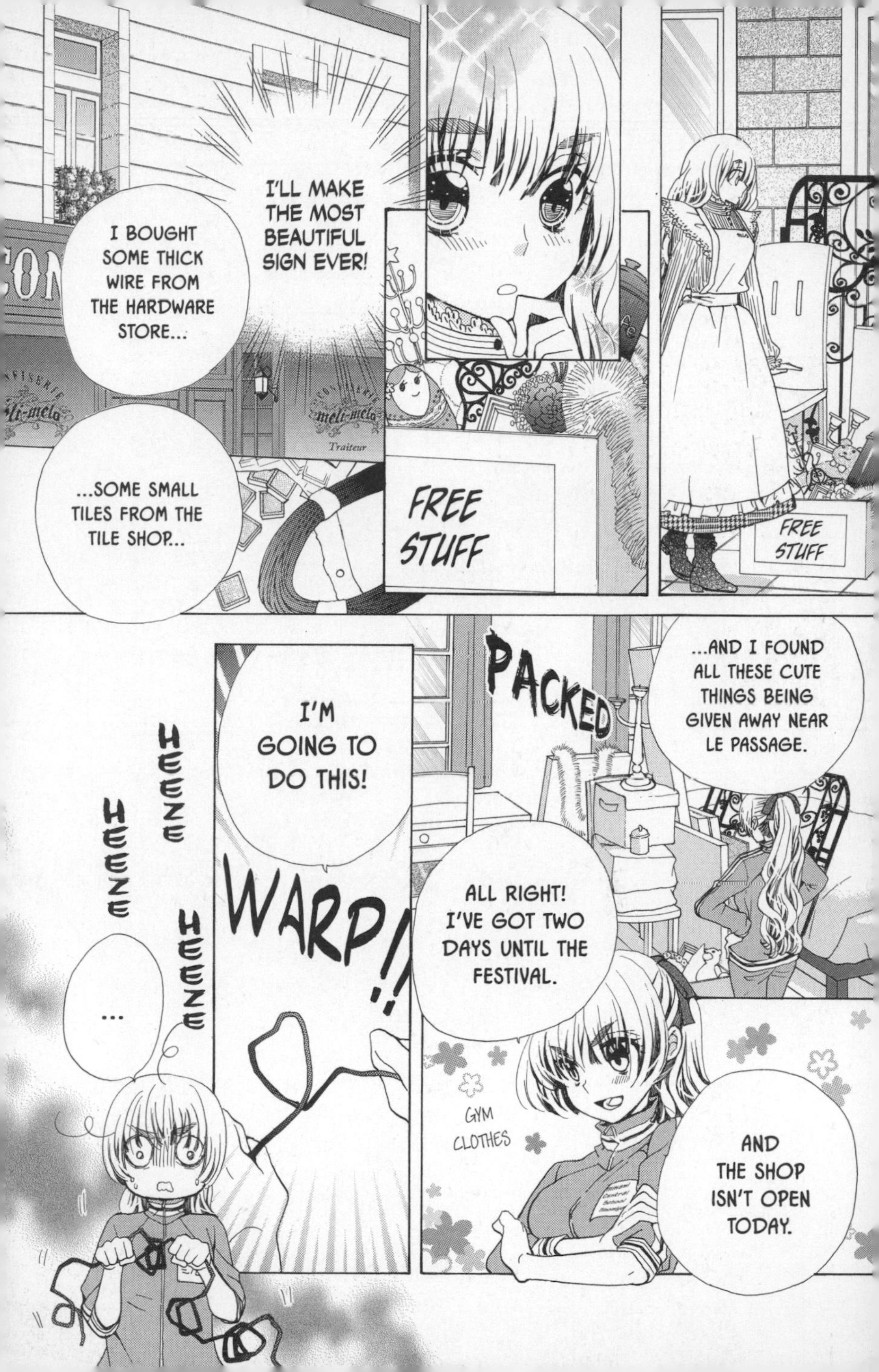
FREE STUFF
I'LL MAKE THE MOST BEAUTIFUL SIGN EVER!
FREE STUFF
I BOUGHT SOME THICK WIRE FROM THE HARDWARE STORE...
meli-melo
meli-melo
Traiteur
...SOME SMALL TILES FROM THE TILE SHOP...
...AND I FOUND ALL THESE CUTE THINGS BEING GIVEN AWAY NEAR LE PASSAGE.
PACKED
ALL RIGHT! I'VE GOT TWO DAYS UNTIL THE FESTIVAL.
AND THE SHOP ISN'T OPEN TODAY.
GYM CLOTHES
I'M GOING TO DO THIS!
WARP!!
HEEZE
HEEZE
HEEZE
...

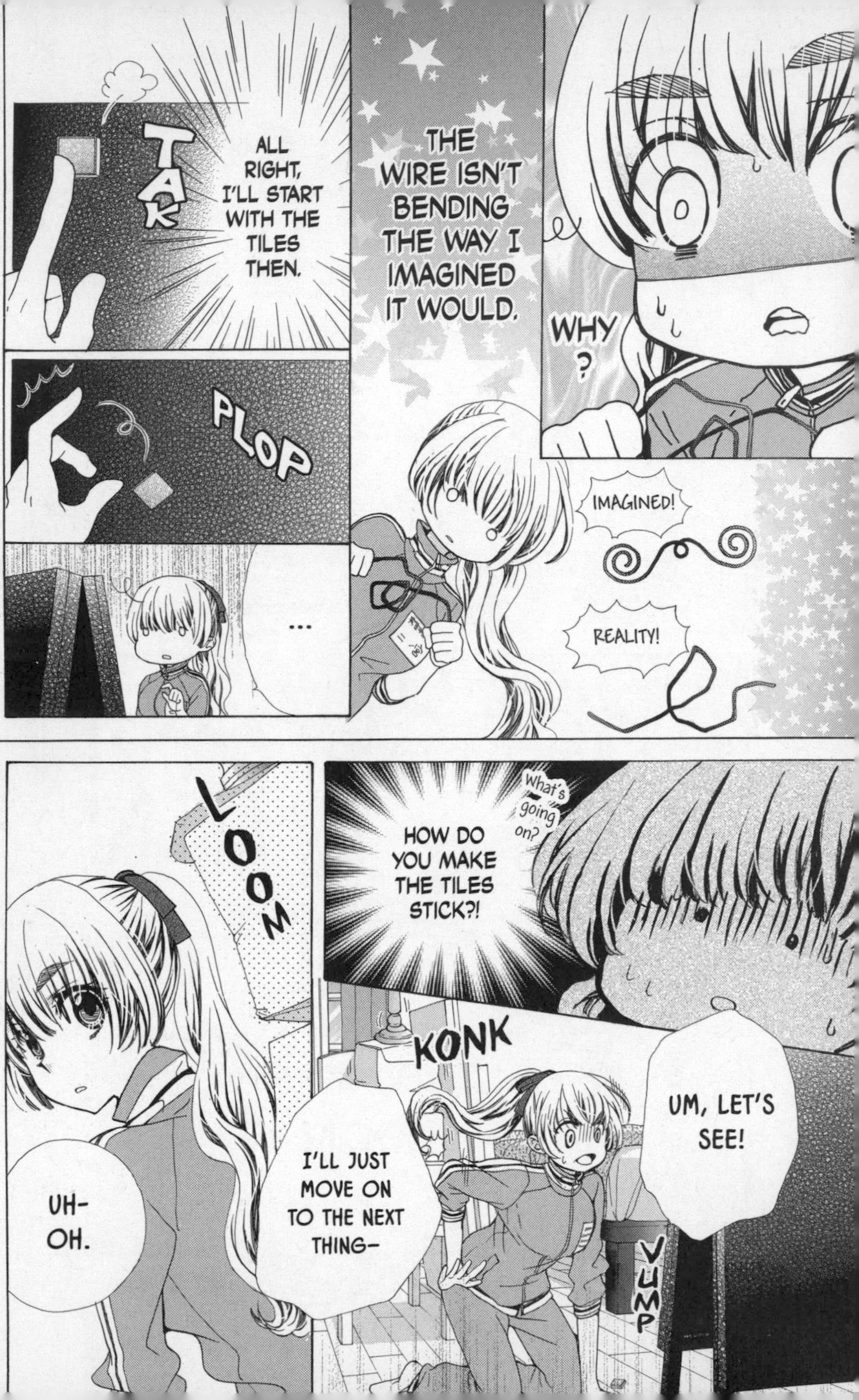
WHY?
THE WIRE ISN'T BENDING THE WAY I IMAGINED IT WOULD.
IMAGINED!
REALITY!
ALL RIGHT, I'LL START WITH THE TILES THEN.
TAK
PLOP
...
HOW DO YOU MAKE THE TILES STICK?!
What's going on?
KONK
UM, LET'S SEE!
I'LL JUST MOVE ON TO THE NEXT THING–
VUMP
LOOM
UH-OH.

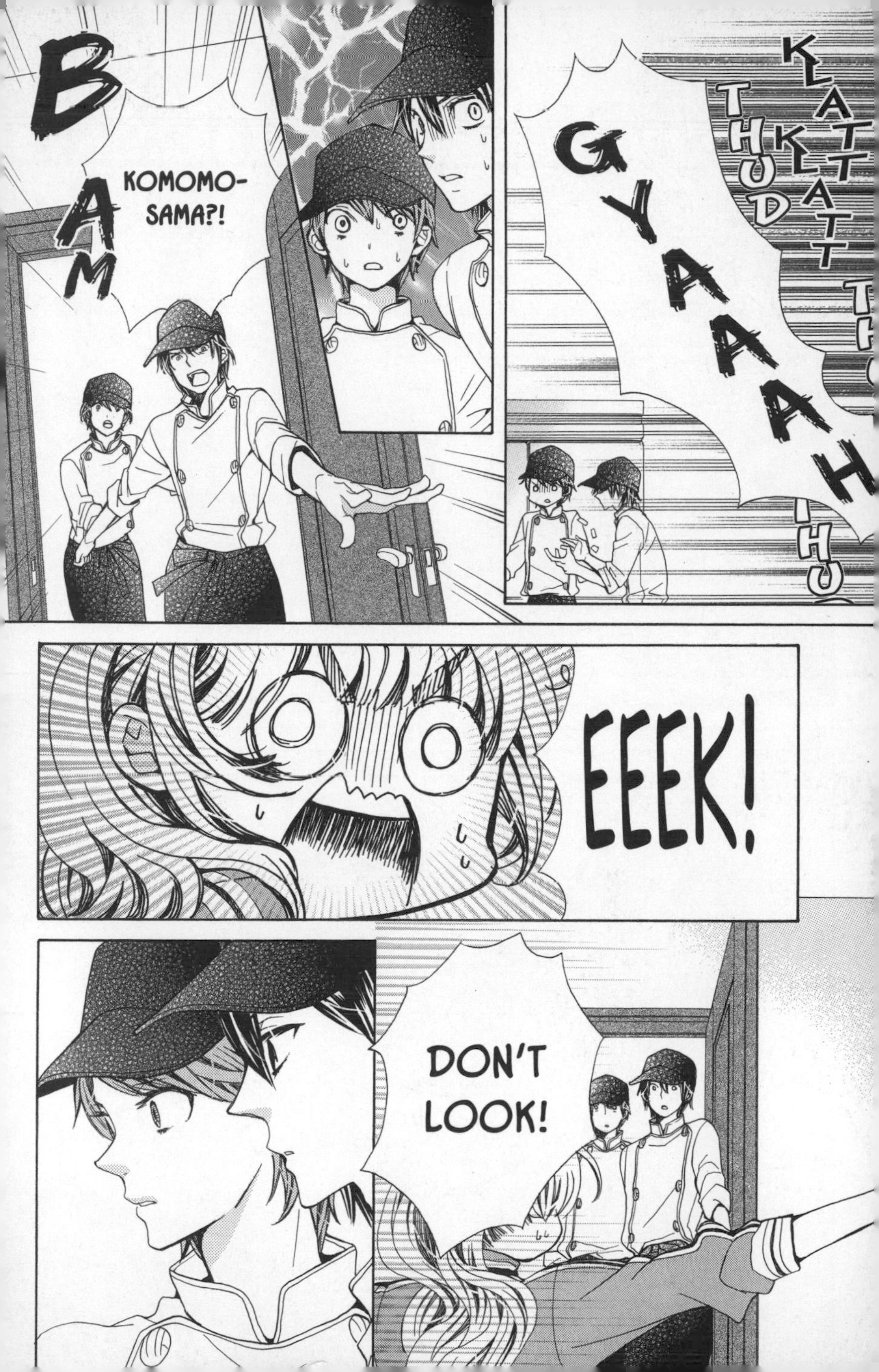
GYAAAH
KLATT KLATT
THUD
BAM
KOMOMO-SAMA?!
EEEK!
DON'T LOOK!

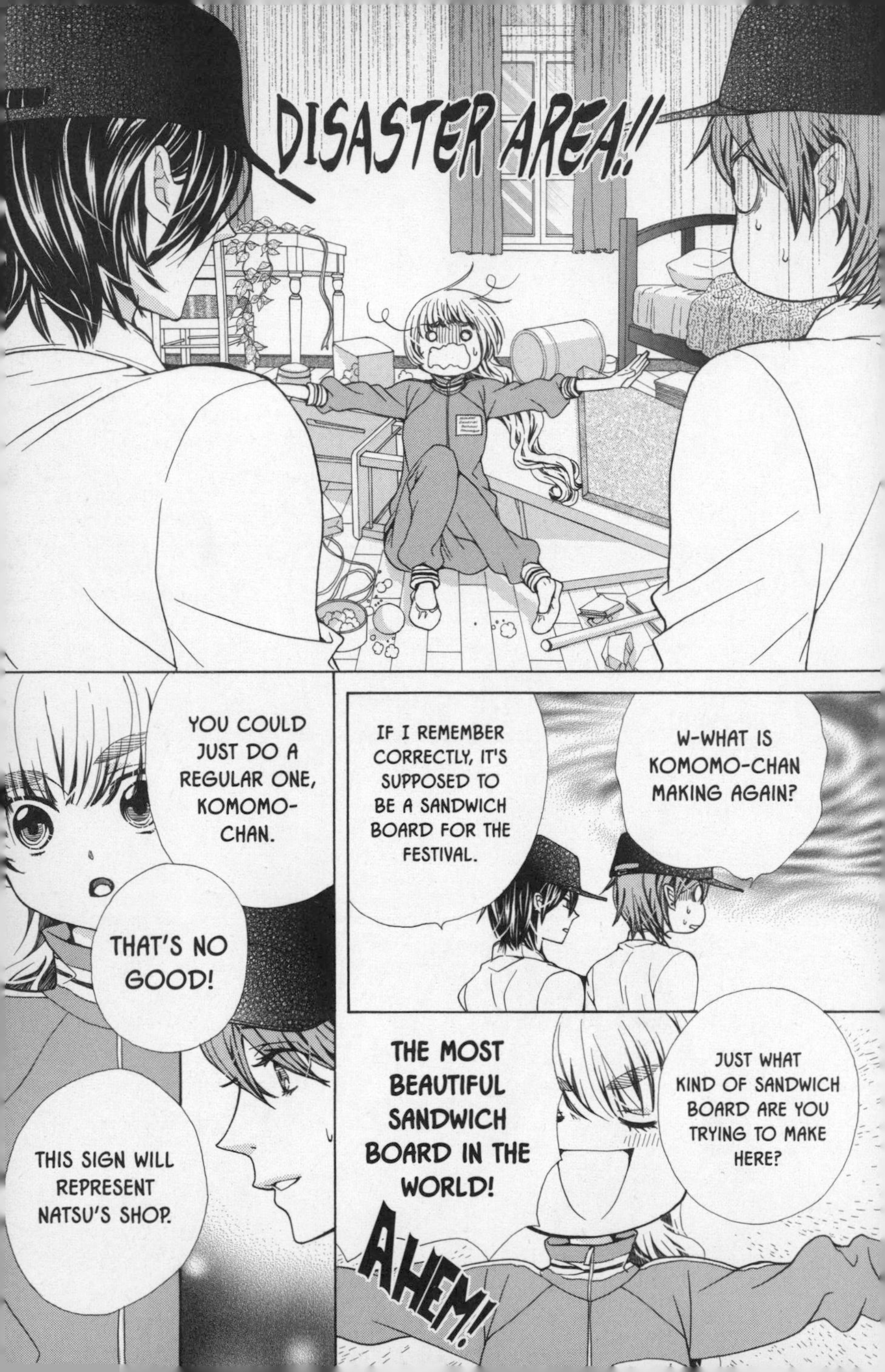
DISASTER AREA!!
W-WHAT IS KOMOMO-CHAN MAKING AGAIN?
IF I REMEMBER CORRECTLY, IT'S SUPPOSED TO BE A SANDWICH BOARD FOR THE FESTIVAL.
JUST WHAT KIND OF SANDWICH BOARD ARE YOU TRYING TO MAKE HERE?
THE MOST BEAUTIFUL SANDWICH BOARD IN THE WORLD!
AHEM!
YOU COULD JUST DO A REGULAR ONE, KOMOMO-CHAN.
THAT'S NO GOOD!
THIS SIGN WILL REPRESENT NATSU'S SHOP.

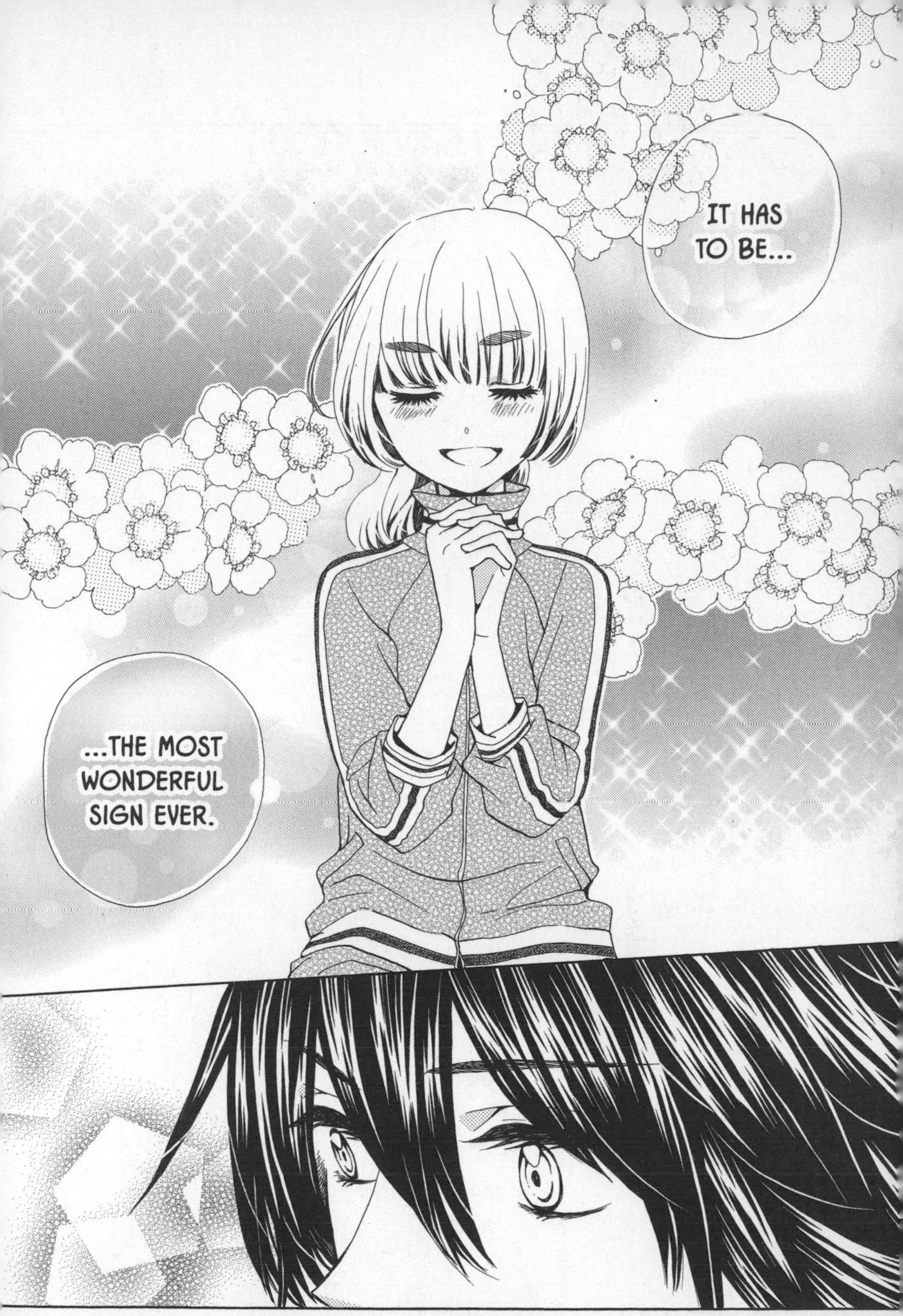
IT HAS TO BE...
...THE MOST WONDERFUL SIGN EVER.

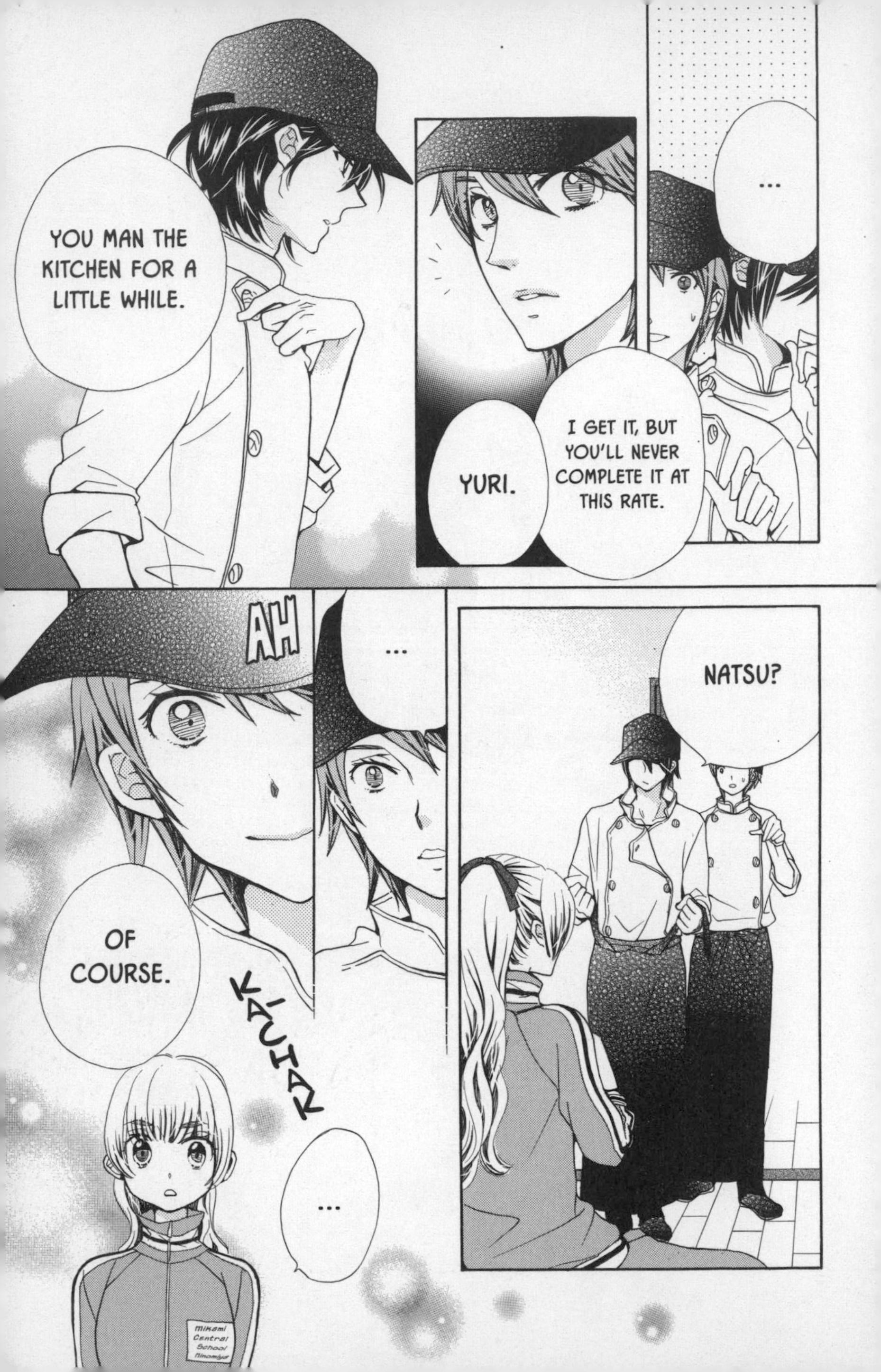
...
I GET IT, BUT YOU'LL NEVER COMPLETE IT AT THIS RATE.
YURI.
YOU MAN THE KITCHEN FOR A LITTLE WHILE.
NATSU?
...
AH
OF COURSE.
KACHAK
...
Mikami Central School Ninomiya

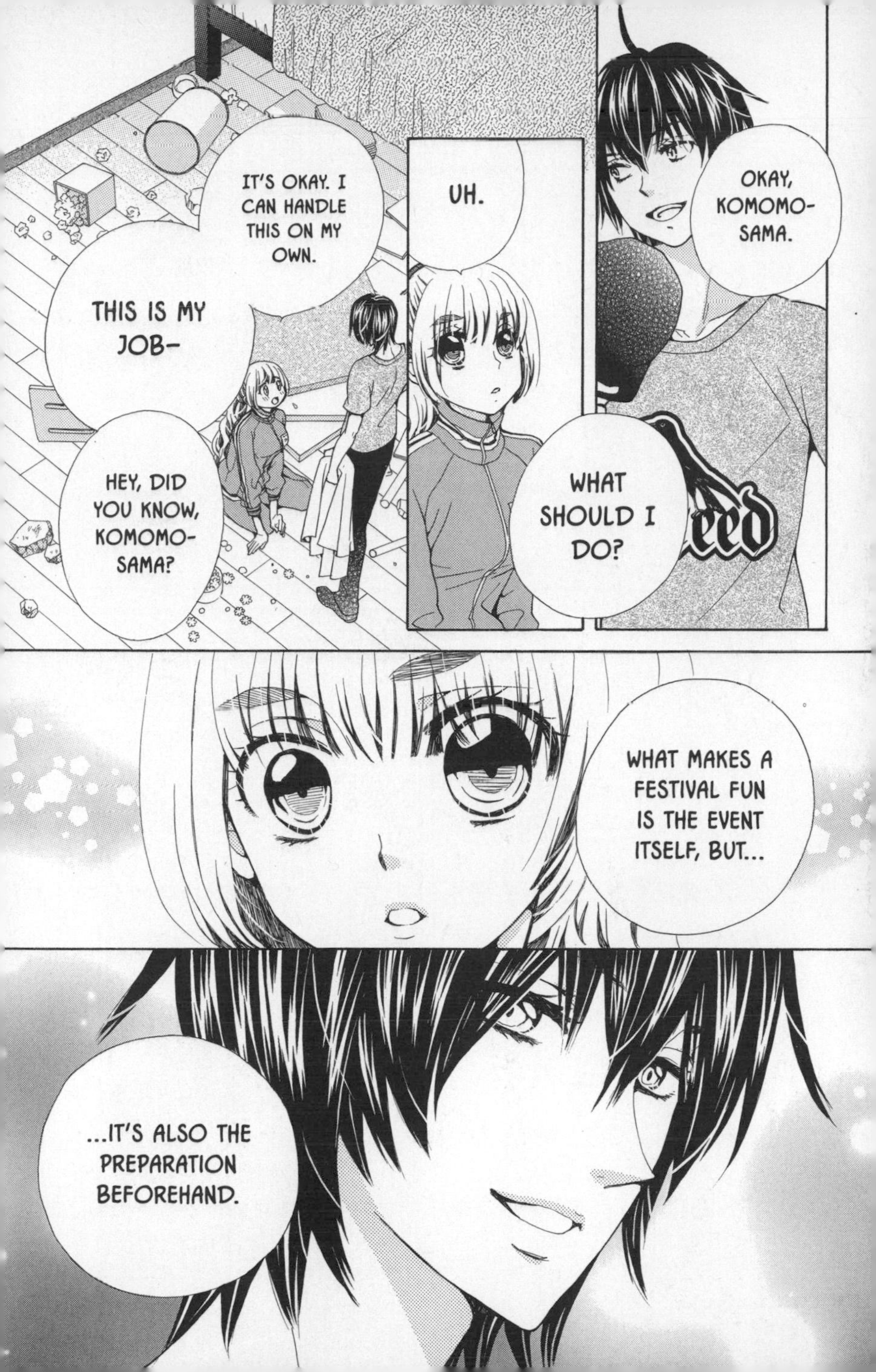
OKAY, KOMOMO-SAMA.
WHAT SHOULD I DO?
UH.
IT'S OKAY. I CAN HANDLE THIS ON MY OWN.
THIS IS MY JOB–
HEY, DID YOU KNOW, KOMOMO-SAMA?
WHAT MAKES A FESTIVAL FUN IS THE EVENT ITSELF, BUT...
...IT'S ALSO THE PREPARATION BEFOREHAND.

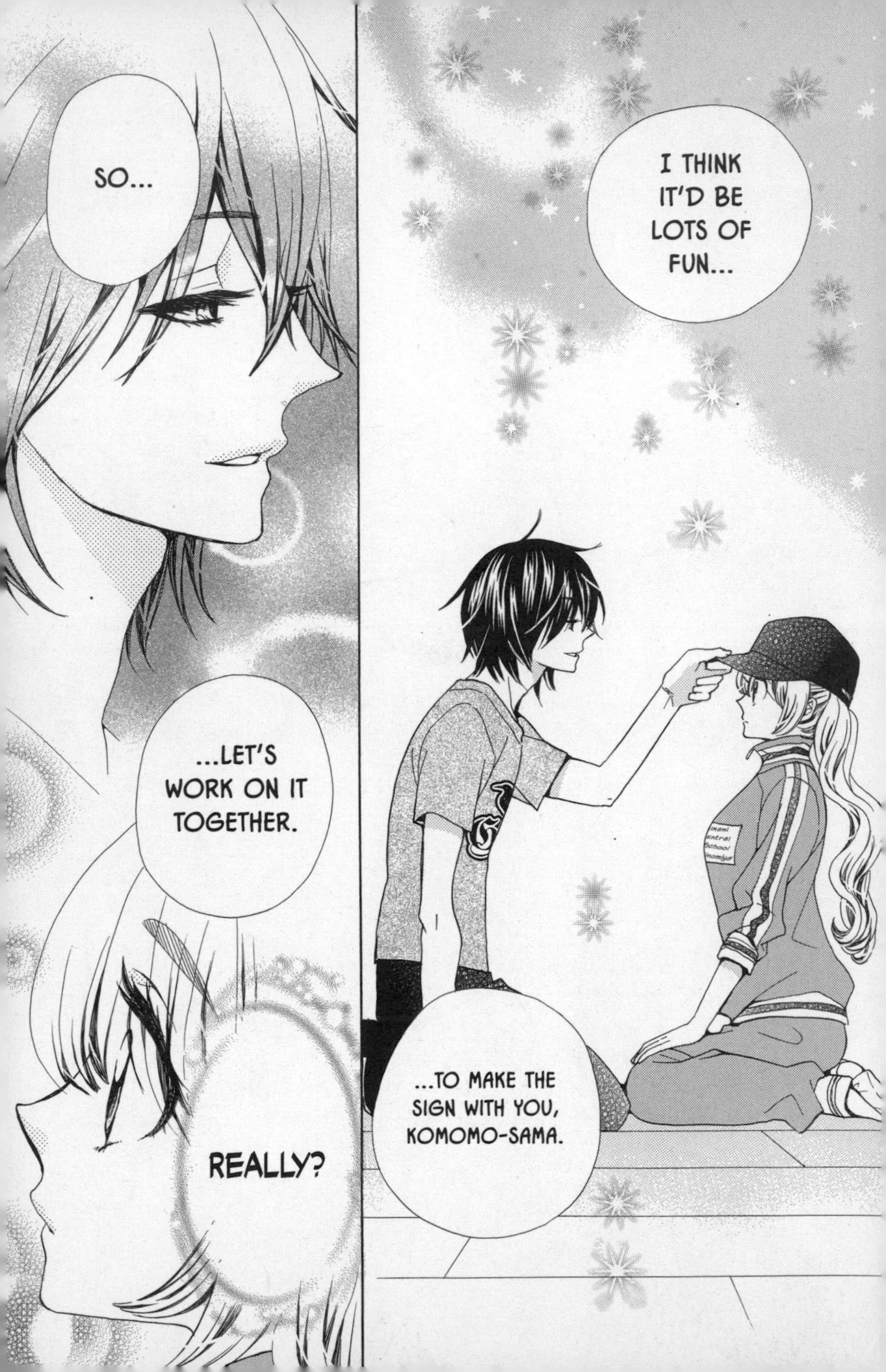
I THINK IT'D BE LOTS OF FUN...
...TO MAKE THE SIGN WITH YOU, KOMOMO-SAMA.
SO...
...LET'S WORK ON IT TOGETHER.
REALLY?

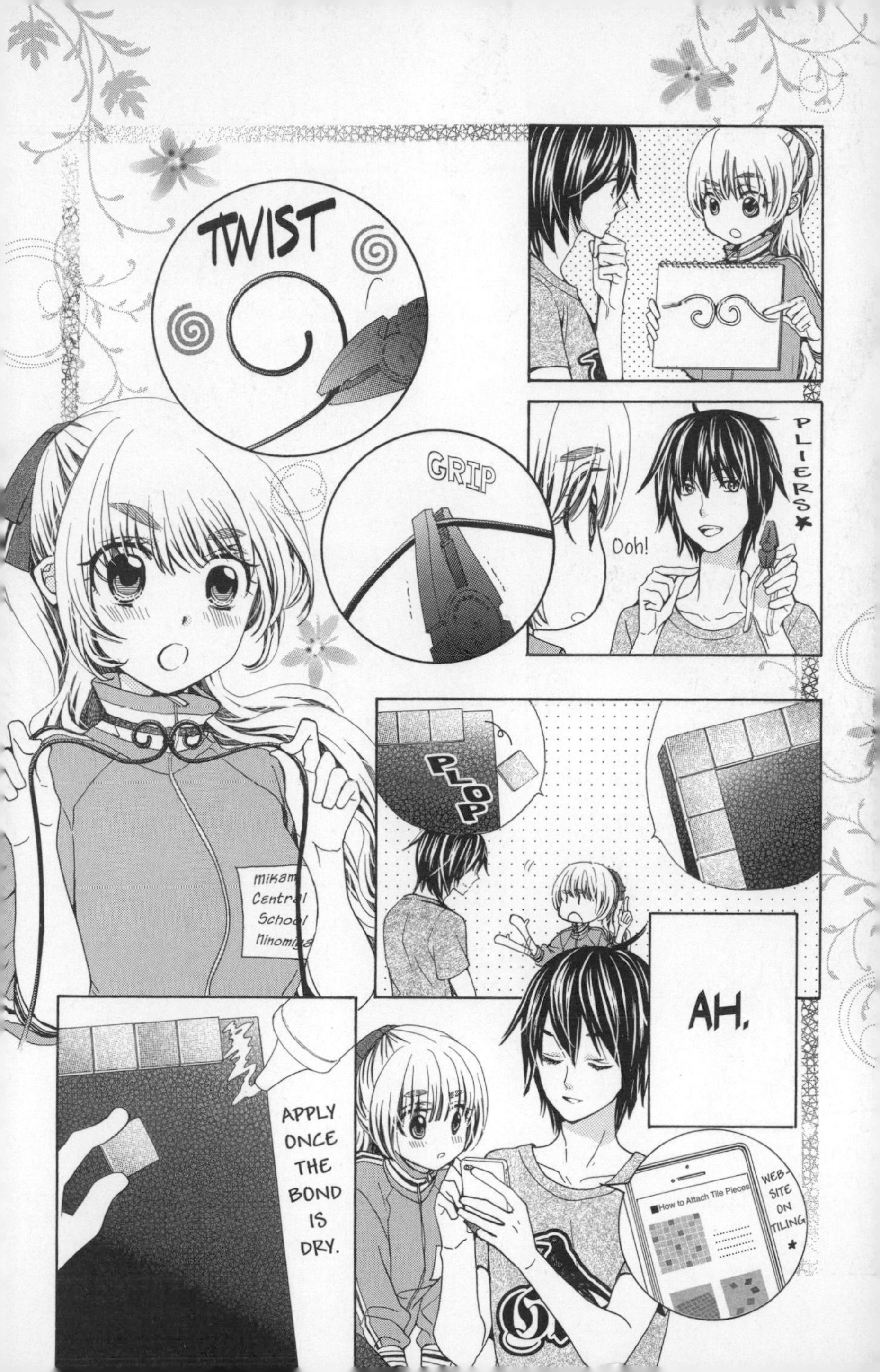
TWIST
PLIERS★
Ooh!
GRIP
Mikam Central School Ninomiya
PLOP
AH.
WEB-SITE ON TILING★
How to Attach Tile Pieces
APPLY ONCE THE BOND IS DRY.

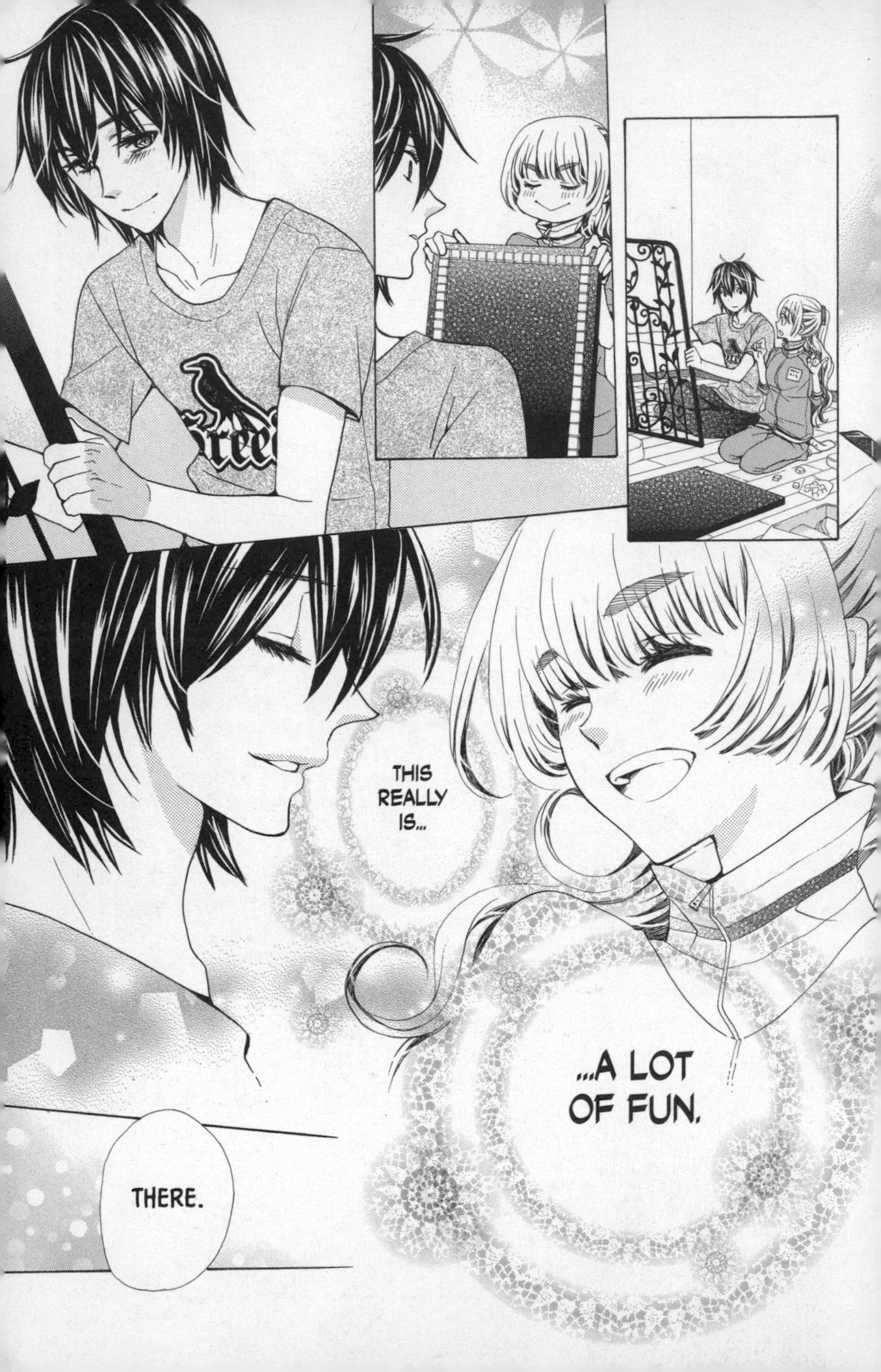
THIS REALLY IS...
...A LOT OF FUN.
THERE.

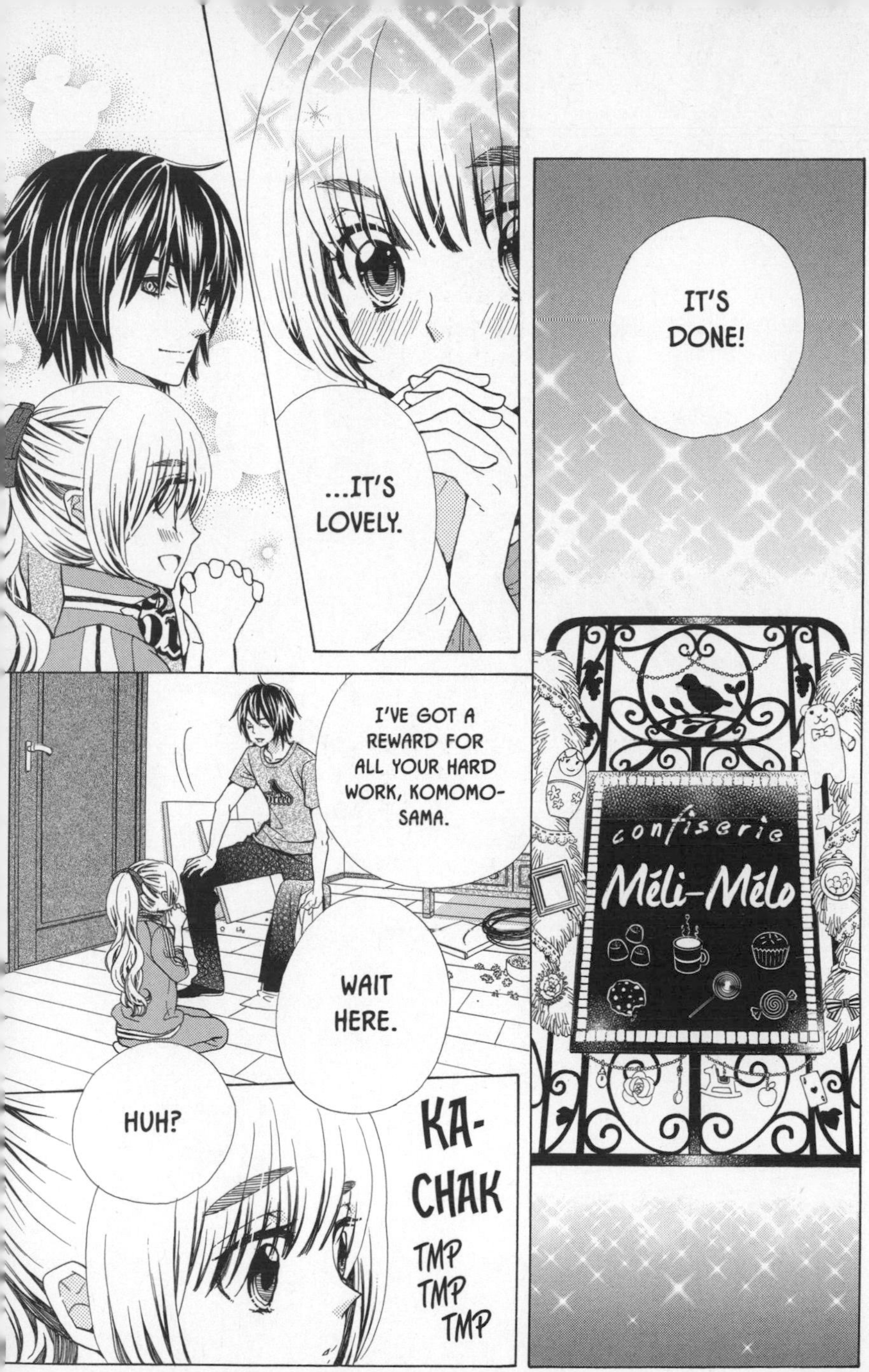
IT'S DONE!
confiserie
Méli-Mélo
...IT'S LOVELY.
I'VE GOT A REWARD FOR ALL YOUR HARD WORK, KOMOMO-SAMA.
WAIT HERE.
HUH?
KA-CHAK
TMP TMP TMP

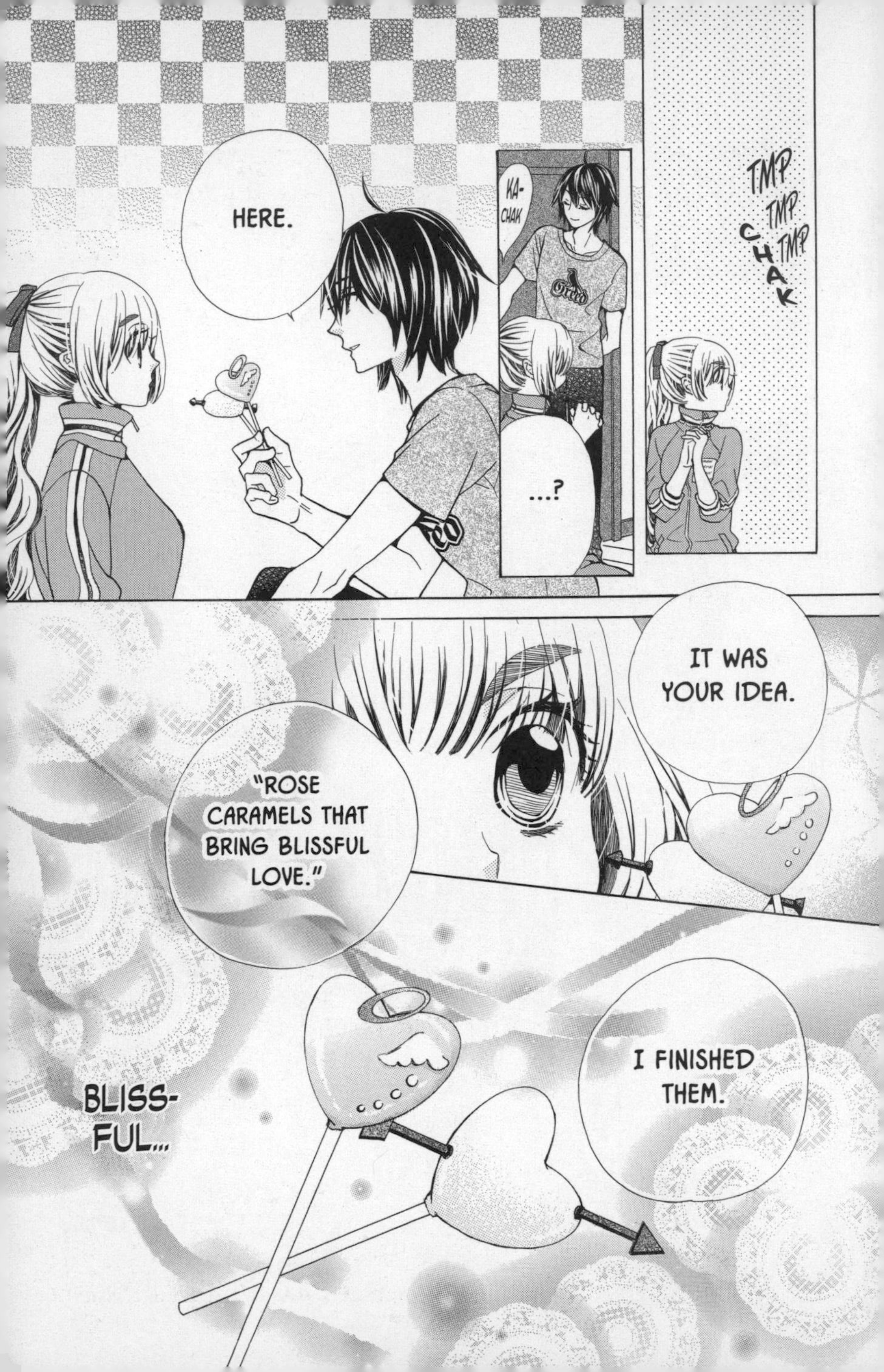
TMP TMP TMP
CHAK
KA-CHAK
...?
HERE.
IT WAS YOUR IDEA.
"ROSE CARAMELS THAT BRING BLISSFUL LOVE."
I FINISHED THEM.
BLISS-FUL...

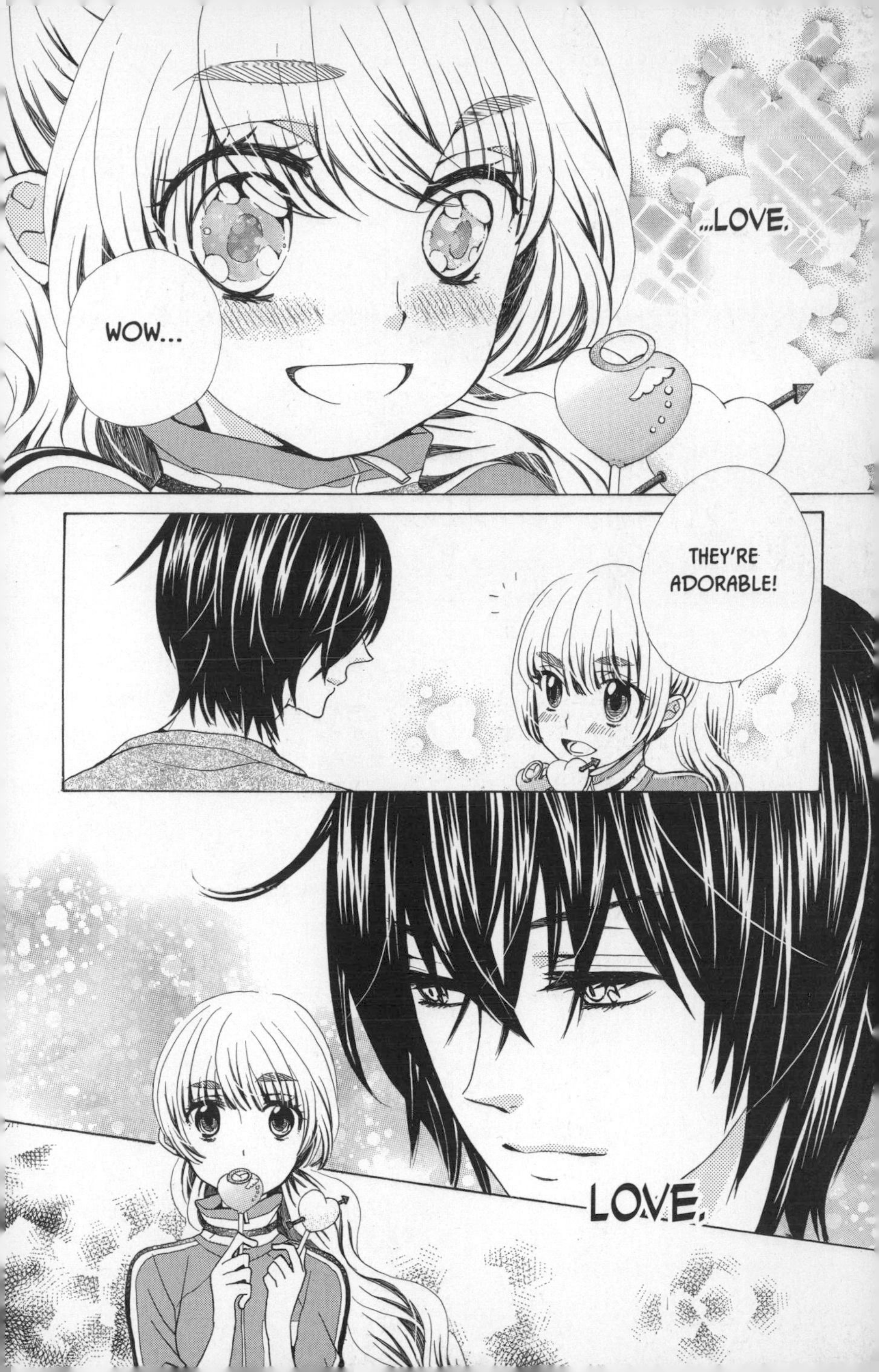
...LOVE.
WOW...
THEY'RE ADORABLE!
LOVE.

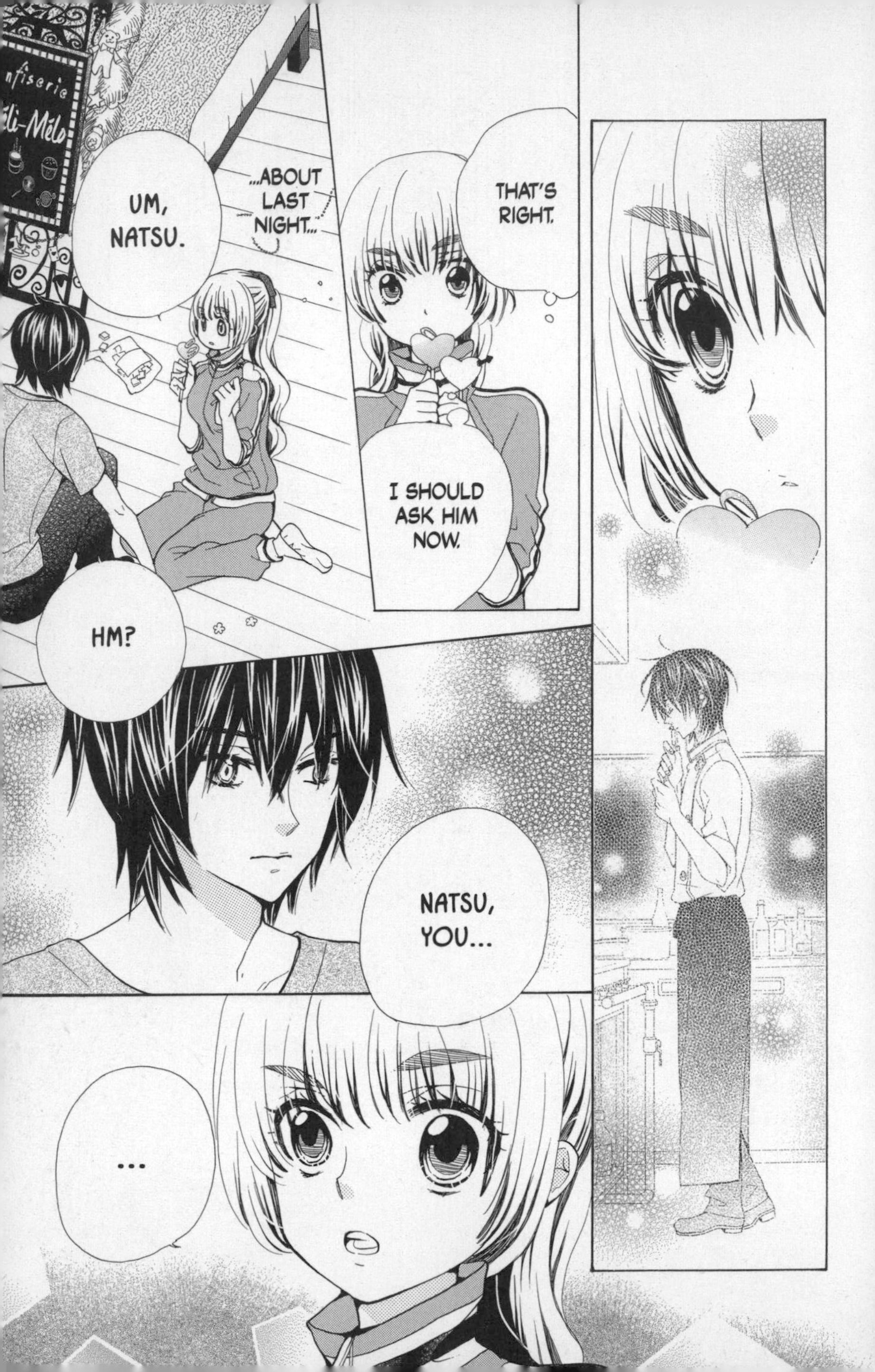
THAT'S RIGHT.
I SHOULD ASK HIM NOW.
UM, NATSU.
...ABOUT LAST NIGHT...
HM?
NATSU, YOU...
...

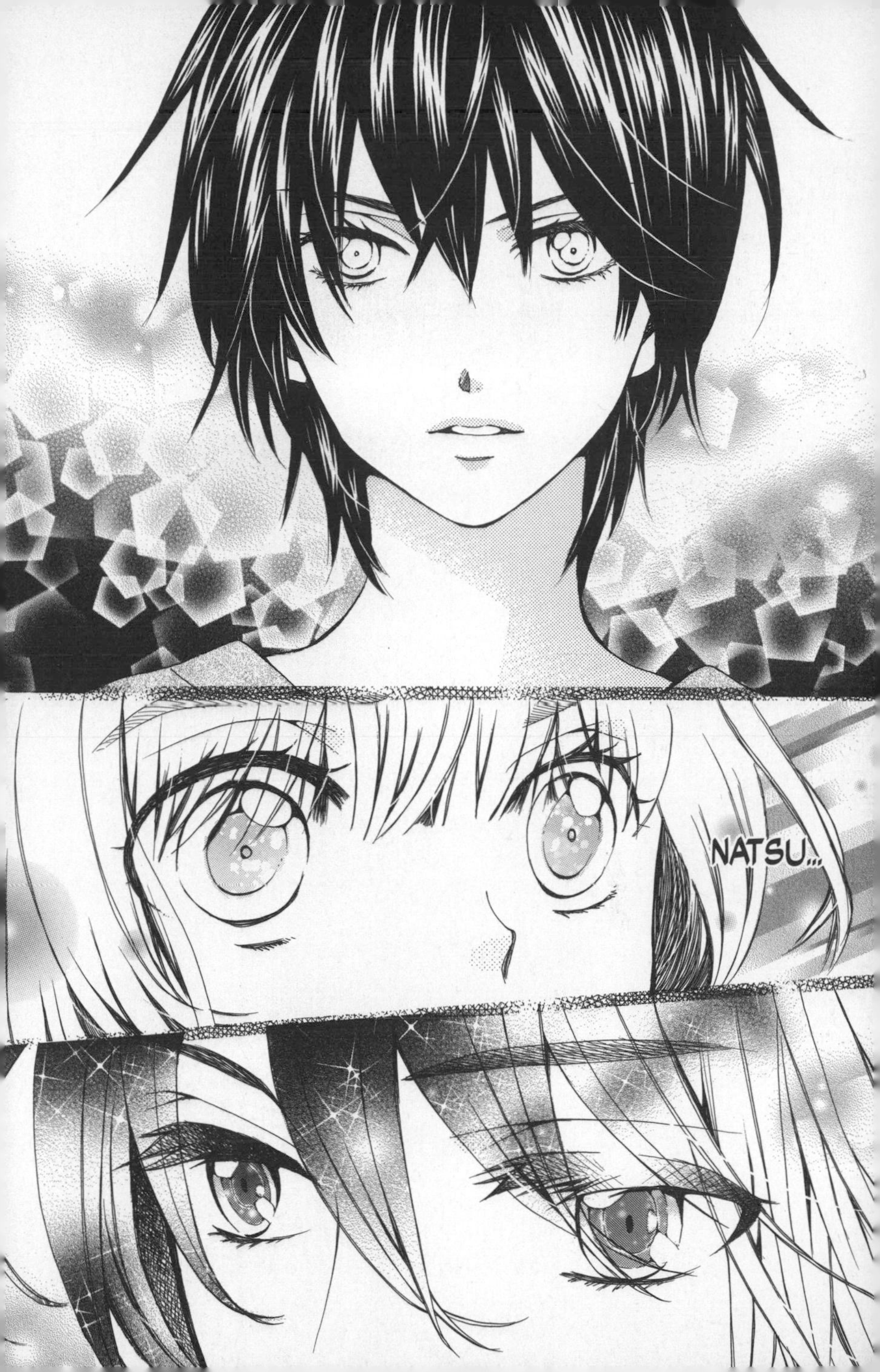
NATSU...

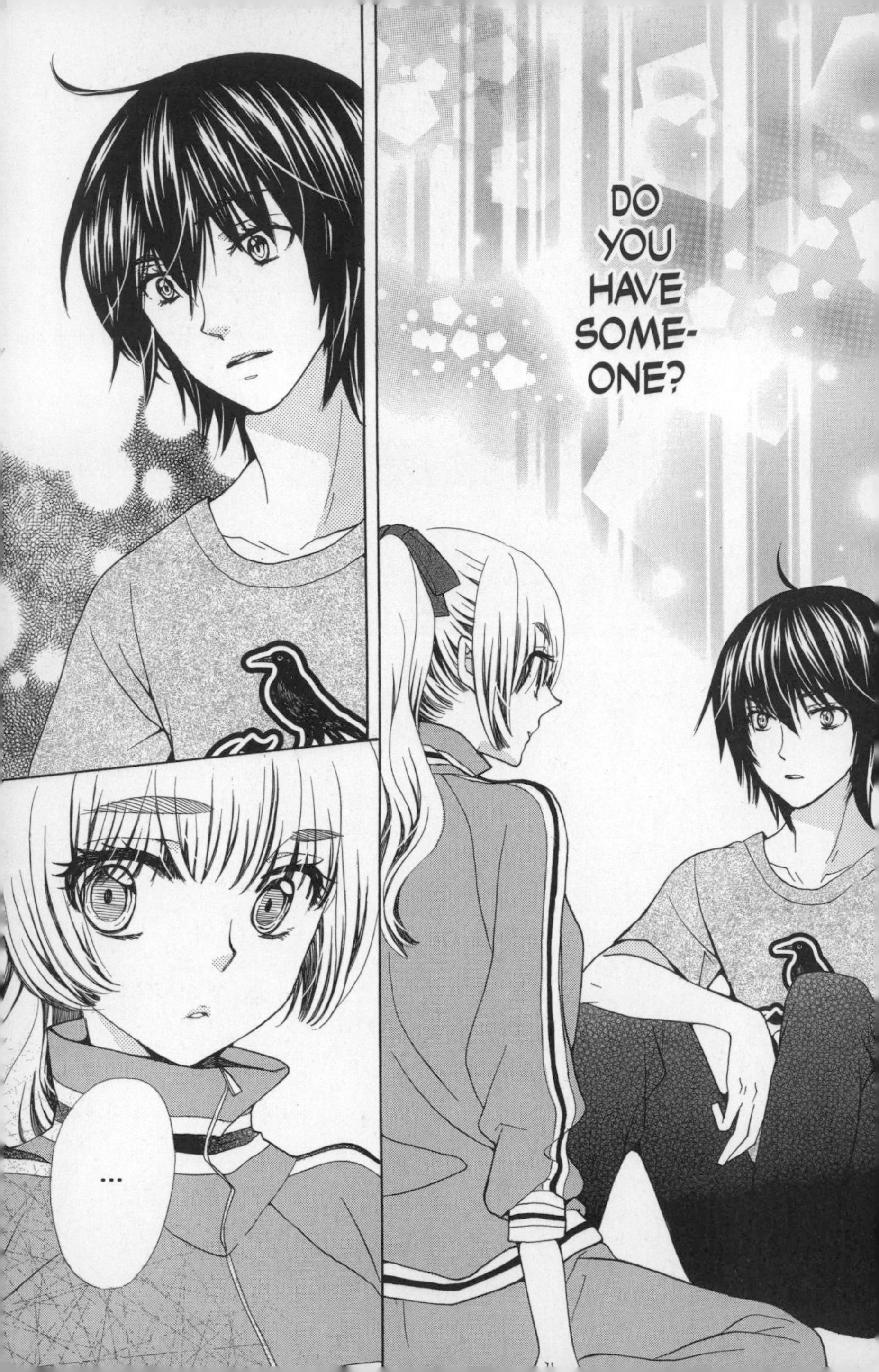
DO YOU HAVE SOME-ONE?
...

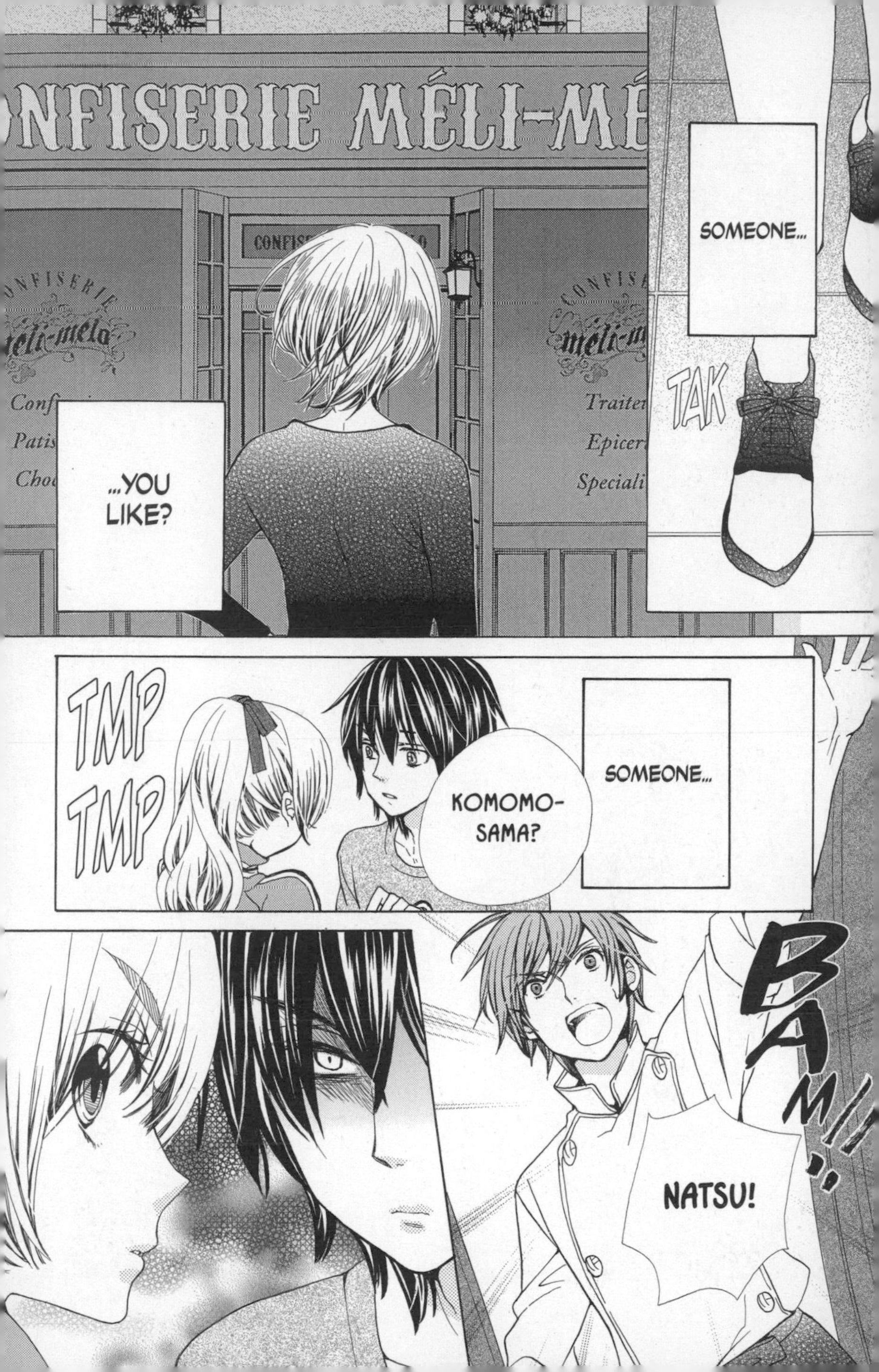
SOMEONE...
TAK
...YOU LIKE?
SOMEONE...
KOMOMO-SAMA?
TMP TMP
BAM!!
NATSU!

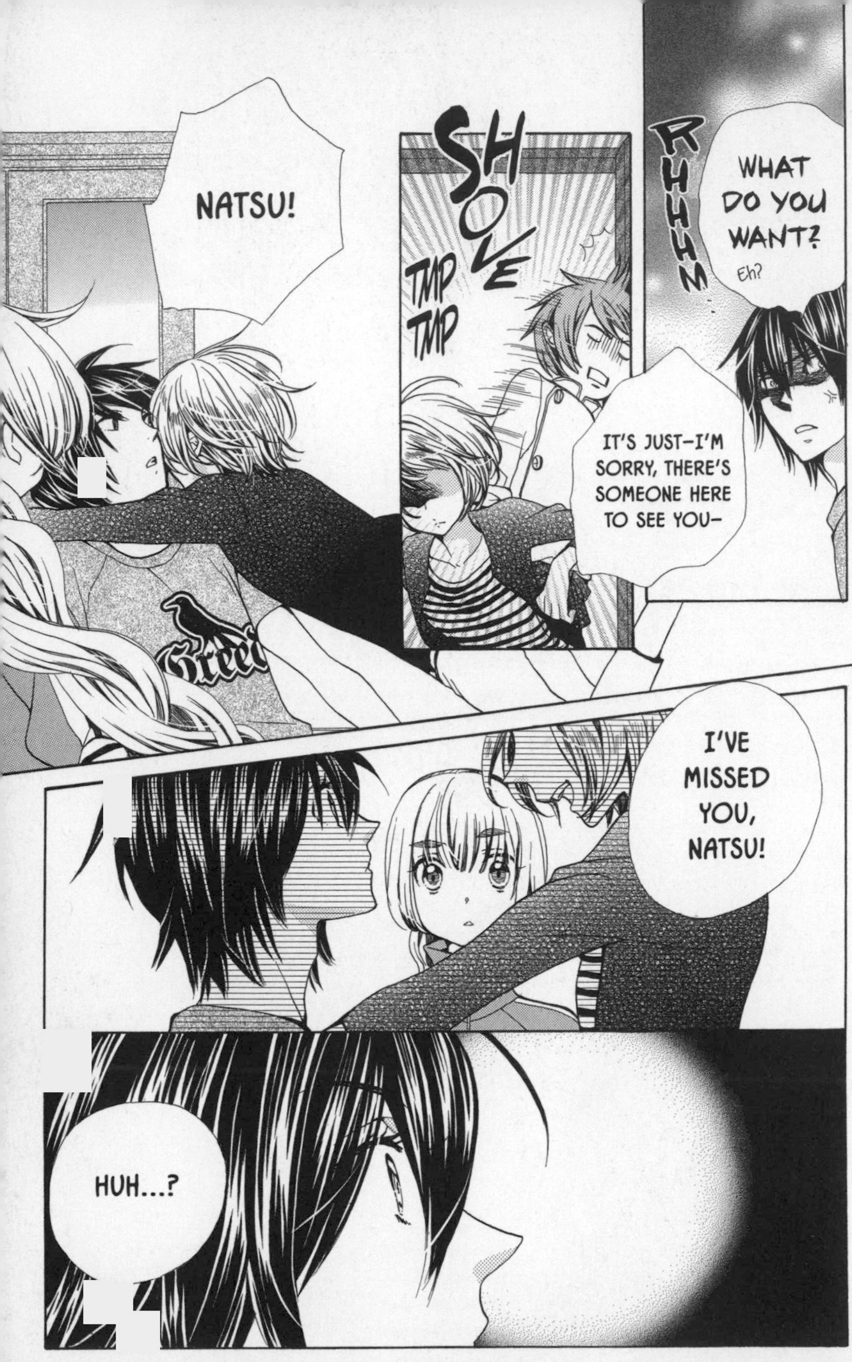
RHHHM
WHAT DO YOU WANT?
Eh?
SHOVE
TMP TMP
IT'S JUST—I'M SORRY, THERE'S SOMEONE HERE TO SEE YOU—
NATSU!
I'VE MISSED YOU, NATSU!
HUH...?

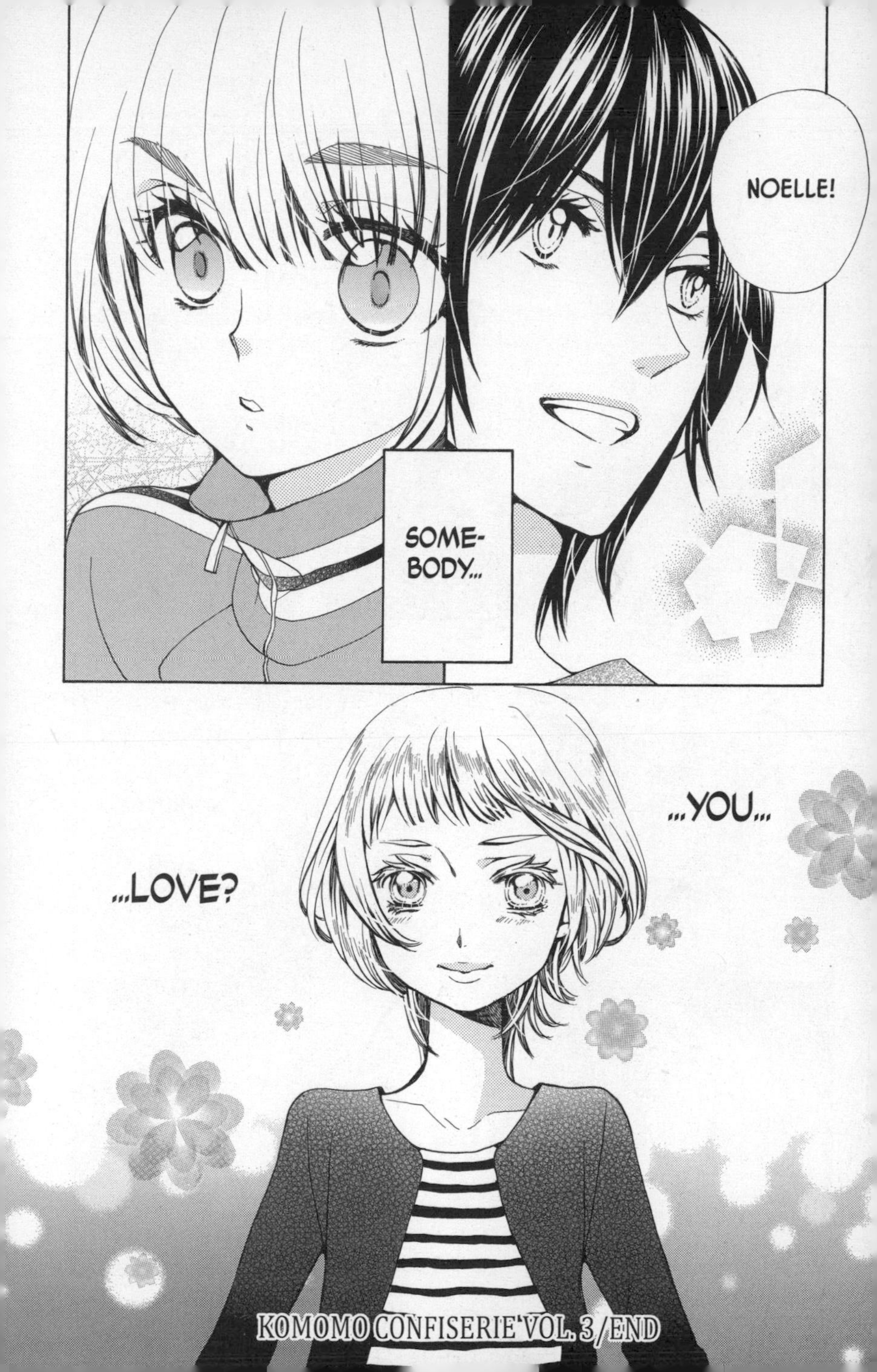
NOELLE!
SOME-BODY...
...YOU...
...LOVE?
KOMOMO CONFISERIE VOL. 3/END

BONUS PAGES

RISE & HER SERIOUS FRIENDS

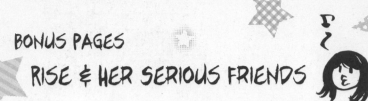

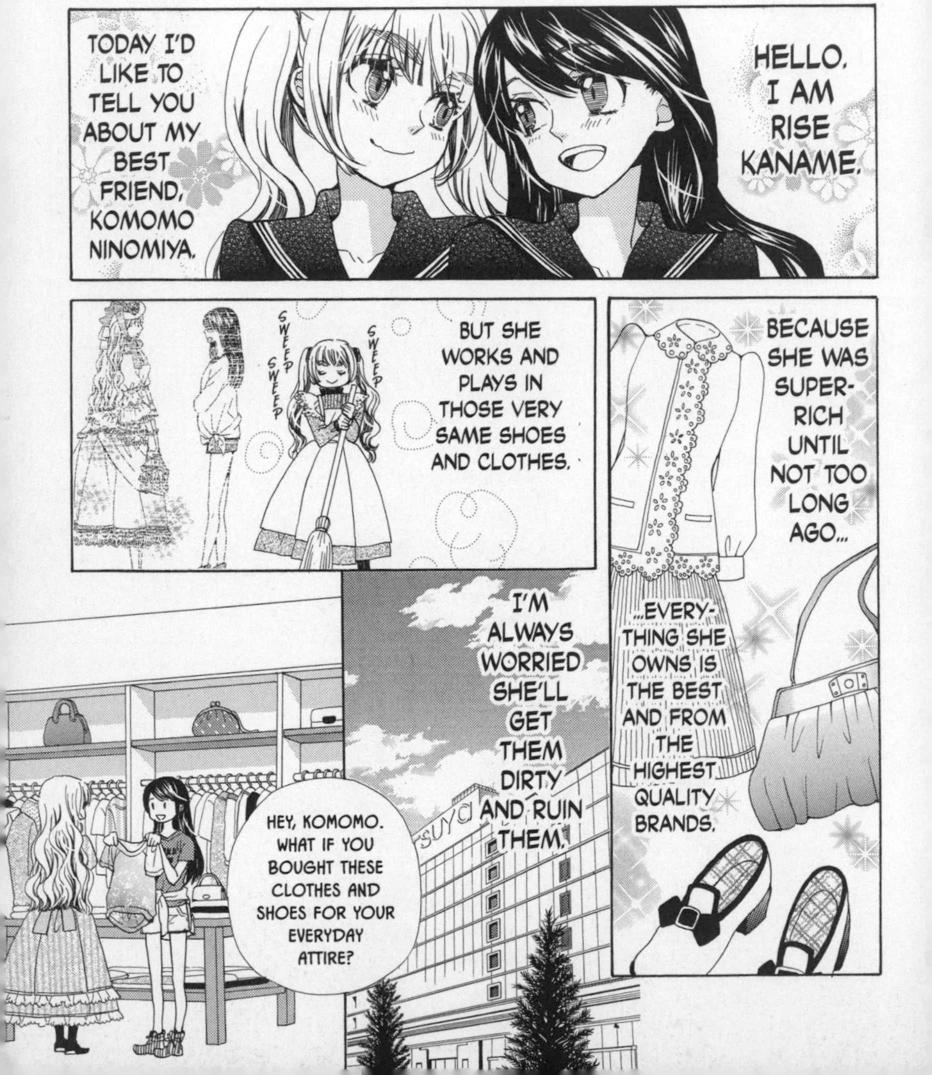
HELLO. I AM RISE KANAME.
TODAY I'D LIKE TO TELL YOU ABOUT MY BEST FRIEND, KOMOMO NINOMIYA.
BECAUSE SHE WAS SUPER-RICH UNTIL NOT TOO LONG AGO...
...EVERYTHING SHE OWNS IS THE BEST AND FROM THE HIGHEST QUALITY BRANDS.
BUT SHE WORKS AND PLAYS IN THOSE VERY SAME SHOES AND CLOTHES.
SWEEP
SWEEP
SWEEP
I'M ALWAYS WORRIED SHE'LL GET THEM DIRTY AND RUIN THEM.
HEY, KOMOMO. WHAT IF YOU BOUGHT THESE CLOTHES AND SHOES FOR YOUR EVERYDAY ATTIRE?

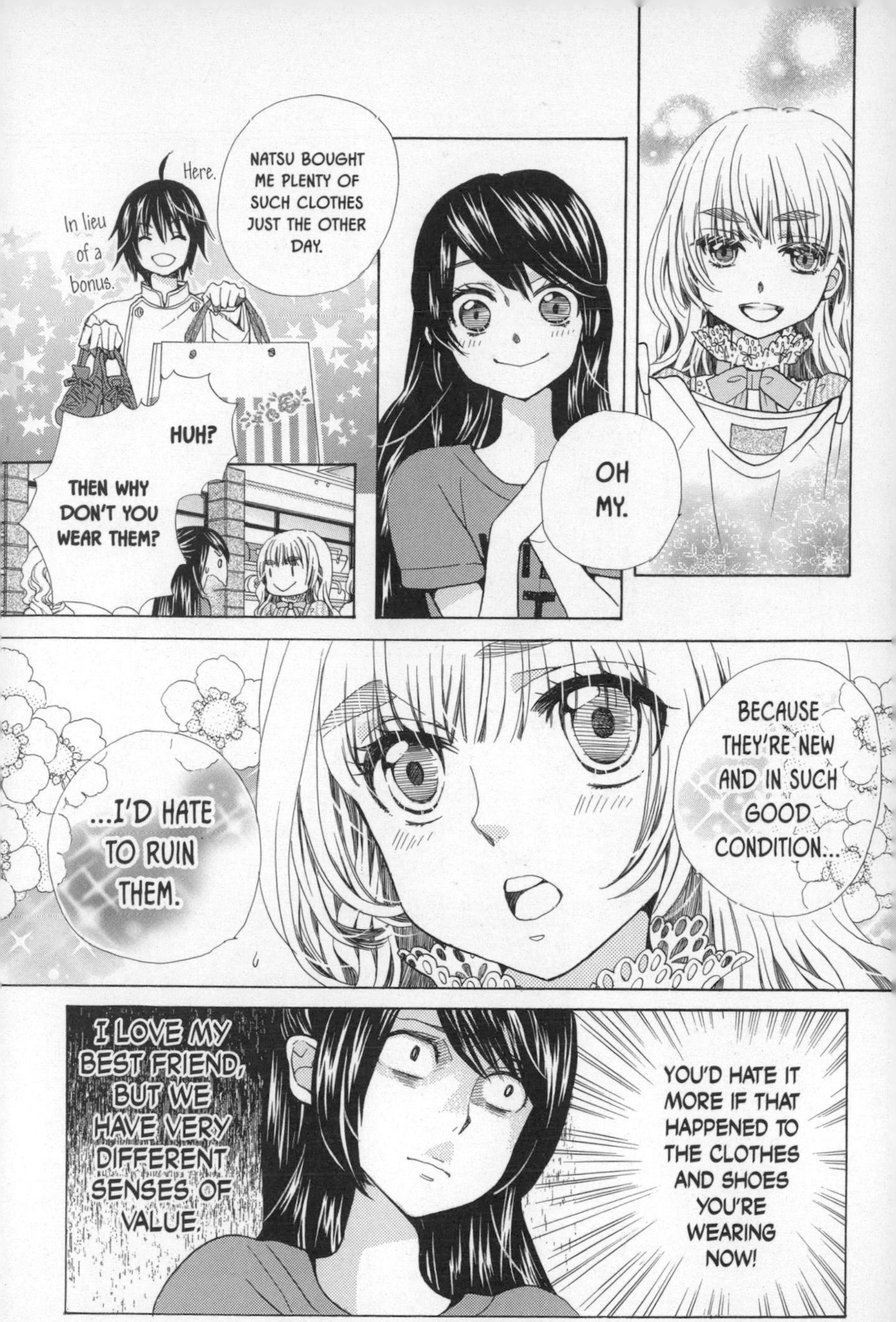
OH MY.
NATSU BOUGHT ME PLENTY OF SUCH CLOTHES JUST THE OTHER DAY.
Here.
In lieu of a bonus.
HUH?
THEN WHY DON'T YOU WEAR THEM?
BECAUSE THEY'RE NEW AND IN SUCH GOOD CONDITION...
...I'D HATE TO RUIN THEM.
YOU'D HATE IT MORE IF THAT HAPPENED TO THE CLOTHES AND SHOES YOU'RE WEARING NOW!
I LOVE MY BEST FRIEND, BUT WE HAVE VERY DIFFERENT SENSES OF VALUE.

BONUS PAGES/END